A YEAR

366 PAC　　　　READINGS

A Year with Bible Prophecy

A YEAR WITH BIBLE PROPHECY

366 PAGE TO A DAY READINGS

Donald CB Cameron BTh MA PhD Cert Ed

John Ritchie Publishing

40 Beansburn, Kilmarnock, Scotland

ISBN-13: 978 1 912522 41 5

Typeset by John Ritchie Ltd., Kilmarnock
Printed by Bell & Bain Ltd., Glasgow

Contents

Abbreviations

ASV	American Standard Version
AV	Authorised Version, now often referred to as the King James Version
DBY	New Translation by JN Darby
ESV	English Standard Version
KJV	King James Version, formerly better known as the Authorised Version
NIV	New International Version
NKJV	New King James Version
RSV	Revised Standard Version
RV	Revised Version
YLT	Young's Literal Translation

The arrangement of readings - please read!

This is not designed as a prophetic text book, distinguished only by being divided into one reading per day. Nor does it assume that the reader knows nothing about prophecy on 1st January and everything by 31st December. Many readers are likely to be familiar with many of the chosen texts; others may not be, and I have tried to cater for both. By the end of the year we will have covered a great deal of Bible prophecy, both fulfilled and unfulfilled, but in bite-size chunks.

I have chosen the New King James Version, with its retained familiar wording, as an excellent compromise between the much loved Authorised/King James Version and modern translations, which are more easily understood by younger people, but not necessarily as accurate.

In line with what we find in Scripture, some readings are informative or expository, some are devotional or practical, whilst others combine these features. Please expect contrasts! During the year we shall look at prophecies in both the Old Testament and New Testament. We will see some which were fulfilled almost immediately and others which are waiting for thousands of years. We will see some conditional prophecies, but many more unconditional ones. Some prophecies are thrilling, some comforting, some challenging and others terrifying, though this will depend upon our relationship with God. Some prophecies can be easily understood on their own; others have to be taken together to be comprehensible. As currently the signs of the times, harbingers of Christ's Return, are multiplying and accelerating dramatically, special attention will be devoted to what we call eschatology – prophecies concerning the last things. We will be reminded that all prophecy is inspired by God and that so much centres round the Person of the Lord Jesus Christ, who was Prophet as well as Priest and King.

The Psalmist wrote: *"Your word is a lamp to my feet* (the immediate future) *and a light to my path"* (the distant destination). (Ps 119:105). God's word throws light on both. In fact much of the "distant scene" is revealed in the pages of Holy Scripture; it is the individual "steps along the way" which are rarely revealed and which therefore encourage us to walk hand-in-hand with our Lord.

In the month of January we cover systematically thirty-one key prophecies regarding God's plan of redemption from the Garden of Eden to the end of the world and beyond. This should give any readers not familiar with Bible prophecy a framework into which to fit others. Thereafter I have grouped daily readings into a number of clearly labelled themes, some of which will display continuity and some contrasts.

Often I would have loved to give fuller quotations, but, having limited myself to a page per day, this has often proved impossible, and reluctantly I have sometimes had to skip sentences, indicating with dotted lines where I have done this. Sometimes it will be necessary to explain the context briefly, as lifting verses out of their setting can be a problem with almost any book of selected readings. There are plenty of good commentaries on Revelation. However, over the year most of Revelation will be covered; the Index of Readings will help identify these..

Amos wrote: *"Surely the Lord GOD does nothing, unless He reveals His secret to His servants the prophets"* (Amos 3:7). In Holy Scripture we have an amazing resource of God's future dealings with the world, not all of which apply equally at any given time, but which combine to cover the whole of human history. Believers should count it a privilege to be entrusted with prophecies which the outside world may scorn; Jesus told His disciples: *""No longer do I call you servants, for a servant does not know what his master is doing; but I have called you friends, for all things that I heard from My Father I have made known to you."* (Jn 15:15). For the unbeliever, the current state of the world is becoming unbearably stressful and alarming. For the believer who takes time to study end-time prophecy prayerfully, the stress is removed, because we are reassured that everything is on course for the next wonderful stage in God's prophetic programme.

Each of the prophetic books of the Bible has its own personal human author's style. God has very wonderfully woven them into a single book. I have deliberately varied my style, moving from reading to reading or section to section, even occasionally reverting to personal reminiscences. It is better to please all the readers some of the time than some of the readers all the time!

Acknowledgements

I wish to thank Mr Fraser Munro for his meticulous, painstaking survey and scrutiny of both the text and the spiritual content of the finished book.

My thanks also to Rev Neil Combe, faithful expositor of the Word, for his expertise in supporting, in panic conditions, authors less proficient than himself in computing matters.

Brief Glossary of Prophetic Terms

Each will be enlarged upon during the year.

Amillennialism The teaching that that the present Church Age is the Millennium.

Abomination of Desolation   A blasphemous image of the Beast which is to be set up in the Jerusalem temple.

Armageddon, Battle of   The demon-driven concentration of the world's armies to confront the Lord Jesus Christ at the end of the Great Tribulation.

Beasts Satan's two deputies who will be dominant between the Rapture and Coming in Power. One is sometimes referred to as the Antichrist, although this may be better applied to the second Beast or False Prophet.

Bowls of Wrath   Seven final plagues or bowls of the wrath of God poured out on earth in quick succession.

Church Age   The period or dispensation from Pentecost to the Rapture.

Coming in Power   The visible, literal, bodily return to earth of the Lord Jesus Christ in great glory as King of Kings and Lord of Lords at the end of the Great Tribulation, to execute judgment upon Satan, the Beast, the False Prophet and their armies,

Diaspora The long, but nevertheless temporary, judgmental exile of Israel from the Promised Land, for failure over many centuries to meet the conditions laid down by God.

First Resurrection The resurrection of the righteous or redeemed. It is likened to a harvest, with Jesus Christ as the Firstfruits, the Church as the Main Harvest and others as the Gleanings.

Great Tribulation The second half of the Tribulation Period; with life on the brink of extinction; an unprecedented, unrepeatable time of suffering for the world.

Great White Throne The judgment following the Millennium, the end of this world and the Second Resurrection; for the unsaved only – those whose names are not written in the Lamb's Book of Life.

Heaven (1) God's dwelling place, not of this creation. (2) The visible universe or 'starry heavens'. (3) Earth's atmosphere.

Hell Also Gehenna and the Lake of Fire. As yet unoccupied, but eternal. Not to be confused with Sheol (Hebrew) and Hades (Greek), the present abode of the souls and spirits of the unbelieving dead.

Judgment of the Nations On earth following Christ's Coming in Power. For Gentile survivors of the Great Tribulation, who will be divided by Christ as a shepherd separates sheep and goats. The 'sheep' in mortal bodies are to repopulate the Millennial earth.

Judgment Seat of Christ, (also referred to as the Bema), in Heaven following the Rapture and preceding the Marriage of the Lamb. There the deeds and service of believers will be evaluated and, if found truly worthy, rewarded. Sins, already forgiven, will not be judged there.

Millennium Earth's final age or dispensation. The thousand year righteous rule of Christ on earth following the Battle of Armageddon, when numerous prophecies of blessing and restoration will at last be fulfilled.

Mystery Babylon The final flowering of the global blasphemous multi-faith false church; guilty of the blood of the martyrs.

Post-Millennialism The belief that the world, through the efforts of the Church and the preaching of the Gospel, will be 'Christianised' and spiritually restored to make it 'fit' for Christ's personal return.

Pre-Millennialism The belief that the Church will be raptured and that Jesus will return to earth before the Millennium. Held exclusively by evangelicals and the stand-point of this book.

Preterism The teaching that most or all end-time promises concerning events on earth had been fulfilled before, during or shortly after the Apostolic Age.

Rapture The future collective snatching or catching up to meet the Lord in the air of the newly resurrected bodies of the dead in Christ and the translated bodies of the living saints, with onward progress to the prepared place in Heaven. From the Latin verb meaning 'to catch up'.

Replacement Theology The teaching that, since their rejection of their Messiah, the Jews have no present or future place in God's plans, and that the Church has eternally inherited all the blessings and privileges (but apparently not the curses!) accorded to Israel.

Seals A series of seven seals is to be opened in Heaven by Jesus Christ, in His role as the Lamb of God. The Seals authorise and set in motion the stages of the Tribulation Period.

Second Death Following the Millennium at the end of the world, when the unsaved dead will be raised bodily to face Christ at His Great White Throne.

Times of the Gentiles Announced by Daniel in his interpretation of King Nebuchadnezzar's dream and confirmed to be on-going by Jesus Himself in His Olivet Discourse. They end at Christ's Coming in Power.

Tribulation Period The seven years before Christ's Coming in Power. The first half may be referred to as 'the Beginning of Sorrows'; the second and more severe half as 'The Great Tribulation' or 'Time of Jacob's Trouble'.

Trumpets A series of seven heavenly trumpets blasts announcing severe judgments upon earth during the Tribulation Period; the final three of these are also called woes.

List of Sections

Practical Prophecies in the Psalms
2 July to 12 July

The Facts of the Millennium
13 July to 21 July

Major Prophecies from a Minor Prophet
22 July to 31 July

Some General Prophecies from the Gospels
1 August to 13 August

Short and Long Term Prophecies of Ezekiel
14 August to 26 August

Seven Trumpet Blasts of Revelation
27 August to 2 September

Prophetic Gleanings from Jeremiah
3 September to 8 September

The Holy City – The New Jerusalem
9 September to 16 September

A Selection from the Minor Prophets
17 September to 8 October

Personalities and Parentheses in Revelation
9 October to 19 October

Prophecies in the Pauline Epistles
20 October to 12 November

More Prophecies from Isaiah
13 November to 24 November

Seven Bowls of Wrath of Revelation
25 November to 1 December

Prophecies in Hebrews to Jude
2 December to 17 December

Christ's Seven Rewards for Overcomers
18 December to 24 December

The Zeal of the Lord of Hosts will Perform This
25 December to 31 December

A Thirty-One Day Tour of Key Prophecies

1 January

"But of the tree of the knowledge of good and evil you shall not eat, for in the day that you eat of it you shall surely die." (Gen 2:17)

Here is an unconditional prophecy given by God to Adam and Eve. Initially there was perfect harmony and communion between Adam and Eve and their Creator; we are not told what form God's manifestation took, but we know that it was very real. Perhaps a century elapsed before the Fall, perhaps very much less. We do not need to know. Other happenings we do need to know, because we are involved! Before Eve was formed, God put Adam on trust, having given him a free will. Adam and Eve had to be tested. The Tempter saw the potential for attack, what the Apostle John later described as "the lust of the flesh, and the lust of the eyes, and the pride of life" (I Jn 2:16). He used this triple appeal on Eve when she was on her own: He still uses the same tactics, and when he catches us out of fellowship, they are that much more effective.

Satan appeared in the form of a serpent and told Eve what appeared to be a half-truth but was in fact a lie, one of his favourite ploys: "Ye shall not surely die" (Gen 3:4 KJV); it is "ye", not singular "thou". All humankind would share in the Fall. They did not immediately die physically, but, having disobeyed God and broken His law, they instantly died spiritually. Without Christ, we share the same condition, and we are not yet free from its constraints. Paul tells us (Eph 2:5) that we are dead in sins; without God's intervention we are hell-bound. Paul confessed that he experienced internal warfare and described himself as a wretched man while still within this "body of death", but went on to thank God through Jesus Christ our Lord for his deliverance (Rom 7:22-24).

Adam and Eve succumbed and fell. Death, the last enemy to be destroyed, entered and has yet to be eliminated. But, as we will be reminded, it will be, and we can share the victory. So, within the opening chapter of the Bible we find that one of Satan's numerous attacks is against Bible prophecy – little wonder, because his fate is foretold there. Let us not give him the temporary satisfaction of ignoring God's faithful promises.

2 January

" I will put enmity between you and the woman, and between your seed and her Seed; He shall bruise your head, and you shall bruise His heel." (Gen 3:15)

God addresses the Tempter in the form of a prophecy, apparently within the hearing of Adam and Eve. It has been recorded for every succeeding generation. It was the Serpent who was cursed, but mankind and creation in general suffered the consequences of that curse. There were specific curses on Adam and Eve individually. However, even at that point, with eviction from the Garden of Eden and a new hostile environment imminent, Adam and Eve were given the hope of a coming Redeemer, the future virgin-born Seed of the woman. While the Serpent was to be permitted to inflict the severest temporary pain on the coming Seed or Descendant of Eve, the Serpent's ultimate fate at the hand of this promised One would be lethal and final. So we have the first shadowy prophecy of both Calvary, where defeat would be turned to victory, and Satan's ultimate consignment to the Lake of Fire.

Conflict between good and evil features in many religions, but usually takes the form of some sort of perpetual balancing act between the two, and any form of divine intervention is incidental. Let those of us who trust in the Lord Jesus Christ as our Saviour be constantly aware that, through Him and Him alone, we are on the victory side in this battle. His victory is our guarantee; but let us never forget that our freedom from the penalty of sin cost Him dear.

Bearing shame and scoffing rude, In my place, condemned, He stood; Sealed my pardon with His blood, Hallelujah, what a Saviour!

Paul reminds us: "For if by the one man's offence death reigned through the one, much more those who receive abundance of grace and of the gift of righteousness will reign in life through the One, Jesus Christ" (Rom 5:17). God had made provision even before Adam and Eve were in a position to break God's law by sinning. God's plan of the ages as revealed in Bible prophecy is not a feature that was added piecemeal as the need arose, but something which was meticulously and lovingly planned before the creation, of which we are a part.

3 January

"Now the LORD had said to Abram: 'Get out of your country.....
To a land that I will show you. I will make you a great nation; I will
bless you and make your name great; and you shall be a blessing.
I will bless those who bless you, and I will curse him who curses
you; and in you all the families of the earth shall be blessed.'"
(Gen 12:1-3)

Here is a major complex prophecy to one of the most pivotal characters in human history, recognised in Judaism, Christianity and Islam. Every part of it still holds good. Abraham, as God renamed him, is highly commended as a man of faith, but eventually his patience wore thin, and, instead of trusting totally in God regarding his promised descendants, he had a son, Ishmael, by Hagar, leading to long-term complications. However God narrowed down the promised blessing to Isaac, the son born to him and his wife, Sarah, in their old age. Later it was to be narrowed down further to Jacob, whom God renamed Israel, hence the "Children of Israel".

God called Abram out from his background; he had to come apart, as does every believer, though in a less dramatic way. God was selecting a family into which, many centuries later, His Son would be born. Jesus was a Jew! It was to become a unique nation, with a host of special blessings and privileges, balanced with a host of responsibilities and potential penalties. Those who have blessed Israel have been blessed, and those who have cursed her have paid the consequences. Christians who play fast and loose with God's faithful promises suffer.

Apostate Jews disinherit themselves. Jesus told the scribes and Pharisees, "If you were Abraham's children, you would do the works of Abraham" (Jn 8:39). In His covenant with Abraham, God was looking beyond the coming Levitical law, which cannot save, to salvation which comes through faith. We all may be brought into the spiritual inheritance through faith, but that does not turn Gentiles into Jews; "Christ has redeemed us from the curse of the law..... that the blessing of Abraham might come upon the Gentiles in Christ Jesus" (Gal 3:13-16). Israel is at present side-lined: "Concerning the gospel they are enemies for your sake, but concerning the election they are beloved for the sake of the fathers" (Rom 11:28).

4 January

"And Abraham said, 'My son, God will provide for Himself the lamb for a burnt offering.' So the two of them went together." (Gen 22:8)

Here Abraham's faith did not fail; indeed, it is an outstanding example to us all, for there are times in our Christian experience where God tests us, though rarely as severely as He did Abraham. Blessing ensues when we pass the test. Abraham had already cast out Ishmael, so now had only Isaac. He had told Abraham to take his young son and heir, whom he loved, to Moriah, later identified with the Temple Mount of Jerusalem, and sacrifice him. Isaac, who was carrying the wood, even as Jesus later bore His cross, had enquired where the lamb for the sacrifice was. Abraham's heart must have been aching as he gave the above answer. At the last second God stopped Abraham slaying his son, and a ram, providentially caught by the horns in a thicket, provided an undamaged or unblemished substitute. Isaac, the beloved son laid upon the altar and raised from it, is a "type" of Christ.

The need for a lamb and the acceptability of that lamb as a sacrifice for sin had been established with Cain and Abel. That was the first indication of salvation being of grace and not works, a lesson still rejected by many. Abraham's answer envisaged only the immediate future, but God recorded the answer for posterity, because He was going to provide THE Lamb, "the Lamb of God who takes away the sin of the world" (Jn 1:29). God was looking further ahead to Calvary, where there could be no convenient stand-in for the precious Lamb of God, for it was He who was to become our substitute. We will see more of this doctrine of the Lamb over the next three days. Darby appropriately renders v 14: "And Abraham called the name of that place Jehovah-jireh; as it is said at the present day, On the mount of Jehovah will be provided"; Jehovah was the precious covenant name of God, rather than a title.

God addresses Abraham: "By Myself I have sworn, says the LORD, because you have done this thing, and have not withheld your son, your only son" (Gen 22:16). Each child of God should be able to bless God, using virtually the same words – "Your only Son".

5 January

"The blood shall be a sign for you on the houses where you are.
And when I see the blood, I will pass over you; and the plague
shall not be on you to destroy you when I strike the land of Egypt."
(Ex 12:13)

Here is another prophecy with both an immediate and a long-term fulfilment. Despite numerous warnings and miraculous signs, the Egyptians had persistently defied God and refused to allow the Children of Israel, their main source of slave labour, to go. Sooner or later God acts decisively against human and demonic defiance; the gods of Egypt were to be judged too. Few understand the full implications of direct conflict with Almighty God. He had announced the slaying of the eldest son of each family that very night. He had instituted for the Children of Israel the Passover feast, which involving the killing of a lamb for each household. They were to eat it fully dressed and prepared for the start of the Exodus journey. But God carefully commanded a precautionary act to exempt them from the punishment about to strike Egypt; they were to apply the lamb's blood to the doorposts and lintel of each house. There was no alternative.

We have already noted the need, acceptability and divine provision of the lamb. Now the emphasis is on the blood. In Leviticus we learn that the life is in the blood. This all pointed forward to Calvary: "But Christ came as High Priest of the good things to come, with the greater and more perfect tabernacle not made with hands, that is, not of this creation. Not with the blood of goats and calves, but with His own blood He entered the Most Holy Place once for all, having obtained eternal redemption" (Heb 9:11-12). What the suffering Lord Jesus Christ accomplished as His body hung upon the cross during those three earthly hours of darkness is more than human tongue can tell. But it was effective, and as with the Israelite families of long ago, there is no other protection for us from the wrath of God for our sin, other than the blood of His Son, our Sin Bearer. "Without shedding of blood there is no remission" (Heb 9:22). As in Egypt, God provides no alternative.

6 January

"He was oppressed and He was afflicted, yet He opened not His mouth; He was led as a lamb to the slaughter, and as a sheep before its shearers is silent, so He opened not His mouth."
(Isa 53:7)

Any who doubts that this was prophetic should recall that this was the passage that the Ethiopian eunuch was reading when Philip the Evangelist encountered him. He asked Philip whom the prophet was speaking of, and, "beginning at this Scripture, (he) preached Jesus to him" (Acts 8:35). We are reminded of the One who remained silent before the High Priest (Matt 26:63). We are reminded that when the mockers cried, "He trusted in the LORD, let Him rescue Him; Let Him deliver Him, since He delights in Him!" (Ps 22:8), He could expect no rescue, because, bearing our sins, He was entitled to none. The final vindication before those mockers is still ahead.

Isaiah was the first to look forward seven hundred years or so and reveal that the actual Lamb, of which the various prototypes had been merely symbolic, was a Man. It was left to John the Baptist to confirm which Man. This was the Man who, as the Lamb of God, "was wounded for our transgressions and bruised for our iniquities" (v 5). Isaiah tells us so eloquently of His vicarious or substitutionary sin-bearing role, but then goes on to tell us what seems the amazing fact that "it pleased the Lord to bruise Him" (v 10), because of the salvation which was being wrought. But we are also told that He (Christ) "shall see the travail of His soul and be satisfied" (v 11). The Lamb Himself was satisfied that what He had accomplished was worth the awful price He had paid. This wonderful chapter 53 may at first sight appear to be repetitive, but various aspects of sin have to be dealt with in order to clear us of both the guilt and penalty. The One who took upon Himself the form of a Servant satisfied all the demands of God's righteous laws.

To us it is an utterly incredible fact that God considered our salvation worthwhile, involving His Son taking human flesh; "being found in appearance as a man, He humbled Himself and became obedient to the point of death, even the death of the cross" (Phil 2:8).

7 January

"Rejoice greatly, O daughter of Zion! Shout, O daughter of Jerusalem! Behold, your King is coming to you; He is just and having salvation, lowly and riding on a donkey, a colt, the foal of a donkey." (Zech 9:9)

This is a distinctive, unambiguous prophecy of the Messiah as the coming King, of which the city of Jerusalem should have been aware and awaiting. All the signs had all been there in Jesus' wonderful ministry; He had clearly demonstrated His qualifications and authority, together with love and mercy. But this lovely prophecy of Zechariah did not foretell here the kind of king whom they really wished for, one who would have advanced their status. Lowliness and true justice were not qualities which they admired or desired. When the pilgrims cried the Messianic acclamation, "Blessed is the King who comes in the name of the Lord" (Ps 118:26, Matt 21:9), they actually dared to call upon Jesus to rebuke His disciples. The blindness of the national spiritual leaders, invested with the authority to appraise, recognise and acclaim their prophesied Messiah, was inexcusable.

Previously Zechariah had been prophesying about events in the intervening centuries, when there would be no king of David's line on the throne. These prophecies would be important to the believing minority, just as end-time prophecies are today to those who choose to heed them. But then Zechariah moved forward five hundred years to Christ's first coming, and made this wonderful promise. Their King was coming, bringing salvation with Him; and although He knew that He would be rejected, His presentation of Himself for their acceptance was absolutely genuine.

Following the fulfilment of this prophecy lies the prophetic gap which we call the Church Age, which was to follow the King's rejection, crucifixion, and ascension. By chapter 14 Zechariah foretells what will happen after the Church Age, namely the world-wide assault on Jerusalem and the rescuing Second Coming in Power which is to usher in the Millennial kingdom, which the prophet goes on to describe briefly, and which half-believers dismiss as allegories. We will return to these important passages later.

8 January

"That which is conceived in her is of the Holy Spirit. And she will bring forth a Son, and you shall call His name JESUS, for He will save His people from their sins." (Matt 1:20-21)

It is Joseph who is addressed here as the legal head of the family. In the past God had sent Israel "saviours". Israel had been warned in Deuteronomy 28 and elsewhere that their sin would lead to God withdrawing His protection and allow enemies to attack and sometimes overwhelm them, till they repented and cried to Him. The saviours whom He sent delivered them from their earthly enemies, but did not save them from their sin; any repentance was almost invariably very temporary. Even at this juncture the remaining tribe in the Land, Judah with Benjamin, and many Levites, wanted a saviour from their enemies, the occupying Romans; but few were prepared to welcome a Saviour from their sins. The spiritual implications of repentance leading to renewal were too demanding. Even today more and more who call themselves Christians resent God interfering in their morals and imposing His laws. It is a prominent sign of the times and points to Christ's Return.

An old chorus says, "And when we call Him Jesus, we call Him by His name." This is absolutely true, though in accepting Him as Saviour we accept Him as our Lord, and indeed as God incarnate. Here at last is the promised Seed of the woman. Here, as forecast by Isaiah (9:6), a child is born, an everyday occurrence, and a Son is given, an utterly unique act on the part of God, who so loved the world. His work of salvation was to be accomplished three and a half decades later. He had come unto His own, but collectively His own would reject Him, though there was always to be a faithful remnant. The way would be made open to the "whosoever believes" of the world. It is open to each one of us today.

9 January

"He will be great, and will be called the Son of the Highest; and the Lord God will give Him the throne of His father David. And He will reign over the house of Jacob forever, and of His kingdom there will be no end." (Lk 1:32-33)

This is part of the message which God commissioned Gabriel to deliver to Mary. We know from Hebrews chapter 1 that the holy angels recognised and worshipped Him when God brought His Firstborn into the world. But Nathaniel's confession, "Rabbi, You are the Son of God! You are the King of Israel!" (Jn 1:49), was almost unique among humankind before Pentecost. It is now of course a central belief of the Christian Church. Matthew then confirms that this was the fulfilment of Isaiah's prophecy (7:14), which concludes with: "They shall call His name Immanuel, which is translated 'God with us'." But the Jewish leaders were not prepared for such a stupendous revelation. When Jesus said or did things which indicated that He was God or equal with the Father, instead of identifying Him with Isaiah's prophecy, they accused Him of blasphemy.

As we noted in yesterday's reading, Joseph had already been told that this was the One who would save His people. But now we come to a prophecy which tends either to be misunderstood or glossed over. To the largely Gentile Church it may appear to be secondary, but we have no right to downgrade any of God's prophecies. The house of Jacob is not the Church; the words are surely carefully chosen. This is not about some imaginary "New Israel"; this is about the old Israel which had still to undergo two thousand years of dispersal and Holocaust. The Lord Jesus Christ is now set down on His Father's throne in Heaven, not the earthly throne of David, whatever a very foolish modern hymn, says to the contrary.

Christ's enthronement on David's throne in Jerusalem follows His Second Coming to earth, and is one element of the Father's vindication on this planet of His once-rejected Son. Yes, the world will eventually end, but Christ's Kingdom, which He will one day hand over to His Father, is an everlasting Kingdom. These unfulfilled prophetic matters are no peripheral doctrines, but are given due prominence throughout Holy Scripture.

10 January

"From that time Jesus began to show to His disciples that He must go to Jerusalem, and suffer many things from the elders and chief priests and scribes, and be killed, and be raised the third day."
(Matt 16:21)

This event, recorded in three Gospels, is the first of Jesus' three such announcements of what was due to happen shortly, some being repeated in other Gospels. It was a prophecy which did not meet with Peter's approval, and he was quick to react. We are not told whether the others felt the same or whether he was acting as a spokesman. Clearly he felt strongly about it himself. Peter took Him aside to say, "Far be it from You, Lord; this shall not happen to You!", and received the sternest rebuke. Of course one cannot say "Lord" and mean it, if one is not prepared to submit to Him in all things; there is always a likelihood of personal inconvenience or even suffering in following Jesus. Peter's had been misguided loyalty. The way of the cross is still offensive and defeatist to some well-meaning folk. Would they only pause to consider the implications, which would be that that their sins do not need Christ's atoning sacrifice.

Peter was still hoping that, despite Jesus' unmilitaristic approach, He would in due course "restore the kingdom to Israel", overthrowing Roman colonial occupation – it was indeed still the hope of the Eleven, right up to the time of their Lord's ascension. When, ten days after that event, the Holy Spirit was given, the wonderful newly accomplished plan of salvation suddenly made sense to them, and they were able to preach with authority. We cannot hope to convince men and women of their need of salvation through Christ's death and resurrection if we do not have the convincing and convicting support of the Holy Spirit.

The disciples' original fallacy has given way to a second even more serious one. The first was that the Messianic kingdom on earth was to follow immediately Jesus' earthly ministry, or at least His resurrection, without any intervening Church Age. The second is that there will be no earthly Messianic Kingdom on earth following the Church Age. There is less excuse for the second, inasmuch as the Church Age was a mystery not revealed in the Old Testament, whereas in the New Testament we have ample confirmation.

11 January

"So they asked Him, saying, 'Teacher, but when will these things be? And what sign will there be when these things are about to take place?..... And they will fall by the edge of the sword, and be led away captive into all nations. And Jerusalem will be trampled by Gentiles until the times of the Gentiles are fulfilled.'" (Lk 21: 7, 24)

This is part of Jesus' great Olivet Discourse, so neglected by many, delivered to Peter, Andrew, John and James during the crucifixion week. The fullest account is found in Matthew. But, whereas in Matthew and Mark only latter day events are covered, Luke records our Lord's earlier warning of events little more than thirty years ahead, before saying anything about the more distant future. He had just told them that one stone of the Temple, which they could see, would not be left on another.

Jesus first warned of coming perilous conditions as the coming Roman siege drew near. Christian Jews did indeed heed the warnings of verses 21 and 22 and duly fled. Ten tribes had already been deported by the Assyrians, never to return, except with a scattering of individuals, until a yet future day of reunification. The siege and slaughter of Jerusalem's unbelieving citizens was as graphically described by Jesus as were the days of vengeance (v 23). They had rejected their only Saviour; His Return could not be expected until the "times of the Gentiles are fulfilled".

This was to be the time of Gentile sovereignty over Israel and Jerusalem in particular; even today Israel cannot have such sovereignty, because the conditions laid down by God have yet to be fulfilled. A pagan mosque dominates the Temple Mount. But fulfilled they will be, and the excuses made by those Christians who deny a future return are pathetic – more than pathetic; they are defiant. In 1980 it was my duty to inform the major general who commanded the Soviet military liaison mission in West Germany that a certain day would be a public holiday – 'Reunification Day'. He was absolutely livid. Reunification with the then Soviet satellite East Germany was unthinkable to him. But it happened! The idea of the twelve tribes of Israel being eventually reunited in the Promised Land, what they call Palestine, would make Muslims equally livid; but God says that it will happen.

12 January

"For then there will be great tribulation, such as has not been since the beginning of the world until this time, no, nor ever shall be. And unless those days were shortened, no flesh would be saved; but for the elect's sake those days will be shortened." (Matt 24:21-22)

The Matthew account of the Olivet Discourse omits the earlier enquiry about the fate of the Temple which Luke includes. The disciples had further asked what are, in fact, two questions: "What will be the sign of Your coming, and of the end of the age?" (24:3). Jesus had much to tell them, but we must leave most of this to further readings. Clearly this situation is to be the climax to a number of events.

This prophecy should alert doubters, for, until recent decades, the above statement of Jesus seemed very much less feasible than it does today – a world on the brink of extinction but for divine intervention. The form of divine intervention, the glorious visible Return of the Lord Jesus Christ to earth, is prophesied with various degrees of detail in several passages as well as this Discourse. We will quote one of these in two days' time and return to the others later. This is about God's mercy as well as His judgment. However it is chiefly for the sake of "the elect" that impending disaster will at that time be averted. Would that the outside world recognised this and sought to be reconciled to the Saviour! We have such a message to declare. Some of the greatest evangelists of the past, before the current scoffing generation, have used the preaching of Christ's Second Coming to win souls.

What must happen in due course will be totally unprecedented in world history, though not nearly as overwhelmingly destructive of life as the Flood of Noah's day. This coming Great Tribulation had been forecast in similar terms in the Old Testament at Daniel 12:1, and features in many other prophecies. It was no sudden decision, because it is to be the precursor of other happenings, both glorious and disastrous, depending upon the standing of individuals before God. We will be reminded tomorrow that something else wonderful must happen first. Signs of its nearness now proliferate with terrifying rapidity for those who have not yet sought a refuge in Christ. But few heed God's gracious warnings.

13 January

"When the Son of Man comes in His glory, and all the holy angels with Him, then He will sit on the throne of His glory. All the nations will be gathered before Him, and He will separate them one from another, as a shepherd divides his sheep from the goats."
(Matt 25:31-32)

Untold mischief has been caused by the 17th Century compilers adding a section title to this passage, "The Last Judgment", to verses 31 to 46 of Matthew 25. Some versions still retain this. Apart from the identity of the Judge, it bears little resemblance to THE last judgment recorded in Revelation 20. What is worse is that, as a result of this misunderstanding, people have assumed that good works, especially charity, or lack of it, can eternally save or condemn an individual. I once heard a young man with an evangelical background preach such a sermon on this passage; so serious was the error that he had courteously but firmly to be corrected. We take on a huge responsibility when we preach the Gospel, and dare not approach it casually. But we are all fallible. If in doubt, we should have reliable sources to consult. James tells us that charity is a mark of pure religion; it must not be dismissed out of hand. But it cannot replace grace and can never save.

This is a major prophecy and not a parable; it is an account of how, following Christ's return to earth in power and glory, He will segregate the survivors of the dreadful Tribulation Period. The Gospel of the Kingdom will have been preached with unprecedented vigour and world-wide coverage. We must look at the details later.

Segregation of flocks of sheep and goats would have been a familiar sight to the disciples to whom Jesus was speaking. It is still comprehensible and very apt. Those likened to sheep are to repopulate the devastated world in their mortal bodies at the start of the Millennium, and raise children. They are already saved, but only at the end of the Millennium will receive their incorruptible bodies. Like raptured believers earlier, they will not taste death. Those likened to goats are to be consigned to Hell, for, so sharp will be the division between the redeemed and unredeemed during the Tribulation, that these are they who will have given their allegiance to Satan.

14 January

"In My Father's house are many mansions; if it were not so, I would have told you. I go to prepare a place for you. And if I go and prepare a place for you, I will come again and receive you to Myself; that where I am, there you may be also." (Jn 14:2-3)

This was the evening of Jesus' betrayal. Judas Iscariot had just gone out into the darkness, and Jesus was left alone with the nucleus of the Church which was soon to be born. This is the first mention in Scripture of a happening which is never revealed in the Old Testament, because it was inappropriate. Even the idea of humans, with the exception of Enoch and Elijah, being in Heaven was new, because up till Calvary even the righteous were known to go down to Sheol (Hades in Greek), though to a separate part, to await their resurrection. What a comfort to the about-to-be-bereaved disciples to know that Jesus was going away to do something in preparation for them! This is not about His coming back to earth; that was prophesied, albeit not in detail, in the Old Testament. This is coming FOR. The Bridegroom coming to take the Bride, His Church, a concept which they did not yet comprehend, to the place He was to prepare in His Father's House, Heaven. "Mansions" is not a good translation – it gives an idea of splendid isolation.

The Eleven had followed Him faithfully during His earthly ministry and would soon be parted. But it was to be temporary. Jesus left it to the Church epistles to tell us more. There are now millions upon millions at rest in dwelling places in the Father's House, but, as we shall see, the prepared place is still unoccupied and perhaps only now nearing completion. It has to be occupied suddenly by the entire body of New Testament believers.

"If it were not so, I would have told you" is a reassurance rarely commented on when there is so much else of importance in these verses. Jesus had not called these men from their homes and families **ultimately to abandon them.** Sometimes courageous and sometimes timorous, they should have had more faith in the power and authority of the One whom they called Lord and Master. Are we any better than they?

15 January

"It is to your advantage that I go away; for if I do not go away, the Helper will not come to you; but if I depart, I will send Him to you. And when He has come, He will convict the world of sin, and of righteousness, and of judgment." (Jn 16:7-8)

Here Jesus presents the Holy Spirit in contrasting roles. To the believer He is a Comforter, Helper and Advocate, and to the world at large, He convicts of sin and points to the cross; but, in accordance with the "whosoever will" principle He does not compel acceptance.

The Holy Spirit is recorded as being active from the very first verses of Genesis. In the Old Testament He came upon various people, such as Samson and King Saul, but later withdrew, to their cost. He inspired the prophets, He inspired the Psalms, but David, after his affair with Bathsheba could cry: "Do not take your Holy Spirit from me" (Ps 51:11); for him it was a real possibility.

But this is different. Never before had the Holy Spirit been given to individuals in perpetuity, as He would be from Pentecost onwards. John had earlier remarked: "The Holy Spirit was not yet given, because Jesus was not yet glorified" (Jn 7:39). Professor Heading comments: "Both divine Persons would not work at the same time on earth. One would go and the Other would come." Jesus then went on to explain how the Spirit of truth would give them understanding; hitherto they had often been puzzled by what Jesus had said. The contrast is so very noticeable in the Apostles from Pentecost on.

The permanence of the Holy Spirit is a characteristic of the Church saint: "Having believed, you were sealed with the Holy Spirit of promise" (Eph 1:13); "Do not grieve the Holy Spirit of God, by whom you were sealed for the day of redemption" (Eph 4:30); we do not have to wait for some "second blessing".

The evidence of the indwelling of the Holy Spirit is our bearing of fruit, through which His Father is glorified, about which Jesus had had been talking earlier that evening (Jn 15:8), rather than the exercising of gifts, which can be counterfeited and are therefore not in themselves evidence. What an incredible gift is the Holy Spirit! No wonder we are warned not to grieve Him.

16 January

"But Jesus kept silent. And the high priest answered and said to Him, 'I put You under oath by the living God: Tell us if You are the Christ, the Son of God!' Jesus said to him, 'It is as you said. Nevertheless, I say to you, hereafter you will see the Son of Man sitting at the right hand of the Power, and coming on the clouds of heaven.'" (Matt 26:63-64)

Under the terms of His own law (Lev 5:1), Jesus was bound to answer the High Priest. Now this is not the most common passage to introduce the subject of the Return of the Lord Jesus in Power, the climactic event of His Second Coming, the juncture when His feet shall next alight on the Mount of Olives, the very spot from which He ascended. However when we ponder that this cross-examination was a matter of hours before His shameful sin-bearing death to which this apology for a servant of God was daring to pronounce judgment, we must surely compare what Jesus was foretelling and what Caiaphas was planning.

Christ was glorified in Heaven from the moment of His ascension, now bearing the honours of the Victor over death. But among vast swathes of humanity He is still regarded as an irrelevant anachronism or merely an outstandingly good man who is an example to us all, but not much else. His ascension was private, with at the departure point only a handful of followers.

Revelation 1:7 declares: "Behold, He is coming with clouds, and every eye will see Him, even they who pierced Him. And all the tribes of the earth will mourn because of Him." I have no idea how this will be accomplished; I simply know that it will be. When one considers how petty human technology, manipulated by people with limited intelligence or education, can flash images around the world from mobile phones, can we doubt that He who created the ages, time itself, will ensure that those souls, including Caiaphas, his Sanhedrin, Pontius Pilate and the Roman soldiers, most still awaiting the second resurrection, will be able to see vividly the Lord Jesus Christ, King of Kings and Lord of Lords, returning in power and great glory?

If we already trust Him as our Lord and Saviour, we shall be among the armies who follow Him, rather than horrified spectators!

17 January

"Then he said to Jesus, 'Lord, remember me when You come into Your kingdom.' And Jesus said to him, 'Assuredly, I say to you, today you will be with Me in Paradise.'" (Lk 23:42-43)

Before darkness fell at noon, the penitent thief on the neighbouring cross made this plea. Jesus did not, in fact, explain that the hoped for Kingdom which the thief visualised lay beyond the coming Church Age; He simply said that they would be together **that day** in Paradise (there were only six hours of the Friday left before the Sabbath. Before sunset the legs of crucified bodies still alive had to be broken to allow the lungs to collapse and bring on immediate death). The timescales were indicated in the same way as Jesus' earlier prediction of Peter denying Him that very night.

On earth three hours of darkness were about to fall. When they ended, Jesus was able to declare: "It is finished". The heavy Temple veil was rent from top to bottom. Out of the sphere of time, with His body hanging on the cross, what agonies was His soul enduring and how long did they last? Krummacher perceptively wrote regarding the dark hours: "That which during this time passed between Him and His Father, lies in the present sealed as with seven seals, hidden in the depths of eternity. We only know that, behind that veil, He was engaged in the most ardent conflict, gained the most brilliant victory, and adorned His representative obedience with its final crown. We know that the grave of our sins was then dug; the handwriting on the wall against us was then taken out of the way; and the wall which separated us from our God removed." By sunset that day they were together in the Father's House, as at long last were Old Testament believers who had been in Sheol. Suddenly, as a new dispensation was dawning, the believer's death was now to involve the soul going upwards, and not, as previously, downwards, to a waiting place, whatever the temporary state of the lifeless body awaiting the resurrection.

The redeemed believer since Calvary has been able to say, like Paul a little later, "For to me to live is Christ, and to die is gain". (Phil 1:21). *Death cannot keep its prey, Jesus, my Saviour; He tore the bars away, Jesus, my Lord.*

18 January

"Simon has declared how God at the first visited the Gentiles to take out of them a people for His name. And with this the words of the prophets agree, just as it is written: 'After this I will return and will rebuild the tabernacle of David, which has fallen down; I will rebuild its ruins, and I will set it up.'" (Acts15:14-16)

A week ago we saw how, in Luke's account of the Olivet Discourse, what was left of Israel within the Promised Land was to be dispersed until the Times of the Gentiles are fulfilled. People who have no difficulty in accepting a delay of forty years under Moses in entering the Promised Land do not like the idea of this much longer parenthesis, before their mass return to truly sovereign nationhood and spiritual enlightenment under their New Covenant: "Again I will build you, and you shall be rebuilt, O virgin of Israel!..... This is the covenant that I will make with the house of Israel after those days, says the LORD: I will put My law in their minds, and write it on their hearts; and I will be their God, and they shall be My people" (Jer 31:4,33).

Yet here is the positive side, where (Simon) Peter had reminded the Jerusalem church leaders that the prophets support this, and cited Amos chapter 9 as an example. Before David's kingdom on earth, represented by the tabernacle, can be restored, God was to take out from the Gentiles a "people for His name". The great parenthesis is in fact the Church Age, which is due to terminate with the Rapture. Our prospects are even more blessed than Israel's, as we wait eagerly for our Lord's return FOR us, rather, as in their case, TO them.

The history of the Church is not described in New Testament prophecy. In Matthew chapter 13 Jesus told a number of parables, which He interpreted for His disciples, but not for the hard of heart, spiritually deaf and blind Jewish leaders, as explained in Isa 6:10. These parables describe conditions during the Church Age, to be understood only by believers. These were at that point "the mysteries of the kingdom of heaven" (Matt 13:11). They should not be mysteries to us; but we should understand how they fit into God's plan of the ages.

19 January

"For the Lord Himself will descend from heaven with a shout, with the voice of an archangel, and with the trumpet of God. And the dead in Christ will rise first. Then we who are alive and remain shall be caught up together with them in the clouds to meet the Lord in the air. And thus we shall always be with the Lord."
(I Thess 4:16-17)

This is what Paul, writing to Titus, describes as the "blessed hope and glorious appearing". Just as Christ's First Coming took place over a number of years and included numerous events, so will His Second. This is the opening event of His Second Coming, and the first major prophecy to be fulfilled since the sack of Jerusalem in 70 AD. It is what our hearts should be longing for, as a bride for her Bridegroom: "My beloved put his hand by the latch of the door, and my heart yearned for him" (Song of Solomon 5:4) - even more intimate than the Old Testament's: "Your eyes will see the King in His beauty" (Isa 33:17).

Involved in this stupendous reunion in the clouds, the meeting point between Heaven and earth, will be (1) Christ Himself, long since resurrected from the dead, (2) the souls of Church Age believers leaving their resting places in the Father's House, (3) their bodies, which have been in the grave since death and (4) "we who are alive and remain", waiting to be raptured (from the Latin word to catch or snatch up, as with raptors). They converge from different directions, but proceed together to the place He has gone to prepare. "And thus we shall always be with the Lord." The sequence is natural, with the dead rising first and living believers following immediately. The glorious, incorruptible resurrection bodies, fit for Heaven and eternity, are described in I Corinthians 15, which we look at later.

The contrasts between this event, generally called the Rapture, and Christ's later Return to earth in power are numerous. Denying that they are separate events would mean that we would not be included in Enoch's prophecy: "Behold, the Lord comes with ten thousands of His saints" (Jude 1:14), or that it is our privilege "to wait for His Son from heaven, whom He raised from the dead, even Jesus who delivers us from the wrath to come" (I Thess 1:10).

20 January

"For we must all appear before the judgment seat of Christ, that each one may receive the things done in the body, according to what he has done, whether good or bad." (II Cor 5:10)

After the thrill of the expectation of the Rapture. at which we looked yesterday, we turn now to a sobering fact. Let us be quite clear that the Judgment Seat of Christ, or *Bema* from the Greek sports arena judges' rostrum, is not the same as the Great White Throne following the end of the world. Only unbelievers stand there; our sins were judged in Christ at Calvary. We find more details in I Corinthians 3:14-15, to which we can return. What is clear is that the Judgment Seat of Christ will take place in Heaven after the Rapture, but before the Marriage of the Lamb. Indeed, the sight in Revelation 4 of crowned saints strongly suggests that it will precede Christ's authorising of the first of the judgments on earth which will follow the Rapture.

A number of crowns are referred to in the epistles and Revelation, such as crowns of life, incorruptible crowns, crowns of glory. Whether they are actually different we cannot say – eternity will tell. I cannot help but think of my short row of Army medals, and of civilians who ask, "And what was this one for?" For instance, I Peter 5:4 gives the impression that the crown of glory will be specifically for the faithful pastor or leader of God's flock. At the Bema we can be rewarded for service, denied rewards for having failed to serve, or indeed both. Jesus Christ paid our entry fee; rewards are less important, but nevertheless significant, as we shall evidently keep them throughout eternity.

Is it possible that we could be ashamed before Him when our works are tested in the Refiner's fire? That which may have impressed neighbours on earth may be found to have been valueless, through wrong motivation. What about the scores of missed opportunities which might have brought blessing to ourselves or others? Jesus **wants** to be able to reward us; He said: "Lay up for yourselves treasures in heaven, where neither moth nor rust destroys and where thieves do not break in and steal" (Matt 6:20), and added that where our treasure is our heart will be also. Where is our treasure?

21 January

"And then the lawless one will be revealed, whom the Lord will consume with the breath of His mouth and destroy with the brightness of His coming. The coming of the lawless one is according to the working of Satan, with all power, signs, and lying wonders." (II Thess 2:8-9)

John, in the opening verses of his First Epistle, tells us that there have been many antichrists, false Christs or opposers of Christ, and that the spirit of antichrist is already in the world, but he added that a final Antichrist is coming. "Let no one deceive you by any means; for that Day" (the Day of the Lord or Great Tribulation) "will not come unless the falling away comes first, and the man of sin is revealed, the son of perdition, who opposes and exalts himself above all that is called God or that is worshipped" (II Thess 2:2-4). Just as God the Father is glorified through Christ, so Satan's ancient ambition is to be glorified and worshipped through his Antichrist or First Beast (Rev 13:2,12).

He is to be allowed by God to reign for forty-two months and will be marvelled at by the world at large. As long as the Church, indwelt by the Holy Spirit, is on earth, he cannot be released; "For the mystery of lawlessness already works; only there is he who restrains now until he be gone, and then the lawless one shall be revealed, whom the Lord Jesus shall consume with the breath of his mouth, and shall annul by the appearing of his coming." (II Thess 2:7-8 DBY).

Following the Rapture the world will suffer an unprecedented lack of competent leadership; initially chaos will reign. Any strong figure who can take control and restore some order will be welcomed. For three and a half years (we can discuss this later) he is to have a measure of success. God's first series of judgments, as the second third and fourth Horses of the Apocalypse go forth, will frustrate and limit his success. Evidently he will use their effects to orchestrate hatred against God. There will no longer be any middle ground between worshipping and blaspheming God. All this is in the future, and those saved before the Rapture will be spared, like Noah's family in the Ark. We return to these ominous matters in future months.

22 January

"But know this, that in the last days perilous times will come: For men will be lovers of themselves, lovers of money, boasters, proud, blasphemers, disobedient to parents, unthankful, unholy."
(II Tim 3:1-2)

There is a similar passage in I Timothy 4:1-3; however the "last days" of this passage is more specifically about the End Times than the other passage, which we can look at on another occasion. Jesus asked the rhetorical question, which demands the answer, "No!", "Nevertheless, when the Son of Man comes, will He really find faith on the earth?" (Lk 18:8). During the second half of the 20th Century there was a revival of a movement which began around the 18th Century, almost died with the Napoleonic Wars, and again with the 1st World War. It was called Post-Millennialism. The teaching was that, through missionary effort and other initiatives, the world was getting better and better and being increasingly "Christianised"; it seemed to flourish for three decades and spawned numerous songs which are still being sung. The supposition was that the world was going to be made fit by our efforts, supported by the Holy Spirit, for Christ's eventual Return. Those of us who pointed out that the Holy Spirit recorded nothing in Scripture about such a programme were accused of defeatism.

Now debunking the false teachings of other Christians is never a pleasant task. Paul in his opening chapters of Galatians found it essential to do so. Saying nothing is not an option. It is much better to take both unbelievers and misinformed believers to passages such as the above, to establish or strengthen their faith. We will have more to say about the signs of the times later, but just pause to reconsider the above prophecy. We are surely right on track for the Rapture. Each of the above characteristics is not only flourishing, but, in a way unprecedented in Church history, is being promoted and flaunted by governments and judiciaries.

One of our responsibilities is to emphasise that what is happening is fully in accordance with Scripture, and that the Bible's latter prophecies warn us that time is drawing short. "Now when these things begin to happen, look up and lift up your heads, because your redemption draws near"(Lk 21:28). Our redemption? Hallelujah! But what about our loved ones, friends and neighbours? Are they aware of the unfolding signs of the times?

23 January

"But one of the elders said to me, 'Do not weep. Behold, the Lion of the tribe of Judah, the Root of David, has prevailed to open the scroll and to loose its seven seals.' And I looked, and behold, in the midst of the throne and of the four living creatures, and in the midst of the elders, stood a Lamb as though it had been slain."
(Rev 5:5-6).

This is our first excursion into the wonderful Book of Revelation, the only book in the Bible personally introduced by our risen Lord. From chapter 4 on it concerns what is still future. This is part of the opening vision which tells what happens in Heaven after the Rapture and Judgment Seat of Christ; saints are seen with crowns.

John has been weeping, because none had come forward to open the scroll which is to release the first series of judgments upon the rebellious world below. Throughout the ages God's people have been crying for justice; there are many instances in the Psalms, for instance: "Do not keep silent, O God! Do not hold Your peace, And do not be still, O God!" (Ps 83:1). John records: "I saw under the altar the souls of those who had been slain for the word of God   and for the testimony which they held. And they cried with a loud voice, saying, 'How long, O Lord, holy and true, until You judge and avenge our blood on those who dwell on the earth?'" (Rev 6:9-10). Not only the living but the righteous dead appeal for justice. The absence of a champion would indeed be cause for lamentation, for evil would have prevailed

But, at first sight, nobody in Heaven or on earth is qualified. Then from the midst of His Father's throne comes forth Christ, described majestically. But when John looks, he sees Him in a very different role, that of the Lamb, still bearing in Heaven the marks of His death, which makes Him alone the righteous Judge: And they sang a new song, saying: "You are worthy to take the scroll, and to open its seals; for You were slain, and have redeemed us to God by Your blood out of every tribe and tongue and people and nation" (Rev 5:9). The following verses foretell sevenfold praise from redeemed in Heaven and fourfold praise from redeemed on earth.

24 January

"Then one of the elders answered, saying to me, 'Who are these arrayed in white robes, and where did they come from?' And I said to him, 'Sir, you know.' So he said to me, 'These are the ones who come out of the great tribulation, and washed their robes and made them white in the blood of the Lamb.'" (Rev 7:13-14)

Too often the Book of Revelation is pictured as being full of doom and gloom. It is also full of victory and glory; it depends whose side one is on! Chapters 1 to 3 cover the Church Age. From chapter 4 it will be too late to be part of the Bride, the Church; but then, before Calvary it was too early! John is shown "a multitude of all nations, tribes, peoples, and tongues, standing before the throne and before the Lamb, clothed with white robes, with palm branches in their hands, and crying out with a loud voice, saying, 'Salvation belongs to our God who sits on the throne, and to the Lamb!'" (Rev 7:9-10). Before the worst happens on earth, John is given a glimpse of those who are to be saved during the Great Tribulation, which is about to start, who will survive to enter the Millennial earth. There is some debate, but most agree that these are the Tribulation martyrs, rather than redeemed Tribulation survivors. We will return to all these amazing matters.

But do remember the description which Jesus gave of the Great Tribulation in His Olivet Discourse. While it will indeed be glorious to survive it, it will be dreadful to endure it: "Therefore rejoice, O heavens, and you who dwell in them! Woe to the inhabitants of the earth and the sea! For the devil has come down to you, having great wrath, because he knows that he has a short time" (Rev 12:12). This will be the period in which the Antichrist, supported by his False Prophet, will not only rule, but will demand direct worship through himself for his Satanic master.

Those who refuse to give allegiance, by accepting the Mark of the Beast in either right hand or forehead, will suffer dreadful persecution, and Satan's wrath. Chapters 13 and 14 cover these events; there can be no reprieve, no alternative to Hell, for those who will accept the Mark of the Beast and what it signifies.

25 January

*"They are spirits of demons, performing signs, which go out to the
kings of the earth and of the whole world, to gather them to the
battle of that great day of God Almighty.....And they gathered them
together to the place called in Hebrew, Armageddon."*
(Rev 16:14,16)

Armageddon is a place in north-eastern Israel, a natural battlefield.
I have looked down on it from Mount Carmel. Lest we are tempted
to deplore this coming battle, let us remember that it is to be Christ's
personal victory over Satan, the Antichrist, the False Prophet and
their massed armies. And we, following from Heaven, are to witness
it, but not take part. It is doubtful whether even the holy angels will do
so, though they have been used in this way before. This is the mighty
power of the One who created the worlds. It is the final act of the
Great Tribulation. This challenge not only seems like madness; it is
madness. Those have given themselves over to demons will be totally
subject to their devices. The unrepentant nations of the whole world
are to send their armies to Israel, and they will evidently cover much
of the Land, at least as far as Jerusalem, which will have been under
siege. Nobody is likely to want to destroy the city totally, because of
the enormous prestige of capturing, occupying and holding it.

Naturally we are not given all the details, but Zechariah chapters
12 to 14, although mentioning Megiddo, tell of what we might call
the Jerusalem Front and describe the fate of the combatants: "Their
flesh shall dissolve while they stand on their feet, Their eyes shall
dissolve in their sockets, and their tongues shall dissolve in their
mouths" (Zech 14:12).

Why do we need to know this? Note that today's text omits erse
15; a timely message from the Lord to believers is inserted into the
campaign account: "Behold, I am coming as a thief. Blessed is he
who watches, and keeps his garments, lest he walk naked and they
see his shame" (Rev 16:15). The first statement indicates that the
demon-maddened armies will be utterly oblivious of Christ's imminent
intervention. But we are alerted as to His plans, and should ever be
watchful, like somebody clothed, prepared and therefore unlikely to
be embarrassed, sitting up at night awaiting the arrival of a dear friend.

26 January

"'Let us be glad and rejoice and give Him glory, for the marriage of the Lamb has come, and His wife has made herself ready.' And to her it was granted to be arrayed in fine linen, clean and bright, for the fine linen is the righteous acts of the saints." (Rev 19:7-8)

Mystery Babylon, the harlot faith which, since the Flood, has embraced all the apparently diverse false religions including apostate Christianity, will now have been judged and destroyed. The true Church will have been in Heaven since the Rapture. Collectively, not individually, she is the Bride of the Lamb. "Christ also loved the church and gave Himself for her, that He might sanctify and cleanse her with the washing of water by the word" (Eph 5:25-26). Note that that cleansing will at this point be in the past.

The marriage of the Lamb takes place in Heaven, in conformity with the Jewish traditions often referred to in the New Testament. The marriage feast will be on earth, with Old Testament and Tribulation saints as the guests. It is possible for those of us who call ourselves evangelicals to become so preoccupied with the fact that works cannot save, that we forget that our Lord does not forget, and, as we were reminded on 20th January, worthy works will be commended at the Bema or Judgment Seat of Christ. It is the heavenly Bridegroom's will that His Bride should be arrayed in her own glory. This, if we think about it, will in no way detract from His own glory – rather the opposite in such a loving relationship. It has been through His grace that we have on earth been able to do that which brings Him glory. Probably most of us, when we have badly let down our Lord, have felt that we will one day be left empty-handed, with nothing to contribute on that glorious marriage day. However, a rarely noticed but reassuring promise tells us that, "Each one will receive his own reward according to his own labour" (I Cor 3:8).

Again, let us remember the timing. Paul warned the Athenians: "He (God) has appointed a day on which He will judge the world in righteousness by the Man whom He has ordained." (Acts 17:31). That will now be over, and we are to accompany our Lord as He descends.

27 January

"Now I saw heaven opened, and behold, a white horse. And He who sat on him was called Faithful and True, and in righteousness He judges and makes war..... Out of His mouth goes a sharp sword, that with it He should strike the nations. And He Himself will rule them with a rod of iron. He Himself treads the winepress of the fierceness and wrath of Almighty God." (Rev 19:11,15)

We will periodically return to this awesome passage during the course of a year's readings. There is far too much of importance to condense into the four hundred words I allow myself daily. Two days ago we looked briefly at the Battle of Armageddon and Christ's personal role in the destruction of His enemies, both demonic and human.

What I propose to look at briefly today is not the immediate hugely important and decisive purpose of Christ's Coming in Power, when alone He treads "the winepress of the fierceness and wrath of Almighty God", but at what He purposes to do thereafter, ruling the nations with a rod of iron. It is important that we should observe that clear statement, because millions of churchgoers are never told about this, despite it being confirmed by numerous clear-cut unfulfilled prophecies. The 4th Century Nicene Creed, which many congregations recite weekly, is partly to blame. In it end-time prophecy is squeezed into the statement: "He shall come again with glory to judge both the quick and the dead; Whose Kingdom shall have no end." Where in this inadequate Creed is the Millennial Kingdom, and the literal fulfilment of a host of prophecies?

This is not a matter of bickering among different groups of Christians. It is about Christian credibility in a global crisis when, as foretold "The rulers take counsel together, against the LORD and against His Anointed, saying, 'Let us break Their bonds in pieces and cast away their cords from us'" (Ps: 2:2-3). It is a matter of believing a promise made by God the Father to God the Son and recorded for our information: "Ask of Me, and I will give You the nations for Your inheritance, and the ends of the earth for Your possession. You shall break them with a rod of iron; You shall dash them to pieces like a potter's vessel." (Ps 2:8-9). That has yet to happen, but it will happen.

28 January

"Blessed and holy is he who has part in the first resurrection. Over such the second death has no power, but they shall be priests of God and of Christ, and shall reign with Him a thousand years."
(Rev 20:6)

The context makes it clear that there are two distinct resurrections. "The hour is coming in which all who are in the graves will hear His voice and come forth - those who have done good, to the resurrection of life, and those who have done evil, to the resurrection of condemnation" (Jn 5:28-29). The first is likened to Old Testament harvests, with Christ as the firstfruits, the Church as the main harvest and others as the gleanings. Those involved are exempt the Second. There has to be the clearest of gaps between the completion of the First and the Second. Six times this thousand year interval is mention in Revelation 20.

The moment we deny this or pretend that the Millennium is the present age, as many do, we are compelled to interpret allegorically vast numbers of other prophecies. In coming months we will look   at many Old Testament Messianic prophecies fulfilled literally at Christ's First Coming, as well as many yet to be fulfilled at His Second. First Coming fulfilments provide excellent precedents for how prophecy is fulfilled. Why interpret less literally those to be fulfilled at His Second? In these precarious times we Christians should be confident in the face of the scepticism of unbelievers and the scoffing of those on the fringe of the churches. If we fail in this, we can hardly expect to be taken seriously.

The ruling of the rod of iron which we looked at yesterday does not imply oppression or cruelty; but it does imply the strictest of regimes to ensure peace, stability, prosperity and worship. We will see more of the administration of this reigning on 30th January. Those classed as blessed and holy are those already resurrected. Those entering the Millennium in mortal bodies are earlier addressed by Jesus thus: "Come, you blessed of My Father, inherit the kingdom prepared for you from the foundation of the world" (Matt 25:34). While death will still be a possibility for those born during the Millennium, the potential human life span, severely curtailed back in Genesis, will extend to the thousand years which even Methuselah did not achieve.

29 January

"Then I saw a great white throne and Him who sat on it, from whose face the earth and the heaven fled away. And there was found no place for them. And I saw the dead, small and great, standing before God, and books were opened. And another book was opened, which is the Book of Life. And the dead were judged according to their works, by the things which were written in the books." (Rev 20:11-12)

There is much in the Bible which human tongue has no power to describe, be it glorious or dreadful. This passage describes the latter – an event which is to follow a final brief failed rebellion and the end of our world and perhaps also its starry surroundings. This is timelessness – eternity. God has committed all judgment to His Son. Christ is to judge the living and the dead (II Tim 4:1). The sins of the believer were judged at Calvary and our board is wiped clean. Living unbelievers will have been judged either before the Millennium (Matt 25:31-32), or in the rebellion at the end of the Millennium (Rev 20:7-9). Now the unsaved dead are to be resurrected to stand bodily to face the One whom they rejected.

The book of life will demonstrate that their names are absent; thereafter they will be judged according their works. When we consider how, with techniques developed over a few decades, mankind has learned to record and replay vast quantities of data, how much more will God's records be free of hackers and viruses? What folly for any to have said during this life, that, as they are going to Hell anyway, they might as well carry on in their wickedness. Several times Jesus talked about Hell being more tolerable for some than others; clearly He meant it, but no further light is thrown on such fearsome matters.

Remember that Jesus spoke of Hell more than anyone else in the Bible – Jesus who "is not slack concerning His promise..... but is longsuffering toward us, not willing that any should perish but that all should come to repentance" (II Pet 3:9). Even the most devout believer has no concept of what, during the hours of darkness at Calvary, was involved in purchasing our salvation. Were we to comprehend *that*, and what people fail to avail themselves of, we would understand better the righteousness of God's judgments.

30 January

"Now I saw a new heaven and a new earth, for the first heaven and the first earth had passed away. Also there was no more sea. Then I, John, saw the holy city, New Jerusalem, coming down out of heaven from God, prepared as a bride adorned for her husband." (Rev 21:1-2)

Compared with yesterday's, today's text is thrilling beyond our imagination. If we look carefully at this chapter, we find that the holy city, New Jerusalem, is actually to descend twice, once during the Millennium, to be withdrawn at the end of this world, and once in the following eternal state. Let us look briefly at the first. We will return to the second descent in due course. This is the place that our Lord went to prepare for us, the bridal home, where the city and its inhabitants are so closely integrated that they are considered one. Resurrected redeemed of other ages will be there too. But of course it and the earth below are parts of different creations, so it is well nigh impossible at present to visualise how its citizens can be so closely associated with the earth below. We cannot be adamant about the details.

But consider. Ever since the time of Abraham we have encountered angels coming and going about God's business between Heaven and earth, and often being seen by those on earth with whom they could communicate. Jacob had his famous God-given dream (Gen 28:12) of a ladder, with angels descending and ascending. That gives us at least a picture of how we, who will be immortal but not angels, will carry out such duties on earth as we are entrusted. We are not told whether all will have this privilege. Jesus told the Twelve, "Assuredly I say to you, that in the regeneration, when the Son of Man sits on the throne of His glory, you who have followed Me will also sit on twelve thrones, judging the twelve tribes of Israel" (Matt 19:28).

In the New Jerusalem we, who are to be "ever with the Lord", will see His face. However the fact that He will be represented in the Jerusalem Temple by His Shekinah Glory, as with the Israelites in the wilderness, makes it uncertain whether mortals will see Him after the "sheep and goats" segregation. But we can say, "Wait and see!" and mean it!

31 January

"He who testifies to these things says, 'Surely I am coming quickly.' Amen. Even so, come, Lord Jesus!" (Rev 22:20)

Our Lord's promise, "Surely I am coming quickly", occurs three times in the epilogue to Revelation (22:6 to 21). Each of the three is immensely significant. The sceptic points to the fact that these words were recorded over nineteen hundred years ago, and asks how He could be coming soon. Well, in the light of eternity we may very well say that nineteen centuries are nothing. Even now we may say: "Our light affliction, which is but for a moment, is working for us a far more exceeding and eternal weight of glory" (II Cor 4:17). However the word translated "quickly" does not necessarily imply "soon". It can also mean rapidly, implying that all the events of His future coming will occur in quick succession

The first occurrence is in verse 7: "Behold, I am coming quickly! Blessed is he who keeps the words of the prophecy of this book." This is one of our Saviour's final recorded blessings, and how lightly it is esteemed in thousands of churches. As we read through the myriad of Bible prophecies and, in particular, this final book, let us ensure that we claim this wonderful blessing. The second instance, in verse 12, is followed by: "and My reward is with Me, to give to every one according to his work". Our Lord is intensely interested in our work for Him – our labour of love, if this is indeed what it is. It is one of the many things He has in mind, and evidently He is thinking of His coming for the redeemed at the Rapture, rather than His later Coming in Power. If we are looking forward to the Rapture, how much more is our heavenly Bridegroom doing the same?

The final occurrence is at verse 20, "He who testifies to these things says, 'Surely I am coming quickly'". And the aged Apostle replies: "Amen. Even so, come, Lord Jesus!" The same aspirations are voiced at I Corinthians 16:22. Many modern translations simply say: "O Lord, come!" But both the Darby and Authorised versions preserve that final plea in the original Greek, *Maranatha!* There is something personal, something unique about this, and many of us who long for our Lord's return often greet each other with "Maranatha!"

"That it might be fulfilled" Prophecies

1 February

*"So all this was done **that it might be fulfilled** which was spoken by the Lord through the prophet, saying: 'Behold, the virgin shall be with child, and bear a Son, and they shall call His name Immanuel,' which is translated, 'God with us.'"* (Matt 1:22-23)

The Holy Spirit often confirms through the Gospel writers that these were prophecies concerning our Lord in His earthly life. The Jews of His day, and indeed of our day, would dispute these. King Ahaz, to whom Isaiah announced his prophecy, was a reluctant hearer, a breaker of God's laws who had sought help from Egypt rather than invoking his right as the anointed king of Israel to turn to God. In fact, he wished to avoid any direct communication from God. He therefore would and could not benefit personally from the prophecy; so it is today with those who shun God, hoping that nobody notices.

"Behold" always introduces something of significance which has yet to happen. This is one of the clearest prophecies of Christ's incarnation. He was foreshadowed by the birth of an ordinary child who would have been little more than a toddler at the time of the Assyrian invasion of Judah and the sacking of several Judean cities. But the Septuagint scholars who translated this into Greek were in no doubt about the miraculous birth which was being foretold, and used the word which really did mean a virgin, *parthenos*, even although the Hebrew word is less specific. If any doubt is left, we have the benefit of Luke's account of *how* the virgin would conceive, which even Isaiah himself did not comprehend; all he could do was accept the fact. The name Immanuel was unique and would have been blasphemous of any other than the Son of God; it is the expression of divine condescension. The Hebrew indicates that the name, Immanuel was given before the conception. The timing of God's demonstration of His love for this fallen world is marvellous – He planned a way in which He would be with us.

The angels provided the evidence, and the wise men or magi further evidence. Any within churches who deny the truth of the incarnation and virgin birth of the Lord Jesus Christ deny the intervention of God Himself, because it is clearly stated that it was the Lord who spoke through the prophet.

2 February

*"When he arose, he took the young Child and His mother by night
and departed for Egypt and was there until the death of Herod,
that it might be fulfilled which was spoken by the Lord through
the prophet, saying, 'Out of Egypt I called My Son.'"* (Matt 2:14-15)

The prophecy here referred to is Hosea 11:1: "When Israel was
a child, I loved him, and out of Egypt I called My son." Obviously
there is a further application to the Exodus of the nation of Israel,
but this does not negate the clearest of statement in this Gospel
that it is applied to Jesus Christ. When God says "My Son", surely
Christ takes priority over Israel. Once again the deity of Christ is
confirmed as being from His earliest days, and not, as some cults
would contend, only from the time of His baptism. All false teaching
is anticipated and countered in Scripture.

Egypt had been a place of refuge when Jacob and his family of
seventy went there to escape the famine; it was to be only temporary,
but long enough for that family to become a nation. The night-time
flight of Joseph, Mary and the infant Jesus was hastened by God's
angelic messenger. This exile also was to be temporary, until it was
time to return to the Holy Land. Malcolm Davis writes: "Israel and the
Lord Jesus were alike in that both were the objects of the love of the
Father, both were called 'My son', and both were in Egypt. In fact
Christ is the true Israel, who perfectly fulfilled for God what Israel so
sadly failed to fulfil." Ellicott comments: "The passage illustrates the
fact that the true Son of God was also submitted in His youth to the
hard schooling of a cruel exile." Nothing unanticipated or accidental
was involved.

Egypt is often thought of as spiritually representing the world with
all that this entails. As new believers we are called out to new life in
Christ. In that sense we are children of God called out to be separate
from the world, which is at enmity with God. During His ministry
Jesus left Israel to go into the foreign region of Tyre and Sidon; but
He never returned to Egypt. Believers should never be at home in
the alien world, but act as ambassadors for Christ.

3 February

*"Then Herod, when he saw that he was deceived by the wise men, was exceedingly angry; and he sent forth and put to death all the male children who were in Bethlehem and in all its districts, from two years old and under, according to the time which he had determined from the wise men. **Then was fulfilled what was spoken** by Jeremiah the prophet."* (Matt 2:16-17)

Jeremiah's prophecy reads: "Thus says the LORD: 'A voice was heard in Ramah, lamentation and bitter weeping, Rachel weeping for her children, refusing to be comforted for her children, because they are no more'" (Jer 31:15). This is another prophecy with an original significance for the prophet's own generation and a future one for the coming Messiah. Matthew was careful not to quote Jeremiah's next sentence, which would have been inappropriate: "Thus says the LORD: 'Refrain your voice from weeping, and your eyes from tears..... they shall come back from the land of the enemy.'" Jeremiah had recently foretold the seventy years Babylon captivity, God's judgment for their unfaithfulness: "But they mocked the messengers of God, despised His words, and scoffed at His prophets, until the wrath of the LORD arose against His people, till there was no remedy..... And those who escaped from the sword he carried away to Babylon, where they became servants to him and his sons until the rule of the kingdom of Persia" (II Chron 36:16,20). This is a superb illustration of the precision of this type of prophecy. No doubt the smallest infants were put to the sword before the long journey. Ezra (3:12) records that some of those who had left as youngsters returned after seventy years.

But, as Walvoord points out, in both instances the children were slaughtered at times of national apostasy and indifference towards God. There is always a cost. There had been no room in the inn for Joseph and Mary when Jesus was about to be born, and in such a close-knit community there was evidently no preparedness among neighbours to show hospitality, despite knowing Micah's prophecy about the Messianic Ruler due to be born there. Are we any better today? We are even more generously provided with prophecies concerning Christ's Second Coming than they were regarding His First. Are we not now beginning to pay the cost of our indifference along with the secular world?

4 February

*"And he came and dwelt in a city called Nazareth, **that it might be fulfilled** which was spoken by the prophets, 'He shall be called a Nazarene.'"* (Matt 2:23)

An angel was duly dispatched to Egypt to tell Joseph and Mary that Herod was now dead and that they should return forthwith to Israel. However Joseph heard that Herod's son, Archelaus, had succeeded him, and might therefore also wish to murder anyone who had been described as another king. One of his first acts on succeeding his father was to murder three thousand of his subjects; one more would have been seen as no problem. Joseph, being thus wary about returning to the ancestral home of Bethlehem of Judea with its Messianic associations, and, having been warned in another dream, set out for the Galilean town of Nazareth, seventy or so miles further on and separated from Judea by Samaria.

Now, unlike all the other fulfilled prophecies, there is no obvious Old Testament prediction. Sceptics love to latch on to such problems. The marginal reference in several Bibles takes us to Isaiah 11:1: "There shall come forth a Rod from the stem of Jesse, and a Branch shall grow out of his roots." John F Walvoord writes: "No express passage in the Old Testament declares that Christ should be a Nazarene. The most plausible explanation is that it may be an oblique reference to Isaiah 11:1.... Just as a rod has an insignificant beginning, so Nazareth was an insignificant city from which the Messiah would come. There is also the possibility that Matthew referred to an oral prophecy not recorded in Scripture." The city's reputation is confirmed in Nathaniel's question: "Can anything good come out of Nazareth?" (Jn 1:46). In Acts, Jesus is referred to seven times as Jesus or Jesus Christ of Nazareth, including once by Himself (Acts 22:8). This is doubly important, as He was thus associated not only with Judea, which had long since returned from exile, but with the absent Northern tribes. But also He was prepared to be given what those in Jerusalem who had rejected Him considered a disparaging title. Our Saviour was prepared to be associated with the mean and lowly. The foolish, stubborn pride of Jerusalem has over the centuries cost them dear.

5 February

*"**As it is written in the Prophets**: 'Behold, I send My messenger before Your face, Who will prepare Your way before You.'"*
(Mk 1:2)

John the Baptist is given considerable prominence in the Gospels. It was in the Jerusalem temple that his priestly father was told by Gabriel of his coming birth and mission: "For he will be great in the sight of the Lord, and shall drink neither wine nor strong drink. He will also be filled with the Holy Spirit, even from his mother's womb" (Lk 1:15).

Today's text quoted Malachi 3:1. Malachi then goes on immediately to foretell the Messiah who was to follow this messenger: "'Behold, I send My messenger, And he will prepare the way before Me. And the Lord, whom you seek, will suddenly come to His temple, even the Messenger of the covenant, in whom you delight. Behold, He is coming,' says the LORD of hosts." Both are described as messengers. But who can endure the day of His coming? And who can stand when He appears? For He is like a refiner's fire and like launderer's soap" (Mal 3:1-2). This is one of the sternest Messianic prophecies.

What we must continually bear in mind is that, at His First Coming, the Lord Jesus Christ genuinely presented Himself to His people, Israel, despite knowing that He would be rejected by the nation as a whole. There is an enigmatic reference to John being potentially Elijah who is to come before the Second Coming. We return to this important fact later. The initial criterion for acceptance at His First coming was repentance: John first preached it: "Repent, for the kingdom of heaven is at hand!" (Matt 3:2); then Jesus preached it: "From that time Jesus began to preach and to say, 'Repent, for the kingdom of heaven is at hand.'" (Matt 4:17). It was what Jesus sent the disciples out to do: "So they went out and preached that people should repent" (Mk 6:12); it is part of our great commission: "and that repentance and remission of sins should be preached in His name to all nations, beginning at Jerusalem" (Lk 24:47). Repentance recognises the need of a Saviour; repentance is essential for restoration from backsliding, repentance is the prerequisite for revival. "As many as I love, I rebuke and chasten. Therefore be zealous and repent" (Rev 3:19).

6 February

*"**That it might be fulfilled** which was spoken by Isaiah the prophet, saying: 'The land of Zebulun and the land of Naphtali, By the way of the sea, beyond the Jordan, Galilee of the Gentiles: The people who sat in darkness have seen a great light, and upon those who sat in the region and shadow of death light has dawned.'"* (Matt 4:14-16)

This was an important prophecy to which to refer, inasmuch as many of Jesus' mighty works were to be done in the region of Galilee, and Scriptural authority was required to demonstrate that this was appropriate. The tribes of Zebulon and Naphtali had of course been deported by the Assyrians many centuries before, but the allocation of land under Joshua had never been formerly revoked. Many Gentiles had settled there in the interim period. In Roman times it was a separate province from Judea, not under the administrative jurisdiction of Jerusalem.

Jesus was now about to make His temporary base in Capernaum. It is a lovely hilly area around that little Sea of Galilee or Tiberias, which is really a large lake on the river Jordan. As a Scotsman I felt very much at home on the one occasion that I visited it. Some of the New Testament sites have been confirmed; others are traditional. Some of the least well-identified ones had unnecessary commemorative buildings erected by the enthusiastic Helena, mother of the Emperor Constantine, a few by the Crusaders and a few more recently, when the Ottoman Empire was relaxing its influence in the area.

It is worth pondering how many of the greatest achievements of the Christian Church down through the Centuries have been far from the Holy Land. The Gospel came to many pagan lands like our own, and the light of the glorious Gospel shone in what seemed the most unlikely places. In the days of the great missionary initiatives, from the late 17th Century until the Post-War period of receding empires, that light continued to shine. More recently it has become common for the newly evangelised lands to take over the torch from those whose nations have abandoned the faith of their fathers. The blessings which were once ours have been passed on, and we cannot but wonder whether we in "the West" are now the ones under judgment.

55

7 February

*"When evening had come, they brought to Him many who were demon-possessed. And He cast out the spirits with a word, and healed all who were sick, **that it might be fulfilled** which was spoken by Isaiah the prophet, saying: 'He Himself took our infirmities and bore our sicknesses.'"* (Matt 8:16-17)

Here we are reminded of the Lord's compassion, something which was so greatly enhanced by His becoming flesh and dwelling among us. The quote is from Isaiah 53:4: "Surely he hath borne our griefs, and carried our sorrows: yet we did esteem him stricken, smitten of God, and afflicted" (KJV). Now that well-known Isaiah verse is very properly primarily thought of in connection with Christ's vicarious sin bearing. But here it is shown to mean even more than that. John Heading perceptively remarks: "Since the NT gives no indication that the Lord's body sustained illnesses taken from others as the result of His miracles, we interpret the quotation as referring to the Lord's grief and sympathy at the misery around Him." Although we know that He was often weary and sometimes hungry, we are not actually told that Jesus never suffered illnesses. We must be careful not to make generalisations, but can safely emphasise that He was to die as the Lamb without spot and blemish. In the Temple no imperfect beast was acceptable as a sacrifice for sins, much less the Lamb of God.

Jesus was able to do the unthinkable and touch the leper in a unique example of empathy. When the woman who secretively touched the hem of His garment and was healed, He perceived that power or virtue had gone out of Him. Everything He did for fallen mankind was costly. He was able to grieve, to weep and to show compassion. The sheer cost of God's redeeming work in Christ is utterly beyond our comprehension.

As believers, we have been born of the Spirit and should display, however feebly, something of our Saviour's love and compassion. The media love to portray Christians as austere, judgmental people. Jude tells us: "On some have compassion, making a distinction; but others save with fear, pulling them out of the fire, hating even the garment defiled by the flesh" (vv 22-23). Ours can be a difficult balancing act in a critical and demanding world, requiring both grace and wisdom, firmness and love.

8 February

*"**That it might be fulfilled** which was spoken by Isaiah the prophet, saying: 'Behold! My Servant whom I have chosen, My Beloved in whom My soul is well pleased! I will put My Spirit upon Him, and He will declare justice to the Gentiles. He will not quarrel nor cry out, nor will anyone hear His voice in the streets. A bruised reed He will not break, and smoking flax He will not quench, till He sends forth justice to victory; and in His name Gentiles will trust.'"*
(Matt 12:17-21)

The Isaiah reference, with minor modifications, is from chapter 42:1-3. Many of the rabbis puzzled over the prophesied contrasting roles of the promised Messiah, some concluding that there were to be two Messiahs, a non-intrusive suffering one, who would be gracious to the downtrodden and an authoritative, conquering one who would establish justice with a new covenant to replace the broken and therefore obsolete one.

The title "servant" occurs sixteen times between chapters 41 and 53 of Isaiah and alternates in meaning between Christ, who would not fail, and Israel, the nation-servant with its unique appointment in God's redemptive purposes for the human race, which often failed in its Divine mission. But here, in this Isaiah passage, is confirmation that both roles are fulfilled in a single Messiah or Christ; and of course the Gospel writer confirms in these verses that Isaiah in this lovely "Servant Song" was foretelling Jesus Christ. That remarkable title of Servant – the Servant of Jehovah – is applied. He is the Servant who is also the Beloved. Six times in the Gospels we find statements such as: "a voice came from heaven which said, 'You are My beloved Son; in You I am well pleased.'" (Lk 3:22). He Himself said: "For even the Son of Man did not come to be served, but to serve, and to give His life a ransom for many." (Mk 10:45).

The Deity and voluntary servitude are mentioned in those key verses of Phillipians 2:5-7, which we look at in greater depth elsewhere: "Let this mind be in you which was also in Christ Jesus, who, being in the form of God, did not consider it robbery to be equal with God, but made Himself of no reputation, taking the form of a **bondservant**, and coming in the likeness of men." Isaiah had been given a privileged preview.

9 February

*"And **in them the prophecy of Isaiah is fulfilled**, which says: 'Hearing you will hear and shall not understand, and seeing you will see and not perceive; for the hearts of this people have grown dull. Their ears are hard of hearing, and their eyes they have closed, lest they should see with their eyes and hear with their ears, lest they should understand with their hearts and turn, so that I should heal them.'"* (Matt 13:14-15)

These verses are quoted in full or in part several times in the Gospels, Acts and Epistles; they are always associated with the failure as a nation of Israel and the long term, rather than eternal, consequences. It is so important to understand the timing of this passage. Jesus had preached openly and ambiguously presenting His Messianic credentials until the point where the religious hierarchy had either to accept or reject Him. There could no longer be any vacillating. Having seen Jesus cast out what was considered impossible, a blind-mute demon, the crowds enquired whether this was not the Son of David, meaning the Messiah. Their leaders were compelled to giving a verdict. "This fellow does not cast out demons except by Beelzebub, the ruler of the demons." (Matt 12:24). What a dreadful human assessment of the Son of God! What catastrophic national consequences! This was the first major stage in Christ's rejection. It was following this that Matthew quotes the above sentence, with an added clause to the effect that they, the leaders, had, for the time being, placed themselves beyond healing. Healing demands recognition of the symptoms, rather than resistance to remedies on offer. The symptoms were hardened hearts, deafened ears and closed eyes. When "at last He sent His Son", they acted like their forebears, who "mocked the messengers of God, despised His words, and scoffed at His prophets, until the wrath of the LORD arose against His people, till there was no remedy" (II Chron 36:16), The ultimate healing of these symptoms is predicted in many prophecies, but much has had to happen first, and in the meantime, it has been the Church's responsibility to keep hearts, ears and eyes active. For any believer of any age, such spiritual barrenness as Israel suffered is self-imposed and cannot be overlooked. How many congregations can be said never to suffer from any of these symptoms?

10 February

*"**That it might be fulfilled** which was spoken by the prophet, saying: 'I will open My mouth in parables; I will utter things kept secret from the foundation of the world.'"* (Matt 13:35)

Jesus' switch from plain speaking to parables is the direct result of what we considered yesterday. In Matthew 13 He told a number of important parables, many with prophetic significance, which we will look at later. Not surprisingly the disciples enquired why. In addition to Jesus' explanation given yesterday, citing Isaiah 6:8-9, one of the most quoted Old Testament passages in the New Testament, Matthew refers to Psalm 78:1-2: "Give ear, O my people, to my law; Incline your ears to the words of my mouth. I will open my mouth in a parable; I will utter dark sayings of old." The "dark sayings" signify riddles or enigmas and are sometimes described as allegories, as with Paul in Galatians 4:21-23, drawing lessons from Sarah and Hagar. We are meant to ponder upon and learn from God's dealings of old.

Let us bear in mind that Jesus did not hesitate to give brief but lucid explanations to the disciples, those whom He loved and who loved Him. They were excluded from this restricted understanding. Jim Flanigan in his excellent Psalms commentary writes: "These will be appreciated by the spiritual, exercised heart, but will be unintelligible and unprofitable to the carnal mind..... There was much to be said, and much to be learned, from the history of the nation, for those who sincerely wish to be taught."

Progressively revealed in the Holy Scriptures is much that was previously inaccessible. The Psalmist wrote: "The entrance of Your words gives light; it gives understanding to the simple" (Ps 119:130). Are we in a spiritual state to "give entrance"? The disciples had evidently been hanging on His every word and asked for, and therefore received, explanations. Are we equally eager to learn and to apply lessons? There is much of prophetic significance in this chapter of Matthew; simple, easily understood lessons are put into a correct perspective regarding the end of the pre-Church Age, the Church Age and what is to follow. But sadly this perspective is lost on many, because doors are closed to the idea of the Church Age ending long before the end of the world. We look at this in another section.

11 February

*"All this was done **that it might be fulfilled** which was spoken by the prophet, saying: 'Tell the daughter of Zion, "Behold, your King is coming to you, lowly, and sitting on a donkey, a colt, the foal of a donkey."'"* (Matt 21:4-5)

Last month we looked this famous Zechariah prophecy; but there is much else to consider. This, for an awaiting people, should have been one of the most instantly recognisable fulfilments of Old Testament prophecy.

We must distinguish between two groups – the enthusiastic multitude who laid their garments and cut down palm fronds to pave the way for the Rider of the donkey, and the religious leaders of Jerusalem. The multitude must have included many of those who at Pentecost identified themselves as being from widely diverse parts of the known world (Acts 2:9-11). Further crowds from the city went out to join in the celebration. The city leaders' reaction was in stark contrast and was to drive our Lord to tears: "And when He had come into Jerusalem, all the city was moved, saying, 'Who is this?'" (Matt 21:10). We are not told how many of the pilgrims and the participating citizens changed sides when the euphoria had died down, or how many were simply disillusioned by subsequent events, or how many still recognised their Messiah in the lowly Figure on the donkey.

The pilgrims were there for the Passover, and sang extracts from what had become the traditional Psalms 113 to 118. Hence it was natural for them to cry "Hosanna!", meaning "Lord, save!" It was natural for them to cry that which so enraged the chief priest and scribes, "Blessed is He who comes in the name of the Lord". It was natural for them to give Him the Messianic title of Son of David. Later Jesus acknowledged to these leaders the correctness of this recognition by identifying Himself as the stone which the builders rejected, implying that they were the neglectful builders (Matt 21:42-45 with Ps 118:22). It is easy to go along with the crowd, particularly when this involves being in a large gathering of believers, though many simply do not have that option, especially with today's dwindling congregations. But it is harder, and indeed sometimes dangerous, to stand alone for the Lord Jesus Christ. Today, as back in those days, the Lord knows who are truly His.

12 February

"But although He had done so many signs before them, they did not believe in Him, **that the word** *of Isaiah the prophet* **might be fulfilled,** *which he spoke: 'Lord, who has believed our report? And to whom has the arm of the LORD been revealed?'"*
(Jn 12:37-38)

The word translated "signs" above appears as "miracles" in the AV/ KJV and Weymouth, but the more common "signs" is better, as it often does mean miraculous acts. But can mean more – evidence or proofs signs of authenticity, signs that the Lord Jesus Christ is indeed Divine, the Son of God. Earlier He had said: "though you do not believe Me, believe the works" (Jn 10:38); evidently the miracles are not intended to be the primary evidence of who Christ is. His later words, "Blessed are those who have not seen and yet have believed" (Jn 20:29), apply to us if we truly believe.

But there is something tragic here. Although He knew that it was to happen and that blessings for others would ensue, to have done all that He had done, and endured all that He had endured, and then come to the point where these comments could be made must have been heart-breaking, despite it having been prophesied.

Isaiah, in the opening two verses of his 53rd chapter, wrote: "Who has believed our report? And to whom has the arm of the LORD been revealed? For He shall grow up before Him as a tender plant, and as a root out of dry ground. He has no form or comeliness; and when we see Him, there is no beauty that we should desire Him." Also, in 52:14: "His visage was marred more than any man, and His form more than the sons of men." Indeed, "He was made to be sin for us, who knew no sin" but the point here is that there was no *desire* on the part of most of those of Israel to whom He had come to see any beauty. As Ironside says, "They failed to see in Jesus the 'arm of the Lord' stretched forth for their salvation, as in the case of the great bulk of mankind today..... to God He was precious beyond words, but to unbelieving man He had no form, no comeliness, that is man did not recognise the moral loveliness that He ever exhibited."

13 February

"I do not speak concerning all of you. I know whom I have chosen;
*but **that the Scripture may be fulfilled**, 'He who eats bread*
with Me has lifted up his heel against Me.' Now I tell you before it
comes, that when it does come to pass, you may believe that I am
He'." (Jn 13:18-19)

We come to what may at first sight be comparatively trivial compared with yesterday's theme, because we are dealing with one treacherous individual, rather a recalcitrant nation. But Jesus did not regard Judas's betrayal as trivial, or the individual's soul as being less precious than the souls of a multitude. Judas Iscariot had been one of those who had accompanied Jesus throughout His ministry, although He had always known of his final disloyalty: "Did I not choose you, the twelve, and one of you is a devil?" (Jn 6:70). The word is correctly "devil" and not the lesser ""demon", because ultimately Satan was to enter him. But in most respects Judas had been treated like the other disciples and had shared the same experiences. Clearly Jesus was personally hurt.

The Old Testament quote is from one of David's Psalms, one where David was recounting his own experiences and feelings: "Even my own familiar friend in whom I trusted, who ate my bread, has lifted up his heel against me." (Ps 41:9). Note that John in his Gospel account did not quote the next verse of this Psalm: "But You, O LORD, be merciful to me, and raise me up, that I may repay them." Jim Flanigan in his commentary writes: "David had these multiple sorrows of remembering his sins, his suffering, his illness and enduring the taunts of his enemies; but perhaps the hardest thing to bear was this, that his own familiar trusted friend should turn against him. This is an undoubted reference to Ahitophel (2 Sam 15:12, 31, 16:20, 23)." The man who had been David's friend and counsellor betrayed him, turning to the usurper Absalom.

Ahitophel did have one legitimate personal grudge against David; Judas had none whatsoever against the Lord Jesus. Jesus said: "Woe to that man by whom the Son of Man is betrayed! It would have been good for that man if he had not been born." (Matt 26:24). That cannot be the believer's position, but each one of can still cause our Saviour sadness.

14 February

"Then they crucified Him, and divided His garments, casting lots,
that it might be fulfilled *which was spoken by the prophet: 'They*
divided My garments among them, and for My clothing they cast
lots.' Sitting down, they kept watch over Him there." (Matt 27:35-36)

It is Matthew who most frequently comments about events in Jesus' life fulfilling specific prophecies. This is understandable in that Gospel which was written primarily for Jews, who should have been familiar with the Old Testament and able to compare the evidence. This is the only time that John in his Gospel does the same (Jn 19:24). In fact the Matthew text may have been added later, but the John text is indubitably original. John adds "Therefore the soldiers did these things", which is significant in that, once God has predicted an event through His prophets, it cannot be cancelled or amended. That may sound obvious, but when we consider even recent Church history, we find thousands of leaders ignoring the clearest of prophecies and forecasting some sort of spiritual Utopia without the prior time of unprecedented tribulation.

The reference is to Ps 22:18: "They divide My garments among them, and for My clothing they cast lots." The Psalmist is no less an authoritative prophet than those who have books named after them. It is confirmation, were any needed, that this amazing Psalm is a God-given personal foresight of Christ's suffering on the Cross. The present tense reflects what the Sufferer was feeling at the time. We will look at other Psalm 22 extracts elsewhere. Soldiers prized souvenirs of their service, and a seamless inner garment (vesture, as in AV/KJV) was too good to be torn apart. Whether some translations are correct in omitting the vesture or changing it to "clothing" is questionable; the Psalm version is unambiguous. I have visited the soldiers' quarters in Jerusalem and seen some of their gambling marks scratched deeply into the stonework – a moving experience.

The cynicism of the observers is summed up in that statement: "Sitting down, they kept watch over Him". Soldiers on important ceremonial duty – and an execution would have been ceremonial in a negative way – required soldiers to stand, as I remember. But here the dying Saviour of the world was turned into a public spectacle until God drew the three hour veil of darkness over the face of the earth.

15 February

*"But when they came to Jesus and saw that He was already dead, they did not break His legs….. For these things were done **that the Scripture should be fulfilled**, 'Not one of His bones shall be broken.'"* (Jn 19:33,36)

It was almost sunset on the crucifixion day. Bodies were not allowed to remain on crosses during the Sabbath which was about to begin, so usually the legs of the victims were broken to allow their lungs to collapse and bring on immediate death. This happened to the two criminals on either side of Jesus, but Jesus was already dead and there was no ritualistic need for Jesus to be dealt with in this way. The Romans bowed to the request of the priests, who were so punctilious in these ceremonial matters, but so blind as to the identity of the Crucified One.

What was more important was that, according to the Passover conditions, no bone of the lamb was allowed to be broken, thus disqualifying it, and this was the Lamb of God. "In one house it shall be eaten;…. nor shall you break one of its bones" (Ex 12:46). The soldiers were, of course, unaware of the Divine overruling which was being applied to this event, so central to the salvation of mankind.

The reference of fulfilment was to Ps 22:16-17: "For dogs have surrounded Me; the congregation of the wicked has enclosed Me. They pierced My hands and My feet; I can count all My bones. They look and stare at Me." Tomorrow we look at the reference to the piercing. David in his extremity had been made a public spectacle, though he of course never suffered the crucifixion that his Descendant both physically and legally (through Mary and Joseph) had to experience. The Holy Spirit was giving King David the most graphic awareness of what his Son according to the flesh was to suffer ten centuries later, and ensured that the record was to be preserved for posterity. With crucifixion the flat cut nails used could be inserted between the bones of the hands and feet, and, as naked or almost naked crucified victims had their bones dislocated through the weight of their suspended bodies, the mocking onlookers could see the very bones staring. The term "dogs" may not seem insulting, but its use here against the mocking onlookers is appropriately degrading.

16 February

"But one of the soldiers pierced His side with a spear, and immediately blood and water came out. And he who has seen has testified, and his testimony is true; and he knows that he is telling the truth, so that you may believe. For these things were done **that the Scripture should be fulfilled..... And again another Scripture says**, *'They shall look on Him whom they pierced.'"*
(Jn 19:34-37)

We are reviewing consecutive verses of John's Gospel here, but, as two separate Old Testament fulfilments are involved, we devote a day to each. Now, before we leave Psalm 22, it is the hands and feet which are pierced while the Victim was still living: "For dogs have surrounded Me; the congregation of the wicked has enclosed Me. They pierced My hands and My feet; I can count all My bones. They look and stare at Me" (Ps 22:16-17).

But the reference here is to Zechariah 12:10: "And I will pour on the house of David and on the inhabitants of Jerusalem the Spirit of grace and supplication; then they will look on Me whom they pierced. Yes, they will mourn for Him as one mourns for his only son, and grieve for Him as one grieves for a first born." What is being fulfilled in this post-crucifixion drama is the national repentance, which still lies ahead and is so vividly portrayed by God through Zechariah. But, as to the actual piercing, David Baron, himself a Jew, wrote: "It was a Roman soldier who did the actual deed; Roman soldiers were they who pierced His blessed brow with the crown of thorns, and His hands and feet with those cruel nails, but the guilt and *responsibility* for the actions will be brought home to the heart and conscience of the Jewish nation in that day."

The personal eyewitness account is significant. As FB Meyer writes: "Finally, from the pierced side of Christ came out blood and water..... This was a symptom that there had been heart-rupture. And that the Lord had literally died of a broken heart. But it was also a symbol of the "double cure" which Jesus has effected. Blood to atone, water to cleanse. 'This is He that came by water and blood, not with the water alone.'" Let us join Thomas in his later confession: "My Lord and my God!"

Important Time Restricted Prophecies

17 February

*"The sceptre shall not depart from Judah, nor a lawgiver from between his feet, **until Shiloh comes**; And to Him shall be the obedience of the people".* (Gen 49:10)

We now look at certain prophecies which are unconditional except inasmuch as they cannot be fulfilled until certain other things have happened. Jacob, on his deathbed, blessed all his twelve sons and Joseph's two, whom he treated as his own. God was clearly over-ruling in these matters. Commentators who fail to recognise this also fail to appreciate the long-term prophetic significance of these blessings. Even during Old Testament history we notice some of the prophesied personal features being worked out in different tribes; but here we are looking further forward than the Old Testament.

Jacob's eldest son, Reuben, had forfeited his right of firstborn. His blessing rested upon Judah, the tribe through whom David, and later the Lord Jesus Christ, would be born. In the immediately preceding chapters of Genesis Judah's leadership qualities are noticeable; Jacob's blessings evidently took character into account – a principle which still prevails with God's treatment of His people. It is the tribe of Judah which would eventually establish its capital in Jerusalem, and Judah which in the time of David would be only reluctantly accepted by the northern tribes. Judah's position, like many of God's appointments, would be resisted, with only Benjamin in close alliance, and retaining the loyalty of most of the priestly tribe of Levi. It was Judah whose first exile was to be only short-lived.

JW Ferguson points out that the Revised Version is correct in rendering the last phrase as "to Him shall the obedience of the peoples (plural) be", and adds: "the verse refers to a coming king who will rule over the nations." Whatever minor variations of interpretation exist, there is no doubt that Shiloh, as a personal rather than a place name, is Messianic. Even its meaning, possibly "sent", "seed" or "peaceable", is debatable. Judah's blessing is evidently looking beyond the rejected Messiah at His First Coming to the time when "the Lion of the Tribe of Judah" (Rev 5:5), who will have set in motion the future Great Tribulation, will thereafter rule with a rod of iron. When we shortly turn to Ezekiel 21, we will see how no king of David's line has ruled Israel since the Babylonian captivity; but One will do so!

18 February

*"The LORD said to my Lord, 'Sit at My right hand, **till I make Your enemies Your footstool**.' The LORD shall send the rod of Your strength out of Zion. Rule in the midst of Your enemies!"*
(Ps 110:1-2)

Not surprisingly this is a Psalm of David, because we are privileged to eavesdrop on a conversation within the Godhead; the Father is addressing the Son. Jesus later in fact challenged the Pharisees with this verse, and included the third Person of the Trinity in His question – "How then does David in the Spirit call Him 'Lord', saying: 'The Lord said to My Lord.....?" (Matthew 24:43).

Jim Flanigan points out that it is the most quoted psalm in the New Testament. Not only does Jesus quote it, but so do Paul, Peter and indirectly John in Revelation. The cults, Orthodox Jews and liberals are all confounded. The text does not say that the Father is telling the Son to sit at His right hand until virtually the end of the world, which Amillennialists have long taught. Rather He is to sit at His right hand **until** He returns to earth in power to reign. David, of course, did not personally understand the sequence of events at and following Christ's First Coming. He wrote as inspired by the Holy Spirit.

Dr Walvoord writes of this psalm: "The crushing judgment on those who oppose Christ is described in verses 5 and 6. The contrast is between Christ's present position in heaven, where He is waiting for the time when judgment will fall on His enemies, at His second coming..... Christ in His resurrection is pictured as ascending into heaven and sitting on the throne of God, waiting until His enemies be made His footstool." We are reminded of Jesus' words: "I also overcame and sat down with My Father on His throne" (Rev 3:21). As the Son of Man He will remain in heaven **until** He goes forth to wage war against His enemies, and to rule with a rod of iron (Rev 19:15). He will do so in His own strength, as the One who conquered sin and death. As believers, we are on His winning side in this long confrontation. Satan, knowing that his time is short, is marshalling his forces, and we may at times feel his wrath, but we overcome by the blood of the Lamb.

19 February

"Then I said, 'Lord, how long?' And He answered: **'Until the cities are laid waste and without inhabitant**, *the houses are without a man, the land is utterly desolate, the LORD has removed men far away, and the forsaken places are many in the midst of the land. But yet a tenth will be in it, and will return and be for consuming, as a terebinth tree or as an oak, whose stump remains when it is cut down. So the holy seed shall be its stump.'"* (Isa 6:11-13)

Recently we looked at the surprising task allocated to Isaiah when he volunteered, "Here am I, send me" (Isa 6:8-9). Isaiah was to inform his people that the hardness of heart and spiritual deafness and blindness which they had allowed to develop would now be reinforced by God Himself. We know, but Isaiah did not, that it would be confirmed by Christ Himself for those who were then in the Land – Judea, long since returned from Babylonian devastation and exile.

Distressed, Isaiah enquired how long this state would continue, and was given the answer contained in today's reading. Isaiah's "Here am I, send me" response is often used out of context in volunteering for various forms of Christian service. Were more to take to look at Isaiah's commission as given by God, there would be less confusion regarding Israel. All the northern tribes were shortly to be exiled and dispersed by Assyria – an exile which has lasted over two and a half thousand years. And yet here God guarantees that the felled "tree" of Israel was to have life preserved in the "stump". The truth concerning what is described as a remnant of Israel is central to understanding God's revealed plans; the "faithful remnant" refers to those who of that remnant who still trust in God.

So although there were to be a variety of timescales, not elaborated in this particular prophecy, for different tribes of Israel, God is always faithful to His promises and always honours the "untils" which He has set. We may not be aware of specific mileposts in our lives, and may, like Israel, forfeit what God had conditionally in mind for us, but we know whom we have believed and should be persuaded that He is able to keep what we have committed to Him until that Day (see II Tim 1:12).

20 February

"Because the palaces will be forsaken, the bustling city will be deserted. The forts and towers will become lairs forever, a joy of wild donkeys, a pasture of flocks **Until the Spirit is poured upon us from on high,** *and the wilderness becomes a fruitful field, and the fruitful field is counted as a forest. Then justice will dwell in the wilderness, and righteousness remain in the fruitful field. The work of righteousness will be peace, and the effect of righteousness, quietness and assurance forever."* (Isa 32:14-17)

The subject of the prophecy is, of course, Jerusalem, the only capital of Israel recognised by God. The common assumption that the only Zion now recognised by God is the Church is folly, as this prophecy confirms. It is abundantly clear that the city which is to be deserted is the same one which is to be restored. Jerusalem was to have the most chequered history for the next two thousand seven hundred years at least. At times, such as during the Babylonian exile, it was to be totally deserted.

This "until" has yet to mature. It was available at Pentecost, but rejected; we think for instance of the words of the city's leaders in Acts: "What shall we do to these men? For, indeed, that a notable miracle has been done through them is evident to all who dwell in Jerusalem, and we cannot deny it. But so that it spreads no further among the people, let us severely threaten them, that from now on they speak to no man in this name." (Acts 4:16-17). The Spirit had indeed been poured out, and the minority who accepted Him formed the nucleus of what was to become a world-wide Church.

But Isaiah looks beyond the two thousand years of Jerusalem-centred dereliction, jealousy and conflict. The worst short episode in the city's history still lies ahead, and only after her rejected Messiah's feet have alighted on the Mount of Olives will the Spirit be poured out and justice and righteousness, which alone can bring peace, prevail. As individual believers and as congregations or assemblies, we are not directly involved in the blessings which follow that "until", but we can learn from this passage that the pouring out of the Holy Spirit is inextricably linked with justice, righteousness and peace, and that these longed-for blessings cannot come without the prior pouring out of God's Spirit.

21 February

*"For Zion's sake I will not hold My peace, and for Jerusalem's sake I will not rest, **Until her righteousness goes forth as brightness**, and her salvation as a lamp that burns. The Gentiles shall see your righteousness, and all kings your glory. You shall be called by a new name, which the mouth of the LORD will name. You shall also be a crown of glory in the hand of the LORD, and a royal diadem in the hand of your God. You shall no longer be termed Forsaken, nor shall your land any more be termed Desolate; but you shall be called Hephzibah, and your land Beulah; for the LORD delights in you, and your land shall be married."* (Isa 62:1-4)

Here we are given a glimpse into the heart of God. Whatever Israel has done in the past and is doing now, it rarely includes demonstrating any long awaited righteousness; but God's love for her is unending. He yearns for this future day spiritual glory. She has time and again forfeited the blessings offered before the death of Moses; she has experienced the curses decreed at the same time, but the door to restitution has ever been open.

Jews of Jesus' day somehow managed to eradicate from their minds the blessings which they would eventually be instrumental in bringing to the Gentiles. Far too many Christians of our own day have managed to convince themselves that God has no future plans for Israel. The speaker here is God Himself. How can so many ears be shut to Him? Yes, Israel is considered by most of the world as being God-forsaken. But God has promised, rather than merely suggested, that she will be seen by all as the Land in which God delights, no longer in a state of self-imposed widowhood.

At the age of twelve I climbed one of the Pentland Hills to see the sun setting in the north-west over the distant Highland mountains. I was so captivated by the wonder of the scene that, without a soul to hear me, I sang the old hymn, Beulah Land..... "As on the highest mount I stand, I look away across the sea, where mansions are prepared for me, and view the shining glory shore, my heaven, my home for ever more." God was using these Isaiah verses to touch my young heart.

22 February

*"I have set watchmen on your walls, O Jerusalem; they shall never hold their peace day or night. You who make mention of the LORD, do not keep silent, and give Him no rest **till He establishes and till He makes Jerusalem a praise in the earth**."* (Isa 62:6-7)

We are still in Isaiah, and are moving on only a verse or two from yesterday's reading, but that prophecy is elaborated with a further "until", emphasising what was still an earthly scene. I return briefly to some personal geography to illustrate an important truth which escapes many. Many years ago I sometimes taught advanced map reading to young soldiers. On a clear day I would take a group to a beach on Ayrshire's Clyde coast and point to a pair of distant pointed mountains to the west and ask them to identify them on the map. They could see the Knapdale hills to the west and would try to find them there. Few immediately realised that the twin peaks were on the Hebridean island of Jura, and that a wide branch of the Atlantic lay, invisible to them, between the mainland and the island. The Old Testament prophet could look over the immediate prospect, as we could with the Firth of Clyde. Often they saw First Coming events as we saw Knapdale; they could even see the distant mountains representing the Millennial Kingdom. But what, like the Atlantic, was completely invisible to them was the intervening Church Age. That is how God wanted them to perceive His latter day promises to Israel. Several of these "until" prophecies give similar Millennial prospects.

God's commitment to Jerusalem is further illustrated. Christ's earthly capital throughout the Millennium will be Jerusalem. The resurrected and Raptured saints will of course be resident in the Holy City, the New Jerusalem, but like Christ Himself, in constant touch with the earth below. Isaiah and Zechariah have most to tell us, and we visit some of these prophecies on other days. The New Testament, which has other priorities, has no need to make more than the occasional brief reference until Revelation chapter 20, when the "window of opportunity" is left wide open.

Currently Jerusalem, fought over by three major religions, is seen more as a curse than a "praise in the earth"; but God has set His watchmen "until". And they never fail.

23 February

"Thus says the Lord GOD: 'Remove the turban, and take off the crown; nothing shall remain the same. Exalt the humble, and humble the exalted. Overthrown, overthrown, I will make it overthrown! It shall be no longer, **Until He comes whose right it is**, *And I will give it to Him.'"* (Ezek 21:26-27)

This "until" was uttered by the prophet Ezekiel in the seventh year of his personal exile to Babylonia, along with ten thousand of his countrymen. The profane puppet king, Coniah, still ruled in Jerusalem, but over a single tribe (Jer 22:30).and, as we know from Ezekiel 8:3-18, heathen abominations were being performed in the Temple. This was the countdown to the final sack of Jerusalem by Nebuchadnezzar's army and the start of the Times of the Gentiles. The turban may be translated as "crown" or "mitre"; it is the insignia of royalty and possibly also of priesthood.

Indicated here is the long interval from the overthrowing of the monarchy till the restoration to the rightful Heir. We are reminded of the Shiloh "to whom shall be the obedience of the people" of Genesis 49:10, which we looked at a week ago in another prophecy: "He shall bear the glory, And shall sit and rule on His throne; So He shall be a priest on His throne" (Zech 6:13). The crown of Israel, the Davidic crown, is not obsolete, but merely suspended until it is one day claimed by *'Him, whose right it is'*, namely the Lord Jesus Christ. In the 2nd Century BC a Levite, was crowned, but subject to the Seleucid Greek emperor, and later the Edomite Herod, who was subject to Rome; but none qualified for Zechariah's restoration.

From Ezekiel 37:15-22 we are reminded that Christ will rule over the united house of all the tribes of Israel: "'Behold, the days are coming,' says the Lord, 'that I will raise to David a Branch of righteousness; a King shall reign and prosper, and execute judgment and righteousness in the earth. In His days Judah will be saved, and Israel will dwell safely'" (Jer 23:5,6). But, more than that; He is to be acclaimed at last "King over all the earth" (Zech 14:9). Sceptics may scoff at the immensity of the miraculous return of a united Israel. We simply trust, crowning Him King of our lives in the meantime.

24 February

*"'But you, Daniel, shut up the words, and seal the book **until the time of the end**; many shall run to and fro, and knowledge shall increase'."..... And he said, 'Go your way, Daniel, for the words are closed up and sealed **till the time of the end**.'"* (Dan 12:4, 9)

Daniel, like Revelation, is an 'apocalypse' or unveiling. Fanciful film-makers ignore the positive significance. Contrast this angelic injunction with another much later angelic injunction: "And he said to me, 'Do not seal the words of the prophecy of this book, for the time is at hand'" (Rev 22:10). Now this sealing is partly for preservation; the book of Daniel is going to be incredibly important in the coming Tribulation when many, even some of those who have previously ignored it, shall run to and fro through its pages for information about what they are to endure and how deliverance will come.

Had the Jews of Jesus' time on earth paid more attention to Daniel 9, they would have recognised the coming of their Prince; the "weeks of years" of Daniel 9 are a miracle of prophecy. There has been a rabbinic curse on Jewish laypeople reading Daniel chapter 9. However, Jesus waited until just before His betrayal to speak of a future event called the Abomination of Desolation foretold by Daniel, and the Gospel writer tells us to understand. Students of prophecy therefore have a very considerable understanding of that prophecy, which we look at in May. But there are details which we may legitimately discuss at present without coming to a complete consensus. In Daniel we find that even angels are intensely interested in these matters. "And at that time your people shall be delivered, every one who is found written in the book" (Dan 12:1). All will have become clear.

However, we, the Church, will not be upon earth when the storm breaks. The tribulation period, unprecedented in its ferocity, is foretold immediately before today's text. The nation of Israel will be the centre of Satan's focus, but Daniel is reassured. The Church will not be going through the Tribulation period. Christ's Olivet Discourse, with the warning of the coming Abomination, is for Tribulation saints at least as much as for us.

25 February

*"O Jerusalem, Jerusalem, the one who kills the prophets and stones those who are sent to her! How often I wanted to gather your children together, as a hen gathers her chicks under her wings, but you were not willing! See! Your house is left to you desolate; for I say to you, you shall see Me no more **till you say,** '**Blessed is He** who comes in the name of the LORD!'"*
(Matt 23:37-39)

No wonder Jesus had wept over Jerusalem. He was now setting the conditions for their seeing Him again. It would not be until they should say, "Blessed is He..." And that still lies ahead.

David Baron sums up the fulfilment of that "until": "But suddenly the noise of war and the shout of triumph is turned into wailing and lamentation as the spirit of grace and supplication takes possession of the heart of the remnant of Israel, and the eyes of the blind are opened, and they behold in the King of Glory..... none other than the one whom they have pierced, and whom for so many centuries they have despised." Isaiah puts it this way: "And it will be said in that day: 'Behold, this is our God; we have waited for Him and He will save us. This is the LORD. We have waited for Him; we will be glad and rejoice in Him; we will be glad and rejoice in His salvation'" (25:9).

FB Meyer compares that future reconciliation with Joseph and His brethren: "It was when his brethren were in their greatest straits that Joseph made himself known unto them; and when the Jews are in their dire extremity, they will cry aloud for help and deliverance from Him whom they rejected. This memorable scene in Egypt will be reproduced in all its pathos, when the long-rejected Brother shall say to His own brethren after the flesh, 'I am Jesus, your Brother, whom ye sold unto Pilate: and now be not grieved, nor angry with yourself, that ye delivered Me up to be crucified; for God did send Me before you to preserve a remnant in the earth, and to save you alive by a great deliverance'" (see Gen 45 1-15)." Our Lord rejoiced in the blessings that would come to His Church in the meantime, but that did not negate His sorrow for His people Israel.

26 February

*"For this is My blood of the new covenant, which is shed for many for the remission of sins. But I say to you, I will not drink of this fruit of the vine from now on **until that day when I drink it new with you in My Father's kingdom.***" (Matt 26:28-29)

Jesus was celebrating with His disciples that Passover feast for which He had longed "with fervent desire" (Lk 22:15) to eat before His suffering. He made this simple unambiguous statement about the next occasion on which He would share wine with them. No, this is not about Heaven. Jesus was talking about a future time on earth ☐ of the Millennium. "And I bestow upon you a kingdom, just as My Father bestowed one on Me, that you may eat and drink at My table in My kingdom, and sit on thrones judging the twelve tribes of Israel" (Lk 22:29-30). We look at that prophecy elsewhere.

The vine, which will be devastated during the Great Tribulation (Rev 8:7), will once again flourish in Israel. "And it will come to pass in that day that the mountains will drip with new wine..... and all the brooks of Judah will be flooded with water" (Joel 3:18). "'I will bring back the captives of My people Israel; they shall build the waste places and inhabit them; they shall plant vineyards and drink wine from them..... no longer shall they be pulled up from the land I have given them', says the Lord your God" (Amos 9:14,15). This is (a) not already fulfilled, (b) not about the Church, (c) not about heaven, but (d) emphatically about the future and about Israel.

In Luke 13:28,29 Jesus told His adversaries (see v 17): "There will be weeping and gnashing of teeth, when you see Abraham and Isaac and Jacob and all the prophets in the kingdom of God and you yourselves thrust out. They will come from the east and the west, from the north and the south, and sit down in the kingdom of God." This cannot be heaven where there are no compass points. And most certainly Jesus' adversaries are not going to be admitted to heaven to witness this event and subsequently be cast out! In the meantime, while   He is still invisible to us, we have the privilege in drinking wine to remember the Lord's death **until He comes**.

27 February

*"And they will fall by the edge of the sword, and be led away
captive into all nations. And Jerusalem will be trampled by Gentiles
until the times of the Gentiles are fulfilled."* (Lk 21:24)

Now the *diaspora* of Israel is a recurring theme in Bible prophecy;
we have already noted it more than once, and will periodically return
to it. Let us make a few short observations now. Firstly, it is only
Jerusalem which is mentioned. The earlier part of Luke's portion
of the Olivet Discourse concerned events leading to the merciless
Roman invasion and capture of Jerusalem. The remainder of Judea
was equally involved, but it was easier for the smaller communities
to escape. The Northern tribes had been exiled many centuries
earlier.

The miracle, and let us not pretend that it is anything else, is that
exiled Israel has survived as a distinct people and never been
integrated into any of the lands of their domicile. They have always
been distinct, "A people dwelling alone, not reckoning itself among
the nations" (Numb 23:9). Genocide is almost as old as human
history. No other nation has survived such deliberate exile. As we
note elsewhere, by Esther's time the Northern tribes had been
dispersed throughout the 127 provinces of the Persian Empire.
Later the Greek and then Roman empires were in control.

Then in 330 AD the Byzantines, nominally Christian, occupied
Jerusalem. In 614 AD the Persians conquered Jerusalem and
destroyed many of the churches and Christian shrines, but in 629
AD Heraclius restored the city to Byzantine rule and rebuilt many
of the churches. But the biggest and longest pagan occupation
was Islamic with only brief breaks as with the Crusaders between
1,099 and 1,244 AD. The Crusaders slaughtered as many Jews
as Arabs. In addition to Arabs, the Egyptian Mamluks, Tartars and
Mongols and ultimately for four hundred years, the Ottomans were
in occupation; all were Muslim. By the 19th Century, with a weakened
Ottoman empire, Greek, Russian, Armenian, Coptic, Marionite,
Ethiopian, Roman and even Protestant shrines were permitted. But
the one thing which was and still is fiercely resisted is the rebuilding
of the Temple on its original site. Jesus said that Jerusalem would
be trampled underfoot by Gentiles, until the Times of the Gentiles
comes to an end. How graphically His prophecy is being fulfilled!

28 February

*"That He may send Jesus Christ, who was preached to you before, whom heaven must receive **until the times of restoration of all things**, which God has spoken by the mouth of all His holy prophets since the world began."* (Acts 3:20-21)

The significance of this statement, so often ignored or avoided, cannot be overestimated. Ten days earlier, as He was about to be taken up to heaven, Jesus was asked by the disciples, "Lord, will You at this time restore the kingdom to Israel?" (Acts 1:6). This, one would think, would have been the appropriate juncture for Jesus to have made it clear that there would be no future restoration of Israel. But He did not.

In Acts chapters 2 and 3 Peter develops the truth that, through their rejection and crucifixion of the Christ, God's plan of salvation has been furthered. "Yet now, brethren, I know that you did it in ignorance, as did also your rulers" (3:17). He then confirmed what they should have known, namely that Christ's suffering had been prophesied (3:18). But Peter was very quick to ensure that they understood that their ignorance did not exonerate them, by immediately demanding their repentance. They may have done it in ignorance, but they had brought that upon themselves by their hardness of heart. They did it of their own free will, but within God's foreknowledge. Jesus Christ is thus said to be remaining in heaven *until* such a future time of restoration of all things on earth. By then it will be even more desperately needed than at present. We are given no information that He is currently restoring anything in heaven. The sin-blighted heaven which will one day be destroyed (Rev 21:1) refers to the visible and atmospheric heaven or firmament. There Satan has his seat as Prince of the Power of the Air (Eph 2:2).

It is clear from the continuous narrative of Revelation chapters 19 and 20, where no change of vision occurs, that the Restoration of all things does not precede, but rather follows, the Great Tribulation and the vanquishing of the leaders of the rebellion which will culminate with the open challenge to God at Armageddon. The restoration is to be both physical and spiritual, to reflect the two aspects lost in the Fall. We occasionally return to these two verses of Acts in our daily readings.

29 February

*"Just as it is written: 'God has given them a spirit of stupor, Eyes that they should not see and ears that they should not hear, To this very day.'..... For I do not desire, brethren, that you should be ignorant of this mystery, lest you should be wise in your own opinion, that blindness in part has happened to Israel **until the fullness of the Gentiles has come in**."* (Rom 11:8, 25)

Two days ago we encountered the term "Times of the Gentiles"; these terminate only at Christ's Return in Power, when He intervenes to save Israel in its very darkest of many dark hours. Jews are one day to resume their appointment as God's witnesses (Isa 43:10-12). However, at the Jerusalem conference James, referring to Simon Peter's earlier words said: "Simon has declared how God at the first visited the Gentiles to take out of them a people for His name" (Acts 15:14). Evidently the "Fullness of the Gentiles" refers to the Rapture of the Church, after which many of Israel are to have their spiritual blindness removed. Paul here indicates that this should no longer be a mystery. Israel's blindness led to the birth of the Church.

Paul here is referring to the well-known statement in Isaiah chapter 6, which Jesus (Matt 13:13) confirmed as being on-going. Ezekiel, who served as prophet to the Babylonian exiles, was commissioned by God: "Son of man, I am sending you to the children of Israel, to a rebellious nation that has rebelled against Me; they and their fathers have transgressed against Me to this very day. (Ezek 2:2-3). Then comes a command which all of us should heed: "You shall speak My words to them, **whether they hear or whether they refuse**" (Ezek 2:7). We should never give up representing God to those for whom we have a responsibility, even when we become discouraged by years of resistance.

God has persisted with Israel for thousands of years, yet still has purposes for them. He demonstrated to Elijah that He is aware of the individuals who still honour Him (I Kings 19:18). Thousands of Jews have recognised Jesus Christ and been saved. As Paul said: "Even so then, at this present time there is a remnant according to the election of grace" (Rom 11:5). Evangelising Jews is a most worthy cause.

Kingdom in Mystery Prophecies

1 March

"In those days John the Baptist came preaching in the wilderness of Judea, and saying, 'Repent, for the kingdom of heaven is at hand!'" (Matt 3:1-2)

It is essential to look at two introductory passages before looking at the seven prophetic Kingdom in Mystery parables of Matthew 13. In our text for today Darby translates "is at hand" as "has drawn nigh" and Young in his Literal Translation as "hath come nigh". John was in effect giving a conditional prophecy – the long-awaited kingdom was potentially imminent. A little later (Matt 4:17) Jesus made precisely the same proclamation at Capernaum. In fact, the King was now present, and, had He been accepted by the nation of Israel, the promised kingdom on earth would have come. Of course, His rejection was foreknown by God, but this did not diminish the genuineness of the offer on hand; it must not be thought of as theoretical.

Matthew uses the term "Kingdom of Heaven" where Mark and Luke frequently and John twice say "Kingdom of God". Matthew, writing primarily to Jews, knew of their reluctance to use the name of God more than necessary, so sensitively he modified the terminology. The Kingdom of Heaven is on earth! It has been argued, comparing the Gospels, that the term "Kingdom of God" includes only believers. John Walvoord, summarising the theme as covered by Matthew, writes: "Matthew then proceeds to account for the fact that Christ did not bring in His prophesied kingdom at His first coming. The growing denunciation of the unbelief of the Jews, and His revelation of truth relating to the period between the two advents (Matt 13) serve to support this point." Once we have grasped this, so many problems are cleared up, including why His triumphal Return has been postponed. In summary, we may state unequivocally that, although the following did not occur at the same time, Jesus presented Himself as the King prophesied in the Old Testament, who was then and there offering a kingdom; He confessed that He was the Son of David privately and publicly; He confessed that He was the Christ and had the right to reign upon earth. We should bear this in mind when we come to the Sermon on the Mount, which was preached when the Kingdom was still on offer. The national resistance which later amounted to rejection had only just begun.

2 March

"In this manner, therefore, pray: 'Our Father in heaven, Hallowed be Your name. Your kingdom come. Your will be done on earth as it is in heaven.'" (Matt 6:9-11)

"Your kingdom come!" was acceptable to Israel because it was assumed to imply status without repentance; many today are prepared to talk loosely of God's "Kingdom", provided it does not involve confession, forgiveness and salvation. Some evangelicals therefore tend to underplay important Kingdom truths, while concentrating on salvation.

The Lord, who gave them this model prayer, had no need to ask for sins to be forgiven; it was their prayer, not the Lord's! Darby writes: "It may have been used as it stands by the disciples previously to the death of our Lord and the gift of the Holy Ghost." There is no record of it being recited in the early Church. Jesus later said: "However, when He, the Spirit of truth, has come, He will guide you into all truth" (Jn 16:13); and that surely includes praying. Acknowledging who it is to whom we pray takes priority. Before making our own requests, we should be aligning ourselves with God's honour and purposes, which must take precedence over our own. Spurgeon writes: "We would have the Lord's will carried out, not only by the great physical forces (he refers to the holy angels) which never fail to be obedient to God..... but by men, once rebellious, but graciously renewed." So while the future Kingdom on earth is primarily in view, it is for every believer here and now to seek to do our Father's will.

The disciples wanted to know how to pray. They were told to desire that God's will should be done on earth in the way that it is in Heaven. Jesus would never have asked them to pray for the impossible. Thanks to the unbelieving hearts of the multitude present and the nation to which they belonged, that was impossible *then and there*. But one day God will create conditions in which it will be possible, when the Devil is bound for a thousand years (Rev 20:2-3). One of the most ludicrous claims of apostate Christianity is that Satan is currently bound. The superficially plausible arguments collapse if one enquires whether currently God's will is being done on earth as in Heaven; clearly it is being scorned. In the Millennium it will be done.

3 March

"Then He spoke many things to them in parables, saying: 'Behold, a sower went out to sow..... But he who received seed on the good ground is he who hears the word and understands it, who indeed bears fruit and produces: some a hundredfold, some sixty, some thirty.'" (Matt 13:3, 23)

The seven parables of Matthew 13 are all prophetic, looking beyond Christ's rejection and ascension, to the Church Age which was to precede His return. The Kingdom was not to be annulled, but to remain in mystery from the unbeliever's point of view, until its future manifestation when He returns in power and glory. One can detect a progression in the parables comparable to the letters to the seven congregations of Revelation 2 and 3; however as both of these series have applications to the entire Church Age, we will leave the progression lessons for the meantime. Christ had been appealing to a nation, but now He concentrates on individuals, albeit millions upon millions of individuals, who were to constitute His Church.

The first two parables are too long to quote in full. The first appears in three Gospels and tells of the seed of the word being sown through the preaching of the Gospel and landing on three unreceptive parts of the field (the world) and one receptive part. Quoted above is only the receptive part, which was to become the nucleus of the Church, although members of the other three   are still to be found within nominal Christianity. Christ Himself is the Sower, although He has commissioned us to share in this work.

The other three parts are, firstly, those who reject the Word outright and have no interest in it whatsoever. The second are those who receive the Word superficially; there is no depth, no preparedness to take the essential step of faith; the third are those who are initially interested and even enthusiastic, until they find that accepting it conflicts with other priorities and could lead to complications and changes of lifestyle. Even the final group has some who, having accepted the Word and accepted Christ as Saviour, prove more committed and fruitful, depending upon their love for their Lord. So it has been throughout the Church Age. What is reassuring is that our Saviour knew that it would be so.

4 March

"Let both grow together until the harvest, and at the time of harvest I will say to the reapers, 'First gather together the tares and bind them in bundles to burn them, but gather the wheat into my barn.'"
(Matt 13:30)

This parable refers to the entire Church Age from sowing to harvest. Jesus described the sowing thus: "He who sows the good seed is the Son of Man. The field is the world, the good seeds are the sons of the kingdom, but the tares are the sons of the wicked one" (vv 37-38). Tares are an old word for darnel, a poisonous weed which looks like wheat until immediately before the harvest, but isn't wheat. The "weeds" of some modern translations is too general and misses the point.

The cults and the secular world make little or no attempt to distinguish between the enormous variety, not only of denominations, but between committed and nominal Christians, between evangelical and non-evangelicals and so on. Some of the cults have flatly refused to accept this lesson of the parable and see only tares in Christendom.

Of course, the common widespread teaching, dating to around the 4th Century and supported by Augustine of Hippo, that both the wheat and the tares are all part of the Church is also false. A Biblical definition of the Church is: "The church of God, which He has purchased with His own blood" (Acts 20:28). Tares are not blood-bought, but co-exist in the world with those who are. Separation is a Christian doctrine; isolation is not. Any given congregation or membership list may include believers and unbelievers, with only the Lord knowing which is which, although genuine believers should have the witness of the Holy Spirit. Only the harvest will tell. "The Son of Man will send out His angels, and they will gather out of His kingdom all things that offend, and those who practice lawlessness, and will cast them into the furnace of fire. There will be wailing and gnashing of teeth. Then the righteous will shine forth as the sun in the kingdom of their Father" (vv 41-43).

Parables are simply to illustrate an important point or points and should not be dredged for every last detail. When we review the parable of the Dragnet and compare the sequence of events, we will see why this is important.

5 March

"Another parable He put forth to them, saying: 'The kingdom of heaven is like a mustard seed, which a man took and sowed in his field, which indeed is the least of all the seeds; but when it is grown it is greater than the herbs and becomes a tree, so that the birds of the air come and nest in its branches.'" (Matt 13:31-32)

This is not the mustard familiar to us as a condiment, but one with dozens of seeds, potential new plants, in each pod. These were the tiniest seeds sown by hand in the Holy Land, but they could grow into large shrubs. We must remember that Jesus was addressing the nucleus of the Church which He was going to build; a little later He said to Peter: "And I also say to you that you are Peter, and on this rock I will build My church" (Matt 16:18). In fact He told Peter that he was *petros*, a diminutive of *petra*, which means a rock. Peter was a little rock, and Jesus was saying that the Church would be built upon Himself. Few verses have been more frequently misinterpreted to justify the assumed status of the Pope.

When Jesus had ascended, the task of building upon Christ, the Cornerstone, must have appeared enormous to the Eleven before the Holy Spirit descended ten days later. Perhaps they recalled this parable; we cannot say, but it certainly illustrated their position. The tiny mustard seed was to expand within twenty-five years to cover much of the then Roman Empire and beyond: "I thank my God through Jesus Christ for you all, that your faith is spoken of throughout the whole world" (Rom 1:8); "the word of the truth of the gospel, which has come to you, as it has also in all the world, and is bringing forth fruit" (Col 1:5-6).

The "birds of the air" are not interpreted for us. Some think that they refer to invasive evil influences that are swift to take advantage of new opportunities. On the other hand, they may be taken to be those who benefit from living within a Christian society. For many centuries within Christian lands charities, health care and other benevolent societies were almost entirely administered by believers, demonstrating practically the love of God. The secular welfare state is a modern phenomenon.

6 March

"Another parable He spoke to them: 'The kingdom of heaven is like leaven, which a woman took and hid in three measures of meal till it was all leavened.'" (Matt 13:33)

This is the second of three parables found only as applying to the Kingdom of Heaven, as opposed to the Kingdom of God. The quantity described would have been appropriate for a family-size loaf of bread. When one adds the leaven, initially the actual quantity appears to remain unchanged; but soon the bulk increases. Leaven permeates and quickly makes its presence felt, as the Gospel penetrates society. This is one way to look at a parable which Jesus did not interpret. No community truly permeated by the Gospel remains unaffected without ensuing benefits, even when there is resistance. Israel had been unique, standing alone among the nations with the task, in which it failed, of representing God. The Church, as the new form of the Kingdom of Heaven in mystery, was to expand within the world, and, although opposed, is still active until the Rapture, when it will be removed.

However, while all this is true, theologians at least as far back as Darby have pointed out that leaven in Scripture is more often associated with evil, and that the Gospel in the earlier parable is the seed. Therefore we may see the leaven as apostasy and false teaching beginning to permeate the Church. Certainly that happened even within the First Century. We think of the Reformation as the return to the true unadulterated faith of the apostolic church, but, while it certainly did restore central truths, even that was only partial. Some false teachers remained unchallenged. The corrupting leaven is still active and needs constant vigilance at every level.

At the first Passover of the Exodus God specified unleavened bread: "Seven days you shall eat unleavened bread..... And they baked unleavened cakes of the dough which they had brought out of Egypt; for it was not leavened, because they were driven out of Egypt and could not wait" (Ex 12:15, 39). We have no time to wait for fermentation to take place or for false doctrine to creep in. The true Church is on a journey from Pentecost to the Rapture. Leaven, once added, works without further interference; let us not give it peace to do its corrupting work.

7 March

"Again, the kingdom of heaven is like treasure hidden in a field,
which a man found and hid; and for joy over it he goes and sells all
that he has and buys that field." (Matt 13:44)

As we read through these Kingdom of Heaven parables, we must remember that the Kingdom was there before the Church and will appear in its final form after the Church and before the end of the world. Currently, within the Church Age it is in what was being introduced as the new mystery form. Walvoord describes this as a 'parable in fulfilment of prophecy'. The common view that we have to sell everything in order to gain salvation simply does not hold true. We were spiritually bankrupt and had nothing with which to pay. "Jesus paid it all", as the old hymn says. Jews who were listening, whether they understood the parable or not, would have responded to the word "treasure", identifying it with themselves: "Now therefore, if you will indeed obey My voice and keep My covenant, then you shall be a special treasure to Me above all people; for all the earth is Mine" (Ex 19:5); "For the LORD has chosen Jacob for Himself, Israel for His special treasure" (Ps 135:4). However, the fact that the treasure was hidden reflects the long period during which Israel did not live up to these qualifications.

Christ came into the world to redeem, to buy back. He came, like the finder in the parable, giving up all to buy the "field". He came firstly to the Jews, who refused redemption, failing to recognise that they needed to be redeemed. A second opportunity was given at Pentecost, but was again nationally rejected. "Therefore let it be known to you that the salvation of God has been sent to the Gentiles, and they will hear it!" (Acts 28:28).

But there is joy for the Redeemer too: "He shall see the labour of His soul, and be satisfied. By His knowledge My righteous Servant shall justify many, for He shall bear their iniquities". (Isa 53:11); "looking unto Jesus, the author and finisher of our faith, who for the joy that was set before Him endured the cross, despising the shame, and has sat down at the right hand of the throne of God." (Heb 12:2). Thus joy is a feature of the Kingdom of Heaven.

8 March

"Again, the kingdom of heaven is like a merchant seeking beautiful pearls, who, when he had found one pearl of great price, went and sold all that he had and bought it." (Matt 13:45-46)

With parables, it is a good idea to ask: Who's who? Who is the merchant? Is this Christ, or, as some have suggested, the individual seeker after God? Surely it is a picture of Christ, and corresponds to the Finder of the treasure and Purchaser of the field in yesterday's reading.

Paul tells us: "Be filled with the Spirit, speaking to one another in psalms and hymns and spiritual songs, singing and making melody in your heart to the Lord" (Eph 5:18-19). But we do have to be discerning, particularly as it has become common for hymns to be written with the flimsiest of Scriptural bases and a serious imbalance of spiritual themes. It can be dangerous to take casually too much theology from hymn books; unlike the Bible, none is infallibly inspired. One old hymn opens with: "I've found the Pearl of greatest price". Its sentiments are lovely and genuinely extol the Lord Jesus Christ, who is seen to be the pearl. I certainly would not regard it as dangerous, and hesitate to be too critical.

As with the Finder of the treasure, the greatest price had to be made to permit the purchase of our salvation. It is beyond human power to measure what our Saviour sacrificed in coming to earth to pay the redemption price. Paul writes: "Husbands, love your wives, just as Christ also loved the church and gave Himself for her" (Eph 5:25). There is a double aptness here, as there is something of the Bride-price paid by the heavenly Bridegroom for the Church, which is the pearl of greatest price. We look elsewhere at the as yet unfulfilled Revelation 19:7-8, but it is worth repeating because of the relevance to the valuable pearl: "Let us be glad and rejoice and give Him glory, for the marriage of the Lamb has come, and His wife has made herself ready. And to her it was granted to be arrayed in fine linen, clean and bright, for the fine linen is the righteous acts of the saints." The main contrast with the Hidden Treasure parable is that it has a special application to Israel, whereas this one applies primarily to the Church.

9 March

"Again, the kingdom of heaven is like a dragnet that was cast into the sea and gathered some of every kind, which, when it was full, they drew to shore; and they sat down and gathered the good into vessels, but threw the bad away. So it will be at the end of the age. The angels will come forth, separate the wicked from among the just, and cast them into the furnace of fire. There will be wailing and gnashing of teeth." (Matt 13:47-50)

The dragnet, familiar to the Galilean fisherman, was so large that it had to be pulled to the shore, where sorting would take place and the bad fish be thrown back. Like the parable of the tares, we see living survivors, foreknown to be either saved or unsaved, co-existing in the world until the Lord's Return in Power and the Judgment of the Nations. Throughout the entire age myriads have died; by the point of death their destinies will have been decided, but during their lifetimes the saved and unsaved have lived together, sometimes easily distinguishable, but all too often not so.

It is important to understand the timing. The AV/KJV, along with the ASV, writes of "the end of the world". Now this certainly does not conform to the end of the world as described in Revelation chapter 20. It is interesting that many, especially Amillennialists, who have long ago discarded the good old Authorised Version for other purposes, are happy to use it when it suits them, even if they realise that a much better rendering is "consummation or end of the **age**", as in DBY. ESV, Montgomery NT, NASV, NIV, NKJV and RSV, rather than "the end of the **world**".

The parable looks beyond the Church Age to the Judgment of the Nations (Matt 25:31-46). Those 'fish', good and bad, who survive the Great Tribulation, will be segregated like sheep and goats, a different illustration. This is the future process whereby the Kingdom is fully transformed from its current mystery status to its glorious Millennial manifestation status. Whether we prefer the word 'just' or the more commonly rendered 'righteous' in verse 49, this justification or being reckoned righteous is of course only on the basis of saving faith in Christ – without that Romans 3:10 applies: "There is none righteous, no, not one" (Rom 3:10 quoting Ps 14).

10 March

"And He said, 'The kingdom of God is as if a man should scatter seed on the ground, and should sleep by night and rise by day, and the seed should sprout and grow, he himself does not know how. For the earth yields crops by itself: first the blade, then the head, after that the full grain in the head. But when the grain ripens, immediately he puts in the sickle, because the harvest has come.'"
(Mk 4:26-29)

Now this parable is still about the Kingdom in mystery, up to the Rapture, or perhaps even until Christ's Return in Power. It is one of the few passages in Mark which appears in no other Gospels. Walvoord notes: "This passage serves to distinguish the Kingdom of Heaven from the Kingdom of God which includes only the righteous."

Harold Paisley says: "It is suitable for the Gospel of the mighty Servant, the Son of God for it is a parable for the servants of Christ." Visiting Venice many years ago, and being very conscious of the consecutive likeness of the four Gospels to the Lion, the Ox, the Man and the Eagle (Ezek 1:10; Rev 4:7), I was amazed to see various sculptures and pictures representing "the Lion of St Mark". Apparently it is the city's symbol, depicted a lion with a Bible and sometimes a sword and halo, the latter being a pagan sun worship symbol with no proper place in Christianity. Mark's is the Gospel with no given genealogy, human or Divine, appropriate to the One who came to serve. "For even the Son of Man did not come to be served, but to serve, and to give His life a ransom for many" (Mk 10:45).

Even within Christians circles some fail to see God's hand in plant life. They may be able to explain cause and effect, but without the Divine Creator the *reason* for this happening cannot be explained. Likewise the Church, contrary to all expectations, has grown. Kelly observes: "The absence and apparent disregard of the Lord are supposed, not His manifestation and active interference. Harvest being come, He reaps, not sending His angels, as in Matthew." As we leave these parables, it is worth remembering that, where no interpretation is given in the text, some flexibility may be permissible, and God may use them in different ways to meet different spiritual needs.

Signs of the Times

11 March

"Then the Pharisees and Sadducees came, and testing Him asked that He would show them a sign from heaven." (Matt 16:1)

I am taking my time to go through four consecutive verses; we will quickly see the prophetic relevance. Up to this point the theologically liberal Sadducees and conservative Pharisees had not joined forces in attacking Jesus. Now they sank their differences in trying to discredit their Messiah. They were equally blind. Jesus was as tough on the latter as on the former. This occurred towards the end of His ministry. They had challenged Jesus in the same way some time previously and had received the same answer (Matt 12:38). Because of their determination not to believe, nothing had changed.

They made an extraordinary demand of Jesus; I say 'demand' rather than 'request', because they were supposedly acting as guardians of the nation's faith. This explains why so often these religious vultures were hanging around to prey upon anything which appeared to be unorthodox or uncomfortable in Jesus' teachings and actions. And Jesus, by such acts as healing most frequently on the Sabbath, had evidently deliberately challenged them, making them take decisions ☐ decisions which were almost always negative, when positive ones might have opened their hearts and minds.

This particular demand was extraordinary; the implications were that the multitude of miracles which Jesus had performed to benefit the needy were not recognised by them as signs from Heaven! What more could they have wanted? Nothing that Jesus had done had been spectacular for the sake of being spectacular. This was proof of whose side these religious leaders were on, and of the kind of miracle, devoid of spiritual demands, which they sought and Satan encouraged: "Then he (the Devil) brought Him to Jerusalem, set Him on the pinnacle of the temple, and said to Him, 'If You are the Son of God, throw Yourself down from here.'" (Lk 4:9). Satan went on to quote a supporting psalm (91:11-12). Quoting Scripture is no guarantee of authenticity! This kind of miracle requires none of the essential saving faith to recognise. The two miracles which might be considered spectacular Jesus performed within sight of only His disciples, namely walking on the water and calming the storm.

12 March

"He answered and said to them, 'When it is evening you say, "It will be fair weather, for the sky is red"; and in the morning, "It will be foul weather today, for the sky is red and threatening."'" (Matt 16:2-3)

Weather forecasting is prophecy based upon observation and experience. Paradoxically the English proverb about the shepherd's 'delight' or 'warning', depending upon the time of day, reminds us that these religious leaders had been appointed by God shepherds of the people: "Son of man, prophesy against the shepherds of Israel, prophesy and say to them, 'Thus says the Lord GOD to the shepherds: "Woe to the shepherds of Israel who feed themselves! Should not the shepherds feed the flocks?"'" (Ezek 34:2).

These Sadducees and Pharisees, as leaders, had a duty towards God. They also had a considerable degree of status even within the land under Roman occupation, with whose officialdom they regularly compromised their religious principles. They lived up to Ezekiel's description, which referred to an earlier period but was being re-enacted: "You eat the fat and clothe yourselves with the wool; you slaughter the fatlings, but you do not feed the flock. The weak you have not strengthened, nor have you healed those who were sick, nor bound up the broken, nor brought back what was driven away, nor sought what was lost; but with force and cruelty you have ruled them." (Ezek 34:3-4). They had for three years seen Jesus doing all those things which they were miserably failing to do, and they did not like it, so they had joined forces for their attack.

In a fallen world God sometimes uses His right to judge and sometimes to warn by means of natural phenomena. But in His wisdom and mercy He has given climatologists and meteorologists the ability to understand the wonderful planetary systems which dictate our weather. When God decides, for His own holy purposes to defy human expectations, people tend to blame Him. Even believers can be irrational, choosing, for instance, a day for some particular weather-dependent activity, and then praying that the weather will be suitable, rather than praying that they will be guided to choose a day when the weather will be good! Also in His mercy and wisdom He has given us the tools to understand where we are in His programme for this world. We consider this next.

13 March

"Hypocrites! You know how to discern the face of the sky, but you cannot discern the signs of the times." (Matt 16:3)

This is the only occurrence of the phrase "signs of the times", but the speaker is Jesus Christ Himself. Signs of the times are those happenings and unprecedented conditions which should alert us to the approaching fulfilment of important God-given prophecies, so that we may be prepared. Even in the Old Testament God sometimes gave in advance precise timings for certain major happenings, such as the four hundred year sojourn of the Children of Israel in Egypt and the seventy year Babylonian captivity. There is in Daniel chapter 9, which we will look at separately, an accurate formula for determining the date of Christ's rejection. But that was sealed for latter day understanding (Dan 12:4); it will be invaluable for authenticating the end-time application of that prophecy.

The signs of the times began to apply at Jesus' First Coming; it is still the responsibility of leaders to be alert and to draw attention to them as His Second draws near. When Herod the Great was questioned by the Magi about the birth of the King, he sought the chief priests and scribes, who were able to quote the relevant passage of Micah. They should from that moment on have been alert for the appearance of their long-awaited Messiah, allowing for the fact that the thirtieth birthday was the point when most holy appointments began. Jesus' ministry should have alerted them; but they were blind to the signs of the times. They knew their Scriptures; several of the "until" prophecies, which we looked at in February, should have alerted them; but they did not. They had no genuine love for their expected Messiah.

So Christ's public appearance, His miracles, His teaching, His formal entry to Jerusalem, His betrayal and crucifixion, and the resurrection (which they tried to deny) were signs of the times which were ignored. We, the New Testament Church, have been given no chronological means of determining our Lord's Second Coming; but we most certain have been given numerous signs of the times. We are about to look at some of these. Are we making sure that we are familiar with what has been prophesied? Can we be sure that our Lord will never address us in the way He addressed the Sadducees and Pharisees?

14 March

"'A wicked and adulterous generation seeks after a sign, and no sign shall be given to it except the sign of the prophet Jonah.' And He left them and departed." (Matt 16:4)

This was not an accusation of basic immorality. Throughout the history of Israel, from the golden calf of Moses' absence on Sinai onwards, any worship or recognition of an idol or image was considered spiritual adultery, because no worship is ever lost; there is always a demonic power ready to accept it. This is why Christians should shun any association with the occult, including star signs and the like; they are described as abominations. The single Greek word *simeion* has a wide range of meanings, including a distinguishing mark, a sign of warning or admonition, miraculous acts as tokens of Divine authority or power, tokens portending future events and confirmatory signs of what had already taken place (WE Vine's *Expository Dictionary*). The challengers sought one kind of sign and were given another.

Now, as we have seen, Jesus had previously been challenged to show what His accusers imagined were signs from Heaven. The miracles which He had already performed, which were the true signs from Heaven, they explained as being demonic, a desperately serious accusation. The healing of the blind-mute demoniac of Matthew 12:22 was a mighty miracle, one never before recorded in Jewish history: "All the multitudes were amazed and said, 'Could this be the Son of David?' Now when the Pharisees heard it they said, 'This fellow does not cast out demons except by Beelzebub, the ruler of the demons'" (Matt 12:23-24). Since then they had given no indications of repentance or change of heart, despite being responsible for the faith of the nation.

There is today a tacit understanding in wider Christian circles that Christ may return some day, just as there was a tacit acceptance among the Sadducees and Pharisees that the Messiah must come eventually. It was an "any time but now" philosophy. Mental barriers go up and shutters come down. The very idea is seen by some as inconvenient, Christ daring to return before the Great Commission of converting the world is complete, a concept never taught in Scripture. As two thousand years ago, preachers of Christ's Return are seen as eccentrics. Are you prepared to be seen as an eccentric for Christ and be ready should He come today?

15 March

"Now as He sat on the Mount of Olives, the disciples came to Him privately, saying, 'Tell us, when will these things be? And what will be the sign of Your coming, and of the end of the age?'" (Matt 24:3)

The 'sign' which the disciples sought was the future indication that their soon-to-depart Lord and Master was about to return. They might actually have assumed that they could still be alive on earth. John Heading points out that the Greek word for 'end' here indicates several things coinciding to reach their climax during the same period. They knew nothing yet about the imminent intervening Church Age; they were enquiring about the current Jewish age.

The truth of the prior Rapture of the Church was soon to be introduced by Jesus (Jn 14:1-3); but this Discourse was about the city whose destruction He had just foretold. He had gone on to tell them about the future Great Tribulation. It is Luke who recorded in his account of that Discourse, the advice appropriate to the Church: "Now when these things **begin** to happen, look up and lift up your heads, because your redemption draws near" (Lk 21:28). **These are our signs of the times**. The Great Tribulation lies beyond our horizon, like the 'loom' or glow visible to the ship at sea of the still invisible lighthouse. We should be watching for the stage being set rather for the 'play' beginning, and keeping our eyes on the Middle East. Our deliverance from the world is to come first: "I, Jesus, have sent My angel to testify to you these things **in the churches**. I am the Root and the Offspring of David, **the Bright and Morning Star**." (Rev 22:16). Morning comes quite suddenly in the Middle East. I recall doing my rounds and visiting sentries in the Gulf States. With no light pollution, the stars could still be incredibly bright not long before dawn.

The Tribulation period which those saved after the Rapture will experience will abound with signs of the times, which will not be neglected as so many signs are today. Malachi had just announced: "For behold, the day is coming, burning like an oven" when he added: "But to you who fear My name **the Sun of Righteousness** shall arise with healing in His wings" (Mal 4:1-2). The Church will not need healing; Israel will do.

16 March

"And you will be hated by all for My name's sake." (Lk 21:17)

When Jesus refers to "you", He means future believing, witnessing Jews. Anti-Semitism has always been one of the characteristic manifestations of Satan's hatred of anything or anyone belonging to or beloved of God; it pervades much of Christendom to its shame and detriment. Now this statement of our Lord's in His Olivet Discourse had a specific period of time in view; other end-time prophecies confirm that Anti-Semitism is on-going.

I recently received an email from someone stating that it was Lord Rothschild who had brought the Jews back to Israel. He had obviously never noted the Divine proclamation recorded in Jeremiah (31:10): "Hear the word of the LORD, O nations, and declare it in the isles afar off, and say, **'He who scattered Israel will gather him**, and keep him as a shepherd does his flock.'" I need hardly remark that Rothschild did not scatter Israel! Of course God often uses human tools, and in Jeremiah 25:9 He refers to "Nebuchadnezzar the king of Babylon, My servant" as the instrument of exile, just as He refers to Cyrus as His instrument for the return from exile: "Who says of Cyrus, 'He is My shepherd, and he shall perform all My pleasure, Saying to Jerusalem, "You shall be built, And to the temple, 'Your foundation shall be laid.'" (Isa 44:28). Later, in Ezra the Holy Spirit records for us: "The LORD stirred up the spirit of Cyrus king of Persia..... And He has commanded me to build Him a house at Jerusalem which is in Judah." (Ezra 1:1-2).

It is not unreasonable to say that the Lord similarly stirred up the spirit of Rothschild some hundred and twenty years ago, and that of Balfour a hundred years ago. But, if we have any spiritual insight, we dare not credit this partial return of Israel to the Promised Land to anyone other than God. Let us never forget that the return of the nation has been in unbelief, the national penitence and confession, prophesied in Zechariah chapter 12, has to take place within the Promised Land. If we believe our Bible, it will happen in God's time. In the meantime He calls out individual Jews, who become members of the Church without losing their Jewish identity (Rom 11:1). Escalating Anti-Semitism is a sign of the times.

17 March

"And Jesus answered and said to them: 'Take heed that no one deceives you. For many will come in My name, saying, "I am the Christ," and will deceive many.'" (Matt 24:4-5)

We now come to some more general signs of the times, where we have to go to other prophecies for further details. There is enough to consider in the above simple statement, providing we recognise that these features are going to escalate rather than diminish. The disciples might have expected otherwise, and such a supposition is still to be found today.

Deception has been rife within the past two centuries. Cults have mushroomed and some are still with us, offering representations of Christ which are anything but Scriptural. Mormons were early on the scene with their American myths and promise of godhood for all their followers, where Christ is Jehovah, a senior son of Elohim. Seventh Day Adventists came soon after with a "Christ" who represents the slain goat while Satan is the scapegoat. So called "Jehovah's Witnesses" deny Christ's divinity, misrepresent His incarnation, refuse to worship Him and do not believe in His physical resurrection. And so we could go on with "Christian Scientists", Christadelphians and so forth. All fail miserably the "What think ye of Christ?" test. Cults might be summarised by John's words: "They went out from us, but they were not of us; for if they had been of us, they would have continued with us; but they went out that they might be made manifest." (I Jn 2:19). It is so important when we encounter cult members to make them stop and think. Try quoting that verse to them and tell them that they are a sign of the times. Sadly they gain certain credibility by pointing out the many imperfections and growing apathy of mainstream believers. It is our responsibility to be alert to the growing trend. Remember that our Lord has warned of the dangers of deception.

Jesus here is looking immediately beyond the Rapture, when there will inevitably be an intense flurry of counterfeit spiritual claims. The world will be thrown into turmoil for the first few years as Satan brings his masterplan into action with his ultimate false or Anti-Christ. What we are currently seeing is nothing compared with the cultish activity which will rush to fulfil the spiritual vacuum left by the raptured Church.

18 March

"And you will hear of wars and rumours of wars. See that you are not troubled; for all these things must come to pass, but the end is not yet." (Matt 24:6)

A different Greek word, *telos* is used here from that in "end of the age"; I quote Professor Heading again: "It means the final completion of the end period just described." Let us pause to contrast this verse with Micah 4:3: "He shall judge between many peoples, and rebuke strong nations afar off; They shall beat their swords into plowshares, and their spears into pruning hooks; Nation shall not lift up sword against nation, neither shall they learn war any more." These two prophecies are equally authoritative; neither is conditional. Both must emphatically be fulfilled sooner or later; God says so.

However, many people choose to quote the second without the first, claiming that the first has already been fulfilled, and that we are now capable of achieving the second with a little goodwill. It is a nice idea, but futile human reasoning. Jesus is talking here of the period before His return as King; that Return is the essential criterion. What a mess of muddled ambitions and expectations people find themselves in when they deny the future Millennium as per the timing of the simple sequence in Revelation 20.

The Church was born in a period referred to as the *Pax Romana*, one of the most peaceful times in the world's history. This greatly facilitated the rapid spread of the Gospel after Pentecost. But, as far as Jerusalem was concerned, it was not to last long, as Titus and his armies laid siege to and sacked the city. Since then there have been periods of greater or lesser warfare throughout the world, but any hopes of lasting peace were always short-lived.

We have no authority to predict or deny further wars or outcomes this side of the Rapture, but we have every reason to anticipate a build-up to conflict in the Middle East, knowing that, as Revelation chapter 6:4 informs us, peace has thereafter to be taken from the earth.

In the meantime, let us remember that for us Church Age believers, and for future Tribulation Period believers, our Lord has personally told us: "See that you are not troubled; for all these things must come to pass." God is still in command.

19 March

"For nation will rise against nation, and kingdom against kingdom. And there will be famines, pestilences, and earthquakes in various places." (Matt 24:7)

When the Bible uses two apparently similar meaning words, such as nation and kingdom, together, there is usually some kind of contrast. *Ethnos* translated 'nation' can also refer to race. It may be, though we cannot be certain, that Jesus was talking about inter-racial conflict. Conflict between races has certainly grown in recent decades, and is one of the underlying causes of terrorism and discord, it may well peak during the Great Tribulation. Its present growth could be considered a sign of the times. With Church still on earth as salt and light, our planet is not yet back at the state before the Flood where, "The earth also was corrupt before God, and the earth was filled with violence" (Gen 6:11). But it will happen.

The many millions of tons of food which are wasted annually whilst there is starvation in parts of Africa is alarming. But we should be aware of the perilous balance between starvation and glut currently preserved by fragile technology and cheap transport. In Revelation chapter 6 we learn that starvation will be widespread as the post-Rapture judgments begin to take their toll. The same chapter, to which we will return in due course, foretells lethal diseases during the same period. Despite incredible advances in science and the eradication of what were once fatal diseases, we have recently come to the point where we can no longer afford all the health care which our aging and expanding population needs. Whether this factor, or growing resilience to antibiotics or new diseases or all three of these will be the cause, we cannot yet tell. But we see here another sign of the times which has already crossed our horizon.

Even now before the Rapture our world is experiencing mounting seismic pressures. Scientists are deeply concerned. Many, including recent earthquakes in Mexico, are closely associated with the volcanic "Fiery Girdle of the Pacific", and Californian San Andreas Fault has the potential for destruction not seen since the Flood. Other areas where seismic plate meets plate have also suffered. Revelation tells of future catastrophic earthquakes. What is truly significant now is that so many signs of the times are coming together at the same time.

20 March

"All these are the beginning of sorrows." (Matt 24:8)

Remember that what we have seen described over the last few days refers to what is to happen following the Rapture of the Church. I make no apology for repeating: "Now when these things begin to happen, look up and lift up your heads, because your redemption draws near" (Luke 21:28). For the Church the signs of the times include the build-up towards judgments and conditions yet to happen. We have no excuse for ignoring them and every reason for informing the outside world that all this is in keeping with what God has foretold. This is one of the greatest tools for evangelisation, as was the Flood and the Ark under construction to the people of Noah's day. Others may not know what the world is coming to; **we do know!**

The term 'Beginning of Sorrows' is usually used in contrast to the Great Tribulation. Jesus did not say "the" Great Tribulation because He was describing it: "For then there will be great tribulation, such as has not been since the beginning of the world until this time, no, nor ever shall be" (Matt 24:21), but in Revelation 7:4 the elder whom John questioned referred to something already revealed, and added "the" as most commentators would do today: "These are the ones who come out of **the** great tribulation, and washed their robes and made them white in the blood of the Lamb". (Rev 7:14). We will see these verses again.

Thus it is appropriate to refer to the whole period between the Rapture and Christ's Return in Power as "the Tribulation Period", with the first part being "The Beginning of Sorrows" and the second as "the Great Tribulation". Capitals are for emphasis but are not in the original text. When we look at Daniel chapter 9 and related passages, we will see how the Tribulation Period is split into two. The term "sorrows" is also used to mean birth pains or travail. The travail preceding the rebirth of Israel is in view: "Who has heard such a thing? Who has seen such things? Shall the earth be made to give birth in one day? Or shall a nation be born at once? For as soon as Zion was in labour, she gave birth to her children" (Isa 66:8).

Christ's Crucifixion and Resurrection in Prophecy

21 March

"Your father Abraham rejoiced to see My day, and he saw it and was glad." (Jn 8:56)

Because most recognised Christian festivals, other than Christmas, follow the lunar calendar, it is impossible to relate them to diary dates. However, as we are coming to the earliest date for Easter, it seems appropriate now to look at some of the great prophecies concerning our Lord's crucifixion and resurrection.

I was seven when my parents were saved. I recall a new book with what seemed to me a curious title suddenly appearing in our bookcase, AM Hodgkin's *"Christ in All the Scriptures"*. I still own and treasure it. From what I had learned at school, Christ was a central Person in the New Testament and had nothing to do with the Old Testament. Sadly this is an all too common perception among adults, let alone children. Christ was there at the creation: "For by Him all things were created" (Col 1:16); then the promise of Christ the Redeemer followed the Fall: "And I will put enmity between you and the woman, And between your seed and her Seed; He shall bruise your head, And you shall bruise His heel." (Gen 3:15). Hodgkin opens the first chapter with today's text, and follows it up with: "Moses wrote of Me" (Jn 5:46) and "David called [Me] Lord" (Matt 22:45). Christ was there before and throughout the Old Testament and not only in prophecy. These are really very elementary truths, but they need to be re-emphasised.

Abraham evidently had prophetic insight, which must have helped to underpin the faith for which he was renowned; Abraham in his day knew Christ; indeed, he talked with Him: "Then the LORD appeared to Abram and said, 'To your descendants I will give this land.' And there he built an altar to the LORD, who had appeared to him" (Gen 12:7). Some have suggested that it was the spirit of Abraham awaiting resurrection who had rejoiced and was glad, but the verb tenses do not allow for this. There are at least five occasions in Abraham's life when the above verse may have applied, including the Divine intervention at Isaac's sacrifice and the anticipation of the heavenly country (Heb 11:16). We now turn to some further Old Testament passages which foreshadow, anticipate or prophesy Christ's crucifixion and resurrection.

22 March

"Then he shall kill the goat of the sin offering, which is for the people, bring its blood inside the veil, do with that blood as he did with the blood of the bull, and sprinkle it on the mercy seat and before the mercy seat." (Lev 16:15)

This is one of the passages which foreshadows or anticipates, rather than prophesies, but its links with the New Testament and Christ's crucifixion are so potent that it seems appropriate to use it as an introduction to more specific prophecies. This is what happened annually for Israel on the Day of Atonement (Yom Kippur) and once for all for us at Calvary (Heb 10:12).

Its fulfilment at Calvary could hardly be clearer. "And Jesus cried out again with a loud voice, and yielded up His spirit. Then, behold, the veil of the temple was torn in two from top to bottom; and the earth quaked, and the rocks were split (Matt 27:50-51). The Father had accepted His Son's sacrifice. Two goats were required to represent different aspects of Calvary. My old pastor, J Sidlow Baxter, writes: "The goat offered as a sacrifice typified the Godward aspect of our Lord's atoning work for us, while the *azazel* goat (which we consider tomorrow) typified the outward aspect." The blood of the slain goat, the sin offering, was taken by the High Priest through the veil into the Holy of Holies and sprinkled on the Mercy Seat. But "it is not possible that the blood of bulls and goats could take away sins" (Heb 10:4). Only Christ's death could make open a way through the veil. "God was in Christ reconciling the world to Himself" (II Cor 5:19). Only "God manifest in the flesh" could accomplish this, by becoming Man and suffering for man in man's place.

The flesh of the Sin offering was burnt outside the camp; "Therefore Jesus also, that He might sanctify the people with His own blood, suffered outside the gate. Therefore let us go forth to Him, outside the camp, bearing His reproach" (Heb 13:12-13). Suffering the reproach of the world for our Saviour, when it happens to us, should be a joy and privilege. Can we, like Paul, say: "I consider that the sufferings of this present time are not worthy to be compared with the glory which shall be revealed in us" (Rom 8:18)?

23 March

"But the goat on which the lot fell to be the scapegoat shall be presented alive before the LORD, to make atonement upon it, and to let it go as the scapegoat into the wilderness." (Lev 16:10)

When people use the term "Azazel", it is not to show off their knowledge of Hebrew; it is because the word "scapegoat" is not a good rendering. The Scapegoat is not only the innocent party who takes the blame, but is the one who actually removes the guilt, carrying it far away. This is what the Lord Jesus has done for us. Holman Hunt's famous picture, "The Scapegoat", manages to capture the utter desolation, misery and abandonment of the goat carrying far away the sins of the people. Having completed the sacrifice of the sin offering goat, the High Priest was to turn to the live goat: "Aaron shall lay both his hands on the head of the live goat, confess over it all the iniquities of the children of Israel, and all their transgressions, concerning all their sins, putting them on the head of the goat, and shall send it away into the wilderness by the hand of a suitable man. The goat shall bear on itself all their iniquities to an uninhabited land; and he shall release the goat in the wilderness" (Lev 16:21-22).

John uses a Greek word which means to carry away, rather than merely bear: "The Lamb of God, who takes away the sin of the world" (Jn 1:29). All the iniquities of the nation had been confessed and symbolically transferred to the Azazel goat. We must draw neither more nor less confidence from Jesus' carrying our sins far away than we do for His shed blood being taken through the veil. Leviticus in the Old Testament and Hebrews in the New do more than any other books to emphasise the centrality of the blood: "For the life of the flesh is in the blood, and I have given it to you upon the altar to make atonement for your souls; for it is the blood that makes atonement for the soul." (Lev 17:11); "And according to the law almost all things are purified with blood, and without shedding of blood there is no remission" (Heb 9:22). The Law's demands are satisfied, and in the Azazel goat the evidence against us is eternally removed.

24 March

*"I have become a stranger to my brothers, and an alien to my
mother's children; Because zeal for Your house has eaten me up,
and the reproaches of those who reproach You have fallen on me."*
(Ps 69:8-9)

It is so easy to think of the Crucifixion and Resurrection as being
isolated from His ministry. But of course these are a climax to
the numerous events of His incarnation. Elsewhere we see vivid
evidence of both the impending sorrow and joy, very human emotions
on the part of One who for love "became flesh and dwelt among us"
(Jn 1:14). Psalm 69 is quoted several times in the New Testament,
and by Jesus Himself. It is not always clear what experiences in his
personal life David was recalling which foreshadowed the Messiah.
There are matters which are personal to David and simply do not
apply to Christ. David, for instance, makes confession, which Jesus
most certainly did not need to do.

Having been brought up as the eldest brother in the family at
Nazareth, and, having taken on (one may reasonably assume) the
responsibilities of head of the home and business at Joseph's death,
He was entitled to family respect. Some brothers are named for us:
"Is this not the carpenter's son? Is not His mother called Mary?
And His brothers James, Joses, Simon, and Judas?" (Matt 13:55).
But during His ministry none became disciples but remained aloof:
"Then His brothers and His mother came, and standing outside they
sent to Him, calling Him" (Mk 3:31). Jesus must have been hurt.
After Pentecost some of these brothers became prominent Church
leaders, recognising His Divinity as well as family kinship. He had
lived and worked among His nation, healing, comforting, preaching
and teaching, with a graciousness unknown among the religious
leaders. A minority could look back and say "and we beheld His
glory, the glory as of the only begotten of the Father, full of grace and
truth." But the majority hated Him.

To the Jews, the magnificent Jerusalem Temple, still standing
despite the Roman occupation, was a symbol of nationalism, but
its courts had been corrupted by greed and commerce. He had
symbolically cleansed it: "Then His disciples remembered that it
was written, 'Zeal for Your house has eaten Me up'" (Jn 2:17). The
Temple leaders hated Him the more.

25 March

"Behold, My Servant shall deal prudently; He shall be exalted and extolled and be very high..... So shall He sprinkle many nations. Kings shall shut their mouths at Him; for what had not been told them they shall see, and what they had not heard they shall consider." (Isa 52:13, 15)

We come to two of the most awesome passages of Scripture regarding our Saviour's crucifixion, Psalm 22 and Isaiah 52:13-53:12. The first is prophetically portrayed through the Psalmist's being allowed to relate it experientially; the second consists of God's words recorded more than seven centuries beforehand, and commences with the command, "Behold!". Those who have not heeded that command this side of death must do so beyond the grave. He speaks of "My Servant". The Father speaks of the Son who willingly became a servant for us.

The margin of some versions gives the alternative and more consistent rendering: "My Servant shall prosper". To the world the crucifixion appears to be a defeat. God knows better. It is about victory as the later verses in both passages demonstrate. It was the costliest of all victories, but it was a victory for every believer. Beforehand Jesus had said: "Now My soul is troubled, and what shall I say? 'Father, save Me from this hour'? But for this purpose I came to this hour" (Jn 12:27). There was an immediate audible response from Heaven. His Father gave miraculous confirmation; the unbelieving put it down to thunder. Nothing changes. Jesus went on to declare: "Now is the judgment of this world; now the ruler of this world will be cast out. And I, if I am lifted up from the earth, will draw all peoples to Myself." (vv 31-32). In the light of eternity Satan was already on the verge of defeat, and unable to reverse the accomplishments of the approaching crucifixion. As G Campbell Morgan put it: "Thus the historic utterances of Jesus harmonise with the prophetic foretelling..... Lifted up by conspicuous sorrows, but by them lifted up into the place of conspicuous sovereignty, so that the kings of the earth shut their mouths because of Him." The intermediate verse 14, which we look at elsewhere, describes the astonishment as people behold the marred visage of the Sufferer. Never has there been greater failure among the human rulers of this world to comprehend what in eternity they will mourn.

26 March

"But I am a worm, and no man; A reproach of men, and despised by the people. All those who see Me ridicule Me; They shoot out the lip, they shake the head, saying, 'He trusted in the LORD, let Him rescue Him; Let Him deliver Him, since He delights in Him!'"
(Ps 22:6-8)

The Psalmist again looks prophetically at the Cross. Handel, in his great oratorio "The Messiah", has managed to capture the sheer derision and malice in the words of the spectators at Christ's crucifixion. They were of course right in saying that God could deliver Him had He wanted, so that barb must have hurt doubly. They were also doubly guilty, for they were displaying a knowledge of their Scriptures whilst being deliberately blind to the identity of the Victim for whose death they had clamoured. It was for our sakes that He did not cry out for the deliverance, whether by the twelve angelic legions which He had said were available (Matt 26:53) or by other mighty means.

Equally hurtful must have been the clause "since He delights in Him", spoken cynically, devoid of sincerity. It is easy to forget, simply because it is beyond our powers of imagination, the pain of the Father as the Son was suffering and He was withholding His support. The evidence for the Father delighting in Him comes over so clearly in the Prophets and the Gospels: "Behold! My Servant whom I uphold, My Elect One in whom My soul delights!" (Isa 42:1); at His baptism: "suddenly a voice came from heaven, saying, 'This is My beloved Son, in whom I am well pleased'" (Matt 3:17); also at His Transfiguration (Lk 9:35). The loving relationship which existed within the Trinity before the world began remained unbroken throughout our Saviour's humanity on earth, and had therefore no need to "resume" at His ascension. It is eternal; the nearest it ever came to being broken was at the moment to which we turn in tomorrow's reading.

I quote again Campbell Morgan: "Men are seen waiting for His dying, nay, not even waiting for that dying, for they gambled for His garment ere He died. Thus humanity is seen around that Sufferer in all its ghastly failure, utterly blind to the real meaning of His suffering - mocking, brutal, callous".

"Reproach has broken my heart, and I am full of heaviness; I looked for someone to take pity, but there was none; and for comforters, but I found none. They also gave me gall for my food, and for my thirst they gave me vinegar to drink." (Ps 69:20-21)

This prophetic Psalm takes us far beyond anything that David can have experienced, although he had several times suffered reproach, and God had been aware of this and had in due course vindicated him with great honour when this was merited. But here is the unmerited reproach which the Lord Jesus Christ suffered. We may be called to bear, or may even volunteer to bear, reproach for our Lord's sake, like Moses: "By faith Moses..... esteeming the reproach of Christ greater riches than the treasures in Egypt; for he looked to the reward" (Heb 11:24, 26). The writer to the Hebrews adds: "Therefore let us go forth to Him, outside the camp, bearing His reproach" (13:13). However let us keep this in perspective compared with what Christ endured for us. I know only by the initials "D.R." the person who wrote perceptively: "No matter how near we may be to Him, we shall always be a stone's throw away, as were the disciples in the garden of Gethsemane. Lk 22:41".

While previously "all had forsaken Him and fled", we know that John and at least three of the women were at the cross. This is acknowledged and to their great credit. But the loneliness which none could break into was the sin-bearing which was His and His alone; not a finger could be raised to help Him during those dread hours of darkness. I often pass the cottage of Sunday school teacher Elizabeth Clephane, who wrote words deeply etched on my memory:
But none of the ransomed ever knew how deep were the waters crossed;
Nor how dark was the night that the Lord passed through, 'ere He found His sheep that was lost.

It is recorded that at the cross, before the nailing, "They gave Him sour wine mingled with gall to drink. But when He had tasted it,   He would not drink" (Matt 27:34). He showed His appreciation, but refused anything which would reduce the pain of the burden He was bearing. When the vinegar or sour wine was offered (Matt 27:48) it was all over.

28 March

"My God, My God, why have You forsaken Me? Why are You so far from helping Me, and from the words of My groaning?" (Ps 22:1)

Here is the voice of One who has always been in fellowship with the One addressed, but has now suddenly found that this fellowship has suddenly been broken. Rather than describe this as Jesus quoting Scripture, we should think of the Psalmist prophetically quoting Jesus. That the priests standing by should not have pricked up their ears as they heard this agonised question seems quite incredible.

Were more costly words ever uttered in human history? The Holy Spirit required that they should be recorded for posterity, once in classical Hebrew and once with the Aramaic accent in which they were spoken shortly before His death at the ninth hour (3 p.m.). *"Eli, Eli, lama sabachthani?";* I leave the translation in the KJV to emphasise the singular "Thou": "that is to say, My God, my God, why hast thou forsaken me?" (Matt 27:46). The Aramaic for "El" was "Eloi". Also in the singular it is "Eli" or "Eloi" as opposed to the much more common plural *"Elohim"* for God. This is not a voice of complaint or protest; He still recognises Him as His God, His Sovereign. The question is better rendered: "Why Me has Thou relinquished or left behind?" If we dare put it thus the question is something like; "Why are You of all people relinquishing or abandoning Me of all people?" The sense of dereliction in the question is almost tangible. As they crucified Him He cried out: "**Father**, forgive them, for they do not know what they do." (Lk 23:34). When everything had been accomplished He could again address Him: "**Father**, into Your hands I commit My spirit." (Lk 23:46).

Paul writes of Jesus' condition during that short period thus: "For He made Him who knew no sin to be sin for us, that we might become the righteousness of God in Him" (II Cor 5:21). But now, so agonisingly conscious is He of this, to Him, novel condition, and the fact that the communion which had existed from eternity had suddenly been broken, He was compelled to address Him, not as Father, but as the less intimate, less personal **"My God"**. Tomorrow we will see how it was foretold that Jesus would answer His own question.

29 March

"But You are holy, Enthroned in the praises of Israel." (Ps 22:3).

The voice which cried: "Why have You forsaken Me?" is the voice that answered: "But You are holy." Our Saviour was at that moment the One who "Himself bore our sins in His own body on the tree" (I Pet 2:24). We cannot begin to imagine what it must have been for the pure, holy, sinless Son of God to bear that abominable load of our transgressions, the accumulated sins of countless millions, past, present and future, in His frail human body. The answer to "Why? was "But Thou art Holy" (KJV). **That** was why. Nothing like this had ever happened before or could happen again.

The prophet Habakkuk makes an explanatory statement: "You are of purer eyes than to behold evil, and cannot look on wickedness" (1:13). The hymn writer rightly said: "The Father turns His face away". The deepest agony of the Sufferer was infinitely greater than that of the actual crucifixion, which many thousands of others had endured. In that He was not unique; He even had on either side of Him two fellow sufferers of the cruel death, which had not been invented when the Psalmist wrote. Prophetically the dreadful crucifixion experience is reflected later in the psalm: "I am poured out like water, and all My bones are out of joint; My heart is like wax; it has melted within Me. My strength is dried up like a potsherd, and My tongue clings to My jaws; You have brought Me to the dust of death" (vv 14-15). In order to make the transaction valid, it was the holy God, and not sinful mankind who had slain Him: "**You** have brought Me to the dust of death"

Back in January we looked at that wonderful verse 7 of Isaiah 53: "He was oppressed and He was afflicted, Yet He opened not His mouth". He had not opened His mouth when questioned by the High Priest, "But Jesus kept silent" until put under oath (Matt 26:62-63). When Herod questioned Him, "He answered him nothing" (Lk 23:9). But here there was another, deeper reason for His opening not His mouth. There was no answer for the sins which He was bearing, He was laden with our guilt; "The LORD has laid on Him the iniquity of us all" (Isa 53:6); and **that** is unanswerable.

30 March

"But He was wounded for our transgressions, He was bruised for our iniquities; the chastisement for our peace was upon Him, and by His stripes we are healed." (Isa 53:5)

The significance of this verse is beyond emphasis. WE Vine points out that the words for "wounded" and "bruised" indicate the most extreme violence and remarks that "our" is stressed twice. He adds, "The chastisement which was administered to Him by God is that which makes for our peace (the word *shalom* is comprehensive), and describes not only a peaceful state, but well-being in general." Whoever else, such as the Romans soldiers, were involved, it is God who inflicted on Him the wounds that should have been ours.

Christ's death was vicarious. He was our substitute. He died in our place. He took our punishment. If we are not prepared to accept that central truth of all central truths, we can have no part in His work of salvation. I still sometimes play the organ, and was recently asked to play for the funeral of somebody whom I had never met, but knew of by reputation. I knew nothing of her family, but agreed to play on condition that they did not require "I did it my way" as a voluntary.

The popular song sounds virtuous and noble, but it reflects the religion of Cain and not that of Abel, who recognised the need of the Lamb. The song starts: "And now my end is near and so I face the final curtain…". It ends with: "I faced it all, and I stood tall; I did it my way." It is the antithesis of the Christian Gospel. It is the precise opposite of the old hymn, "Rock of Ages", one verse of which commences, "Nothing in my hand I bring, simply to Thy cross I cling" and ends with: "When I soar through realms unknown, meet Thee on Thy judgment throne, Rock of Ages, cleft for me, let me hide myself in Thee." The "cleft" was the wounding. The confidence here is endorsed by Almighty God in this line from Isaiah. If we turn to the description of Christ's Great White Throne in Revelation, where all unbelievers must ultimately stand, we see the appalling folly of proposing to "stand tall" before the face of One who, for sinful mankind, hung on a cross.

31 March

"For You will not leave my soul in Sheol, nor will You allow Your Holy One to see corruption." (Ps 16:10).

While David may have been speaking of his personal future, Peter, in quoting this verse, made it absolutely clear that this was ultimately about the experiences of Christ. We look at the resurrection applications and Peter's summary tomorrow, but concentrate today on the awful implications of Jesus' soul having been in Sheol (Greek *Hades*). The absent corruption referred of course to Christ's body, which was later seen to be alive "by many infallible proofs". Corruption stems from sin, and Christ was sinless.

His body had remained upon the cross during those awful three hours of darkness. But what of His soul? We are given many details of what happened during daylight hours, but what of the darkness? It may have been **only** three hours outside Jerusalem. But how long did it seem to the One who descended to Sheol when He was purchasing our salvation? We dare not speculate. Krummacher writes: "That which during this time passed between Him and His Father, lies in the present sealed as with seven seals, hidden in the depths of eternity. We only know that, behind that veil, He was engaged in the most ardent conflict, gained the most brilliant victory, and adorned His representative obedience with its final crown. We know that the grave of our sins was then dug; the handwriting on the wall against us was then taken out of the way; and the wall which separated us from our God removed."

Now look at Matthew 27:50-51: "And Jesus cried out again with a loud voice, and yielded up His spirit. Then, behold, the veil of the temple was torn in two from top to bottom; and the earth quaked, and the rocks were split." The eternal transaction had been completed by the moment of death: "Who does not need daily, as those high priests, to offer up sacrifices, first for His own sins and then for the people's, for this He did once for all when He offered up Himself." (Heb 7:27). "Not with the blood of goats and calves, but with His own blood He entered the Most Holy Place once for all, having obtained eternal redemption." (Heb 9:12). The veil was torn not at His ascension, not even at His resurrection, but at His death.

1 April

"You will show me the path of life; In Your presence is fullness of joy; at Your right hand are pleasures forevermore." (Ps 16:11)

We move forward a single verse in Psalm 16. Peter, on the day of Pentecost, with an eloquence and authority which he had never previously possessed, challenged the crowd with: "Him, being delivered by the determined purpose and foreknowledge of God, you have taken by lawless hands, have crucified, and put to death; whom God raised up, having loosed the pains of death, because it was not possible that He should be held by it." (Acts 2:23-24). The first sermon in Christianity was about the death and resurrection of the Lord Jesus Christ. Anything which purports to be Christianity without these is fraudulent and futile. Peter went on to quote yesterday's and today's texts, emphasising that there was much more in them than could apply to David alone: "Men and brethren, let me speak freely to you of the patriarch David, that he is both dead and buried, and his tomb is with us to this day" (Acts 2:29).

For David the "path of life", meaning the resurrection and an incorruptible celestial body, still lies ahead; but for Christ it followed the three days in the tomb. Peter was one of those "to whom He also presented Himself alive after His suffering by many infallible proofs, being seen by them during forty days" (Acts 1:3), but still demanding that vital element of faith in others. Peter was proclaiming the resurrection, and the Holy Spirit was ensuring that all, irrespective of native language, could comprehend.

Paul, in a powerful address in the synagogue in Antioch in Pisidia also quoted Psalm 16 to prove that Jesus Christ was the slain and resurrected Messiah. He said: "Therefore He also says in another Psalm: 'You will not allow Your Holy One to see corruption.' For David, after he had served his own generation by the will of God, fell asleep, was buried with his fathers, and saw corruption; but He whom God raised up saw no corruption'" (Acts 13:35-37). "Therefore let it be known to you, brethren, that through this Man is preached to you the forgiveness of sins; and by Him everyone who believes is justified from all things from which you could not be justified by the law of Moses" (Acts 13:38-39).

2 April

"Yet it pleased the LORD to bruise Him; He has put Him to grief. When You make His soul an offering for sin, He shall see His seed, He shall prolong His days, and the pleasure of the LORD shall prosper in His hand." (Isa 53:10)

When we looked at verse 5 of this amazing chapter, we saw that it was the Father who wounded the Son. The solemnity of that fact overwhelms us; but now we are faced with an even more profound truth as Isaiah gazes forward to Calvary: "It **pleased** the Lord (Jehovah) to bruise Him." God forbid that we should ever see anything cynical or sadistic in this action. It was the outworking of this wounding which brought the pleasure, the joy. We are now taken to the Victim's assessment of whether it had all been worthwhile. If we see it as the heavenly Bridegroom paying the bride-price we might be able to take it in more readily – love enters in. When it is made   about one who has died, the statement, "He shall prolong His days" means so much more; this is endless resurrection. Dead people do not prolong their days. To John He said: "I am He who lives, and was dead, and behold, I am alive forevermore. Amen." (Rev 1:18). A Christ who had never died and risen again could not be our Saviour. He thought that it had all been worthwhile, as did His Father! The prophecy of Isaiah has been in their Tanakh (Old Testament) for nearly twenty-eight centuries, and yet Orthodox Jews are still blind to these sublime truths.

WE Vine, writing of the statement, says: "He shall see His seed", says: "An Israelite was regarded as conspicuously blessed if he had a numerous posterity, and especially if he lived to see them" (Genesis 48:11; Psalm 128:6). Here then we have the intimation of the exceeding joy of Christ in seeing the results of His sacrifice in the countless multitude of His spiritual posterity from among Jews and Gentiles.

FB Meyer speaks of the vindication of all that Christ was seen by Isaiah as having to go through. There is the vindication of the future revelation to those who esteemed Him not and dared assume that God was punishing Him for blasphemy, the vindication of the trust of each individual believing soul and the vindication of His exaltation to the right hand of power.

3 April

"For I know that my Redeemer lives, and He shall stand at last on the earth; and after my skin is destroyed, this I know, that in my flesh I shall see God, Whom I shall see for myself, and my eyes shall behold, and not another. How my heart yearns within me!"
(Job 19:25-27)

This is an outstanding confession of faith in God's role as the Redeemer, in the possibility of personal possession of salvation, in the resurrection of the human body, and in the Redeemer's latter day appearance on earth. It is also a lovely declaration of this man's love for His God. It is all the more remarkable because it was recorded before the Scriptures were written.

Job is one of those mysterious but honourable figures like Melchizedek in early Bible history, who had unique revelations from God. He may have been a prince who was known to have lived somewhere in the desert fringe area in what is now southern Syria or northern Jordan about the time of the Patriarchs. We would have been told, had such details been important. Few have had such a commendation as Job: "Then the LORD said to Satan, 'Have you considered My servant Job, that there is none like him on the earth, a blameless and upright man, one who fears God and shuns evil?'" (Job 1:8). Job's is one of those splendid testimonies where the righteous acknowledge the need for redemption as much as gross sinners do.

Now Job's prophecy refers not to Christ's resurrection, of which he may or may not have been aware, but to the fact that when Job's resurrection takes place at the time of Christ's Return in power, he will see his Redeemer. The clear implication is that the Christ whom we know to have died will be alive when Job is restored to life. The principle is so important. Most of the clearest statements about Christ's resurrection are in the New Testament, but the Old Testament abounds with unconditional, and often hitherto unfulfilled, prophecies, which simply would not be feasible had He remained in His grave. "If Christ is not risen, your faith is futile; you are still in your sins!" (I Cor 15:17). But His latter day appearance on earth still lies ahead. Church saints will see Him first. Can each of us like Job exclaim: "How my heart yearns within me!"?

4 April

"Behold, this Child is destined for the fall and rising of many in Israel, and for a sign which will be spoken against (yes, a sword will pierce through your own soul also), that the thoughts of many hearts may be revealed." (Lk 2:34-35)

Here, in the words of the elderly Simeon, is a very different personal prophecy concerning Jesus' death. Simeon was one of the few truly longing for the "consolation of Israel" in the form of the promised Messiah. Many today have long waited for what we might call the "consolation of the Church", the Rapture, when our heavenly Bridegroom will come to take us to His Father's home. Have any had an absolute guarantee that they will be among the "we who are alive and remain"? But Simeon had been given the promise which allowed him to stand in the Temple, take the Baby in his arms and declare publicly: "My eyes have seen Your salvation."

But for Mary, Simeon had a very different message which in no way negated his public statements. So much nonsense has been invented about our Lord's mother, that we Protestants are reluctant to make too much of Mary. She had no personal "immaculate conception"; she acknowledged a Saviour (Luke 1:47). She is certainly not the Queen of Heaven; that title belonged to a Babylonian goddess referred to five times by Jeremiah. She is in no position to answer prayers or to intercede for us, because, like us, she still awaits her resurrection. Moreover, only Christ can intercede (1s Tim 2:5). She did not remain a virgin; she had several other children.

Nevertheless she has been greatly honoured: "Rejoice, highly favoured one, the Lord is with you; blessed are you among women!"..... "Behold, henceforth all generations will call me blessed." (Luke 1:28, 48). But often when God honours, there is a cost to be borne. During Jesus' ministry, Mary must have had to deal with the protests of the other siblings regarding His wonderful works and unique status. But worst of all, she was the mother who had to stand at the cross and watch her Son die. That in effect was the piercing by the great sword. But even in His extreme agony He lovingly catered for the future care of His mother (John 19:25-26). His death has indeed "revealed the thoughts of many hearts", determining eternal destinies.

5 April

"On that very day some Pharisees came, saying to Him, 'Get out and depart from here, for Herod wants to kill You.' And He said to them, 'Go, tell that fox, "Behold, I cast out demons and perform cures today and tomorrow, and the third day I shall be perfected."'"
(Lk 13:31-32)

This often overlooked little incident must not be confused with Jesus' warnings to His disciples of His forthcoming crucifixion and resurrection. Jesus was at this time in Galilee, where Herod was governor. The Pharisees' warning was not an honourable one; probably their intention was to get Him to Jerusalem where they would be better able to deal with Him in the manner they wanted, and under the jurisdiction of Pilate. Jesus' description, "that fox", was clearly appropriate. Whether Jesus' message was passed on to the cunning, scheming, decadent Herod we do not know.

Jesus was talking about the present and the immediate future – the idiom of the three days is clear enough. He had being carrying on His ministry of casting out demons and healing the sick, and would continue to do so in the immediate future. But Galilee was not to be the place where He would perfect His purposes. He had already pointed out, "It cannot be that a prophet should perish outside of Jerusalem" (Lk 13:33). It was the city to which He said: "O Jerusalem, Jerusalem, the one who kills the prophets and stones those who are sent to her!" (Lk 13:34). Neither Herod nor the Pharisees could hinder His purposes: "Now it came to pass, when the time had come for Him to be received up, that He steadfastly set His face to go to Jerusalem" (Lk 9:51). Jerusalem was the place with the essential Temple and city walls, outside which the ultimate sacrifice could take place. But that time was still a little ahead, and there were those in Galilee who still needed liberating and healing.

Regarding the term "being perfected", Norman Crawford, points out that elsewhere it is used of the resurrection of Christ and His saints: (Philippians 3:12, Hebrews 11:40, 12:23). We have not space to quote them all, but note Hebrews 5:9: "And having been perfected, He became the author of eternal salvation to all who obey Him". In ignorance the Pharisees became a guilty party in this victory; Herod was not even allowed that dubious honour.

6 April

"From that time Jesus began to show to His disciples that He must go to Jerusalem, and suffer many things from the elders and chief priests and scribes, and be killed, and be raised the third day."
(Matt 16:21)

We have seen many predictions by prophets concerning Jesus' death and resurrection. Now we turn to His own predictions, which were very much literal prophecies and meant to be taken at face value. Several times Jesus warned His disciples of His approaching betrayal, death, the manner of His death and His resurrection on the third day. There had been various reactions, including general sadness and Peter's reprimand. But, until the Holy Spirit came upon them, none could fully grasp the reality. Even today there is widespread reluctance to take any but the most general prophecies to heart. They had Jesus in their midst; we have the gift of the Holy Spirit.

They saw confirmation of the betrayal; they witnessed the crucifixion, they saw or were aware of His burial. In other words they saw the fulfilment of the first part of these prophecies. Therefore they had a precedent for literal fulfilment. Surely, one would have thought, they should have had no doubts about His impending resurrection. Perhaps the two angels at the tomb felt the same; they witnessed the devotion and love of the bereft women who had brought spices as for long-term burial, but they were impelled gently to reprimand them with a question and reminder: "Why do you seek the living among the dead? He is not here, but is risen! Remember how He spoke to you when He was still in Galilee, saying, 'The Son of Man must be delivered into the hands of sinful men, and be crucified, and the third day rise again'" (Lk 24:5-7).

We find Thomas declaring: "Unless I see in His hands the print of the nails, and put my finger into the print of the nails, and put my hand into His side, I will not believe." A little later He said to Thomas, "Reach your finger here, and look at My hands; and reach your hand here, and put it into My side. Do not be unbelieving, but believing." To Thomas's credit, he did not have to reach out; instead, he became the first disciple to confess, "My Lord and my God!" (Jn 20:25, 27-28).

Pentecost to the Rapture Prophecies

7 April

"And I also say to you that you are Peter, and on this rock I will build My church." (Matt 16:18)

The Church was about to be built after Jesus' ascension, not upon Peter but upon Christ, "The stone which the builders rejected has become the chief cornerstone" (Mk 12:10 see also Acts 4:11). "Behold, I lay in Zion a chief cornerstone, elect, precious, and he who believes on Him will by no means be put to shame" (I Pet 2:6). It was Christ who was rejected and in whom we must believe. Peter was described by Jesus as *petros* a small stone.

We have already noticed that the Church Age is a mystery not revealed until Christ's First Coming. The Church was born at Pentecost and is to be completed and removed from earth at the Rapture. How does it relate to the previous and following ages? Paul speaks of an enmity between Israel, who had long been God's witnesses, and the Gentiles whom Jews tended to despise. "For He Himself is our peace, who has made both one, and has broken down the middle wall of separation, having abolished in His flesh the enmity..... so as to create in Himself one new man from the two, thus making peace, and that He might reconcile them both to God in one body through the cross, thereby putting to death the enmity" (Eph 2:14-16). Most Jews have excluded themselves for the duration; their restoration still lies ahead.

Compared with the numerous prophecies fulfilled during Christ's First Coming and the many to be fulfilled following the Rapture, we seem to be living in a comparative prophetic vacuum. Micah talked of "the sun going down on the prophets" (3:6). The first of these prophetic vacuums or parentheses ended at the opening event of Christ's First Coming; the second, in which we currently find ourselves, will end at the opening event of Christ's Second Coming. There are a few very short term prophecies for the few decades in which the Church was being established. But, apart from the 70 AD sack of Jerusalem which chiefly concerned Israel, there are important general predictions, but no specific prophecies of events between then and the Rapture. We simply do not *need* them, because we are always meant to be Rapture-ready, with only the signs of the times to alert us.

8 April

"Behold, I send the Promise of My Father upon you; but tarry in the city of Jerusalem until you are endued with power from on high."
(Lk 24:49)

This is a specific prophecy linked to a command. They had just received their Great Commission and were shortly to receive the means of carrying it out. The promise had been made in the upper room before Jesus' betrayal, and Jesus confirmed that it was His Father's promise, something which the eleven must have noted. The command was not to leave Jerusalem until what proved to be Pentecost. He reinforced this message before His ascension: "And being assembled together with them, He commanded them not to depart from Jerusalem, but to wait for the Promise of the Father, 'which,' He said, 'you have heard from Me'" (Acts 1:4). The two may be variations of Luke's Gospel of the same matter.

When we are sent out to witness and win souls, as the Apostles were soon to be, we too may have to tarry in prayer and preparation so that we may be endued with power from on high. Mere human activity, however well intentioned, does not yield lasting results.

A group of eleven was about to become the nucleus and leadership team of Christ's Bride and Church. On the evening when they were locked away for security and Thomas was absent. Jesus had already imparted the Holy Spirit: "And when He had said this, He breathed on them, and said to them, 'Receive the Holy Spirit'" (Jn 20:22). But, although already indwelling, the Holy Spirit had not come upon them in power and visible manifestation; that was to wait for a more public occasion. The Church was not born in obscurity.

These words were spoken "here in Jerusalem". We are not told whether there was an interval between this and the next part of the narrative, but there is clearly continuity, and one wonders about thoughts and conversations during the two miles crossing the Kedron valley, passing Gethsemane of recent memories, and then climbing to the Olivet hill-top village. "And He led them out as far as Bethany, and He lifted up His hands and blessed them. Now it came to pass, while He blessed them, that He was parted from them and carried up into heaven. And they worshipped Him, and returned to Jerusalem with great joy" (Lk 24:50-52).

9 April

"Then one of them, named Agabus, stood up and showed by the Spirit that there was going to be a great famine throughout all the world, which also happened in the days of Claudius Caesar."
(Acts 11:28)

This is a very different prophecy from most we have considered, but it is intensely practical and demonstrates the need of the new Church to be involved in such mundane matters, reminding us of God's love for mankind and His provision of opportunities. Luke, the author of the Acts, was always very precise with his timings; Claudius was Emperor from 41 to 54 AD. The Greek here indicated the inhabited world. There were several famines about this time, and Josephus tells of one which was particularly severe in Judea and Syria, when the citizens of Jerusalem were in great distress.

The Church was therefore only a few years old, and undergoing persecution, when this new challenge arose. Becoming a Christian is no guarantee of a quiet life and prosperity. The so-called Prosperity Gospel is a hideous modern aberration. We live under a very different covenant from the Levitical one, where obedience guaranteed good harvests (Deuteronomy 28:4 & 8). William Kelly asks: "Is it not of deep interest, the faith and love which responded to this, though it was no charity sermon, without waiting for a call from the saints already impoverished by their generous love after the great Pentecost which first saw the assembly here below? They believed in the coming scarcity, and thought of the saints in Jerusalem as truly 'one body'". Both in Acts and some Pauline epistles, concern for believers in Jerusalem was a feature of the expanding Church. The very fact the Agabus was inspired to make this prophecy is evidence of our Heavenly Father's care for His own. No such predictions were available from the pagan oracles.

Kelly's reference to the selling of land following Pentecost is noteworthy. It may indeed have led to hunger for some: "All who were possessors of lands or houses sold them, and brought the proceeds of the things that were sold, and laid them at the apostles' feet; and they distributed to each as anyone had need" (Acts 4:34-35). What God knew, but they did not, was that, before long, the Roman armies were to lay siege to Jerusalem and consequently the land would be forfeited indefinitely.

10 April

"And see, now I go bound in the spirit to Jerusalem, not knowing the things that will happen to me there, except that the Holy Spirit testifies in every city, saying that chains and tribulations await me."
(Acts 20:22-23)

In human terms what could be less motivational, what more calculated to discourage? But in the Lord's service motivational theory is turned on its head. Paul talks of being "bound in the spirit". Some versions give 'spirit' a capital 'S', but the NKJV and ASV are correct in leaving it as lower case. This is Paul's own spirit which is here under the compulsion of the Holy Spirit; Darby, in his version, actually says "my spirit" to emphasise the contrast. Distinguishing between the soul and spirit, which together comprise two thirds of our being, can be difficult: "For the word of God is living and powerful, and sharper than any two-edged sword, piercing even to the division of soul   and spirit...., and is a discerner of the thoughts and intents of the heart" (Heb 4:12). Our emotions are based in the soul; there we can credit or indeed fail to credit what is truly influenced by God's Holy Spirit. When, like Paul, we are totally surrendered, emotions can be forgotten, and our entire being becomes focused on doing God's will, whatever the cost.

Evidently the Holy Spirit reinforced His programme in every city which Paul visited. He reveals the details of His plans for us only at a pace with which we can cope. It is easy to let our imaginations run riot and say to other believers, "The Lord told me this..... or that." It can make us sound very spiritual, but the evidence of the genuineness of such communication will eventually become apparent. In Paul's case, the genuineness is demonstrated in his further "adventures" in his witnessing, at a pace, with intermittent delays, which were clearly not of human choosing. What epistles might not have been written, what souls not won for Christ, had Paul pushed ahead blindly under this compulsion? I turn again to William Kelly: "Nevertheless God was in it all; for during these very bonds, Paul wrote the Epistles, which furnish, as we happily know, the fullest and brightest light of Christ on heavenly things that was ever vouchsafed for the permanent instruction and comfort of the saints of God."

11 April

"But the following night the Lord stood by him and said, 'Be of good cheer, Paul; for as you have testified for Me in Jerusalem, so you must also bear witness at Rome.'" (Acts 23:11)

Since Paul's declaration recorded in yesterday's reading, the Apostle had made a slow voyage with many stops to the final port of Caesarea. There he had fellowship with other believers, and there Agabus, the confirmed prophet whom we encountered two days ago, foretold Paul's imminent imprisonment should he proceed to Jerusalem (Acts 21:11). The others present reacted by trying to persuade Paul to change his mind. Would we not have done the same, conscious of all the wonderful things Paul might yet have done had he remained free? There was nothing insincere about their attempts to divert Paul; they were in tears. But Paul answered: "What do you mean by weeping and breaking my heart? For I am ready not only to be bound, but also to die at Jerusalem for the name of the Lord Jesus" (Acts 21:13). Who was right and who was wrong? In the Lord's work that is surely a naïve question. If hearts are right, the question is right, and the Lord will overrule to confirm His priority. Some of these local believers accompanied Paul on the two or three day journey to Jerusalem, where a number of dramatic events were to take place, including being taken into Roman protective custody from the intrigue of his own countrymen.

We cannot go into the details of Paul's time in Jerusalem. Secular commentators have criticised Paul's actions in Jerusalem, but the Lord Jesus did not do so. The Roman governor, aware of Paul's status – a providential status it proved to be – as a Roman citizen, was very shortly to send him under heavily armed escort back to Caesarea. But the Lord chose Jerusalem, to which Paul had been so determined to go, despite the advice of others, as the place where He would stand by His faithful bondservant in visionary form. Imagine Christ coming into our home, even if that should be a prison, and greeting us with, "Be of good cheer!" Here was glorious divine confirmation, that, whatever Roman governors and soldiers, Jewish religious leaders and shipwrecks might do, absolutely nothing could prevent his witnessing for Christ in Rome.

12 April

"'Most assuredly, I say to you, when you were younger, you girded yourself and walked where you wished; but when you are old, you will stretch out your hands, and another will gird you and carry you where you do not wish.' This He spoke, signifying by what death he would glorify God. And when He had spoken this, He said to him, 'Follow Me.'" (Jn 21:18-19)

Nobody was more conscious of his failure before Jesus' trial than Peter. How bitterly he had wept when the cock crowed three times. Jesus wanted him and John to be the most prominent leaders of His about-to-be-born Church, and so, before His departure, He ensured that old scores were settled and old wounds healed. No specific prophecy was made for John's future, although it was widely and correctly assumed that he would have a very long life, though emphatically *not* until the Lord's return! The time was soon to come when they would rejoice that they were counted worthy to suffer shame for His name (Acts 5:41). Have we ever rejoiced in such experiences, if in less dramatic ways? It can only bring blessing, because nobody is more aware of our stance than our Saviour.

Immediately before His departure Jesus was demonstrating in a more detailed way than in any prior prophecy what was to happen to individuals, as opposed to nations. Here was further confirmation of the fact that Peter's failings were forgiven and that he would actually follow his Lord in the manner of death; the description could only have implied crucifixion. Surely none of us would have contemplated disclosing such personal details, yet Jesus was actually confirming that Peter would glorify God in such a death. It was to happen when Peter was old, though clearly not as old as John would become. He had therefore much to achieve in the meantime, and would still have many successes and a few failures. But all the time he would have this unique confidence that he was in His Master's hands and plans.

Scoffers have sometimes quoted these words of Jesus as proof that we should not believe in a potentially ever-imminent Rapture. But if we read the Olivet Discourse, it should become obvious that the Rapture could not have taken place before the sack of Jerusalem and a long *diaspora* or exile. Of course, we must constantly be ready.

13 April

"For I know this, that after my departure savage wolves will come in among you, not sparing the flock." (Acts 20:29)

Should we call this a specific or a general prophecy? Both seem appropriate, because what Paul knew was going to happen in the church or assembly at Ephesus would happen regularly throughout the world wherever the Gospel was preached and believers would assemble themselves together. If we need confirmation, we should turn to Revelation (2:1-7) to see that later believers in Ephesus "left their first love" and were called upon to repent. We return to this.

Paul had just said: "Therefore take heed to yourselves and to all the flock, among which the Holy Spirit has made you overseers, to shepherd the church of God which He purchased with His own blood" (Acts 20:28). William MacDonald points out that this is the only place in the Bible where we read of God's blood being shed; God is a Spirit. The explanation is that "God was in Christ reconciling the world to Himself" (II Cor 5:19), and that the Son of God had to become Man to have blood to shed. Darby renders those last words: "which he has purchased with the blood of his own." Paul, Silas and some of the others had laboured long and hard in Ephesus; they had suffered persecution. Each local congregation or assembly is a flock. Paul makes no promises of Divine intervention and banishing of the "wolves"; it is a leadership responsibility to deal with these marauders who hang around every flock, and are increasingly active in the last days. Jesus, the Good Shepherd who gave His life for the sheep, said: "A hireling, he who is not the shepherd, one who does not own the sheep, sees the wolf coming and leaves the sheep and flees; and the wolf catches the sheep and scatters them" (Jn 10:12).

The history of foreign missions is full of stories of faithful under-shepherds who have suffered under the hand of pagan authorities, when the home congregations which sent them out were living in comparative safety. The day is fast approaching in our own lands when taking a stand on the Word of God is becoming dangerous, and where pulpits are increasingly being accessed by "hirelings" who fear more for their own skins than for the welfare of the flock.

14 April

"But when the Helper comes, whom I shall send to you from the Father, the Spirit of truth who proceeds from the Father, He will testify of Me." (Jn 15:26)

A week ago we looked at the promise of the coming of the Holy Spirit as a specific event on the Day of Pentecost. Now we consider the general application of the prophecy, valid throughout the Church Age. Jesus was speaking on the night of His betrayal; around six weeks later He was to be taken from them into Heaven. Judas had departed and He was left with the Eleven who were to be potentially bereaved and leaderless. They needed reassurance. Fifty days after His resurrection the Holy Spirit descended with great power and miraculous signs. But the Church was to last very much longer than even the oldest who were present and who were to be filled with the Spirit on that wonderful day. This ministry of the Holy Spirit is for the entire Church Age. What was true then is still true today. Jesus' prophecy had no "sell-by date".

When people questioned what was happening, Peter declared: "This is what was spoken by the prophet Joel". He did not say that the whole of Joel's prophecy was being fulfilled then and there; indeed, the entire Church Age lay between. He was saying that this wonderful awe-inspiring Holy Spirit who had just come in such power is the same Holy Spirit who will be so active "before the coming of the great and awesome day of the LORD" (Acts 2:20), which means the Great Tribulation. Peter was emphasising the authenticity and authority of the Holy Spirit to people who claimed to honour their (Old Testament) Scriptures.

All twenty-seven books of the New Testament had yet to be written, one of them said, "All Scripture is given by inspiration of God, and is profitable for doctrine, for reproof, for correction, for instruction in righteousness, that the man of God may be complete, thoroughly equipped for every good work" (II Tim 3:16-17). Peter (I Pet 1:11) tells us that the Old Testament prophets were inspired by the Spirit of Christ; and that can hardly change with New Testament prophecies. As the young Church grew and the apostles one by one died, so inspired or Spirit-breathed gospels and epistles would become available to guide, teach, discipline and encourage them.

15 April

"Remember the word that I said to you, 'A servant is not greater than his master.' If they persecuted Me, they will also persecute you. If they kept My word, they will keep yours also." (Jn 15:20)

Here is another important general prophecy valid throughout the Church Age; Christians in some Muslim lands can confirm that the persecution prophecy has rarely been more relevant. The 70 AD sack of Jerusalem by the Romans and consequent exile and dispersion was foretold in Luke chapter 21. At the time that was very important for those involved. But one might expect there to be many more prophecies of specific future events for the Church Age. However, once the Church was established by the end of Acts, such prophecies ceased. We are given other general prophecies for the Church, rather than for individuals, to remind and reassure us that God is still in control and that we are within His will. We must be content with that. As the Lord's return approaches, the signs of the times are coming ever more sharply into focus to warn us to be prepared.

The Apostles felt honoured to suffer for their Lord's sake: "So they departed from the presence of the council, rejoicing that they were counted worthy to suffer shame for His name" (Acts 5:41). Paul later encouraged the Thessalonians: "we ourselves boast of you among the churches of God for your patience and faith in all your persecutions and tribulations that you endure, which is manifest evidence of the righteous judgment of God, that you may be counted worthy of the kingdom of God, for which you also suffer" (II Thess 1:4-5).

Most of us have never undergone persecution on the scale described; but we are expected to be ready should it occur. Christian youngsters are liable to find themselves suffering from increasing internet abuse. Such trials should test us and leave us stronger, being "kept by the power of God through faith for salvation ready to be revealed in the last time. In this you greatly rejoice, though now for a little while, if need be, you have been grieved by various trials, that the genuineness of your faith, being much more precious than gold that perishes, though it is tested by fire, may be found to praise, honour, and glory at the revelation of Jesus Christ" (I Pet 1:5-7).

16 April

"For the hearts of this people have grown dull. Their ears are hard of hearing, and their eyes they have closed..... Therefore let it be known to you that the salvation of God has been sent to the Gentiles, and they will hear it!" (Acts 28:27-28)

We have already looked at the famous Isaiah chapter 6 declaration, which Jesus had earlier quoted. But what a desperately sad ending to the Acts for Israel, and what a joyful one for us Gentiles! Those of Israel who had been saved were now part of the Church, and indeed initially the backbone of that Church. God had been merciful and had given Jerusalem over three decades to repent. We read, for instance, "Then the word of God spread, and the number of the disciples multiplied greatly in Jerusalem, and a great many of the priests were obedient to the faith" (Acts 6:7). Soon the first Samaritan and then Gentile Christians were to be saved, and the Jewish believers became an increasingly tiny proportion of the Church. The Church was already moving forward from its first phase towards its Gentile led phase.

Sadly, a great folly still pervades much of what calls itself Christianity – the assumption that this Acts 28:28 declaration is permanent. It is a folly from the Gentile point of view, giving an utterly unscriptural false sense of security. Gentile believers are addressed in Romans 11:22: "Therefore consider the goodness and severity of God..... Otherwise you also will be cut off" (Rom 11:22) It is a folly from the Jewish point of view, because it effectively refuses to believe a host of unfulfilled prophecies regarding Israel's future in witnessing for Christ, their Messiah following the Church Age. The closing statement of today's reading applies only until the end of the Church Age, in other words, until the Rapture.

We might think of the Church Age as the filling in the "sandwich" of verses 4 and 5 of Hosea 3: "For the children of Israel shall abide many days without king or prince, without sacrifice or sacred pillar, without ephod or teraphim"..... (**here the Church Age fits in**)..... "Afterward the children of Israel shall return and seek the LORD their God and David their king. They shall fear the LORD and His goodness in the latter days." There are several similar Church Age "sandwiches fillings" in Old Testament prophecy.

Our Blessed Hope

17 April

"You turned to God from idols to serve the living and true God, and to wait for His Son from heaven, whom He raised from the dead, even Jesus who delivers us from the wrath to come." (I Thess 1:9-10)

We now devote a week to how the Church moves from the mortal to immortal state. This epistle was written about a decade before the Acts 28 quote which we looked at yesterday. There was a Jewish synagogue in Thessalonica, but here Paul is addressing the many Gentile converts. He referred to his initial ministry and teaching when he was with them. Evidently he had taught them something about the Rapture; would that more Christian teachers did so. But, as we will be reminded soon, some were concerned because members had died since Paul's time there, and they were worried lest they had missed out on the first resurrection. Irrespective of whether we are dead before or alive at the Rapture, waiting "for His Son from heaven" should be natural to every believer. When we consign a believing loved one to the grave, it is merely to "wait for His Son from Heaven". This is such a basic matter of faith.

But here we have a further reassurance; we are to be delivered from the "wrath to come". Both the dead and living at the Rapture are to see from a non-participating heavenly perspective the "wrath to come", the Tribulation Period which is to follow the Rapture. As we see elsewhere from Revelation 5 onward, we will witness the Lamb setting in motion the events of this coming wrath. Those who would accuse God of being unloving in His judgment should take note of what happens in any society in which crime and rebellion are not summarily dealt with.

I close with a quote from my *"Rapture – Sooner Not Later"*. "Post-Tribulationists believe that the Church will go through the entire Tribulation period, and some even regard Pre-Tribulationists as being afraid to undergo this 'time of testing'; some can be quite scathing, mistaking faith for cowardice. Applying the same faulty logic, one might equally well say that Noah was a coward for building the Ark to escape the Flood. Or, worse, one might argue that Jesus' warning of Matthew 24:16 to 'flee to the mountains' is pandering to cowardice by discouraging people from remaining 'on the firing line for God'"!

18 April

"But I do not want you to be ignorant, brethren, concerning those who have fallen asleep, lest you sorrow as others who have no hope." (I Thess 4:13)

Back in January we looked very briefly at two verses of this important passage, to which we now devote six days, interspersing these verses with further verses from 1st Corinthians 15. Even this will not be an in-depth study; this book is not intended to provide that. Not only were these words of assurance for those in the Thessalonian congregation who had recently lost loved ones, they are for all of us, for the entire Church Age, an expansion of Jesus' betrayal evening promise to come **for** us, as opposed to come **to** us. Sadly many in disbelief tend to ignore them because of their spectacular and miraculous elements.

We note that in these verses believers are spoken of three times as being asleep; when death is mentioned, it is the "dead in Christ" – a Church Age term. Unbelievers are never described as being asleep; they feel the sting of death which has been removed for us: "The sting of death is sin, and the strength of sin is the law. But thanks be to God, who gives us the victory through our Lord Jesus Christ" (I Cor 15:56-57). WE Vine writes: "All out of Christ are dead, all in Christ live, or have eternal life (John 6:47, Colossians 3:4). But all, whether living or dead, equally exist and are equally conscious of existence." Our Saviour is never said to have slept in death. He bore our sin, enduring the strength and penalty of the law, and suffered in our place the full horror of death.

Believers in this young church must have been saddened by the phrase "others who have no hope"; and so it is for us today. Grief for the loss of friends is common to all; even Jesus wept at a graveside. It should urge us all the more to preach Christ and Him crucified, that others might believe and have this glorious hope which is simply a justifiable confidence in the One who never lets down those who have placed their trust in Him. When we grieve over believers, it must be for loved ones left behind, not those who have "gone before". Paul described departing to be with Christ as "far better" (Philippians 1:23).

19 April

*"For **if** we believe that Jesus died and rose again, even so God will bring with Him those who sleep in Jesus".* (I Thess 4:14)

"If" introduces the conditions for being a partaker in these prophecies. They are only for believers in Christ's death and resurrection. This cannot reasonably be confused with Christ's Coming in Power, when He certainly is not going to bring with Him newly awoken "dead in Christ" who have never been evaluated and rewarded for their service and or been part of the Bride at the Marriage of the Lamb. This is about various parties converging at a wondrous meeting between Heaven and earth before moving to the "prepared place"; Jesus is to bring with Him those who currently sleep in Him. How they must be longing for that moment! This is the wonderful opening event of Christ's Second Coming.

We must remind ourselves where those who sleep in Christ are at present. In January we recalled Jesus' assurance, "In My Father's House are many mansions" (Jn 14:2). The NKJV did not change the AV/NKJV 'mansions'; but 'dwelling places' or something similar would have avoided this strange sense of splendid isolation. Presumably it was chosen to represent glory; but the real glory lies beyond the resurrection, not in the present temporary dwelling places within the Father's House. Then Jesus went on to promise: "I go to prepare a place for you." Let us be quite clear that that place, the Bridal Home, cannot be occupied this side of the Rapture, when the Church will at last be complete.

Those who sleep in Jesus are currently where Jesus' soul was in the very brief period between His death and resurrection. The penitent thief said to Jesus, "'Lord, remember me when You come into Your kingdom.' And Jesus said to him, 'Assuredly, I say to you, today you will be with Me in Paradise.'" (Lk 23:42-43). That was a promise; Jesus meant just that. The day ended at six o'clock and the thief's legs were broken and he died rather less than three hours after Jesus, but within the time frame Jesus had given. The Kingdom of which the thief had spoken still lies ahead, but Paradise was what had previously been the happier part of Sheol or Hades, and had now moved with the Old Testament saints from being "below" to being within the Father's House "above".

20 April

"For this we say to you by the word of the Lord, that we who are alive and remain until the coming of the Lord will by no means precede those who are asleep." (I Thess 4:15)

Paul has the divine authority for what he is writing to this congregation, and effectively to the whole Church. This is the first of Paul's recorded epistles; teaching about the Rapture was never given an afterthought status. "We who are alive and remain" applies ultimately to those who will survive until the Rapture without tasting death; it is legitimate for us to include ourselves in that number until we are called to be among "those who are asleep".

The Greek word here for 'coming' is *parousia*, which applies to the Rapture and perhaps to what follows immediately. So-called "Jehovah's Witnesses" have been taught half-truths about this word. I mention this in case we should encounter any of them; they need to be saved too. They can be caught totally off-guard if we speak about end-time prophecy. It is an excellent way to introduce Scriptural truths. *Parousia* is a **noun** implying 'a coming' or 'the coming', however it *can* also be translated as "presence", which JWs stick to rigidly to deny our Lord's Coming as described in this passage, ignoring the fact that more often "coming" fits the context much better. The most common Greek New Testament **verb** for going or coming (motion) is ***erchomai***, which cannot mean presence and is often used in conjunction with *Parousia.*

The word "precede" in the RV, NKJV etc is correct. The word "prevent" has changed its meaning since the AV/KJV was completed in 1611. Those who have fallen asleep before the Rapture are not to be at a disadvantage compared to those who will still be in their mortal bodies when they are snatched away or raptured. The Rapture is not to be thought of only for those who remain. The word 'resurrection' applies specifically to the deceased bodies and the moment that these are reunited with soul and spirit to restore the human trinity of which I Thessalonians 5:23 speaks: "Now may the God of peace Himself sanctify you completely; and may your whole spirit, soul, and body be preserved blameless at the coming of our Lord Jesus Christ." Should He come today, would that description fit us?

21 April

"For the Lord Himself will descend from heaven with a shout, with the voice of an archangel, and with the trumpet of God. And the dead in Christ will rise first." (I Thess 4:16)

We will see tomorrow where the meeting-point between Heaven and earth will be. It is stated clearly that Jesus will not return bodily to earth until the restoration of all things foretold by His prophets (Acts 3:21). There are numerous restoration prophecies as yet unfulfilled, but they do not in any way conform to the Rapture of the Church, which is, for very good reasons, not foretold in the Old Testament.

Writing to the Corinthians, Paul foretells elements of the Rapture which had hitherto been a mystery: "Behold, I tell you a mystery: We shall not all sleep, but we shall all be changed - in a moment, in the twinkling of an eye, at the last trumpet. For the trumpet will sound, and the dead will be raised incorruptible, and we shall be changed" (I Cor 15:51-52). He mentions the trumpet call and the voice *as of* an archangel (rather than simply 'of'). We are reminded of the authoritative voice which called Lazarus forth from his tomb (John 11:43). It is a summons which neither the sleeping nor the surviving can ignore. It is the voice of the One who created the worlds and for whom no amount of corruption or disintegration can resist. If the sea can give up the dead at the second resurrection of the unsaved (Rev 20:13), it can certainly do the same for the saved at the first resurrection. What is said to happen in a twinkling of an eye is not the Rapture itself, although that will probably also be true. It is the miraculous change from our past or present state to our new incorruptible state. The older or frailer we become, the greater the appeal. I know from personal experience!

Some have associated this trumpet blast with the last of the seven trumpets of Revelation 8:2 to 11:15, claiming that the Church will go through the Tribulation Period. But those are about future judgments on earth following the Rapture. They conform to the silver trumpets which sounded the advance in Numbers 10:1-8. In military circles the last trumpet, usually of three, was for many centuries a well-known signal to move off; the Thessalonians and Corinthians would have understood this.

22 April

"Then we who are alive and remain shall be caught up together with them in the clouds to meet the Lord in the air. And thus we shall always be with the Lord." (I Thess 4:17)

That initial "then", *epeita*, indicates the order of events and does not imply any interval. The newly resurrected saints will not have to wait in the clouds before returning heavenwards. What a reunion this is going to be, though our attention will surely be centred on the Lord Jesus Christ Himself, our heavenly Bridegroom, before we start looking for departed loved ones. It is He whom we are said to be going to meet. Paul said: "It is sown a natural body, it is raised a spiritual body. There is a natural body, and there is a spiritual body" (I Cor 15:44). Even if we are among those "who are alive and remain", we should not forget that those newly resurrected will also suddenly find themselves in an entirely novel state. We must not think of our loved ones as already being in their ultimate heavenly state, a common misconception.

We cannot be certain about the clouds. Probably they are natural atmospheric clouds divinely ordered to be present. It has been suggested that they represent the Shekinah glory as seen in the Old Testament from Exodus to Ezekiel, suggesting that the world below might be very briefly aware of the glory. Evidently it will be the same kind of vanishing from earthly view which Jesus experienced at His ascension. We are not in fact told whether the "left behind" will see anything at all, or whether people will simply disappear.

What is indisputable is the onward destination. We are not going to the newly vacated resting places within the Father's house. "If I go and prepare a place for you, I will come again and receive you to Myself; that where I am, there you may be also" (Jn 14:3). Those who sleep in Christ awaiting their resurrection are not going to have a preview of the Bridal Home, despite that also being in Heaven. We enter that together. Heaven is a big place. This is "for always" – for ever. When later He returns to earth in power and glory, we will "follow in His train", as says an old hymn, which conjured up strange images for children like me!

23 April

"Therefore comfort one another with these words." (1 Thess 4:18)

The 1st Thessalonians 4 passage both opens and closes with comfort, something which sadly cannot apply to unbelievers once this earthly life is over. Then in chapter 5:9-11 we are given a lovely complex reassurance, tying together several earlier promises in this epistle: (a) "For God did not appoint us to wrath"; the Church, will not have to go through the coming Tribulation Period, because it is to be a pre-tribulational Rapture. (b) "But to obtain salvation through our Lord Jesus Christ, who died for us"; through Christ's death our salvation will at last be complete in every respect, the salvation of the body, one of our three elements, occurring last at our resurrection or being changed. (c) "That whether we wake or sleep, we should live together with Him;" neither has any advantage over the other, all such distinctions cease when we meet our Saviour. (d) "Therefore comfort each other and edify one another, just as you also are doing." Based upon these assurances we should comfort one another, strengthening each other's faith by means of the eternal truths of Holy Scripture.

In the 1st Corinthians chapter to which we have referred, Paul wrote: "Therefore, my beloved brethren, be steadfast, immovable, always abounding in the work of the Lord, knowing that your labour is not in vain in the Lord" (15:58). It constantly comes over in the epistles that these matters are not to be detached from other Christian experiences. Peter writes: "Sanctify the Lord God in your hearts, and always be ready to give a defence to everyone who asks you a reason for the hope that is in you, with meekness and fear" (I Pet 3:15). The Gospel cannot be detached from the coming fullness of the everlasting life which we already possess in Christ. "As it is written: 'Eye has not seen, nor ear heard, nor have entered into the heart of man the things which God has prepared for those who love Him.' But God has revealed them to us through His Spirit. For the Spirit searches all things, yes, the deep things of God" (I Cor 2:9-10). It is common for verse 9 to be quoted without verse 10, but we dare not detach the work and witness of the Holy Spirit, or we miss out on the "deep things of God".

The Future of Seven Churches of Asia

24 April

"Remember therefore from where you have fallen; repent and do the first works, or else I will come to you quickly and remove your lampstand from its place - unless you repent." (Rev 2:5)

This was addressed to the church at Ephesus. The Lord said that that He was aware of their works, their labour, their patience and moral standards; many church leaders would be thrilled to be given such an assessment. But the Lord said that they had lost their first love, and that one negative point more than outweighed all the positives.

The personal epistles of the risen Christ to the seven churches in Ephesus and its hinterland in Revelation 2 and 3 have four purposes: (a) Each was addressed to the "angel" or current leaders or pastors of each church as they existed when John recorded his Revelation at the end of the First Century. (b) Each was to be communicated to the other six for their attention: "He who has an ear, let him hear what the Spirit says to the churches" (verse 7). (c) They were to be applied down through the centuries to other congregations with similar predominant characteristics. (d) The seven in turn were to present a picture of the progress of the Church for the entire Church Age, from the moment they were written until the Rapture. It really does seem to correspond to developing Church history. Each has its own introductory description of the Lord and a promise for the "overcomer". These we will return to in mid-December.

What the Lord said about the Ephesians with their lost first love was becoming common in the young churches, who, though still vigorous, were beginning to take their eyes off their Saviour. We in the countries which sent out so many missionaries, are sometimes put to shame by the spirituality of newly established congregations in previously unevangelised lands. But, like the Ephesian church, which would have been less than fifty years old, love can cool with maturity. The Lord did not recommend training conferences or courses; He demanded **repentance**. That has rarely been a popular word, because it demands a degree of humility and much prayer. Today's society hates that spiritual discipline which attacks or destroys self-image. When we put Him first, we are blessed with an entirely different kind of confidence.

25 April

"I know your works, tribulation, and poverty (but you are rich); and I know the blasphemy of those who say they are Jews and are not, but are a synagogue of Satan. Do not fear any of those things which you are about to suffer. Indeed, the devil is about to throw some of you into prison, that you may be tested, and you will have tribulation ten days." (Rev 2:9-10)

This was addressed to the church at Smyrna, Izmir in modern Turkey, then a very rich and prosperous city renowned for its idolatry and emperor worship. This was one of only two churches not faulted by our Lord. There is so much in these little epistles which invites our attention; we simply cannot do them justice, and our aim is to concentrate on prophetic aspects.

As with Ephesus, their characteristics are mentioned, but here the Divine assessment is that they are rich. Are we rich in this sense; is our congregation? They have been under severe attack, not from secular factions so much as religious parties, yet were proving to be undefiled. Judaism was a recognised and permitted religion within the Roman Empire, provided it kept itself to itself and did not take liberties. Initially Christianity was considered to be a branch of Judaism, but often Jews did everything possible to disassociate themselves and went out of their way to encourage oppression by the civil authorities. This had evidently happened in Smyrna and the Lord refused to recognise them as proper Jews. So Smyrna may be said to represent the persecuted Church before Constantine legitimised it in the 4th Century.

Who but Christ could have said: "Do not fear any of those things which you are about to suffer" and been trusted? Modern believers are given so many assurances, and yet, despite having only the fraction of the tribulation which the Smyrna believers were experiencing, we can appear as worried as our secular neighbours. They were confident that they were in the Lord's will, and that they were suffering for their Saviour's sake, rather than because of any failings. We cannot be sure about these "ten days". Walter Scott suggests: "There may be an allusion here to the 'ten persecutions', and also to the tenth under Diocletian, which lasted just ten years." It was at Smyrna that Polycarp was later martyred for refusing to worship the Emperor.

26 April

"I know your works, and where you dwell, where Satan's throne is. And you hold fast to My name, and did not deny My faith even in the days in which Antipas was My faithful martyr, who was killed among you, where Satan dwells..... Thus you also have those who hold the doctrine of the Nicolaitans, which thing I hate. Repent, or else I will come to you quickly and will fight against them with the sword of My mouth." (Rev 2:13, 15-16)

We now come to the third church, that of Pergamos or Pergamum, with its unenviable description. Many of the pagan teachings, mysteries and practices which were absorbed by Rome, both during its Imperial days and the later Catholic regime, arrived from Pergamum which had taken over as the satanic capital after ancient Babylon's demise. Pergamum had been the stopping point of the title Pontifex Maximus (Great Bridge Builder), whence the Babylonian priests, rejected by the Medo-Persians, had fled, only to be adopted by the Roman Emperors in 44 BC and by Constantine, when he assumed the leadership of the Church which he had newly espoused. It has remained a papal title since, and will meet its end at the Mystery Babylon of Revelation 17.

This is one of the four congregations where both failings and strengths are recognised. I have omitted from today's reading some of the failings, including absorption of Greek philosophy into the faith (v 14), but have included that of a particularly serious departure from the principles of assembly government. These are the type of problems which came to the fore after Constantine "adopted" Christianity. The famous supernatural sign of a cross in the sky was a later invention. Over the course of the 4th Century Christianity became recognised as the state religion. This resulted in numerous compromises in doctrine and practice; efforts were made at Nicea and Chalcedon to stop the rot and safeguard at least some fundamental doctrines. Commenting on verses 14 and 15, Jim Allen writes: "While the Balaamite teaching turned the spiritual liberty of believers into licence, the Nicolaitan teaching turned the scriptural leadership of believers into clericalism." Ecclesiastical hierarchies were beginning to develop, and pagan priesthoods were being adapted to Christianity. Aspiring to high office, pomp and paraphernalia has no place in our faith. The Lord demanded immediate repentance for the entire assembly.

27 April

"Nevertheless I have a few things against you, because you allow that woman Jezebel, who calls herself a prophetess, to teach and seduce My servants to commit sexual immorality and eat things sacrificed to idols..... Now to you I say, and to the rest in Thyatira, as many as do not have this doctrine, who have not known the depths of Satan, as they say, I will put on you no other burden. But hold fast what you have till I come." (Rev 2:20, 24-25)

We now come to the city of Thyatira, whose first convert may have been Lydia, on business in Philippi when Paul and Silas visited. In this epistle the church there is recognised by the Lord for its works, love, service, faith and patience – surely an impressive list indeed by human standards. And yet Christ identified things so serious that they demanded immediate action; they are elaborated in verses 21 to 23. Do we really take time to evaluate our fellowships by Christ's standards, as revealed here, or do we simply tick the boxes for works, love, service etc, and congratulate ourselves?

The downward trend noted at Pergamum, and typical of the 4th to 6th Century Church had continued with the growing dominance of the Papacy and a non-Biblical centralised hierarchical government. Pagan gods had been turned into saints, allowing the old deities to be honoured and worshipped in the pretence of being apostles and martyrs. Mary had suddenly become the 'Mother of God'.

Thyatira had already developed the characteristics of the later centralised church, which boasted that it was the true Church, just as once Jezebel had usurped the rulership of the Northern Kingdom of Israel in puppet King Ahab's day, and had appointed herself the nation's prophetess, controlling eight hundred and fifty prophets, in contrast to God's true prophet Elijah. Every kind of perversion was practised as part of the irreligious rituals. Enforced celibacy led to natural consequences, as it still does. Obviously such statistics did not apply to Thyatira when the epistle was written, but the trends were already there, despite all their other attributes. John de Silva's description of "tolerated apostasy" is apt. This was typical of the Dark Ages when there was so little left of Christianity that the Celtic Church had to send missionaries to convert central Europe. Only the approaching Reformation brought the Dark Ages to an end.

28 April

"I know your works, that you have a name that you are alive, but you are dead..... Remember therefore how you have received and heard; hold fast and repent. Therefore if you will not watch, I will come upon you as a thief, and you will not know what hour I will come upon you." (Rev 3:1, 3)

Here is an ancient congregation which resembles the Post-Reformation Church, something which many of its adherents still assume to be wonderful. Some people are upset if one dares to say a word against Luther, Calvin or Knox. They were great men, fearless men, who did a wonderful work in challenging the spiritual corruption of Rome and restoring belief in the Gospel of Grace, salvation through faith in Christ's finished work of redemption. But they had their faults, such as Luther's Anti-Semitism and Calvin's imbalanced representation of God's love and foreknowledge. The point is that Protestantism is no more a guarantee that an individual will go to Heaven than Catholicism is a guarantee that they will not! The very word "Protestant" tells us what people are not, rather than what they are. The Lord is deeply aware of the blood of His martyrs, but there were various motives for opposing Catholicism, and not all were worthy or spiritual. Sadly there remains a good deal that is sterile within what is left of Protestantism.

Joseph Seiss wrote: "We call the contents of these chapters *Epistles*; but they are not so much messages from an absent Lord as sentences of a present Judge, engaged in the solemn act of inspection and decision." What Thyatira had "received and heard" was indeed appropriate, but they had failed to hold fast, and repentance was absent. Four hundred years after the Reformation Protestantism is largely in disarray and there is still widespread disinterest in the Lord's coming. It is tragic that to so many He is going to come as an unexpected thief in the night, with the signs of the times ignored.

Archbishop Trench once remarked that if the established church calendar were to be rigidly observed, none of these little epistles would ever be read to congregations. Perhaps that is no longer quite so true, but there is still a desperate failure to take to heart what our risen Lord has to say to the churches.

29 April

"Because you have kept My command to persevere, I also will keep you from the hour of trial which shall come upon the whole world, to test those who dwell on the earth. Behold, I am coming quickly! Hold fast what you have, that no one may take your crown." (Rev 3:10-11)

How refreshing to come to a second church against which our Lord records no criticism! He does however include a word of warning, because being seen to be faultless today is no guarantee that one will be so in another fifteen or thirty years. I know this from personal observation, having in the Army been posted back to places where I had served many years before. One may encounter deeply wounded individuals who have "held fast". Many churches have lost any "crown" they once had. History, however, tells us that this church at Philadelphia held fast for many centuries.

There is general agreement among futurist commentators that Philadelphia is likened to the recent age of missionary endeavour, true revivals and widespread evangelism, plus the reawakening of a longing for the Lord's return. Earlier the Lord had commented on the fact that "You have not denied My name". Loyalty to the name of the Lord Jesus Christ in ancient Roman times could be dangerous, and in some British cities is currently becoming so. In Muslim lands it still is perilous, and it is not unreasonable to believe that the Lord views these Christian minorities as being much more Philadelphian than Laodicean. Would that that were true in Great Britain! John Walvoord remarks: "Also they are commended for having kept His Word; that is, that had guarded and kept the truth of God as it was committed to them and had not departed from the faith." The amount of revisionism and reinterpretation of Scripture in modern seminaries compared to a century ago is alarming. "The hour of trial which shall come upon the whole world" seems to indicate that, not only was the Philadelphian church not to go through the coming Great Tribulation, but neither will the faithful latter day Church which resembles it. While a few generations ago there was far more awareness of the signs of the times, it is we, the Post-Philadelphian believers, who have entered the build-up period to the Rapture, where moral conditions are increasingly like those which Noah experienced.

30 April

*"Because you say, 'I am rich, have become wealthy, and have
need of nothing' - and do not know that you are wretched,
miserable, poor, blind, and naked.....As many as I love, I rebuke
and chasten.*
*Therefore be zealous and repent. Behold, I stand at the door and
knock. If anyone hears My voice and opens the door, I will come in
to him and dine with him, and he with Me."* (Rev 3:17, 19-20)

Laodicea has become the most infamous of the early churches, and
is invariably associated with lukewarmness, that feature which leads
to apathy, lethargy and pride. At least those who are cold to the Gospel
may be more easily challenged and won for Christ, compared with
the half-hearted and otherwise preoccupied, features of this age of
affluence and sophistication. Humility is almost totally absent. At first
sight it may seem strange that our Lord did not include the failures of
previously addressed churches, but He did not have a single good
thing to say about this congregation as an entity. He Himself was
excluded and actually presented Himself as being outside the door
and knocking for admission. His appeal is to the individual, as it still
is in apostate churches.

This last epistle mirrors the general state of Christianity as the
Rapture approaches. The centrality of the Gospel of Grace, based
on Christ's vicarious death and resurrection, is variously replaced by
(a) a Kingdom Now Gospel, (b) a Signs and Wonders Gospel and
(c) a Prosperity Gospel - sometimes all three at once. Prominent
"Christian" leaders publicly defy God's command and support
multi-faith initiatives. Need we say more? No wonder we share the
same condemnation as the Laodiceans. A few decades ago false
prophecies were being loudly proclaimed about a glorious near future
of a triumphant church, apparently capable of bypassing the Great
Tribulation which Jesus Christ emphatically foretold. So few seemed
to be aware how contrary such schemes are to the Word of God.

When the Lord returns for the rebuked and chastened ones "whom
He loves", the remainder who are left behind within what is termed
Mystery Babylon who will dare to claim to be the true Church, He will
spew out of His mouth. As we leave Laodicea, Revelation takes us
from "the things which are", to "the things which will take place after
this" (1:19, 4:1).

Short term prophecies - long term consequences

1 May

"And God said to Noah, 'The end of all flesh has come before Me, for the earth is filled with violence through them; and behold, I will destroy them with the earth'" (Gen 6:13)

Before looking at the great prophecies of Daniel in which God has graciously outlined for us His plan of the ages, we pause to consider a few prophecies with short term consequences, whose serious long term consequences were not humanly anticipated. This is a most solemn Genesis verse, in which God communicates to one man His intentions. It is particularly relevant to us today, knowing that, although God will never so comprehensively destroy mankind the way He did in Noah's day, He has nevertheless promised to judge the world in righteousness. "By faith Noah, being divinely warned of things not yet seen, moved with godly fear, prepared an ark for the saving of his household, by which he condemned the world and became heir of the righteousness which is according to faith" (Heb 11:7). Like Noah, we have been divinely warned.

Every congregation or local assembly, every member, should be sharing Noah's commendation. Do we have similar faith in God's promises? Are we moved with godly fear regarding those who are unprepared? Have we shared God's warnings with members of our household? Our "ark" is the salvation which God in Christ has prepared for us, and of which we need only avail ourselves. Do our lives truly condemn the world without being patronising? Are we prepared to be scoffed at in warning society?

I have included this among short term prophecies, because Noah immediately went to work to construct the largest vessel ever built until the 19th Century. It took a hundred years and must have been the object of numerous jokes. Is it a fear of being ridiculed which compels many Christians to avoid the subject of Bible prophecy, the more so as the years pass by? My wife recalls how, around 1949, one of her workmates joked about her being "whisked away", a reference to the Rapture, which the little Baptist church where her family worshipped was known to preach. It was no secret. But times have changed. Are you and your place of worship known to preach the Rapture?

2 May

"And the Angel of the LORD said to her: 'Behold, you are with child, And you shall bear a son. You shall call his name Ishmael, because the LORD has heard your affliction. He shall be a wild man; His hand shall be against every man, and every man's hand against him. And he shall dwell in the presence (face) *of all his brethren.'"* (Gen 16:11-12)

The one who was addressed was Hagar (Hajaraha in the Koran), the servant of Abraham's wife. God had made promises regarding Abraham's descendants. Abraham and Sarah were now elderly and childless, so Sarah offered Hagar as a surrogate mother. Abraham should have continued to trust God, who had intended to stretch their faith to the point where the necessary offspring was to be a miraculous answer to prayer. It was almost as if Abraham and Sarah were offering God a solution to a perceived problem! Endless complications ensued, and Hagar came to despise Sarah. God instructed Abraham to send the pregnant Hagar away, although He took steps to protect her.

How very accurate and descriptive the above prophecy is of both the ancestors and members of Islam. The Quraish (or Quarysh) tribe of Muhammad claimed to be descended directly from Ishmael. It was after this that God enlarged His original covenant with Abraham: "Thou shalt be a father of many nations. And I will give unto thee, and to thy seed after thee, the land wherein thou art a stranger, all the land of Canaan, for an everlasting possession" (Gen 17:4). God added, "But my covenant will I establish with Isaac, which Sarah shall bear unto thee at this set time in the next year" (Gen 17:21). Note the potential for conflict between the Ishmaelite tribes or nations and the twelve tribes of the Children of Jacob or Israel, son of the promised Isaac. This title to the Land has never been revoked, but occupation has always been conditional. For much of human history the Land has been claimed by descendants of Ishmael and Esau.

The consequences of our impatience with or lack of faith in God can be immense. When we read or listen to the news, we are reminded of the consequences of one man's failure four thousand years ago. But unlike the world at large, we know that God has the matter in hand.

3 May

"Now within three days Pharaoh will lift up your head and restore you to your place, and you will put Pharaoh's cup in his hand according to the former manner, when you were his butler." (Gen 40:13)

At first sight this appears to be trivial compared with yesterday's prophecy. The interpreter of the imprisoned butler was his fellow prisoner, Joseph, who had been sold into slavery by his brothers, and was innocent of any crime. He is one of only three major Old Testament characters against whom no fault is recorded. But God had allowed him to be placed in prison for the long-term good of multitudes.

Pharaoh's butler and baker had been jailed for reasons not recorded. Both had dreams which Joseph, who was ever in close communion with God, was able to interpret. The baker's dream foretold his impending death, but the butler's dream was interpreted happily as above. Joseph did ask the butler to mention his predicament when released. But the butler forgot, until two years later when Pharaoh had two visionary dreams for which he was desperate to find an interpreter. Then the butler remembered Joseph, who was quickly sent for. Then Joseph said to Pharaoh, "The dreams of Pharaoh are one; God has shown Pharaoh what He is about to do" (Gen 41:25), going on to describe the coming seven years of plenty and seven of famine. Joseph was appointed as governor and administrator of the colossal administrative measures which had to be undertaken.

Eventually Joseph's father, Jacob, and his eleven brothers reluctantly came down to Egypt, where they were honoured and provided for. It was in Egypt that, over four centuries, the children of Israel grew from being a family of seventy to a nation of around two million. The butler's dream may have seemed trivial at the time; but look what came out of it! Christians use the term "providential" when things work out unexpectedly for the good. Joseph's imprisonment seemed so unfair, but God was in control throughout.

We should start blessing Him here and now, trusting Him, who like Joseph, was for us "separate from his brethren" (Gen 49:26). We need not wait until we are "throned where glory dwelleth" before blessing the hand that guides and the heart that plans.

4 May

"Then the LORD turned to him and said, 'Go in this might of yours, and you shall save Israel from the hand of the Midianites. Have I not sent you?'" (Judg 6:14)

Here is a prophecy addressed to a most unlikely person; that is how Gideon viewed himself. None of us knows what the Lord has in mind for us individually, but the closer we are to Him, the more receptive we are likely to be. Joshua and the following two generations were now long past. The period of the Judges was well under way; it was summarised by "everyone did what was right in his own eyes" (Judg 21:25). One of the penalties of apostasy had taken effect: "The LORD will cause you to be defeated before your enemies; you shall go out one way against them and flee seven ways before them" (Deut 28:25). In formerly Christian nations, people do what is right in their own eyes, ignoring the God of their fathers, and people wonder why we are in such a mess.

A variety of surrounding nations had invaded and plundered Israel. In Gideon's day it was the Midianites who had been beleaguering them for seven years, till eventually the people cried out to Jehovah. When we see "LORD" in capitals, it is Jehovah (as in the Darby and American Standard versions), God's name rather than His title. When we call Him "Lord", effectively we do the same.

It was the pre-incarnate Christ who found Gideon down in a winepress threshing wheat, out of sight of the marauding Midianites. The whole episode is an exciting narrative and should be read. Gideon's speedy victory was assured, but only after "Gideon built there an altar to Jehovah, and called it Jehovah-shalom" (Judg 6:24 DBY), signifying "the LORD is our peace". Then he was ready for God's commission. The nation rallied to Gideon's summons, a huge army mustered. However "the LORD said to Gideon, 'The people who are with you are too many for Me to give the Midianites into their hands, lest Israel claim glory for itself against Me, saying, "My own hand has saved me."'" (Judg 7:2). Eventually it was a miniscule three hundred who defeated Midian. Gideon judged and defended Israel for decades. God still does not require numbers, but He does require obedience, separation and dedication.

5 May

"Then Elijah said to Ahab, 'Go up, eat and drink; for there is the sound of abundance of rain.'" (I Kings 18:41)

Elijah was God's weather forecaster; a confident forecaster, having divine authority. Meteorological conditions did not appear to have changed; the first cloud, "the size of a man's hand", was yet to appear over the Mediterranean. There had been three years of drought, and consequently famine, imposed upon the Northern Kingdom of Israel under that most evil king, Ahab, and his even more evil wife, Jezebel. Both were dedicated Baal worshipers. And now Ahab was being warned to take precautions before the imminent deluge, by the very prophet whom God had authorised to call for the drought in the first place. Ahab was aware of this and hated Elijah.

Sometime before this forecast, when Ahab met Elijah, he said: "Is that you, O troubler of Israel?" (I Kings 18:17). Elijah's reply was: "I have not troubled Israel, but you and your father's house have, in that you have forsaken the commandments of the LORD and have followed the Baals" (18:18). Then followed the episode on Mount Carmel when Elijah exposed the falsity of Baal, and fire came down from Heaven to authenticate Elijah as a man of God, and four hundred and fifty priests were slain on Elijah's instructions.

Later still Elijah experienced a personal crisis of faith, complaining to God: "I have been very zealous for the LORD God of hosts; because the children of Israel have forsaken Your covenant, torn down Your altars, and killed Your prophets with the sword. I alone am left; and they seek to take my life" (I Kings 19:14). "Jealous" may be a better translation than "zealous". In this present age we too may be zealous or jealous for our God. We may even feel like James and John when they felt that Jesus had been offended by a Samaritan village, and asked: "Lord, do You want us to command fire to come down from heaven and consume them, just as Elijah did? But He turned and rebuked them" (Lk 9:54-55).

But a new age or dispensation was dawning. Whatever God permitted Elijah to do, our commission is to preach the Gospel to every creature, and we have been given prophecies which indicate that time is running out. Our loyalty and zeal should be directed to winning souls while yet there is time.

6 May

"For if you remain completely silent at this time, relief and deliverance will arise for the Jews from another place, but you and your father's house will perish. Yet who knows whether you have come to the kingdom for such a time as this?" (Esth 4:14).

This was one of the most potentially dangerous of Anti-Semitic episodes in history. The speaker was the godly Mordecai, uncle and guardian of Esther, who had become queen of the great Persian Empire. He was addressing his niece. A certain ambitious Haman was currying favour with the Emperor Ahasuerus, and had recently been promoted to the point where he expected all citizens to humble themselves and bow down before him. Mordecai considered this to be idolatry and steadfastly refused. Haman told the Emperor: "There is a certain people scattered and dispersed among the people in all the provinces of your kingdom; their laws are different from all other people's, and they do not keep the king's laws. Therefore it is not fitting for the king to let them remain" (Esth 3:8). Those words reflect many later pogroms and holocausts, some in so-called Christian lands. Haman persuaded Ahasuerus to allow him to send dispatches, sealed with the Emperor's signet, to the 127 provinces of the Empire, ordering that all Jews should be slaughtered on a certain day.

The obvious person to intercede was Queen Esther, though it meant taking her life in her hands. But note Mordecai's faith; many of the prophets had already foretold Israel's eventual God-decreed restoration. His personal prophecy recognised that God would provide *somebody* as a deliverer if Esther failed. But Mordecai also recognised that God was giving him and Esther a unique opportunity to be involved in His work. How many blessings are claimed by others, which could have been ours? Well, Esther did intercede successfully. Haman was duly hanged on the gallows he had prepared for Mordecai, and swift messengers were dispatched to revoke the orders.

Consider that question, "Who knows whether you have come to the kingdom for such a time as this?" We may be sure that God placed us where we are for good reasons.

7 May

"But He knows the way that I take; When He has tested me, I shall come forth as gold." (Job 23:10)

In probably the oldest book in the Bible God has allowed dialogues to be recorded for us regarding one of the great mysteries, that of suffering, especially when it affects the godly. The book opens with an insight into spiritual forces that are at work behind the scenes. This is no work of fiction to deal with a philosophical problem; Ezekiel (14:14) talks of Job as one of the three most righteous men who had lived, the others being Noah and Daniel. James writes: "You have heard of the perseverance of Job and seen the end intended by the Lord - that the Lord is very compassionate and merciful." (5:11). Job, at this point, about half-way through his ordeal, did not know this "end", but trusted. He appreciated that he was being tested, and used the illustration of gold which must be refined; though he was still deeply puzzled about why God was allowing this level of suffering, and did not appreciate the underlying compassion. He sought answers.

J Sidlow Baxter comments: "The fact is, Job was *not meant* to know the explanation of his trial; and on this simple fact everything hangs. If Job *had* known, there would have been no place for faith; and the man could never have come forth as gold purified in the fire." Job's three comforters were religious men and deep thinkers, but that was no guarantee of spirituality. They were of the school which assumes that, if one is suffering, it must be for specific sins, and that uprightness is a guarantee of prosperity. One finds this in Islam, and quite often in sterile Christianity. God dealt severely with them: "My wrath is aroused against you and your two friends, for you have not spoken of Me what is right, as My servant Job has" (42:7). Job confessed: "Therefore I have uttered what I did not understand, things too wonderful for me, which I did not know" (42:3). God allowed Job to intercede for them; blessing came to them through Job's travail.

"Now the LORD blessed the latter days of Job more than his beginning" (42:12). God had given Satan limited authority to torment Job (1:12 & 2:6); now He honours His afflicted servant, and Satan is confounded.

8 May

"'This is the interpretation of each word. MENE: God has numbered your kingdom, and finished it; TEKEL: You have been weighed in the balances, and found wanting; PERES: Your kingdom has been divided, and given to the Medes and Persians.' That very night Belshazzar, king of the Chaldeans, was slain". (Dan 5:26-28,30)

This was Daniel's interpretation of the writing on the wall which had appeared, written by a detached hand, during Belshazzar's blasphemous banquet using Temple vessels where their god, Bel, would have thus been honoured. Belshazzar's grandfather, Nebuchadnezzar, had sacked Jerusalem and brought vessels from the Temple. Nebuchadnezzar, having received some very hard lessons, had eventually come to acknowledge God's righteousness and informed his entire empire (Daniel 4). Daniel reminded the now petrified Belshazzar that he had been aware of all this, making him doubly guilty. Daniel quickly declined the honours which he was ready to bestow upon him. We must never compromise our stand with evil in the supposition that we may be an influence for good. That very night the Medo-Persian army entered Babylon and Belshazzar was slain. Babylon, with its massive walls, was considered to be impregnable, but the attackers opened newly-made sluice gates on the Euphrates, diverting its waters, and marched in on the river bed! Those in the world who defy God think of their souls as being impregnable. Jesus told of one such: "And I will say to my soul, 'Soul, you have many goods laid up for many years; take your ease; eat, drink, and be merry.' But God said to him, 'Fool! This night your soul will be required of you; then whose will those things be which you have provided?'" (Lk 12:19-20). Even believers may not be immune from such false confidence, which indicates a lack of spirituality and lingering attachment to this world.

Darius became the provincial king under the Persian Emperor, Cyrus. God had told Nebuchadnezzar (Daniel 2) that the Persians would succeed Babylonia in the succession of empires which would occupy the Holy Land. God still reserves the right to dispossess nations and give to others (Judges 11:23). How long will our land continue the recent policy of overturning God's righteous laws and flaunting such "liberty" which is really bondage?

9 May

"Go into the village opposite you, and immediately you will find a donkey tied, and a colt with her. Loose them and bring them to Me. And if anyone says anything to you, you shall say, 'The Lord has need of them,' and immediately he will send them." (Matt 21:2-3)

We may think of this as a very minor prophecy indeed, but we must never think of anything our Lord says or does as being trivial. We can always learn or benefit. They were on the Mount of Olives when Jesus spoke; we are not told the names of the two disciples tasked here.

Occasionally our work for the Lord may involve a little embarrassment. We are not told of any prior arrangement made by Jesus for this donkey and colt; possibly He had spoken to the owners out of earshot of the disciples; perhaps He just knew that they would be there. Certainly He knew that these would be the first ones they would encounter. Most people would have suggested that, were the owners in sight, the disciples should have explained their position and who it was who wanted them.

But, no, they were being asked to take a step in faith. People were there, and they did indeed question their motives when they loosed them and made to lead them away. The disciples, as instructed, used the standard word for "Lord", when they replied, and this was immediately accepted. Not everyone, even among believers, is so quick to respond positively when we learn that the Lord has need of them, their time, their talents or their possessions. But these people were evidently willing.

Surely neither the owners nor the disciples realised that they were to have a hand in that great prophecy which we looked at last month: "Rejoice greatly, O daughter of Zion! Shout, O daughter of Jerusalem! Behold, your King is coming to you; He is just and having salvation, Lowly and riding on a donkey, a colt, the foal of a donkey" (Zech 9:9). What a privilege to have even the humblest part in the preparations our Lord was making for His acclamation, His rejection and our salvation! If we are saved now, we will have the even greater privilege of being in the throng which will follow His descent, not **from** the Mount of Olives, but on a white horse from Heaven itself to the same Mount.

10 May

"And seeing from afar a fig tree having leaves, He went to see if perhaps He would find something on it. When He came to it, He found nothing but leaves, for it was not the season for figs. In response Jesus said to it, 'Let no one eat fruit from you ever again.' And His disciples heard it.'" (Mk 11:13-14)

Mark's account is more detailed than Matthew's particularly regarding timing. Critics, completely missing the significance of the fig tree, have suggested that our Lord was being unreasonable or even bad-tempered. In fact, before fig trees produce their annual crop of fruit, it is often possible to find a few small early figs, which are not noticeable until one peers among the leaves which precede the main crop, but are perfectly edible. As God the Son He was displaying His authority over all nature in this unusual miracle.

Mark goes on to tell how, when they returned to the city the following morning, Peter drew Jesus' attention to the tree, which had by now withered away completely. There are various lessons to learn here. Peter had evidently been surprised by the result of Jesus' curse, so He said: "Have faith in God. For assuredly, I say to you, whoever says to this mountain, 'Be removed and be cast into the sea,' and does not doubt in his heart, but believes that those things he says will be done, he will have whatever he says." (Mk 11:22-23). We do not currently display faith of this order with such dramatic results. However those to whom He spoke were apostles, who did have considerable miraculous powers during their later ministry, and in the Millennium they and perhaps others will have such authority during the restoration of the planet from the physical disasters of the Great Tribulation.

The cursing of the fig tree had taken place on what we call Palm Sunday – the day of acclamation. Jesus had been entitled to find "fruit" when He came to Jerusalem, but was to be disappointed. The fig tree, which like the vine and olive, was sometimes used to represent the nation; and that was spiritually dead and about to face many centuries of unproductiveness.

It is our privilege and responsibility to be fruitful: "By this My Father is glorified, that you bear much fruit; so you will be My disciples" (Jn 15:8).

11 May

"And he said, I tell thee, Peter, the cock shall not crow this day, before that thou shalt thrice deny that thou knowest me......And the Lord turned, and looked upon Peter. And Peter remembered the word of the Lord, how he had said unto him, 'Before the cock crow, thou shalt deny me thrice.' And Peter went out, and wept bitterly." (Lk 22:34,61-62)

I have reverted to the good old Authorised Version, with a cock rather than a Trans-Atlantic rooster! Why is this account of failure included in Scripture? One can think of several possible reasons and it is not for us to prioritise them. Had Peter been boasting or actually offering Jesus what he thought was his unfailing support? Was it because, as Church history progressed and error after error crept in, Peter should be demonstrated to be fallible, just as earlier it was recorded that he had a mother-in-law; the man claimed to be the first Pope was a married man, and Paul records that Peter took his wife around with him (I Cor 9:5)! Was it because at Pentecost Peter turned out to be the most fearless champion of the new faith?

It is highly probable that in any physical battle Peter would have been to the fore. What Peter could not cope with was that Jesus, the powerful miracle worker, whom he had publicly confessed to be the Christ, was, at the time of denial, being submissive, passive, apparently a lost cause, despite Jesus' earlier prophecy of crucifixion followed by resurrection. Peter had forgotten Isaiah 53.

After the cock crowed, when Jesus turned to look at Peter, Peter recalled the prophecy. He knew that Jesus had known his inner heart. It was a matter of grief to Peter, perhaps to his dying day, despite the words of comfort and personal commission recorded in John 21. His pastoral care was all the better as a result.

When we fail our Lord, do we ever stop to wonder whether our Lord is looking? Do we ever go out and weep bitterly. If we do, we are likely not only to be forgiven, but to be used again in our Master's service.

12 May

"Jesus said to her, 'Your brother will rise again.'" (Jn 11:23)

Jesus was addressing the reproachful grieving sister, Martha. Jesus had deliberately delayed His return to Bethany, and Martha pointed out to Him that Lazarus would not have died had He been present. Most of us have, at one time or other, criticised our Lord for not conforming to our arrangements and time-scales. At least she did it face to face and not behind His back. FB Meyer points out that love permits pain, and that He abstained from hastening, not because He did not love Lazarus's family, but because He did. He writes: "Anything less than an infinite love must have rushed instantly to the relief of those loved and troubled hearts, to stay their grief and have the luxury of wiping their tears. Divine love alone could hold back the impetuosity of the Saviour's tender-heartedness until pain had done her work."

Of course Lazarus would rise again. But surely an immediate resurrection was beyond Martha's wildest dreams. She had sufficient faith, based upon her knowledge of the Old Testament and Jesus' own teaching, to believe in the last day resurrections. He did not immediately reassure her, rather He affirmed His own authority over death in words which have been quoted at many thousands of funerals down through the centuries. Jesus said to her, "I am the resurrection and the life. He who believes in Me, though he may die, he shall live" (Jn 11:25). Jesus Christ, as the Firstborn from the dead, is not restricted by time.

Now Jesus, grieving Himself, had gently to reprimand Martha, who was now perceiving problems like decomposition, which seemed to her to be beyond her Lord's ability to overcome: "Did I not say to you that if you would believe you would see the glory of God?" (11:40). So often we believe; but do we believe *enough*? At this juncture quite a crowd had assembled. "Now when He had said these things, He cried with a loud voice, 'Lazarus, come forth!'" (11:43). This is the voice which will call forth the dead at both the First and Second Resurrections. The very manner of Lazarus' resurrection was a miracle; he came forth bound hand and foot. Later we will see something of the profound and significant effect of this unique miracle on the High Priest and Sanhedrin.

13 May

"And he said, 'Who are You, Lord?' Then the Lord said, 'I am Jesus, whom you are persecuting. It is hard for you to kick against the goads.' So he, trembling and astonished, said, 'Lord, what do You want me to do?' Then the Lord said to him, 'Arise and go into the city, and you will be told what you must do.'" (Acts 9:5-6)

Was there ever a more instant and dramatic conversion? Saul of Tarsus, consumed by hatred of the recently saved followers of the Way, and armed with the written authority of the High Priest to arrest them, was suddenly confronted by the risen and glorified Christ. He who had refused to acknowledge the Lordship of Jesus Christ immediately addressed Him thus. Obedience is one of the first signs of true repentance and conversion; and Saul wanted to obey before even knowing what would be asked of him.

The way our Lord identified Himself is of the greatest significance and solace to suffering and persecuted believers. Although utterly beyond the reach of physical attack, the Lord feels our suffering when it results from our faithful service; the costlier that service, one dares to suggest, the more He feels it. What were Paul's feelings when he was told to go into the city of Damascus? Human nature might have suggested that he was to face some dreadful form of punishment for his activities, for his part, for instance, in Stephen's death. He knew nothing of what the astonished Ananias was about to be told: "Go, for he is a chosen vessel of Mine to bear My name before Gentiles, kings, and the children of Israel. For I will show him how many things he must suffer for My name's sake" (Acts 9:15-16).

Saul little realised that his past deeds, performed in a mistaken zeal for the God of his fathers, would turn out to be one of his prime qualifications for the tremendous task that lay ahead. A good evangelist will be aware of how God can work, and will not show greater respect for the upright citizen in his audience than for the one who looks weighed down by the burden of sin, or indeed considers him- or herself beyond redemption. The prophecy contained in today's text was fulfilled within hours; but the results have benefitted the Church down through the centuries.

God's Plan of the ages in Daniel

14 May

*"There is a God in heaven who reveals secrets, and He has made known to King Nebuchadnezzar what will be in the latter days......
You, O king, are a king of kings. For the God of heaven has given you a kingdom, power, strength, and glory."* (Dan 2:28, 37)

Daniel is classed as a Major Prophet; his book was written during the seventy year Babylonian captivity of Judah and after the last ruling king of David's dynasty until the future Millennium.

Malcolm Davis writes: "God revealed to Daniel probably more concerning the future of both Gentile and Jewish history than to any other Old Testament prophet. The prophecies in his book span the entire period of Gentile rule in the world during the so-called 'Times of the Gentiles', from 605 BC until the Second Coming of Christ." The nations involved in these prophecies all at one time occupied, or will occupy, the Holy Land. The Church Age is not covered in these prophecies, but in each one it is clearly indicated where the present age fits in, before the prophecy switches from the past to the future, that future beginning with the Tribulation Period.

The Babylonian Emperor, Nebuchadnezzar, had been given a dream which only Daniel was able to interpret. Nebuchadnezzar had seen an image with a head of gold, arms and chest of silver, loins and thighs of brass and legs of iron. The feet and toes are described as iron mingled with incompatible potter's clay. The interpretation was that Nebuchadnezzar, the conqueror of Judah, depicted as the head of gold, ruled the first listed empire only by God's authority. It was to be replaced by the silver Medo-Persian Empire, which was in turn to fall to the bronze Greek Empire of Alexander the Great. In chapter 8 these latter are identified by name. Nebuchadnezzar was told: "And the fourth kingdom shall be as strong as iron, inasmuch as iron breaks in pieces and shatters everything; and like iron that crushes, that kingdom will break in pieces and crush all the others" (2:40). This was Rome, still unheard of in Babylon, which was to conquer Greece and be in occupation when Christ was born. We know from other visions that the Church Age was to fit in between that (the legs) and the latter Antichrist's 'feet kingdom' of iron mingled with clay, which will briefly triumph between the Rapture and Christ's Coming in Power.

15 May

"And in the days of these kings the God of heaven will set up a kingdom which shall never be destroyed; and the kingdom shall not be left to other people; it shall break in pieces and consume all these kingdoms, and it shall stand forever." (Dan 2:44)

We continue in the same vision. Godless empires have dominated the Middle East and have defied God within the Promised Land. Other nations have been doing this throughout the Church Age, but are not touched on here. We will see in Daniel 9:26 that a latter day prince of the Romans, the nation which in 70 AD destroyed Jerusalem, will appear with what is sometimes called his Revived Roman Empire, and will desecrate the rebuilt Jerusalem temple and blaspheme God. This is one of the two wild Beasts of Revelation chapters 13 to 19, who are to lead the final disastrous revolt of unredeemed mankind against Christ at Armageddon. We will see more of these matters in visions given by God through angels to Daniel himself, rather than to others who required an interpreter. But this earthly monarch had first here, and later in chapter 4, to be reminded that "The Most High rules in the kingdom of men, gives it to whomever He will, and sets over it the lowest of men" (4:17).

Many, including the Church of Rome, have, with fertile imaginations, concluded that this Kingdom which shall never be destroyed is the Christian Church. But the Great Commission of the Church never included such campaign directives. Imagine missionaries arriving in unevangelised lands and proclaiming such an agenda – "breaking in pieces and consuming all these kingdoms"! The Church will be in Heaven during the short rule of the 'feet and toes kingdom', although those alive till the Rapture will perhaps have witnessed the re- emergence of that empire, whether they recognise it or not. In his dream which Daniel interpreted, Nebuchadnezzar saw a stone "cut out without hands" strike the image and the iron, the clay, the bronze, the silver, and the gold being crushed and blown away as chaff. "And the stone that struck the image became a great mountain and filled the whole earth" (2:35). That Stone is the returning Lord Jesus Christ, whose kingdom will be established for a thousand years on earth, before being handed over to His Father.

16 May

"After this I saw in the night visions, and behold, a fourth beast, dreadful and terrible, exceedingly strong..... It was different from   all the beasts that were before it, and it had ten horns. I was considering the horns, and there was another horn, a little one, coming up among them, before whom three of the first horns were plucked out by the roots. And there, in this horn, were eyes like the eyes of a man, and a mouth speaking pompous words." (Dan 7:7-8)

This is the first of four visions given directly to Daniel by God. It concerns four latter day empires striving for dominance in the area of the Great (Mediterranean) Sea. The four beasts should not be confused with those seen by Nebuchadnezzar, except inasmuch as the fourth beast of chapter 7 is the reappearance after many centuries of the fourth beast (the Roman Empire) of the earlier vision. Daniel sees this fourth beast as having ten horns, which parallel the ten toes of the chapter 2 image.

Again the Church Age is passed over, and we pass from ancient history to what is to happen speedily on earth following the Rapture. We will see more of this latter day form of the Roman Empire when we look at Revelation 17. It seems unlikely that these four latter-day empires will be fully in place when the Rapture occurs. If not, they will very rapidly materialise, and a "Little Horn" or aspiring world leader will suddenly appear and take control, overthrowing three of the existing nations or kings. In the meantime we may consider the build-up of international tensions in the Mediterranean as a sign of the times. We may speculate intelligently but cautiously, having been given this privileged preview.

In verses 21 and 25 we see how this Little Horn will be permitted for three and a half years to persecute the Tribulation saints, the multitude saved after the Rapture, before he meets his fiery fate as the first occupant of Hell. These visions are given chiefly for the benefit of those sufficiently interested in God's revelation of the end of the age to repent and be saved and called Heavenwards before these things happen, and also for those who repent later and will have to undergo this persecution. Tomorrow we see in this vision the victory of Christ and His saints.

17 May

"I was watching in the night visions, and behold, One like the Son of Man, coming with the clouds of heaven! He came to the Ancient of Days, and they brought Him near before Him. Then to Him was given dominion and glory and a kingdom, that all peoples, nations, and languages should serve Him. His dominion is an everlasting dominion, which shall not pass away, and His kingdom the one which shall not be destroyed." (Dan 7:13-14)

We continue with the same vision and what we might call "Meantime in Heaven". When things look bad on earth, particularly when believers are involved, we need to be reminded that God is fully aware and totally in control. This is about the Great Tribulation, the three and a half years of the temporary triumph of the "Little Horn", Satan's Man of Sin's brief reign. Satan will no longer have access to Heaven, and in any case, the Judge's decision will allow no appeal. Daniel in vision has seen a heavenly court convened, thrones set up (not set down as in the AV/KJV) and the Ancient of Days, God the Father, take His place in judgment. The Lord Jesus Christ as the Son of Man, the title He used of Himself particularly in prophetic contexts, is formally brought before Him.

Two thousand years ago He was despised and rejected of men. His own nation, to whom He came, had cried: "We will not have this Man to reign over us". The Church, those who *would* have Him reign over them, was born, witnessed on earth for around twenty centuries, and is to be taken to Heaven. Thereafter, through the preaching of the Kingdom, "A great multitude which no one could number, of all nations, tribes, peoples, and tongues," will have endured the Great Tribulation (Revelation 7:9,14), will have been saved and will have felt the wrath of the Little Horn. At the court's decision the Blasphemer will be slain, the Kingdom to which his master, Satan, has long aspired, will be given in perpetuity to the Son of Man and His victory will be shared by His saints on earth who have endured so much. Israel, which will have suffered most, will be "the head and not the tail". It is easy to be a half-hearted believer now; but not then.

18 May

*"And you will be hated by all for My name's sake. But he who
endures to the end shall be saved. So when you see the
'abomination of desolation,' spoken of by Daniel the prophet,
standing where it ought not" (let the reader understand), "then let
those who are in Judea flee to the mountains."* (Mk 13:13-14).

Lest any should object to so much of Daniel's prophecies, let us
note that, two days before His betrayal, Jesus took time to give
the above warning; it is also recorded in Matthew 24. Moreover,
it is the only occurrence of either Matthew's or Mark's Gospels
commanding the reader to understand. And that applies to Gentile
as well as Jewish readers, although it is the latter who chiefly will
have to heed the warning immediately before the start of the Great
Tribulation, as the ensuing verses indicate. Enduring to the end is
not about our soul's salvation, but about physical survival in that
future time of unsurpassed tribulation. It serves as another reminder
that prophecies concerning the time of the Lord's Second Coming
are as relevant to us today as were those about His First Coming;
let us not come under the same accusation: "Then He said to them,
'O foolish ones, and slow of heart to believe in all that the prophets
have spoken!'" (Lk 24:25). And that was said to disciples!

The original Abomination was erected by 2nd Century BC Antiochus
Epiphanes. The final one is to be erected by the "Little Horn" of
Daniel 8, but the prophecy referred to is in Daniel 9. Jesus spoke
of it as being yet future, demonstrating that prophecies may
intentionally have secondary or even tertiary relevance, with the
earlier fulfilment being less important than the final one. A further
secondary fulfilment was when the Emperor Caligula, against the
advice of Herod Agrippa I, tried to set up an image of himself in the
temple a few years into the Church Age; he died in 41 AD before his
orders could be carried out. That was not God's sanctioned timing.
According to the church historian Eusebius, Christians in Judea in
70 and 135 AD saw their situation foreshadowed here. They were
certainly not wrong in taking heed and fleeing to the desert in 135
AD during the further rebellion against Rome. Tomorrow we look at
Gabriel's message to Daniel.

19 May

"Seventy weeks are determined for your people and for your holy city, to finish the transgression, to make an end of sins, to make reconciliation for iniquity, to bring in everlasting righteousness, to seal up vision and prophecy, and to anoint the Most Holy."
(Dan 9:24)

This is a most remarkable and significant chapter. It is all about Daniel's people, the Jews, though ultimately the timing impinges upon the entire Millennial world. Daniel had been reading Jeremiah's scroll, prophesying the seventy year exile, and realised that it would soon be over. He immediately prayed passionately in intercession for his nation. Gabriel told Daniel that, as soon he had started praying, he was instructed to fly quickly and tell Daniel the following. The word 'week' here means any group of seven or heptad, and, when it is applied to years, a septennium. The breakdown of the seventy septennia is given in verse 25, and calculations were to start "from the going forth of the command to restore and build Jerusalem". This was 445 BC (Nehemiah 2:1-8).

Thus 490 years were determined or allocated to Israel and Jerusalem, in three groups, consisting of 7 (49 years), 62 (434 years) and 1 (7 years). The first division was fulfilled long ago, leaving us with 434 years and 7 years. So at the end of the 490 years, all the above must be completed. That takes us just beyond Christ's Coming in Power to the very start of the Millennium. Some have maintained that this puts the entire Church Age into the Millennium, but that in no way conforms to the above description.

Verse 26 starts: "And after the sixty-two weeks Messiah shall be cut off, but not for Himself"; thus, after the second of the periods, Christ, the Messiah, was to die His vicarious death. Sir Robert Anderson calculated that from the command to rebuild Jerusalem was precisely 483 years! As in the other prophecies, the entire Church Age is passed over, apart from the mention (with no date attached, but which we now know to be 70 AD) that "the people of the prince who is to come shall destroy the city and the sanctuary". The detached seven years are held over until after the Rapture, because, as we have seen, the whole seventy years, allowing for the interval, was to be allocated to Daniel's people, not to the Church.

20 May

"Then he shall confirm a covenant with many for one week; but in the middle of the week He shall bring an end to sacrifice and offering. And on the wing of abominations shall be one who makes desolate, even until the consummation, which is determined, is poured out on the desolate (or desolator)." (Dan 9:27)

Yesterday we read of "the people of the prince who is to come", the people being the Romans in 70 AD. Now we read of that future prince of Roman extraction. He is the First Beast of Revelation 13, who, shortly after the Rapture, is to impose a seven year covenant with the many of Israel, as opposed to the faithful remnant who will reject his claim to be the Messiah. Like his master, Satan, he will hate Israel, but will nevertheless wish to be acclaimed Messiah. In order to achieve this, he will have to sanction the rebuilding of the Jerusalem Temple and its sacrifices and ceremonies. The subtlety is frightening.

But after three and a half years he is to break the covenant, discard the sacrifices and offerings, which have been vainly offered to God, and turn on his supporters, as he, "the man of sin is revealed, the son of perdition, who opposes and exalts himself above all that is called God or that is worshipped, so that he sits as God in the temple of God, showing himself that he is God" (II Thess 2:3-4). We will see more of this Abomination elsewhere.

I quote from my *"Christ's Second Coming – Seven Crucial Questions"*: "Lest any should doubt the "statistics" involved, the two 3½ year periods are also found in Daniel 7:25; 12:7, Revelation 11:2, 3; 12:6; 12:14 and 13:5, with their duration described in various ways, namely *"three and a half years"*, *"time and times and half a time"*, *"42 months"* and *"1,260 days"*. For instance, the two witnesses of Revelation 11 are to testify for 1,260 days (v 3), and the woman in Revelation 12 is to be given a wilderness refuge for 1,260 days (v 14)." It was at the beginning of this vision that Gabriel said to Daniel: "I have come to tell you, for you are greatly beloved; therefore consider the matter, and understand the vision" (Dan 9:23). How privileged we are through God's Holy Spirit to share that understanding!

21 May

"Then the king shall do according to his own will: he shall exalt and magnify himself above every god, shall speak blasphemies against the God of gods, and shall prosper till the wrath has been accomplished; for what has been determined shall be done."
(Dan 11:36)

Chapters 10 and 11 of Daniel are divided into three parts. In chapter 10 an angel confides in the aged prophet, who has for three weeks been in mourning because of the future of his own people, a unique insight into his personal battles against what Paul calls "the rulers of the darkness of this age….. spiritual hosts of wickedness in the heavenly places" (Eph 6:12). Then chapter 11 gives a most remarkable, and of course accurate, preview of the warfare in the 4th to 2nd Centuries BC between the Seleucid and Ptolemaic Kings of the North and South. Unbelieving historians assumed Daniel to have been written after the events, but have been confounded. God retains the right to disclose the future even to unbelievers, who naturally tend not to believe, to their cost! Then from 11:36 to the end of that chapter the prophecy leaps forward to the Tribulation Period.

Within the second part we are told more about the Little Horn, of chapter 7, Antiochus Epiphanes and his original Abomination of Desolation (9:27), and see how he foreshadowed the future First Beast: "And forces shall be mustered by him, and they shall defile the sanctuary fortress; then they shall take away the daily sacrifices, and place there the abomination of desolation. Those who do wickedly against the covenant he shall corrupt with flattery; but the people who know their God shall be strong, and carry out great exploits" (Daniel 11:31-32). Again we see the "many", in contrast with the "few" of 9:27, foreshadowed by the heroic Maccabees of the 2nd Century BC.

Then we come to today's text and to the future Beast. Just as Antiochus came to power through flattery and intrigue, so the Beast, symbolised in Revelation 6:2 as the rider of the white horse with a bow and no arrow, will initially deceive the many in Israel and the Gentile nations as, for three and a half years, he increasingly blasphemes God. Much of this is fascinating and revealing history, but some is future and to be witnessed by us from our Heavenly home and sanctuary.

22 May

*"At that time Michael shall stand up, the great prince who stands
watch over the sons of your people; and there shall be a time of
trouble, such as never was since there was a nation, even to that
time. And at that time your people shall be delivered, every one
who is found written in the book."* (Dan 12:1)

Now here is an awesome statement. This is the Great Tribulation.
Various aspects are foretold in other Old Testament prophetical
books, it is described here in Daniel, and is confirmed by the Lord
Jesus Christ Himself in very much the same terms as in Daniel,
though with the added statement that all flesh would be destroyed,
but for Divine intervention on behalf of the elect. It is simply not
negotiable and it is emphatically stated here to be unprecedented.
And yet in recent years many churches were ignoring these
graciously revealed truths and warnings, and loudly telling the world
at large that the Church was triumphantly leading the planet to a
golden age fit for Christ's eventual Return. Any one of us may have
to turn the attention of fellow believers to what the Bible actually
foretells. I was once one of a minority resisting this prophecy-
ignoring movement. We were classed as negative resisters of the
Holy Spirit. Even God's holy prophets were classed as wet blankets
in their day! But it was the Holy Spirit who inspired Daniel to record
what we now read in his book. We have been vindicated by ensuing
events. We dare not reinvent the Word of God.

The Great Tribulation will be catastrophic throughout the world.
The wrath of God will be poured out on the fallen angelic host and
its leaders, as well as upon unbelieving mankind. But Daniel was
assured by God, that his people, Israel, who would, as ever, be a
focal point of Satan's wrath, would have a champion appointed by
God. This is Michael, the only one specifically called an archangel in
the Bible (Jude 1:9), but also seen as a mighty being in Daniel 10,
whilst, in Revelation 12, we read of his victory and final supremacy
over the Devil. Daniel is assured that his people will be delivered,
but only those whose names are "written in the book". This principle
applies of course to all classes of all ages, and Zechariah describes
how it will yet apply to Israel.

23 May

"Then I heard the man clothed in linen, who was above the waters of the river, when he held up his right hand and his left hand to heaven, and swore by Him who lives forever, that it shall be for a time, times, and half a time; and when the power of the holy people has been completely shattered, all these things shall be finished."
(Dan 12:7)

Now this "man greatly beloved", prophet and statesman, Daniel, around ninety years of age, a true patriot, despite recognising his people's massive shortcomings, has been through many traumatic experiences, and probably had more divinely revealed to him than anyone since Moses. Now he has to have a glimpse of the pre-incarnate Christ, and be given a little more chronological data. As ever we must remember that the prophetic 'clock' stopped ticking about the time of Jesus' rejection and is not due to start again until following the Rapture, with the seven year remainder of the 490 years assigned to Israel. Verses 2 and 3 concern the resurrection and are very important; we will return to them in another section.

Then Daniel sees two figures, one on either side of the banks of what appears to be the Tigris. Evidently neither is human, and one is described as being above the river. Most commentators agree that this is one of a number of theophanies in the Old Testament from Genesis on, a pre-incarnate appearance of Christ. The other figure asks Him how long it will be before these things come to an end. Then the Lord, assuming it is He, "held up his right hand and his left hand to heaven, and swore by Him who lives forever, that it shall be for a time, times, and half a time; and when the power of the holy people has been completely shattered, all these things shall be finished" (Dan12:7). We read in Hebrews 6:13 that, "When God made a promise to Abraham, because He could swear by no one greater, He swore by Himself;" there is nothing incongruous here.

Now, as we saw a few days ago, this "time, times and half a time" is one way of expressing the three and a half years, in this case the latter half of the seven, or the Great Tribulation. This is final confirmation that these shattering experiences for Israel will end at Christ's Return in Power.

24 May

"And he said, 'Go your way, Daniel, for the words are closed up and sealed till the time of the end. Many shall be purified, made white, and refined, but the wicked shall do wickedly; and none of the wicked shall understand, but the wise shall understand.'" (Dan 12:9-10)

Daniel has been told much, but not everything. We, even with our many New Testament prophetic passages, are in the same position, and must make use of all that we have. Those righteous of Israel who survive the Great Tribulation will be purified, having all eternity to reap the benefits. The remainder will resist God and become even more wicked. There will be no middle ground in those grim days. The wise will understand what has hitherto been partly or totally incomprehensible.

The One speaking gives two further time periods, starting with the mid-tribulation breaking of the Beast's covenant, 1,290 and 1,335 days respectively, thus adding 30 and a further 45 days to the 1,260 days of the Great Tribulation; those who attain the 1,335 are said to be blessed. These are exactly what they claim to be, days, not years as cults have claimed and been proved to be wrong.

We can only conclude that the added periods follow Christ's Coming in Power and relate to the miraculously swift restoration of earth and conditions of entry - "Whom heaven must receive until the times of restoration of all things, which God has spoken by the mouth of all His holy prophets since the world began" (Acts 3:21). Daniel is thus identified as one of these prophets. Indeed, Jesus spoke of "Daniel the prophet". The "Blessed" would appear to be those of Israel described in Ezekiel 20:35: "And I will bring you into the wilderness of the peoples, and there I will plead My case with you face to face". The Gentile blessed are those likened to sheep at the Judgment of the Nations (Matthew 25:31-46). Thereafter this hero of prophetic students is allowed to go into retirement: "But you, go your way till the end; for you shall rest, and will arise to your inheritance at the end of the days." (12:13). What a lovely commendation!

Reluctant Prophets and Prophecies

25 May

"I see Him, but not now; I behold Him, but not near; a Star shall come out of Jacob; a Sceptre shall rise out of Israel, and batter the brow of Moab, and destroy all the sons of tumult." (Numb 24:17)

The prophet here is the Babylonian magician, Balaam, hired at great expense by the king of Moab to curse the Children of Israel, who, towards the end of their exodus from Egypt, had sought permission to pass through Moabite territory *en route* to their crossing of Jordan. Moab, being descended from Isaac via Esau, was regarded as a relation and potential friend, compared with the peoples whom they were shortly to dispossess. But their king was afraid of Israel and did not trust their credibility, despite the evidence of God's miraculous preservation. Such power as Balaam could employ was, of course, occult. When Christians have to contend with such power, we overcome by the blood of the Lamb (Revelation 12:11). God signalled His disapproval via Balaam's suddenly vocal donkey, which crushed his foot when it encountered an angel invisible to Balaam, and was given power to rebuke its master.

Balaam was a most reluctant prophet, in that God kept overruling him and putting other words in his mouth – "Balaam raised his eyes, and saw Israel encamped according to their tribes; and the Spirit of God came upon him" (Numb 24:2). Moreover he was reluctant, because he was greedy for reward, as Jude recorded, "Woe to them! For they..... have run greedily in the error of Balaam for profit" (1:11). The frustrated Balaam asked Balak: "How shall I curse whom God has not cursed? And how shall I denounce whom the LORD has not denounced?" As he surveyed Israel, he made the most significant observation: "There! A people dwelling alone, not reckoning itself among the nations" (chapter 23:9). Israel, under God's authority, has never been able to be integrated with any other nation, even though recently foolish world statesmen have tried to encourage this.

Much that we see happening in the world around us may appear to impinge adversely upon God's people, whoever we may be. The storm clouds are gathering. But God is ever watchful and in control; He will never be thwarted. Overcoming by the blood of the Lamb is no formula or magic spell; it is our identification with the greatest Victor and victory in earth's history.

26 May

"And he (Eli) *said, 'What is the word that the LORD spoke to you? Please do not hide it from me. God do so to you, and more also, if you hide anything from me of all the things that He said to you.' Then Samuel told him everything, and hid nothing from him. And he said, 'It is the LORD. Let Him do what seems good to Him.'"*
(I Sam 3:17-18)

This is one of the many sad episodes in Israel's history. Soon the Philistines were to carry off the Ark of the Covenant. The comment was to be made, "Ichabod" – "the Glory of the Lord is departed from Israel". God removes His glory at appropriate times. One can today visit churches where members boast about what the Lord has done there in the past, unaware that His glory has departed.

This was back in the days of the Tabernacle. Eli, the High Priest, was a devout man, but weak. His two sons were taking advantage of their place in society and horribly desecrating the Tabernacle: "Now Eli was very old; and he heard everything his sons did to all Israel, and how they lay with the women who assembled at the door of the tabernacle of meeting" (2:22). Eli had failed to discipline them, and God chose to deal through Samuel, the Temple child, rather than with Eli himself. God had spoken to Samuel during the night. "Behold, I will do something in Israel at which both ears of everyone who hears it will tingle" (I Sam 3:11). God was about to end completely Eli's house (or family).

Eli knew that God had spoken to the boy. One can feel for Samuel, being asked by God to deliver to his spiritual guardian and employer such a dire message. Had the message been for Hophni and Phinehas, the two wicked sons, he would at least have had the satisfaction of feeling that the fate which he was to communicate would have been deserved. But Eli's sin was weakness, unacceptable in view of his spiritual responsibility for the nation. Eli was humble enough to ask Samuel for an unexpurgated version of God's message. Having proved himself faithful, Samuel went on to be the last of the Judges (Acts 13:20) and first of the Prophets (Acts 3:24), with his name in the Hebrews 11 roll call of honour (11:32).

27 May

"The LORD said to me: 'Do not say, "I am a youth," For you shall go to all to whom I send you, and whatever I command you, you shall speak.'" (Jer 1:7)

Jeremiah, the Weeping Prophet, was unique in his ministry, which was to continue until the deportation of Judah and sack of Jerusalem by the Babylonians. He was not unique, however, in making excuses, such as youthfulness and lack of eloquence, for not passing on God's warnings to his nation. The Northern Kingdom had already been deported by the Assyrians, and Judah had not learned the appropriate lessons. She had had some good kings and temporary revivals, but the general trend was a downward spiral.

God had anticipated Jeremiah's reluctance. Being a prophet of God in a rebellious society involves challenging national morals in His name, and often condemning both civil and religious powers, or even confronting neighbouring nations. God did not choose a recognised, self-confident orator; so often He chooses the weak things of the world to confound the wise. He had already chosen Jeremiah; His decision was not negotiable: "Before I formed you in the womb I knew you; before you were born I sanctified you; I ordained you a prophet to the nations" (1:5). Having chosen him, He empowered him. God never fails to do this.

Having obeyed God, and been filled with His Spirit for this great task, Jeremiah confesses to be desperate to deliver God's word: "His word was in my heart like a burning fire shut up in my bones; I was weary of holding it back, and I could not" (Jer 20:9). Jeremiah with its 52 chapters is virtually as long as Isaiah with its 66, and Jeremiah also wrote Lamentations. In God's hands the reluctant youth became the major major prophet! It was Jeremiah who was tasked with foretelling, not only the Babylonian captivity, but also its seventy year duration (25:11-12). But when God commissions us to impart bad news, so often it is accompanied by good news, with or without conditions attached. Some of the most lovely, as yet unfulfilled, long-term prophecies were given to Jeremiah by God to pass on to His wayward people.

28 May

"I will heal their backsliding, I will love them freely, for My anger has turned away from him. I will be like the dew to Israel; he shall grow like the lily, and lengthen his roots like Lebanon." (Hos 14:4-5)

Hosea's is a book with a happy ending, but much sorrow before this can be achieved. Being a prophet resulted in Hosea enduring heart-breaking experiences and acting as an illustration of what God was suffering with His unfaithful people, Israel. Feinberg writes, "Just as Luke presents the prodigal son, so Hosea presents the prodigal wife". In the first three chapters, God told Hosea to enter into a marriage with a potentially unfaithful woman, Gomer, whose conduct would reflect Israel's conduct towards her Husband, Jehovah.

The second child was to be called Lo-Ammi, meaning 'not My people'. Thousands of years had to elapse between verses 9 and 10. Verse 9 reads: "Call his name Lo-Ammi, for you are not My people, and I will not be your God;" whereas verse 10 reads: "Yet the number of the children of Israel shall be as the sand of the sea..... And it shall come to pass in the place where it was said to them, 'You are not My people,' there it shall be said to them, 'You are sons of the living God.'"

What God does **not** say is that He is discarding them as His people and replacing them with another people, such as the Church! Christians may be rather glad that Israel is not the Church. God has some exceedingly uncomplimentary things to say to Israel through Hosea. The Church would not like to think of itself as having been divorced, or, as in Isaiah 54:4-5, widowed before being re-married. Having excluded the Church from this major application of Hosea, we have to admit that the Church is full of individuals, congregations and even denominations who have been no less unfaithful. Those long-term backsliders who are truly redeemed will be fully restored, to appear almost empty handed one day at the Judgment Seat of Christ. There is something in Hosea for each one of us. People who never bother to read the Old Testament assume it to be negative and austere. But God's love, which is displayed in unprecedented measure towards the end of the Gospels, is demonstrated time and again in the Old Testament, as here.

29 May

"'Behold, the days are coming,' says the Lord GOD, 'that I will send a famine on the land, not a famine of bread, nor a thirst for water, but of hearing the words of the LORD. They shall wander from sea to sea, and from north to east; they shall run to and fro, seeking the word of the LORD, but shall not find it.'" (Amos 8:11-12)

Amos's own country of Judah had had both good and bad kings since the death of Solomon, and was yet to experience brief revivals. The Northern Kingdom had had only bad kings, and would be first to be exiled. To preach a message like this in one's own country would be a formidable task, but to be instructed to preach it in the neighbouring rival country, would be frightening indeed, especially if one was a humble herdsman and fig gatherer from an obscure Judean village! Amos was sent by God to deliver a number of 'burdens'. Are we burdened by the spiritual state of our land? Many are burdened by its economic state and other problems, but these were not the burdens which God laid upon His prophet. There is much else in Amos' book; but let us consider the above quotation from chapter 8.

As William Kelly remarked: "Their worst famine would be one of the word; they shall feel the want of what they despised." Does this not strike us as familiar? The outcome of progressive neglect of the Word of God will result in our not being able to access it when we need it most. Limited thirst or hunger may allow some hope. In Eli's day it was recorded: "The word of the LORD was rare in those days" (1 Sam 3:1). But, when water is absent and famine sets in, panic follows. In Britain we are in a situation where regular attenders of a congregation have to be told the page number of the "pew Bible", because they are so unfamiliar with the Scriptures! Whatever has happened to "From childhood you have known the Holy Scriptures, which are able to make you wise for salvation" (II Tim 3:15)? Possession of a Bible is not enough; it is every parent's responsibility, and not an onerous one, to impart to youngsters a love of the Bible.

Ours is still in an Eli situation, rather than an Amos one!

30 May

"And Jonah began to enter the city on the first day's walk. Then he cried out and said, 'Yet forty days, and Nineveh shall be overthrown!'" (Jonah 3:4)

Jonah can certainly be classed as a reluctant prophet. Tasked by God to deliver a prophecy of judgment to the cruel, bloodthirsty Assyrian capital city of Nineveh, Jonah took a boat to Tarshish, at the opposite end of the Mediterranean. He simply did not want his nation's most vindictive and powerful enemy warned of God's forthcoming judgment; moreover, telling of God's love and concern for Gentiles was not a favourite Jewish pastime. Even believers can be more like Jonah than we care to admit, when we hear of dreadful atrocities, and wish that God would strike the perpetrators dead there and then, forgetting that "God is not willing that any should perish" (II Pet 3:9); and "I have no pleasure in the death of the wicked, but that the wicked turn from his way and live" (Ezek 33:11).

Jonah had established his credibility locally as a prophet by foretelling King Jeroboam's military successes (II Kings 14:25). Perhaps God deliberately sent to Nineveh a prophet with a good track record. We all know about the great fish which God prepared – a special fish – to swallow Jonah, who, whilst in its stomach, experienced a personal spiritual revival! Which of us has not received second chances and more from God when we have failed in His service?

Jonah must have been extremely eloquent and convincing to make the whole city, from the king downwards, repent so wholeheartedly. It was no mere outward show. God recognised its sincerity. Jesus told the Pharisees: "The men of Nineveh will rise up in the judgment with this generation and condemn it, because they repented at the preaching of Jonah; and indeed a greater than Jonah is here" (Matt 12:41). The main contemporary message of Jonah is that God is witness to evil and demands repentance. If that is truly forthcoming, He will relent and either forgive, or at least postpone retribution, which He did by over a century in Nineveh's case.

In the final verse God tells Jonah of His concern for 120,000 who cannot discern between their right and left hand - probably the children under the age of responsibility - and even for livestock. To God they are all individuals, not mere statistics.

31 May

"Then the chief priests and the Pharisees gathered a council and said, 'What shall we do? For this Man works many signs..... nor do you consider that it is expedient for us that one man should die for the people, and not that the whole nation should perish.' Now this he did not say on his own authority; but being high priest that year he prophesied that Jesus would die for the nation." (Jn 11: 47,50-51)

Earlier in John chapter 11 we read of that spectacular and public miracle of Jesus, the raising of Lazarus, already four days in the tomb. When Jesus had turned water into wine, it was recorded: "This beginning of **signs** Jesus did in Cana of Galilee, and manifested His glory; and His disciples believed in Him" (Jn 2:11). Here He had asked Martha: "Did I not say to you that if you would believe you would see the glory of God?" (Jn 11:40).

This happened only a couple of miles from Jerusalem, and Lazarus had become a veritable tourist attraction. The High Priest and Sanhedrin had either to recognise and acclaim Jesus as Messiah or Christ or reject Him. The excuse was pathetic: "If we let Him alone like this, everyone will believe in Him, and the Romans will come and take away both our place and nation" (Jn 11:48). They were secure in their 'don't rock the boat' compromise with the Roman occupying power. The status quo, which gave them a position in society, suited them very well.

But God over-ruled. The High Priestly office had been ordained by God, even though the present incumbent was the most ungodly individual. What he said was on God's authority, not his own. Formally he prophesied that Jesus would die for the nation. Central to the offering of the lamb in Old Testament theology was the vicarious, substitutionary office of the victim. One should die for the many. The Lamb of God should die for the whole world, but Caiaphas' jurisdiction was over Israel only – the nation. Here, immediately before the events leading up to the crucifixion, God ensured that the pronouncement was made by the High Priest, whose office was about to be made obsolete – "Christ came as High Priest of the good things to come, with the greater and more perfect tabernacle not made with hands, that is, not of this creation" (Heb 9:11).

The Perfected Church in Heaven

1 June

"Who will transform our lowly body that it may be conformed to His glorious body, according to the working by which He is able even to subdue all things to Himself." (Phil 3:21)

Last month we reviewed the main Rapture prophecies, but certainly did not exhaust them. We look now at a few verses which link our present condition with our glorious status in Christ in the home which He has been preparing for us, which He and we will temporarily vacate when later He descends in glory to judge. What happens in Heaven between the Rapture and that stunning event?

We have seen how "this mortal must put on immortality" (I Cor 15:53). We need constantly to be reminded that we are following our Saviour, "the Firstfruits of them that sleep", and that our resurrection is through His merits and not our own: "For if we have been united together in the likeness of His death, certainly we also shall be in the likeness of His resurrection" (Rom 6:5). We must be aware of the part of the Holy Spirit in our future status: "He who raised Christ from the dead will also give life to your mortal bodies through His Spirit who dwells in you" (Rom 8:11). Apart from the indwelling Holy Spirit we have no hope; the evidence which we can show to the world is the fruits, not the gifts, of the Holy Spirit.

We are eternally saved from the moment we confess our sins and place our faith in the Lamb of God, who died in our place and shed His precious blood for us, but on earth neither we nor our family and friends see the complete work of redemption. We should be "eagerly waiting for the adoption, the redemption of our body" (Rom 8:23). No truly saved person should have any doubt whatsoever about Heaven being our ultimate destination. To others this may seem arrogance, so we have to emphasise that it is entirely of Christ's doing, and that they are invited to place the same saving trust in Him. "So we are always confident, knowing that while we are at home in the body we are absent from the Lord" (II Cor 5:6). We long to be "at home with the Lord". We return to this verse and its context on 6th November.

2 June

"Being confident of this very thing, that He who has begun a good work in you will complete it until **the day of Jesus Christ.**"
(Phil 1:6)

For many centuries there has been widespread failure to distinguish between the Rapture and Christ's Return in Power, in other words between the *Parousia* and the Coming in Judgment, or between the Day of Christ and the Day of the Lord. The Rapture, like the Church itself, is never spoken of in the Old Testament. The Day of the Lord is referred to by most of the Prophets and, unlike the Rapture in the New Testament, is described as being terrifying, another contrast with the Rapture. For instance: "Wail, for the day of the LORD is at hand!" (Isa 13:6); "Alas for the day! For the day of the LORD is at hand; It shall come as destruction from the Almighty" (Joel 1:15); "Is not the day of the LORD darkness, and not light?" (Amos 5:20). In the New Testament we read: "But **the day of the Lord** will come as a thief in the night, in which the heavens will pass away with a great noise" (II Pet 3:10, also I Thess 5:2). Some feel that the Day of the Lord will extend to the end of the world.

While the Day of Christ is to start with the Rapture, it seems that everything thereafter up to the Return in Power is included. He will have the glory in His Church. Paul talks about our spirituality up to the Rapture: "that you may be blameless in **the day of our Lord Jesus Christ**".....that we are your boast as you also are ours, in **the day of the Lord Jesus**" (I Cor 1:8; II Cor 1:14). Church discipline must be exercised until the Rapture, for instance: "deliver such a one to Satan for the destruction of the flesh, that his spirit may be saved in **the day of the Lord Jesus**" (I Cor 5:5). We must never fear that the Rapture has already occurred: "And we ask you, brethren, in regard to the presence of our Lord Jesus Christ, and of our gathering together unto him, that ye be not quickly shaken in mind, nor be troubled, neither through spirit, neither through word, neither through letters as through us, as that **the day of Christ** hath arrived" (II Thess 2:1-2 YLT, as per Textus Receptus).

3 June

"After these things I looked, and behold, a door standing open in heaven. And the first voice which I heard was like a trumpet speaking with me, saying, 'Come up here, and I will show you things which must take place after this.'" (Rev 4:1)

We have seen how the Church is to be taken to Heaven. In contrast, John is taken there only in vision, but all that he sees is reality, which he has to describe in terms that we can understand. He has witnessed the progress of the Church on earth up to its Rapture. Now John sees the Church in Heaven, where she is to experience the Bema or Judgment Seat of Christ and the Marriage of the Lamb, before accompanying her Lord back to earth in triumph. Here the Lamb is central, and the Church secondary.

"Immediately I was in the Spirit; and behold, a throne set in heaven, and One sat on the throne" (Rev 4:2). We had a brief glimpse back in January of this august heavenly scene. A few verses before, the Lord had promised to "overcomers" of the church of Laodicea: "I will grant to sit with Me on My throne, as I also overcame and sat down with My Father on His throne" (3:21). John sees the Father's throne, where we are later shown that the Lamb is "in the midst", and we also see around that throne the priestly number of twenty-four crowned "elders", who seem to represent the raptured church in their resurrection bodies, though they may be individuals. Tomorrow we consider this crowning.

John is about to see mighty angels in their delegated roles during a time of judgment on earth below, because the Tribulation Period begins virtually immediately. To the vast majority of those on earth it will seem to be calamity after calamity, following a very brief period of false optimism, as Satan's powerful Man of Sin, under a cloak of benign authority, is seen to take control. But from a heavenly point of view, John sees the systematic pattern of escalating judgments in Seals, Trumpets and Bowls of Wrath. John was to see in scenes which alternate between Heaven and earth, the reception by the minority of the Gospel of the Kingdom, and the calamitous fate of the majority who accept Satan's alternative, and its demonically-inspired progress to Armageddon.

4 June

"And He who sat there was like a jasper and a sardius stone in appearance; and there was a rainbow around the throne, in appearance like an emerald. Around the throne were twenty-four thrones, and on the thrones I saw twenty-four elders sitting, clothed in white robes; and they had crowns of gold on their heads."
(Rev 4:3-4)

John was unable to describe God the Father in any other way; he simply described what he saw; and that was beyond human understanding. But the twenty-four surrounding thrones are clear enough - resurrected saints crowned. Why does Revelation not describe the crowning ceremony, which at this point is now past? The answer is simple; it would have been inappropriate in a book which is about to describe God's judgment on the rebellious world: "For the time has come for judgment to begin at the house of God; and if it begins with us first, what will be the end of those who do not obey the gospel of God?" (I Pet 4:17). It is in the Epistles we learn about the crowning.

Hebrews 9:27 tells us that, "It is appointed for men to die once, but after this the judgment." Even believers are not exempt. But all emphatically do not appear to be judged at the same time. The legacy of inadequate Creeds still pervades much of Protestantism. If you regularly attend one of the major Protestant churches, I would ask you when you last heard a sermon about the Judgment Seat of Christ. I never have; this is an Amillennial hangover. And yet there are still faithful preachers of an undiluted Gospel within denominations where the majority of congregations, Laodicean- like, have departed from the truth. One of the major Creeds says, speaking of Heaven, "From thence He shall come to judge the quick and the dead." That is at best a half truth. Christ is not **coming** to judge the Church. That judgment is to take place in Heaven. It must do, because the judgment in all cases follows the resurrection – the whole person is to be judged – and, following our resurrection, we will be in Heaven, and will be seen there, as in today's text, having been through that judgment.

I am devoting more time to the subject of the Judgment Seat of Christ than I had planned, having observed the effects of confusion regarding these truths.

5 June

"Why do you judge your brother? Or why do you show contempt for your brother? For we shall all stand before the judgment seat of Christ. For it is written: 'As I live', says the LORD, 'Every knee shall bow to Me, And every tongue shall confess to God.' So then each of us shall give account of himself to God." (Rom 14:10-12)

Here we are brought up sharply. There is a grave danger in putting ourselves above younger or weaker brothers and sisters. Admittedly leaders have a responsibility for discipline and conduct within the congregation or assembly, but this must be done with a mixture of compassion and humility, as well as the exercise of delegated authority, rarely an easy balance to maintain! The above quote by Paul from Isaiah 45 is more often associated with Philippians 2, where we are reminded that "every tongue" includes the ungodly. Here we find ourselves included, and are not allowed to forget that our Saviour is also our Judge.

The word "judgment" is frightening; the fact that fire is mentioned in one of the relevant texts makes some think of Purgatory, a Pagan concept absorbed long ago by Catholicism, which claims that sins not confessed to a priest and, therefore, purportedly unforgiven, must be purged in this imaginary temporary place of torture. It is a most serious misinterpretation of the Judgment Seat of Christ. Absolutely nobody appears at the Judgment Seat of Christ bearing any of their sins; only those whose sins were dealt with by Christ at Calvary will be there. Such fears are in effect an insult to Christ's redeeming work.

Vengeance is the prerogative of God. But there is no hint of vengeance in this judgment. This is not God's eternal throne; it is specifically the Judgment Seat of Christ. It is a necessary act of love: "Christ also loved the church and gave Himself for her, that He might sanctify and cleanse her with the washing of water by the word, that He might present her to Himself a glorious church, not having spot or wrinkle or any such thing, but that she should be holy and without blemish" (Eph 5:25-27). This is why it takes place before the Marriage of the Lamb, and that is why most Amillennialists do not preach it. It simply does not fit their truncated programme. So what is left to be judged if Christ paid the penalty of our sins, in a way that makes further punishment impossible?

6 June

"Now if anyone builds on this foundation with gold, silver, precious stones, wood, hay, straw, each one's work will become clear; for the Day will declare it, because it will be revealed by fire; and the fire will test each one's work, of what sort it is." (I Cor 3:12-13)

The foundation of our faith is our Redeemer and His work, not our own "For no other foundation can anyone lay than that which is laid, which is Jesus Christ." (verse 11). "Be diligent to present yourself approved to God, a worker who does not need to be ashamed" (II Tim 2:15). It is our work, our stewardship which is tested. All impurities are exposed, and what is left is assessed. Peter puts it this way: "That the genuineness of your faith, being much more precious than gold that perishes, though it is tested by fire, may be found to praise, honour, and glory at the revelation of Jesus Christ" (I Pet 1:7). This supports the idea that the gold represents that which we have done in our mortal bodies, which has brought glory and honour to our Lord. It is rarely the most spectacular work which does that; but He values it.

Sadly, long Christian lives may be shown to have little to commend them. One of the shortest has been demonstrated to be of eternal value by the number of death-bed conversions it has encouraged. It is that of the repentant thief, who, with hours to live when he made his plea to Jesus, was told that he would be with Him in Paradise by the end of the day.

I John 1:9 is sometimes wrongly quoted as referring to this judgment: "If we confess our sins, He is faithful and just to forgive us our sins and to cleanse us from all unrighteousness". Let us not ignore such verses. But, as John Walvoord remarks, "The context is that of fellowship with God. It is not talking about ultimate reward, but rather the daily experience of Christians who walk with God. As sin comes into their lives and some disobedience or departure from God becomes evident, they will lose the experience of fellowship with God even though their salvation is intact. In order to restore this fellowship, it is necessary for Christians to confess their sins to God."

7 June

"Do not lay up for yourselves treasures on earth, where moth and rust destroy and where thieves break in and steal; but lay up for yourselves treasures in heaven, where neither moth nor rust destroys and where thieves do not break in and steal. For where your treasure is, there your heart will be also." (Matt 6:19-21)

Now those words of Jesus were not specifically for the Church, but apply to all believers. Old Testament saints and Tribulation saints will have their service evaluated and rewarded as appropriate at other times. But the principle applies to us; rewards in Heaven are everlasting - "an inheritance incorruptible and undefiled and that does not fade away" (I Pet 1:4). Paul writes: "of the hope which is laid up for you in heaven, of which you heard before in the word of the truth of the gospel" (Col 1:5). He also writes, reminding us of the essential conditions: "Everyone who competes for the prize is temperate in all things. Now they do it to obtain a perishable crown, but we for an imperishable crown" (I Cor 9:25). We cannot even be certain how many will actually witness rewards for stewardship being given; we only know that both the individual and the Lord will be involved, though likening it to a sports competition suggests that others will share our joy.

The Greek word for judgment seat is *bema*, which is also used for the judges' rostrum at Greek sporting events, deciding who was worthy to receive the great honour of the victor's crown of leaves. Before Christ's *Bema* we will not be competing against each other for a limited number of crowns, though of course others may in life take the initiative, when we fail to perform some required service.

Some of the crowns appear to be for specific forms of faithful service and qualities: "Finally, there is laid up for me the crown of **righteousness**, which the Lord, the righteous Judge, will give to me on that Day, and not to me only but also to all who have loved His appearing" (II Tim 4:8); "When the Chief Shepherd appears, you will receive the crown of **glory** that does not fade away" (I Pet 5:4). And a final thought: "Let us not grow weary while doing good, for in due season we shall reap if we do not lose heart" (Gal 6:9).

8 June

"Then the four living creatures said, 'Amen!' And the twenty-four elders fell down and worshipped Him who lives forever and ever."
(Rev 5:14)

Thereafter in Revelation there are only the briefest mentions of the elders, and none specifically of the Church, until we come to chapter 19 and the marriage of the Lamb. In chapter 5 the Church, represented by the twenty-four elders, has been very much in evidence as the Lamb asserts His right to open the seals, thus inaugurating the Tribulation Period. In chapter 5 it is confirmed that we are a **kingdom of priests** (not kings and priests as in some versions). The number twenty-four confirms the completion of the Church. Attention is turned from the elders to the Lamb and to those awesome things He is about to command from Heaven, which will immediately impact upon the earth. The scene thereafter alternates between Heaven and earth, between cause and effect. The Lamb is referred to twenty-two times from chapter 5 to 19, building up to the wrath of the Lamb. Only He, as "the Lamb as it had been slain", has the authority and right to do this; He alone has earned it.

In the interim chapters we see three sequences of seven judgments, learn of the false bride as opposed to true bride, are told of God's bountiful provision for acceptance of the Gospel of the Kingdom, and of salvation in the midst of tribulation; we learn of those who will preach that Gospel. We see the souls of Tribulation martyrs awaiting vindication; we see God's two divinely-commissioned witnesses; we see Satan's pursuit of the faithful remnant of Israel; we see how Satan is cast down and how he empowers his two deputies; we see the destruction of the world's religions, and then its political system, we see the build up to Armageddon, but, until chapter 19, we are told no more about the Church! We are there, in Heaven, but, from the point of view of those on earth, kept in the background, whilst the venom of rebellious mankind is directed against our espoused Bridegroom.

We are inclined to talk of ourselves, the Church, as the Bride of Christ. In fact we are still the **espoused** Bride, but, when He returns with us in power and glory, He has planned that we will appear as His Bride.

9 June

"And I heard, as it were, the voice of a great multitude, as the sound of many waters and as the sound of mighty thunderings, saying, 'Alleluia! For the Lord God Omnipotent reigns! Let us be glad and rejoice and give Him glory, for the marriage of the Lamb has come, and His wife has made herself ready.'" (Rev 19:6-7)

At first sight there appears to be discontinuity, a complete change of subject, between these two verses. But the voice of the heavenly multitude demonstrates the significance of the timing of the Marriage of the Lamb. The rejoicing, which ends at verse 6, has been largely over the destruction of the multi-faith persecuting and blaspheming false church, Mystery Babylon, (we say more about this elsewhere). "For true and righteous are His judgments, because He has judged the great harlot who corrupted the earth with her fornication; and He has avenged on her the blood of His servants shed by her." (19:2). Until the harlot church, Satan's counterfeit, is utterly removed, it is inappropriate for Christ to take to Himself His long-espoused wife, His true Church.

I quote from my *"Rapture – Sooner Not Later"*: "Contemporary Jewish marriage customs are often referred to in the New Testament from the Gospels through to Revelation, and prophetically from Matthew 25:1 onwards. The custom was that the bridegroom;
- paid the bride-price, consecrating his betrothed to himself
- returned to the father's home to prepare a place for her
- came back often suddenly, usually at midnight, to claim
his bride, whom he would take to his father's house where the marriage would be consummated
- returned to the bride's original home where those invited by
the bridegroom's father would be waiting for the wedding feast"

We see Christ, having taking human flesh, coming into this world and paying the precious bride-price with His blood on the Cross. He returned to His Father's House, fulfilling His promise to go to prepare a place, and returned at the Rapture to claim His Bride. At this juncture in Revelation 19 the wedding feast is about to be announced, but the consummation must come first. We see more tomorrow.

10 June

"And to her it was granted to be arrayed in fine linen, clean and bright, for the fine linen is the righteous acts of the saints"
(Rev 19:8).

We have already observed the standard of perfection: "that He might present her to Himself a glorious church, not having spot or wrinkle or any such thing, but that she should be holy and without blemish" (Eph 5:27). This is possible only as the result of the grace given to her, accepted and applied, and evaluated at the earlier Judgment Seat of Christ. The status of the Church following the Rapture will have already been glorious. Now it is to be even more glorious. "According to the working of His mighty power which He worked in Christ when He raised Him from the dead and seated Him at His right hand in the heavenly places..... And He put all things under His feet, and gave Him to be head over all things to the church, which is His body, the fullness of Him who fills all in all. (Eph 1:19-23)

Later, to the Ephesians, Paul writes: "(He) raised us up together, and made us sit together in the heavenly places in Christ Jesus, that in the ages to come He might show the exceeding riches of His grace in His kindness toward us in Christ Jesus" (2:6-7).This is not momentary; not only will we see it reflected during the Millennium in the Holy City, with which the Church is so closely related that it is almost indistinguishable; it is in fact eternal.

The final stage of the Marriage is the Bridegroom bringing His new Bride back to her original home, the earth, for the marriage feast or supper: "Then he said to me, 'Write: "Blessed are those who are called to the marriage supper of the Lamb!"' And he said to me, 'These are the true sayings of God.'" (Rev 19:9). This follows Armageddon, at the inauguration of the Millennium, and indicates the timing of the resurrection of Old Testament saints, of whom John the Baptist was one of the last and most honoured, a sort of 'best man': "He who has the bride is the bridegroom; but **the friend of the bridegroom,** who stands and hears him, rejoices greatly because of the bridegroom's voice. Therefore this joy of mine is fulfilled" (Jn 3:29).

Israel in Bible Prophecy

11 June

"I will bless those who bless you, And I will curse him who curses you; And in you all the families of the earth shall be blessed." (Gen 12:3)

These words were addressed by God to Abraham, as he later became known. This subject is so central to understanding Bible prophecy that we introduced it back in early January and have constantly had further glimpses of it. I can do no better than quote, for succinctness, John De Silva's brilliant *"Outlines In Bible Prophecy"*: "Israel is God's principal nation *prophetically*. The high mark of its privilege in both history and prophecy is that Christ, the principal Person in both history and prophecy, was born into it and to it. It comes as no surprise that in the purposes of God, it is 'to the Jew first.'"

History has borne out the validity of this prophecy for four thousand years. Everything in prophecy due to be fulfilled until now in God's programme has indeed been fulfilled. Israel has been unique among the nations. As the signs of the times accelerate, Israel remains, as a multitude of prophecies foretell, at the centre of world attention and a source of frustration, hatred and potential conflict among the many who curse her, and a source of blessing to those who still dare to defy international opinion and bless her. Much remains to be fulfilled before long. Keep your eyes on Israel! The Pope's 2017 Christmas message supports a two nation state in the Holy Land; how sad that the poor man thus invites God's condemnation in Joel 3:2: "they have divided up **My** Land." Mind you, if he wants to seek world-wide acclaim, this is one way to go about it. The opponents of Jeremiah's prophesying used the same tactics – and were judged.

Today's text is part of the opening words of one of God's unconditional covenants; it cannot be annulled; but many of the benefits have been put into suspension until an appropriate future day. This is the Abrahamic Covenant, which must never be confused with the conditional Levitical Covenant, given to the Children of Israel through Moses and eventually irreparably broken. That is to be replaced at the outset of the Millennium with a new one. That new covenant must not be confused with the Church's current unconditional covenant, which we remember in the "cup of the new covenant in My blood" (I Cor 11:25).

12 June

"Now the LORD had said to Abram: 'Get out of your country, from your family and from your father's house, to a land that I will show you.'" (Gen 12:1)

Abram, as he was then known, was required by God to abandon two things, his kindred and his homeland. He had evidently been influential and wealthy in the godless Ur of the Chaldees. When God calls us for a special duty, He may ask us to take a huge step of faith, and to sacrifice much of what we hold dear. As we look back on our lives, we may see how God has been leading us. Very often we have to confess to disobedience, doubts and delays, with consequent disappointments. It is not for us to know the what-might-have-beens. But, just as God had narrowed His plans for preserving mankind, following the death of Abel at the hand of Cain, through Seth and his descendants until Noah, so now, since Nimrod's challenge at Babel, He had been narrowing down Noah's Semite (Shemite) descendants to Terah, the father of Abram, the progenitor of a new race.

Terah set off for Haran with his son Abram, daughter-in-law Sarah, and Lot. But he lingered in Haran and eventually died there, allowing Abram, free of filial responsibility, to head towards Canaan to raise the great family, which, under God's oversight, was to become more than a nation, but rather a family of nations. It is so easy to assume that, once we are in the place God wants us to be, all will run smoothly. In fact Abraham, his son Isaac and grandson Jacob (whom He renamed Israel) underwent a successions of immense trials of faith, jealousies and rivalries, battles, wanderings and indeed miracles, before being told that his descendants would be "strangers in a land that is not theirs, and will serve them, and they will afflict them four hundred years" (Gen 15:13), emerging as a fully-fledged nation.

Throughout history there has been opposition from all who resented these plans of God. The Psalmist could cry: "They have said, 'Come, and let us cut them off from being a nation, that the name of Israel may be remembered no more.'" (Ps 83:4). The ultimate aim is justified: "That they may know that You, whose name alone is the LORD, are the Most High over all the earth" (Ps 83:18).

13 June

"Then Abraham fell on his face and laughed, and said in his heart, 'Shall a child be born to a man who is one hundred years old? And shall Sarah, who is ninety years old, bear a child?' And Abraham said to God, 'Oh, that Ishmael might live before You!'"
(Gen 17:17-18)

Any of us can doubt God within our heart, but cannot hope to conceal it from Him. Even faithful Abraham faltered as he approach old age and infertility; Sarah, also doubting, gave her handmaiden to Abraham to raise a family. We looked at the conflict between Isaac and Ishmael and their respective mothers several weeks ago, as an example of a short-term prophecy with long-term consequences. Today we note the narrowing down of the Messianic line and Israel's unique purposes. Some years previously the Lord had told Hagar: "Behold, you are with child, and you shall bear a son. You shall call his name Ishmael..... He shall be a wild man; his hand shall be against every man, and every man's hand against him. And he shall dwell in the presence (or face) of all his brethren." (Gen 16:11-12). How descriptive that last prophecy is of an acknowledged ancestor of Islam! Abraham had no control over the nature of his son by Hagar; that was not the type of man that God wanted in His Son's human ancestry.

Abraham pleaded that Ishmael, by then a teenager, might fulfil the terms of the covenant. But God said: "No, Sarah your wife shall bear you a son, and you shall call his name Isaac; I will establish My covenant with him for an everlasting covenant, and with his descendants after him. And as for Ishmael, I have heard you. Behold, I have blessed him, and will make him fruitful, and will multiply him exceedingly. He shall beget twelve princes, and I will make him a great nation. But My covenant I will establish with Isaac, whom Sarah shall bear to you at this set time next year" (Gen 17:19-21).

The reinvigorated Abraham when he was 137 years old married again and had six sons by Keturah! In time their identity became merged with the Ishmaelites. Most of Abraham's children by Hagar and Keturah and their descendants, settled to the east, the future cradle of Islam. Abraham was indeed also the father of nations other than Israel.

14 June

"The children struggled together within her; and she said, 'If all is well, why am I like this?' So she went to inquire of the LORD. And the LORD said to her: 'Two nations are in your womb, two peoples shall be separated from your body; one people shall be stronger than the other, and the older shall serve the younger.'"
(Gen 25:22-23)

Today we consider what God said to the expectant Rebekah. Of the three nations whose territory the Israelites had later to pass through during their Exodus, Ammon and Moab were descendants of Lot by his two daughters, but Edom was descended from Esau. They opposed the Children of Israel during the Exodus, despite a courteous request for right of passage with payment offered (Numbers 20:14). The Herods, illegitimate client puppet kings of the Roman Empire, were of Edomite stock. Edom survived long as an entity. The territories of Ammon, Moab and Edom form a significant part of what is currently the Kingdom of Jordon.

God renamed Jacob, meaning 'supplanter', 'Israel', which means 'ruling with God', (Gen 35:10). Rebekah has been criticised for her part in deceiving the almost blind Isaac into giving his blessing to the younger twin, Jacob (Genesis 27). But it was Rebekah, rather than Isaac, who first perceived God's will. That struggle has never really ended, and for long the famous birthright has never been allowed to be forgotten. It became a running sore, the cause of enmity throughout succeeding generations; Antisemitism still thrives on it. Isaac was unhappy about having given his blessing to Jacob, rather than to Esau, but he was perceptive enough to realise that God had over-ruled and that he could not undo Jacob's blessing, though he was able to give a lesser blessing to Esau, to whom he said "**By your sword you shall live**, and you shall serve your brother; but when you break loose you shall break his yoke from your neck'" (Gen 27:39-40 RSV). Need we comment about the sword? Muslims still confess that theirs is a religion of the sword. We find much about Edom in Major and Minor Prophets, notably: "Who is He that comes from Edom.....for the day of vengeance is in My heart" (Isa 63:1,4). Obadiah's prophecy is devoted largely to the sins of Esau's family and its punishment.

15 June

"On the same day the LORD made a covenant with Abram, saying: 'To your descendants I have given this land, from the river of Egypt to the great river, the River Euphrates.'" (Gen 15:18).

These are almost the concluding words of God's great covenant, most provisions of which He later narrowed down, firstly to Isaac and then to Jacob. The following verse lists the nations who were at that moment in possession of the Land; this shows how ridiculous is the quite common claim, wrongly based on Hebrews 11:10, that what God was promising was only a heavenly home: "For he (Abraham) waited for the city which has foundations, whose builder and maker is God". Heaven was never occupied by the Hittites, Amorites, Canaanites etc!

The River of Egypt is not the Nile, but a seasonal river between the "Gaza Strip" and the Nile. Much of the territory of present Israel, Lebanon, parts of Jordan and even Iraq are included. Except briefly, at the end of David's life and throughout Solomon's reign, the territory has never been fully subjected and incorporated. Judges chapter 1 records that there remained much land to be possessed after the conquest under Joshua; they were content with less than God had promised. Are we not all guilty of such behaviour? Only those of the future faithful remnant at Christ's Return in Power will fulfil that 4,000 year old covenant territorial promise!

The title to the land (and after all it is God who owns the title deeds) was to be handed to Jacob and his twelve sons and their descendants. Other descendants of Abraham and Isaac were excluded. It was to be an everlasting possession as long as earth shall last. So, while title was unconditional, occupation was to be conditional both depending upon God's plans for them, such as the four hundred years in Egypt, and their own faithfulness, or lack of faithfulness, to God, hence the forty year extension of the Exodus, and the later long captivities. In 721 BC the ten Northern tribes were expelled, but their future reoccupation is guaranteed as much as the Judah-dominated Southern tribes, exiled to Babylon, restored kingless, only to be re-exiled by the Romans. Whatever the decisions of modern Zionism, the Balfour Declaration and the First United Nations Declaration, while possession remains Jewish, unopposed occupation awaits the Messiah's return.

16 June

"My covenant I will not break, nor alter the word that has gone out of My lips. Once I have sworn by My holiness; I will not lie to David: His seed shall endure forever, and his throne as the sun before Me." (Ps 89:34-36)

Whether we think of the Davidic Covenant as being an extension of the Abrahamic one is not the most important issue. What is important to note is that both are unconditional, guaranteed by God, and refer to the earth as long as it shall endure. Both II Samuel 7 and I Chronicles 17 record God's promises to David. David had been embarrassed by living in a grand palace while the Ark of the Covenant was still in an elderly tabernacle or marquee. Through the prophet, Nathan, God told David that his descendants or family would last for ever, and that his son would build the Temple. His successor, Solomon, did indeed build the Temple, but because of his later unfaithfulness, his seed did not endure. If we compare the genealogies of Matthew and Luke, we find that Solomon's line died out with Joseph, whilst Nathan's line (the son, not the prophet) would continue through Mary, to whom the assurance was given: "He will be great, and will be called the Son of the Highest; and the Lord God will give Him the throne of His father David" (Lk 1:32).

In Psalm 89 and elsewhere, it was made clear that David's line would often fail, but that God's faithfulness to His covenant would not. Those provisions will be fulfilled during the Millennium, when the resurrected David will evidently be a visible vice-regent under Christ Himself. Prophetic programmes which do not allow for these provisions of an everlasting covenant are fatally flawed.

Nothing like this has happened during the Church age; as we saw elsewhere: "Simon has declared how God at the first **visited the Gentiles to take out of them a people for His name**. And with this the words of the prophets agree, just as it is written: **'After this I will return** and will rebuild the tabernacle of David, which has fallen down; I will rebuild its ruins, and I will set it up'" (Acts 15:14-16). The Davidic Covenant is inactive during the Church Age, but it will be fully promulgated after Christ's Return to earth.

17 June

"For I could wish that I myself were accursed from Christ for my brethren, my countrymen according to the flesh, who are Israelites, to whom pertain the adoption, the glory, the covenants, the giving of the law, the service of God, and the promises." (Rom 9:3-4)

The most virulent anti-Semitic attitudes within Christendom stem from failure to accept what the New Testament says about Israel. Romans chapters 9 to 11, particularly 11, are ignored. When Paul was writing not long before the destruction of Jerusalem and the *Diaspora*, he emphasised that the promises, among other things, were still valid. There are, however, different stages in the development of Israel. In the past she was likened to a vine, in the present to a fig tree and in the future to an olive tree. This is a vast topic, but let us note briefly some of the evidence. "You have brought a **vine** out of Egypt; You have cast out the nations, and planted it" (Ps 80:8). Israel was planted by God in the Promised Land. "Yet I had planted you a noble vine, a seed of highest quality. How then have you turned before Me into the degenerate plant of an alien vine?" (Jer 2:21). By the time Jeremiah wrote, ten of the tribes had already been uprooted.

Jesus told this parable: "A certain man had a **fig tree** planted in his vineyard, and he came seeking fruit on it and found none." (Lk 13:6). God is the owner; eventually He removed the tree from the Land. "Now learn this parable from the fig tree: When its branch has already become tender, and puts forth leaves, you know that summer is near" (Mk 13:28). Israel's being partially back in the Land should draw our attention to the end of this age and start of the next.

"If **you** were cut out of the olive tree which is wild by nature, and were grafted contrary to nature into a cultivated **olive tree**, how much more will these, who are natural branches, be grafted into their own olive tree?" (Rom 11:24). Paul addresses Gentiles and reminds them of the historical source of their newly-found faith, warning against the heretical assumption that God has no future purposes for Israel, whereas a multitude of prophecies await fruition. We are encountering many of these as we proceed through the year.

18 June

"And the name of the city from that day shall be, Jehovah is there (Jehovah Shammah)." (Ezek 48:35 ASV)

God revealed Himself to Israel progressively, as He disclosed His names. These names do not apply exclusively to Israel; as we list them briefly, we should see that we can apply them to our situations too. With some translations, we have to look to the margins of our Bibles for the Hebrew renderings. Jehovah, we recall, is the covenant name rather than simply a title, and reveals our Holy God. As Elohim He is the Creator to whom all have a responsibility as created beings. To Abraham He revealed Himself as *El Shaddai*, the God who sustains and protects, under Whom His people may take shelter, as in Ps 91:1-2: "He who dwells in the secret place of the Most High shall abide under the shadow of the Almighty. I will say of the LORD, 'He is my refuge and my fortress; My God, in Him I will trust.'" Back in March, when we found Isaac enquiring about the apparently absent lamb for the burnt offering, Abraham spoke of *Jehovah-Jireh,* God who provides, pointing forward to the Lamb of God (Genesis 22:8,14).

When Israel was attacked by the Amalekites, and Moses had been helped to hold his hands up in intercession to Heaven, he raised an altar named *Jehovah-Nissi*, "the LORD is my Banner" (Ex 17:15). After many decades of attacks and oppression from neighbouring nations, when Gideon was personally called by God to lead His people in victory over the Midianites, he did not wait until after the victory, but erected an altar which he named *Jehovah-Shalom*, meaning "the LORD is our peace" (Judg 6:24); in an alien world we should share such confidence.

We now look towards the future Millennium: "Behold, the days come, saith Jehovah, that I will raise unto David a righteous Branch, and he shall reign as king and deal wisely, and shall execute justice and righteousness in the land. In his days Judah shall be saved, and Israel shall dwell safely; and this is his name whereby he shall be called: 'Jehovah our righteousness', (*Jehovah-Tsidkenu*)" (Jer 23:5-6 ASV) – the imputed righteousness of Christ, effective for us. Ezekiel wrote from Babylonian captivity, with Jerusalem sacked; but he was privileged to view the Millennial Jerusalem, as described in today's text: *Jehovah-Shammah*, "the LORD is there".

19 June

"Do not fear, for you will not be ashamed; neither be disgraced, for you will not be put to shame; for you will forget the shame of your youth, and will not remember the reproach of your widowhood anymore. For your Maker is your husband, the LORD of hosts is His name; and your Redeemer is the Holy One of Israel; He is called the God of the whole earth." (Isa 54:4-5)

Here is a theme which many theologians prefer to ignore; yet it is often referred to in Scripture as something which is by no means obsolete or exhausted – Israel as the "Wife of Jehovah"; we touched on it briefly last month with Hosea. It must not be confused with the Church, though, as there is also unfaithfulness within the Church, lessons may apply. The Church, the espoused Bride of Christ whilst on earth, was not born until Pentecost.

"For your Maker is your husband, the LORD of hosts is His name; and your Redeemer is the Holy One of Israel; He is called the God of the whole earth" (Isa 54:5). The privileges extended to Israel had been stupendous, but ever since she had become a nation, she had continually transgressed. The nature of this transgression is adultery with alien deities. It started back in Exodus near the foot of Mount Sinai with the golden calf. Even Solomon was drawn away: "When Solomon was old..... his wives turned his heart after other gods; and his heart was not loyal to the LORD his God, as was the heart of his father David." The subsequent division of the Kingdom was the result of idolatry, "because they have forsaken Me, and worshipped Ashtoreth the goddess of the Sidonians, Chemosh the god of the Moabites, and Milcom the god of the people of Ammon." (I Kings 11:4,33).

Through Jeremiah God pleaded with the remaining tribes as a husband with an unfaithful wife: "Only acknowledge your iniquity, that you have transgressed against the LORD your God, and have scattered your charms to alien deities under every green tree, and you have not obeyed My voice', says the LORD. 'Return, O backsliding children,' says the LORD; 'for I am married to you. I will take you, one from a city and two from a family, and I will bring you to Zion'" (3:13-14). The relationship will be renewed in the Millennium!

20 June

"And so all Israel will be saved, as it is written: 'The Deliverer will come out of Zion, and He will turn away ungodliness from Jacob; for this is My covenant with them, when I take away their sins.'"
(Rom 11:26-27)

Paul is quoting Isaiah 59. We must not take the opening statement out of context. A few Christians treat Israel as if she can do no wrong. This can give them a false sense of security, because their worst time has to precede their best time. Only when their Deliverer, their Messiah, returns to earth will all those of Israel who have survived the Great Tribulation be saved. We made brief comments back in February, and will see more when we turn to certain passages of Zechariah. The Hebrew original actually talks of the Deliverer coming **to** Zion, while Paul here quotes the Septuagint **'out of'**, but, as WE Vine says, both prepositions have support from other passages. This is emphatically following Christ's Return in Power, when there will be a great national mourning among those who have survived God's sifting.

Earlier Paul had written: "Isaiah also cries out concerning Israel: 'Though the number of the children of Israel be as the sand of the sea, the **remnant** will be saved'" (Rom 9:27); that does not contradict the "all" of 11:26. When Christ returns to Israel, only the remnant will have survived to be saved, firstly as to their mortal life and secondly from their sins. Some of these will be the 144,000 witnesses, some those who escaped to the wilderness, some will have participated in the defence of Jerusalem and yet others may still be scattered. But all will welcome their Messiah; those who had rejected Him beyond the point of repentance will have already perished.

Paul adds a comment about Israel in the Church Age: "Concerning the gospel they are enemies for your sake, but concerning the election they are beloved for the sake of the fathers" (11:28). Campbell Morgan writes: "As touching the Gospel, Israel is for the period treated as an enemy..... Thus through the maintenance of a remnant God keeps His covenant with the fathers through the period of national rejection, but at last the nation as a whole will be restored. Unbelieving Israel has been rejected as a nation, in order that the outside world they failed to bless may receive salvation."

21 June

"'Thus says the LORD, who created you, O Jacob, and He who formed you, O Israel: 'Fear not, for I have redeemed you; I have called you by your name; You are Mine..... You are My witnesses,' says the LORD, 'and My servant whom I have chosen, that you may know and believe Me, and understand that I am He. Before Me there was no God formed, nor shall there be after Me.'"
(Isa 43:1,10)

The atheist who compares Bible prophecy with the history of Israel is confounded, and must either repent and acknowledge his Creator or remain a fool – "The fool has said in his heart, 'There is no God'" (Ps 53:1), and must face the awful eternal consequences, when salvation had been on offer.

If we read Deuteronomy chapters 28 and 30, we see how accurately and in what detail God's warnings for obedience and disobedience, for blessing or cursing, have been fulfilled for three and a half thousand years. Not all of Israel's history can been authenticated by contemporary secular records, but most can be. The sceptics of former years have progressively been proved wrong by Babylonian, Persian and other ancient records written after the fulfilment of proven prior prophecies.

The 721 BC exile of the Northern tribes has yet to be reversed; but it will be. The 70 AD exile of the reminder has been only partly reversed, but it will be: "Fear not, for I am with you; I will bring your descendants from the east, And gather you from the west; I will say to the north, 'Give them up!' and to the south, 'Do not keep them back!' Bring My sons from afar, and My daughters from the ends of the earth" (Isa 43:5-6). No other exiled nation has survived as such for more than two or three generations. But Israel has survived for hundreds, while its language has astonishingly been resurrected as promised. The greater number of Nobel laureates than from any other race is typical, as is their 20th Century military survival against overwhelming odds. The present situation of the partially restored nation is precisely what one would expect from Scripture, with the very alliances of future invading states listed by name in Ezekiel. More atheists among Jews than among most other races has been anticipated, as has their final future Holocaust. Indeed, they are God's witnesses, in spite of themselves.

Seven opened seals of Revelation

22 June

*"I am He who lives, and was dead, and behold, I am alive
forevermore. Amen. And I have the keys of Hades and of Death.
Write the things which you have seen, and the things which are,
and the things which will take place after this."* (Rev 1:18-19)

We have already seen in Revelation chapters 2 and 3 the "things
that are" in seven actual, but also typical, Church Age congregations
or assemblies. We have noted that, thereafter, John was caught up
in spirit to Heaven to see and record for us things which will take
place after this, beginning with the newly-raptured Church. We
have seen how the "Lamb as it had been slain" will alone be found
worthy to open the seals of a scroll, which will inaugurate on earth
the Tribulation Period. As we proceed through Revelation, we find
that there are to be three successive series of judgments, namely
opened seals, trumpet blasts and emptied bowls of God's wrath,
followed by Christ's Return in Power at the Battle of Armageddon,
defeating Satan's demonically-led armies and incarcerating Satan
himself, thus preparing for the new world order of the Millennium.
There are other important visionary scenes of happenings and
personalities which apply to all or part of the period between the
Rapture and Christ's Return.

When the Lord Jesus Christ Himself has graciously revealed so
much, we dare not ignore or dismiss as too difficult these visionary
prophecies of the future – what accelerating signs of the times
suggest may start very soon indeed. I learned at school that the
world's population was approximately two thousand million; recently
it surpassed seven thousand million! We are approaching the state
where succeeding judgments will render this overcrowded world
barely habitable. So, as believers look up, awaiting our ever nearing
redemption, we must prayerfully study Revelation and other end-
time passages. But let us also tread carefully, because the only
chronological data we are given between the Rapture and the start
of the Millennium is, as we found in Daniel 9:27, the seven years of
a covenant, imposed by Satan's man, not by God, though within His
permissive will, and divided into two three-and-a-half year periods.
Those saved after the Rapture are likely to know exactly how they fit
into the revealed programme.

23 June

"Now I saw when the Lamb opened one of the seals; and I heard one of the four living creatures saying with a voice like thunder, 'Come and see.' And I looked, and behold, a white horse. He who sat on it had a bow; and a crown was given to him, and he went out conquering and to conquer." (Rev 6:1-2)

This is the first of the celebrated 'Horsemen of the Apocalypse', which have captured the imagination of film makers and others. We remember that it is Christ who opens the seals and permits the powers on earth to do their worst with fateful consequences. It seems that, in the seals, God is exercising His permissive will, allowing mankind to bring judgments upon himself, in contrast to the later direct intervention of the Trumpet and Bowls of Wrath judgments. John Heading appropriately entitles his section on the seven seals as "God's judgments on moral and social apostasy". The horsemen should not all be thought of as personalities, though the first does indeed depict the false or Anti-Christ, whom Satan will have primed to take on progressively a global leadership role, from his power base of a Revived Roman Empire, as Daniel 9:26 indicates, presumably with its capital in Europe.

Despite the white horse, the first rider is emphatically not Christ, though he will strive for recognition as the saviour of a world facing potential chaos. His lesser crown or *stephanos* is awarded by men, not by God. He is portrayed with no short-range sword or medium-range spear, but only a long-range arrowless bow, suggesting that he is to come to international power through force of personality and persuasion, rather than by open warfare. Such is the world-wide fear of open warfare using nuclear, biological, chemical and cybernetic weaponry, that, with Satan's personal backing, any promising alternative will be welcomed, whatever the moral and social cost.

In 1920 Henry Ironside perceptively remarked: "It will be man's last effort to bring in a reign of order and peace while Christ is still rejected. It will be the world's greatest attempt to pull things together after the church is gone. It will be the devil's cunning scheme for bringing in a mock millennium without Christ." In the intervening years the cry has increasingly been: "Let us break Their bonds in pieces and cast away Their cords from us" (Ps 2:3).

24 June

"When He opened the second seal, I heard the second living creature saying, 'Come and see.' Another horse, fiery red, went out. And it was granted to the one who sat on it to take peace from the earth, and that people should kill one another; and there was given to him a great sword." (Rev 6:3-4)

The rider of the white horse will be unable to restrain the loosing of the second. The brief attempt of the Man of Sin to maintain peace with his iron rule is doomed to failure: "For when they say, 'Peace and safety!' then sudden destruction comes upon them, as labour pains upon a pregnant woman. And they shall not escape" (I Thess 5:3).

Now at this point we cannot point to specific prophesied wars, but we know from Matthew 24:7-8 that this and the following seals are to be opened during the three and a half years before the Great Tribulation begins. "For nation will rise against nation, and kingdom against kingdom. And there will be famines, pestilences, and earthquakes in various places. All these are **the beginning** of sorrows."

There will be endless scope for wars, riots, class warfare, criminal violence and local and family strife. No particular geographical area is specified. The very colour of the horse is suggestive. New converts to Christ may expect to be martyred even at this stage. It may be that the abortive invasion of Israel by Russia, Iran, Libya and other less clearly identified allied nations described in Ezekiel 38 and 39 will take place fairly soon after the Rapture, and following the opening of the second seal. We look at this in more detail later, when we review Ezekiel, but have to agree with other commentators that God has deliberately left the precise timing enigmatically questionable. It may even occur *before* the Rapture, but must never be thought of as a prerequisite. When it occurs, with invader destroying fellow-invader and devastating meteorological phenomena, Israel will not have to lift a finger, except to bury invaders. It will be a massive demonstration of God's righteous fury, and one of the mightiest calls ever to the world, to repent and turn to Him. Whatever the timing of this invasion, God is going to furnish unprecedented evidence of His power at a time when Satan is challenging in a way unknown since the Flood.

25 June

*"When He opened the third seal, I heard the third living creature
say, 'Come and see.' So I looked, and behold, a black horse,
and he who sat on it had a pair of scales in his hand. And I heard
a voice in the midst of the four living creatures saying,'A quart of
wheat for a denarius, and three quarts of barley for a denarius; and
do not harm the oil and the wine.'"* (Rev 6:5-6)

Here we have the inevitable economic consequences of war, namely famine and inflation. It is a remarkable reflection of the trends of modern society, because the luxury items which only the rich and powerful can afford are to be the least affected, whereas the staple cereals are to become so scarce that what was, at the time of writing, a day's pay will buy what amounts to approximately an eighth of a staple diet, barely sufficient for survival. And one wonders about the children and elderly, unable to do a day's work. By the sixth seal no class will be exempt.

Famine following war has been the norm throughout history. What is to be different, is that this has to be global, and is sanctioned by Heaven. Using one's wealth and influence to emigrate to a more favourable area will no longer be an option. The voice of one of the four angelic beings around the Divine throne makes the announcement of a further step in bringing humankind to a decision point during the mercifully short Beginning of Sorrows, by the end of which, as the Great Tribulation takes effect, it will be too late to change one's mind.

We rarely notice how often in the present age God delivers people from the natural consequences of folly, carelessness, disobedience and sometimes sin. Often society as a whole benefits from the presence of God's people. The "salt of the earth", one of the titles of God's people, helps to keep society from going rotten. But, following the Rapture, the world will be under a different regime, when God will allow those who reject Christ to bear the full consequences. When, a little later, they have either to repent or to accept Satan's Mark of the Beast, they will have the experiences of the Beginning of Sorrows to look back upon, and to weigh up before making calculated responses.

26 June

"When He opened the fourth seal, I heard the voice of the fourth living creature saying, 'Come and see.' So I looked, and behold, a pale horse. And the name of him who sat on it was Death, and Hades followed with him. And power was given to them over a fourth of the earth, to kill with sword, with hunger, with death, and by the beasts of the earth." (Rev 6:7-8)

The horse here is of a livid greenish colour, almost corpse-like. The accumulated consequences of the first three seals seem to combine to mark the progress of the Beginning of Sorrows, to the point where even Satan's human representative, the Man of Sin, cannot halt the plummeting state of the earth. Death and Hades are linked, so this refers exclusively to the unsaved, whose souls go immediately to Hades; such will be the constant peril of death, that the fear of Hades will grip those on earth. The complacency that allows true atheism to survive will have gone.

There are two ways to interpret the "fourth part of the earth". One is that only a quarter of the globe will be affected, the quarter which is the Beast's or Antichrist's power base, the Mediterranean centred Revived Roman Empire, and its latter day prince of the empire which destroyed Jerusalem and exiled the Jews in AD 70. The alternative, and probably more likely explanation, is that a quarter of humankind will perish at this stage.

We have already seen under the previous two opened seals the effects of war and famine; added to these is now "death", which, in similar contexts, seems to indicate disease leading to death. Already modern medicine with all its wonderful remedies and cures is doing little more than holding the tide of threatening new diseases and epidemics. A very recent phenomenon is that of our health services, even in peace time, no longer being able to cope – a sign of the times? When war breaks out and famine sets in, hospitals are stretched   to breaking point, and who knows what new forms of disease may arise? The Greek for 'beast' here is *therion*, or wild beast including reptiles, and is also used (as in Revelation 13 etc) of Satan's two chief emissaries. In most modern societies wild animals, snakes and so on are not seen as major threats. Only time will tell.

27 June

"When He opened the fifth seal, I saw under the altar the souls of those who had been slain for the word of God and for the testimony which they held. And they cried with a loud voice, saying, 'How long, O Lord, holy and true, until You judge and avenge our blood on those who dwell on the earth?' Then a white robe was given to each of them; and it was said to them that they should rest a little while longer, until both the number of their fellow servants and their brethren, who would be killed as they were, was completed." (Rev 6:9-11)

With this seal our attention is drawn to something in Heaven, which will have resulted from events on earth. It tells us much about the new vitriolic anti-Christian, anti-God character of the regime set up under the first seal. The souls seen here are of those who will be saved and then martyred for their faith after the Rapture. Their bodies will remain on earth, collectively awaiting their resurrection, which will not take place until Christ's Return, when the perpetrators will be destroyed. But individually each soul and spirit will be caught up to Heaven at death, with each being seen as an accepted sacrifice, hence the position relative to the heavenly altar.

It is the soul which enquires "How long?", addressing Christ by the rare title of *despotes*, the One with supreme authority. Further confirmation that these souls are not from the Church Age is the fact that they are calling for vengeance, as Old Testament saints might have done. In the Church we are told: "But I say to you, love your enemies, bless those who curse you, do good to those who hate you, and pray for those who spitefully use you and persecute you" (Matt 5:44).

Their plea will be answered, firstly by the granting of white robes and secondly by being told to rest a little longer, until their surviving brethren are similarly martyred. In the light of eternity, we will understand better the Divine love and wisdom which has planned, guided, recognised and rewarded. These robes are not indicative of their having washed their robes in the blood of the Lamb, which is how they will have gained Heaven in the first place; rather they seem to be a Divine acknowledgement of their sacrifice and victory.

28 June

*"I looked when He opened the sixth seal, and behold, there was a great earthquake; and the sun became black **as** sackcloth of hair, and the moon became **like** blood. And the stars of heaven fell to the earth, as a fig tree drops its late figs when it is shaken by a mighty wind. Then the sky receded as a scroll when it is rolled up, and every mountain and island was moved out of its place."* (Rev 6:12-14)

John records how the sun and moon and other phenomena are to appear to people on earth. This is largely about God-inspired terror to the unbelieving world and is to be taken literally, not allegorically. What follows the opening of the sixth seal is so portentous that it cannot be overlooked, especially when we recall that each seal is opened by the Lamb of God Himself. At first sight it seems to be a description of the end of the world; but it isn't; much has to follow even before the Lord's Return. Some futurist commentators are probably too eager to give a precise date within the Tribulation Period, others feel that, although the Seals, Trumpets and Bowls of Wrath start sequentially, they all terminate at the Lord's Return. However most simply place this event at or about the start of the Great Tribulation, and distinguish this earthquake from the utterly disastrous one described in chapter 16:18. Whether seismologists can explain earthquakes is unimportant here. God is to use His natural processes at precisely the right time and with the intensity which He dictates for the appropriate result.

Later in Revelation we will see more of what are described as stars falling. Again, what is important to realise is that, whether they are comets, asteroids or simply man-made satellites, the spectacle, as vividly described in this passage, will be petrifying, and probably visible all over the inhabited world. Such happenings have been anticipated by alarmed learned specialists, based upon scientific observation.

As for the sky being seen by John to roll up, all the worst fears of environmentalists, conservationists, climatologists and meteorologists are to be exceeded. If this is only roughly at the point where the Beginning of Sorrows gives way to the Great Tribulation, God is evidently going to allow a degree of recovery, or life during the following three and a half years would be impossible.

29 June

"And the kings of the earth, the great men, the rich men, the commanders, the mighty men, every slave and every free man, hid themselves in the caves and in the rocks of the mountains, and said to the mountains and rocks, 'Fall on us and hide us from the face of Him who sits on the throne and from the wrath of the Lamb! For the great day of His wrath has come, and who is able to stand?'" (Rev 6:15-17)

We are reminded of Jesus' Olivet Discourse: "And there will be signs in the sun, in the moon, and in the stars; and on the earth distress of nations, with perplexity, the sea and the waves roaring; men's hearts failing them from fear and the expectation of those things which are coming on the earth, for the powers of heaven will be shaken" (Lk 21:25-26).

Precisely how people of every rank and class are suddenly to become so intensely aware of God the Father and Son we are not told. It may or may not be visionary, but it will be effective. We know from elsewhere in Revelation that this is about the time when a furious Devil will be cast out of Heaven, and his two Beasts, who have attempted to be seen as benign and appealing alternatives to a holy God, will reveal themselves in their true Satanic colours, demanding worship, and allegiance to their master. A way to "stand" will be provided, as we will be reminded over the next two days, but those who have already deliberately set themselves against the Lamb will be so petrified that they will seek to hide from His face in the earth, as far as possible from the heavenly throne.

Already the signs of the times indicate that the "great day of His wrath" is becoming ever closer, even although other things, notably the Rapture, must come first. Even some who call themselves Christians scoff at both the Rapture and the Day of Wrath and publicly undermine the authority of the Bible. Whatever men may conclude at that awful time, they are at last to be left in no doubt that this, and what is to follow under the Trumpets and Bowls of Wrath, are conscious acts of God, who, to challenge a fallen world, is utilising visibly His own wonderfully created natural laws.

30 June

"'Do not harm the earth, the sea, or the trees till we have sealed the servants of our God on their foreheads.' And I heard the number of those who were sealed. One hundred and forty-four thousand of all the tribes of the children of Israel were sealed."
(Rev 7:3-4)

Before the seventh seal is opened we are given a parenthetical glimpse ahead at the Gospel and its preachers in that otherwise dreadful future period. God the Holy Spirit has recorded a list of 144,000 carefully identified Jews. God has a blessed mission for these sealed Jews in that final 'week of years', which, as we saw in Daniel 9:24, has been reserved for Daniel's people. God is not going to allow an evangelisation vacuum or absence of witnesses after the Rapture of the Church. Since Jesus was rejected by His City and nation, the Church has filled the vacuum left by the side-lined Jews. But the Church is to be taken to Heaven just before the storm breaks. So witnessing Jews, genuine faithful, spiritual remnant Jews, are going to do what their ancestors failed to do effectively nearly two thousand years ago. They are going to be God's sealed witnesses.

Now we are not specifically told that these are evangelists, but they are evidently sealed for some purpose other than merely protection, and, immediately after their tribes are listed, we read of the great crowd of Tribulation saints, evidently saved after the Rapture. We return to these tomorrow. Even today there are tens of thousands of Orthodox Jews who are steeped in the Old Testament Scriptures, just as Paul was nearly two thousand years ago. Like Paul, they will be (and perhaps already are) zealous for God, but blind to the identity of their Messiah, until God's Holy Spirit comes upon them with power, as with Paul (Acts 9:17-18, 20). Just as long ago Saul of Tarsus became the Apostle Paul in an instant, so, probably very soon after the Rapture, God will seal His witnesses – He is going to need them to preach the Gospel of the Kingdom throughout the whole world (Matthew 24:14). Consider the impact of 144,000 Spirit-filled witnesses dispersed world-wide under Divine control. Going roughly by present population statistics, this would leave around twelve hundred Wesleys or Spurgeons for Great Britain and around five thousand Moodies or Grahams for the United States!

1 July

"After these things I looked, and behold, a great multitude which no one could number, of all nations, tribes, peoples, and tongues, standing before the throne and before the Lamb, clothed with white robes, with palm branches in their hands, and crying out with a loud voice, saying, 'Salvation belongs to our God who sits on the throne, and to the Lamb!'" (Rev 7:9-10)

This follows the identifying of the 144,000. These are their converts; some may have been saved through Bibles and literature left behind at the Rapture, but most will have been reached by these sealed witnesses. John is evidently puzzled by the multitude's identity, as, while, like the Church, they are washed in the blood of the Lamb, sharing a common salvation, they have certain distinguishing features. They are said to be an innumerable company, so it is not us for to attempt to quantify them! However, as a great many, both believers and unbelievers, will have already perished under the Seals and before the Great Tribulation, we are able to appreciate the mercy of God in this multitude. It is reasonable to assume that *proportionately* as many are to be saved after the Church Age as during it. The word "apocalypse" (meaning "revelation") may have taken on purely negative connotations in the secular world, but, in eternity, countless millions will be able to look back at this time and bless God.

"These are the ones who **come** out of the great tribulation, and washed their robes and made them white in the blood of the Lamb" (Rev 7:14), or literally, "out of tribulation, the great one", confirming that this is that which Jesus foretold (Matt 24:21). The "came" in the AV/KJV is wrong. They had not already "come" at this point before the seventh seal. Their position before the throne, the palm branches, the suffering and deprivation from which they are assured of freedom henceforth, and the heavenly roles they are promised, all distinguish them: "They are before the throne of God, and serve Him day and night in His temple. And He who sits on the throne will dwell among them. They shall neither hunger anymore nor thirst anymore; the sun shall not strike them, nor any heat" (7:15-16).

Only after this encouraging interlude is the seventh seal opened, leading to the sounding of the Trumpets. We will leave this to a later section.

Practical prophecies in the Psalms

2 July

*"Blessed is the man who walks not in the counsel of the ungodly, nor stands in the path of sinners, nor sits in the seat of the scornful..... **He shall be like a tree** planted by the rivers of water, that brings forth its fruit in its season, whose leaf also shall not wither; and **whatever he does shall prosper.**"* (Ps 1:1, 3)

We have looked at some of the great Messianic psalms, and others concentrating on long-term fulfilment. Now we turn to a few which apply to everyday life, where fulfilment can be on-going. Many of them, like Psalm 1, are conditional. They are in no way less reliable, but we, for our part, must fulfil the conditions.

Some translations replace "blessed" with "happy"; but it can mean rather more than happy when God is the One who blesses. In fact, it is more often the greater who blesses the lesser, as here. The blessings come upon those who, on life's journey, press on, and do not linger where sinners could distract, or make themselves comfortable where scoffers scorn the things of God.

Verse 2 tells of their delighting in the law of the Lord, that which modern society is ever less willing to do, thus hastening judgment. The blessed person hides God's word in the heart and meditates on it day and night. Without modern drugs, sleeplessness was probably at least as prevalent in the Psalmist's day as nowadays. But there is much evidence in Scripture of people having learned passages by heart, to meditate upon them later. The person blessed by God is beautifully described, in a way more vivid to dwellers in the Middle East than to those in our Northern climes. A tree planted by the water puts down deep roots and draws up the moisture, making it more attractive to look at, more resistant to wind, and, above all, more fruitful. Jesus frequently made reference to our bearing fruit – it is a mark of blessedness. The blessedness, seen in the light of the New Testament, is a step beyond the strong consolation which we have through having in the first place "fled for refuge to lay hold of the hope set before us..... an anchor of the soul, both sure and steadfast" (see Hebrews 6:18-19). All believers are saved, but some are more blessed than others, thanks to more godly conduct.

3 July

*"The ungodly are not so, but are like the chaff which the wind drives away. Therefore the ungodly **shall not stand** in the judgment, **nor sinners** in the congregation of the righteous."*
(Ps 1:4-5)

Many sermons and even commentaries on Psalm 1 are quick to expand on the delightful opening verses, but slow to mention these closing verses. However this contrast between the righteous and unrighteous is a common sequence in the Psalms, and must be respected, to give us a balanced insight into God's dealings with humankind. The secular world has the opposite tendency, that of concentrating cynically on the judgmental aspect of our faith and neglecting the positive. While God knows who will or will not be saved, our duty is to preach that, while life shall last, the way leading to eternal life is open to all. Both cases are conditional. We cannot expect blessing without obedience. The unbeliever is judged for his ungodliness, his ignoring the reasonable demands of his Creator. Eventually all must appear before their Creator, but not all will be able to stand. The illustration of chaff driven by the wind contrasts with the security the believer has in Christ.

Note that the Psalmist refers to the "ungodly", rendered the "wicked" by Darby, the ASV and RSV. The Hebrew word denotes those who have done wrong, are living in sin and intent on continuing to do wrong (WE Vine). Evangelicals avoid categorising degrees of wickedness, because ultimately people are either saved or unsaved; there is no middle ground. However Jesus Christ Himself on several occasions talked about degrees of eternal punishment – more or less tolerable, and it is wise to bear this in mind as we present a just God in our preaching. The Psalmist's comments seem to be directed against those who had deliberately spurned and defied God. Joel (1:12) presents a vivid picture of those who were once potentially right with God, but who have neglected to trust Him. It is a marked contrast with the fruitfulness of the Spirit-filled believer: "The vine has dried up, and the fig tree has withered; the pomegranate tree, the palm tree also, and the apple tree - All the trees of the field are withered; surely joy has withered away from the sons of men."

4 July

*"I will praise You, O LORD, with my whole heart; I will tell of all Your marvellous works. I will be glad and rejoice in You; I will sing praise to Your name, O Most High. When my enemies turn back, **they shall fall and perish at Your presence**.... You have blotted out their name forever and ever. O enemy, destructions are finished forever! And you have destroyed cities; Even their memory has perished. But **the LORD shall endure forever**; He has prepared His throne for judgment."* (Ps 9:1-3,5-7)

Many books of Bible readings make much of the Psalms, but we are covering mainly prophetic aspects. We go through a few sequentially rather than thematically. This is one of the many Psalms of David where he draws on his own experience; it is tried and tested by a man whom God loved and honoured. The Septuagint treats it and Psalm 10 as a single unit, because of its arrangement and continuity. David was often the victim of undeserved jealousy and hatred, and sometimes had to take refuge. In some parts of the world Christians are regularly subjected to such treatment, and any one of us may experience such trials. David got his priorities right; he started with praise, not petition. It came naturally to him, rather than as a formula which he hoped would work. It should still be natural to any believer, whatever our circumstances. Drawing the attention of our adversaries to our God's mighty works gives us an impregnable foundation. Jim Flanigan writes: "By that name will Jehovah be known in that day when He reigns unchallenged and supreme in kingdom splendour. But David recognises this supremacy already and ascribes praise accordingly." Furthermore, David recognises, as we should, that this One is on our side, maintaining our cause. David, as a man of faith, anticipates the ultimate victories, but, even in his own varied experience and tribulations in this life, he had witnessed the evidence.

The contrast between the impermanence of mortal man and the permanence of God is so overwhelming, that we either put our confidence in His saving and keeping power or we try to convince ourselves that there is "no one out there", and hope for the best. A universe without order, without laws would be chaotic. Scientists keep discovering ancient laws and formulae; the more we know, the greater our responsibility.

5 July

*"The LORD is my shepherd; **I shall not want.** He makes me to lie down in green pastures; He leads me beside the still waters. He restores my soul; He leads me in the paths of righteousness for His name's sake. Yea, though I walk through the valley of the shadow of death, **I will fear no evil**; For You are with me; Your rod and Your staff, they comfort me. You prepare a table before me in the presence of my enemies; You anoint my head with oil; my cup runs over. **Surely goodness and mercy shall follow** me all the days of my life; and **I will dwell in the house of the LORD** forever."*
(Ps 23:1-6)

In these Psalm readings I am highlighting those words which in English clearly imply the future. Sometimes the future is implied in the Hebrew elsewhere. Campbell Morgan summarises it thus: "The Lord is my Shepherd, I shall not want; the Lord is my Guide, I shall be rightly led; the Lord is my King, I shall reach His palace by and by." Both the present and the future are catered for. There are believers who actually feel guilty when we are made to lie down in green pastures, and we forget who it is who is leading us by the still waters - a powerful image in arid regions. "Come ye apart and rest while" were the words of a compassionate and caring Saviour

The well-known metrical version reads, "In death's dark vale I fear no ill", which explains its popularity at funeral services. But the valley of the shadow of death is something which David had already encountered, and found to be less oppressive through his Lord's presence throughout. Bunyan was correct in putting Christian's 'Valley of the Shadow' episode quite early in his pilgrimage. In actual death, with our soul and spirit safe in the Father's house and our body silent in the grave, we are beyond any attacks from the powers of darkness. But, in this life, we are not immune and need His presence to say, "Begone, foul fiend!"

As long as life lasts in this fallen world we are in the presence of enemies. But the Lord it is who furnishes tables, anoints heads and fills cups to overflowing. Believers' lives which reflect a calm consciousness of this Divine Presence cannot fail to impress.

6 July

*"The LORD is my light and my salvation; **whom shall I fear**? The LORD is the strength of my life; of whom shall I be afraid? When the wicked came against me to eat up my flesh, my enemies and foes, they stumbled and fell. Though an army may encamp against me, **my heart shall not fear**; though war should rise against me, **in this I will be confident**. One thing I have desired of the LORD, that will I seek: **that I may dwell in the house of the LORD** all the days of my life, to behold the beauty of the LORD, and to inquire in His temple."* (Ps 27:1-4)

This is like the 23rd Psalm in some respects, although here other experience comes into play. With neither light nor salvation we would have cause to fear. Countless millions currently have neither, and blame everybody but themselves. Who would be a politician?

David had challenged earthly armies. By defying their champion, Goliath, he had effectively taken on a nation: "Then David said to the Philistine, 'You come to me with a sword, with a spear, and with a javelin. But I come to you in the name of the LORD of hosts, the God of the armies of Israel, whom you have defied. This day the LORD will deliver you into my hand, and I will strike you and take your head from you.... that all the earth may know that there is a God in Israel.'" (I Sam 17:45-46). Later in this psalm David's confidence seems to wane somewhat, but rallies at the end. Perhaps we have had similar experiences. We depend upon the Lord in critical situations, but not when things calm down and the threat diminishes.

John Heading mentions that the last phrase of our reading should probably be "look with pleasure upon his temple." Even although it was still only a tabernacle with a courtyard in David's day, he knew that it was the place where the Ark of the Covenant was kept, the place of the offerings, the place where God chose to meet with His people, the place with the altars. For David, being permanently there was impossible; he was the king, not the High Priest! The desire was appropriate, but God's service often calls us to meet for worship and fellowship, and then to return to the battlefield.

7 July

*"Out of Zion, the perfection of beauty, **God will shine forth. Our
God shall come, and shall not keep silent;** a fire shall devour
before Him, and it shall be very tempestuous all around Him.....
Offer to God thanksgiving, and pay your vows to the Most High.
Call upon Me in the day of trouble; **I will deliver you, and you
shall glorify Me**."* (Ps 50:2-3,14-15)

Many Psalms start by looking to the immediate future, move to
the intermediate future and culminate in the Millennium. Here the
sequence is reversed, and we are taken to Messiah's Second
Coming, which is first to the Mount of Olives outside Jerusalem
(Zechariah 14:4 etc). The beauty is attributed to Zion, the place of
His Shekinah glory when He returns from the heavenly Zion. The
shining forth is to be accompanied by fire and tempest, consistent
with other Return in Power passages.

Some assume that He has been keeping silent down through the
centuries, this is not so, but **then** all will be compelled to listen. We
are in an intermediate state: "God, who at various times and in various
ways spoke in time past to the fathers by the prophets, has in these
last days spoken to us by His Son, whom He has appointed heir of all
things, through whom also He made the worlds" (Heb 1:1-2).

The scene is one of judgment of His own, not in this case of the
world at large, though the world is called to witness it. It is primarily
of course about Israel. The Pastoral Epistles give the prior New
Testament aspects: "For the time has come for judgment to begin at
the house of God; and if it begins with us first, what will be the end
of those who do not obey the gospel of God?" (I Pet 4:17).

In the intermediate verses God states that He will not reject Israel's
sacrifices, but reminds them that "the cattle on a thousand hills" are
His, and that at best they only give back what is His. The very fact that
we are disciplined, and therefore not exempt from trouble, and that
God disciplines those whom He loves, should give us confidence to
call upon Him and be delivered. When we gladly yield to Him, even
in adversity, and demonstrate this to the world, we bring glory to His
Name.

8 July

*"Purge me with hyssop, and **I shall be clean**; Wash me, and **I shall be whiter than snow**. Make me hear joy and gladness, that the bones You have broken may rejoice."* (Ps 51:7-8)

The background to this Psalm and this plea is well known. We read in 2nd Samuel 11 how David remained in Jerusalem and sent Joab out in command of the army, with Uriah the Hittite as one of his officers. David was attracted by Uriah's beautiful wife, committed adultery with her and made her pregnant. David then committed the greater sin, by ordering Joab to put Uriah in a position in battle where he was bound to be slain. What happened thereafter is important, and tells us much about God's dealings with the truly penitent. He sent the prophet Nathan to David, describing his action in the form of a parable. When David's wrath rose, Nathan declared: "You are the man!" and summarised the magnitude of the crime, in view of how God had so blessed David.

David did not attempt to defend himself: "'I have sinned against the LORD.' And Nathan said to David, 'The LORD also has put away your sin; you shall not die.'" (12:13). But David wanted assurance of forgiveness, hence the above classic prayer. The shrub hyssop had been used to apply the blood of the Passover lamb at the Exodus. David needed to anticipate: "'Come now, and let us reason together,' says the LORD, 'Though your sins are like scarlet, They shall be as white as snow; though they are red like crimson, they shall be as wool'" (Isa 1:18). His joy and gladness were restored, the spiritual crushing he had experienced was lifted, and some of his finest psalms were written thereafter.

So often, although our salvation remains intact, there is a temporal price to pay, sometime a large one: "Now therefore, the sword shall never depart from your house, because you have despised Me, and have taken the wife of Uriah the Hittite to be your wife" (12:10). This was fulfilled in subsequent history. "Because by this deed you have given great occasion to the enemies of the LORD to blaspheme, the child also who is born to you shall surely die" (12:14). When we sin, our Saviour's name may be blasphemed. It is wonderful to have sins forgiven, but more wonderful never to have committed them.

9 July

"Return, we beseech You, O God of hosts; Look down from heaven and see, and visit this vine and the vineyard which Your right hand has planted, and the branch that You made strong for Yourself..... **Then we will not turn back from You; revive us, and we will call upon Your name.** *restore us, O LORD God of hosts;* **cause Your face to shine, and we shall be saved!"** (Ps 80:14-15,18-19)

Now this was written about Israel, whose ultimate revival lies ahead; we have already seen that the vine illustrates Israel past. In Israel of old there were no revivals in the Northern Kingdom. Their first king, Jeroboam I, "asked advice, made two calves of gold, and said to the people, 'It is too much for you to go up to Jerusalem. Here are your gods, O Israel, which brought you up from the land of Egypt!'" (I Kings 12:28). As a nation they had thus quickly come to the point of no return, though many individuals remained loyal to God, as Elijah later discovered. The Southern Kingdom had revivals under Jehoshaphat, Hezekiah and Joash, though not permanent enough to halt eventual exile; Habakkuk could pray: "O LORD, I have heard Your speech and was afraid; O LORD, revive Your work in the midst of the years! In the midst of the years make it known; in wrath remember mercy" (3:2).

However, provided we recognise dispensational differences, we find invaluable principles which can be applied to New Testament congregations. We can sense the sadness of God "looking down from heaven" upon some of our congregations. In fact, as Jim Flanigan says, God was asked to return, to look down, to behold and to visit; it is a sequence which cannot be reversed, even if we may not have reached the Laodicean point of being a church in which He is no longer present. This prayer was for restoration as well as revival. One wonders how many churches, having experienced a brief revival, have never been fully restored. AE Phillips writes: "His prayer is for restoration to fruitfulness and to be able to sense afresh the glory and presence of God." Jesus said: "I chose you and appointed you that you should go and bear fruit, and that your fruit should **remain**, that whatever you ask the Father in My name He may give you" (Jn 15:16).

10 July

"He who dwells in the secret place of the Most High shall abide under the shadow of the Almighty. I will say of the LORD, 'He is my refuge and my fortress; My God, in Him I will trust.' Surely He shall deliver you from the snare of the fowler and from the perilous pestilence. He shall cover you with His feathers, and under His wings you shall take refuge; His truth shall be your shield and buckler. You shall not be afraid of the terror by night, nor of the arrow that flies by day, nor of the pestilence that walks in darkness, nor of the destruction that lays waste at noonday." (Ps 91:1-6)

What an incredibly reassuring statement for fragile humanity is found in these opening words, and what a declaration of infinite authority supports it! What safer place can there be in the universe than beneath the shadow of the Almighty? The tenderness of the mother bird brooding over her nestlings is there; but so is the protection of the invincible warrior.

Forty years ago I was billeted for three months in an ancient Gloucestershire priory which was reputed to be haunted. I do not believe in ghosts as the spirits of deceased people, but recognise that spiritual powers of darkness may associate themselves with certain locations. I deposited my belongings and knelt to pray, committing my situation to the Lord. When I arose I noticed that my Bible was lying open on the table, and these were the first words that I read! No, the Bible did not open magically; I must have put it down like that unconsciously but providentially. And no, I cannot regale readers with a host of similar experiences. That one was enough to give me perfect peace for the rest of my stay. Most believers can recount at least one or two such experiences.

This is the psalm that Satan dared to quote when tempting Jesus in the wilderness: "'For it is written: 'He shall give His angels charge over you, to keep you,' and, 'In their hands they shall bear you up, lest you dash your foot against a stone.'" (Lk 4:10-11). The promise in fact had been made only for all who "dwell in the secret place of the Most High", as well as for our Saviour whilst on earth. Let us not stray from such refuge.

11 July

*"LORD, how long will the wicked, How long will the wicked triumph?..... For the **LORD will not cast off His people, nor will He forsake His inheritance.**"* (Ps 94:3,14)

When we looked at the Fifth Seal of Revelation, we saw the souls of the Tribulation martyrs calling for vengeance, and noted that this was more typical of the Old Testament than the New. Jim Flanigan comments: "It is important to note the difference between revenge and vengeance. It has been said that revenge is an act of passion, and vengeance is an act of justice." Perhaps the greatest contrast here is in the patience and longsuffering of God, and the impatience and frustration of believers. It is another of those many cases where we will have to wait to eternity for a full answer. But even now we can stop and consider how any one of us might have suffered had God listened to those who had earlier been calling for vengeance. The temporary "triumph" of the wicked may have been allowing some of those wicked time to repent.

In the meantime, God is very much aware of His own, and of their crying to Him to "shine forth" as the God of vengeance, if that is what they are doing; although, as we remarked earlier, the Church's commission does not provide for such pleading. As the psalm progresses (verse 12), we find that God's timing allows for His own to be instructed and chastised, both marks of His care and love, resulting in blessing and that ultimate fruitfulness which merits eternal rewards.

Then we come to today's prophecy, about the Lord not casting off His people, or forsaking His inheritance. It is almost as if we were having to being reminded that God is capable of bearing in mind two opposite priorities. When we looked at Job 23, where the oppressor was Satan himself, rather than unspecified wicked, he could say of God: "But He knows the way that I take; When He has tested me, I shall come forth as gold" (v 10). Each child of God should be familiar with the permissive will of God, which never fails to remember His people, His inheritance. That expression "His inheritance" reminds us of the price He paid for us: "Since you were precious in My sight, You have been honoured, and I have loved you" (Isa 43:4).

12 July

*"The LORD is merciful and gracious, slow to anger, and abounding in mercy. **He will not always strive with us, nor will He keep His anger forever.**"* (Ps 103:8-9)

The whole of this Psalm is a song of praise, without a single request. There is a danger that, when we pray and remind God of His wondrous attributes, we almost try to manipulate Him, reminding Him of promises which He most certainly has never forgotten! There is nothing of this in Psalm 103. It opens with the psalmist's spirit speaking to his soul: "Bless the LORD, O my soul; And all that is within me, bless His holy name! Bless the LORD, O my soul, and forget not all His benefits (vv1-2). It is we, not He, who can be forgetful. Soon the singer's whole being is praising God. However, when praise is purely physical, it can be almost indistinguishable from the popular culture of the world. We must beware.

Today's text is, of course, primarily about Israel, but, bearing in mind that we are under a different covenant, we Gentiles can still claim most of the provisions, plus some others. This is about the character of God. He does anger, but is slow to do so, and He does not nurse that anger, to keep it warm, as the poet said. Those of Israel who feared the Lord were only saved inasmuch as their salvation still had to be accomplished on the Cross. This psalmist is evidently a man of saving faith, and had personally experienced reassurance when he sang: "He has not dealt with us according to our sins, nor punished us according to our iniquities" (verse 10). What he could not know is what we now know, namely the means of salvation to which the law and prophets were pointing.

But in faith he could still claim: "As far as the east is from the west, so far has He removed our transgressions from us. As a father pities his children, so the LORD pities those who fear Him" (vv 12-13). The distance between East and West is infinite, and demonstrates the extent of the effectiveness of our redemption. While our position. as Church saints, is more blessed than that of the Pre-Calvary Old Testament saints, we can still be challenged and even humbled by these men and women of old.

The facts of the Millennium

13 July

"Then I saw an angel coming down from heaven, having the key to the bottomless pit and a great chain in his hand. He laid hold of the dragon, that serpent of old, who is the Devil and Satan, and bound him for a thousand years." (Rev 20:1-2)

'Millennium' simply means a thousand years. There are numerous unconditional, unfulfilled prophecies in both Old and New Testaments which must wait for what has been aptly described as their 'window of opportunity'. Some, of course fit into the Tribulation Period; but others, beautiful, thrilling, glorious prophecies, about earth rather than Heaven, which need neither exaggeration nor understatement, can only find fulfilment in the Millennial 'window'. Since the Fall in Eden, God has been keeping the best till last. In January we looked very briefly at the subject of the Millennium, and we have since then mentioned it frequently in other prophetic contexts. After almost seventy years as a Pre-Millennialist, and having in my varied career and experience visited a wide variety of churches in this and other countries, I am more than ever convinced that the general apathy towards end-time prophecy results in the first place from failing to take Revelation 19 and 20 seriously, and for failing to observe the continuity between them. Pre-Millennialism is the central position, requiring no manipulation of plainly stated facts. It involves the simplest interpretation of Scripture. The widespread Amillennialism, shared with Catholicism, sees the Church Age as the Millennium and no future on earth beyond Christ's Return in Power, as described in Revelation 19. Post-Millennialism teaches that the world is to get better, "fit for the Lord's Return", without any future Great Tribulation. It supposes that most of the dramatic apocalyptic prophecies were fulfilled long ago. In effect they accuse Jesus Christ and the prophets of gross exaggeration.

Those who inserted the chapter divisions a few centuries ago, and incongruously separated the fates of Satan's deputies, the Beast and False Prophet, from that of Satan himself, have done a grave disservice. Satan's fate is separated by a couple of verses in order to explain the different timescale of God's dealing with him. Over the next few days we will see why God has chosen not to consign Satan immediately to Hell, unlike the other two members of the "trinity of evil".

14 July

"All the nations will be gathered before Him, and He will separate them one from another, as a shepherd divides his sheep from the goats. And He will set the sheep on His right hand, but the goats on the left." (Matt 25:32-33)

Back on 13th January we looked at the preceding verse: "When the Son of Man comes in His glory, and all the holy angels with Him, then He will sit on the throne of His glory." We noted the timing, which is immediately following Christ's Return in Power; we also noted that it is not a parable, but a straightforward prophecy. The contrast with the earlier Rapture is too great to avoid confusion. This is about His Coming to earth in glory, as recorded in Revelation 19. We have just seen that the Millennium is predicted to follow that Return, so this is about who is to enter, or not enter, as the case may be, the Millennial kingdom, where the Lord Jesus Christ is at last seen to be King by the world which rejected Him.

Angels are mentioned, because they will be responsible for gathering the surviving population of the world before Christ. Does this seem unlikely or impossible? Consider the situation. The concluding events of the Great Tribulation, of which we will see more when we come to the Bowls of Wrath, will include the following: "There was a great earthquake, such a mighty and great earthquake as had not occurred **since men were on the earth**..... Then every island fled away, and the mountains were not found" (Rev 16:18-20). This earthquake, the final of many Tribulation period quakes, will exceed the Flood! During the Flood ocean floors were uplifted to mountain top levels and vice versa. The entire world was massively reshaped. Christian geologists perceive the answers to so many of the puzzles which face scientists who deny God's ability to act as swiftly and decisively as at creation: "saying, 'Where is the promise of His coming? For since the fathers fell asleep, all things continue as they were from the beginning of creation'" (II Pet 3:4). This is the "dogma of continuity". The world will be so utterly devastated, and the small surviving percentage of the world's former population be so impoverished and helpless, that it will require angels to gather them, probably miraculously, before that throne of glory, briefly allowing the rest of our planet, free of people, to be comprehensively restored.

15 July

"Then the King will say to those on His right hand, 'Come, you blessed of My Father, inherit the kingdom prepared for you from the foundation of the world: for I was hungry and you gave Me food; I was thirsty and you gave Me drink; I was a stranger and you took Me in; I was naked and you clothed Me; I was sick and you visited Me; I was in prison and you came to Me.'" (Matt 25:34-36)

The criteria for separation are quite different from any other judgment described in Scripture. Whether a person will be put on Christ's right hand side for entry to His Kingdom, or His left hand side for rejection, will depend upon how he or she has treated "these My brethren" (vv 40 & 45). Those in one group are described as blessed and righteous (vv 34 & 46); those in the other group are described as cursed, due to be consigned to everlasting punishment (vv 41 & 46). Both groups are to be allowed to question the Judge's decision. The 'sheep' are told: "Inasmuch as you did it to one of the least of **these My brethren**, you did it to Me" (v 40).

Walvoord writes: "In mentioning 'My brethren', He is referring to a third class, neither sheep nor goats, which can only be identified as Israel, the only remaining people who are in contrast to all the Gentiles." William Kelly writes: "But who are the King's brethren? Those whom the Lord will send out before He comes in the glory of the Kingdom; men sent out to announce that He is coming in His kingdom..... The King's 144,000 messengers, shortly before He appears in glory, will go forth preaching the gospel of the kingdom everywhere.... the Lord remembers this, and counts what was done to His messengers as done to Himself."

Thus the "sheep" are those who will support them physically, respond to their message, and be saved. One can imagine how incredibly difficult it will be for "these My brethren", with the double handicap of Jewishness and lack of the Beast's deadly 666 Mark, to survive, if they can neither buy nor sell. They will be almost entirely dependent upon charity – charity which is virtually certain to put the lives of donors and sympathisers at risk of martyrdom from Satan's and the Beast's False Prophet.

16 July

"And the King will answer and say to them, 'Assuredly, I say to you, inasmuch as you did it to one of the least of these My brethren, you did it to Me.' Then He will also say to those on the left hand, 'Depart from Me, you cursed, into the everlasting fire prepared for the devil and his angels.'" (Matt 25:40-41)

Those likened to goats will have had their opportunity to query the Judge's verdict, and are given the explanation recorded above. There will be no appeal. John de Silva writes: "We note here that the unbelievers, the 'goats', are cast into eternal punishment without any scrutiny of their works, since their evil works have already been manifested against 'the least of these' – the Lord's brethren – 'ye did it unto Me.'"

These 'goats', we know from Revelation 14:9-10, will have the double condemnation of the Mark of the Beast, and the penalty of rejecting the Gospel of the Kingdom, which they will have heard preached. They may plead ignorance, but no excuse will be accepted for having rejected their opportunity. They will, from quite early in the Great Tribulation, have been fully aware of the call for repentance and of the angelic confirmation of the message of these sealed missionaries (Revelation 14:6-7). This is the last we hear of the 'goats'; like the Beast and False Prophet, they will not have to wait until the Great White Throne. Kelly writes: "Observe, He does not say, 'Cursed of My Father' answering to 'Blessed of My Father'. God hates putting away. So when the awful moment comes for the curse to be pronounced on these wicked Gentiles, it is simply, 'Depart from Me, ye cursed.'"

It is here that we learn that the Lake of Fire is prepared not for humans, but for the Devil and his angels (verse 41), but that humans can and will occupy it along with those for whom it is prepared. It is here that Jesus adds His personal testimony, that it is everlasting (verses 41 and 46). "JWs" who come to your door think they know better than Christ. These are clear statements, not parables, but plainly stated by the One who, in love, was about to lay down His life for the 'whosoever'. Is the awful cost of rejecting God's salvation in Jesus Christ ever more clearly emphasised?

17 July

"When..... you return to the LORD your God and obey His voice, according to all that I command you today, you and your children, with all your heart and with all your soul, that the LORD your God will bring you back from captivity, and have compassion on you, and gather you again from all the nations where the LORD your God has scattered you." (Deut 30:1-3)

We return to a theme which we encounter in so many contexts, a theme which our Enemy hates and has, down through the centuries, been determined that Christians will refuse to believe. We have elsewhere quoted the solemnly introduced Jeremiah 31:10 to demonstrate that there can be no replacement for Israel: "He who scattered Israel will gather him." Here we simply consider the basic fact that the same Israel will be regathered. However what we saw yesterday prophesied in Matthew 25 concerns the Gentiles – "all nations" in verse 32. Indeed, "The Judgment of the Nations" is an appropriate title; Israel is also to be judged, but separately, because of her special roles. We will see later that at this juncture the unredeemed of Israel will have by now been "refined", "sifted in a sieve", but will have failed the test.

The contexts of the passages which we will look at over the next three days all have mentions, so there is no need to quote them. The only conditions imposed in this promise delivered by God through Moses are clear enough, and need not be repeated. At national level they have never been complied with..... yet! But dozens of prophecies confirm that they will be. Both major and minor prophets confirm them. Zechariah, which we will look at in the next section, alternates, without due warning, much less often than Isaiah and Jeremiah, between the past to the future, so identifying Millennial applications can sometimes be easier. Take for instance Zechariah 10:6-8: "They shall be as though I had not cast them aside; For I am the LORD their God, And I will hear them .... I will whistle for them and gather them, for I will redeem them." But Isaiah also uses this most descriptive expression, demonstrating God's longing to call back His own: "And will whistle to them from the end of the earth; surely they shall come with speed, swiftly." (5:26). The conditions of Deuteronomy 30 will be fulfilled at last.

18 July

"The wilderness and the wasteland shall be glad for them, and the desert shall rejoice and blossom as the rose; It shall blossom abundantly and rejoice, even with joy and singing. The glory of Lebanon shall be given to it, The excellence of Carmel and Sharon. They shall see the glory of the LORD, the excellency of our God." (Isa 35:1-2)

I recall attending in 1949 an exhibition in Edinburgh about the amazing horticultural progress brought about by Zionism, with impressive illustrations from *kibbutzim* and much more. We were told that this fulfilled the Isaiah 35 prophecy, and I was duly impressed. In 2007 I actually visited a kibbutz; I was still impressed, but realised that, while this might have been a tiny foretaste, the fulfilment, which is to be a miraculous restoration of the entire planet, must await our Lord's Return. In the meantime Lebanon, part of the Promised Land, is still in alien hands; the glory of the Lord has yet to be seen.

The physical state of most of the 'sheep' survivors of the Great Tribulation will be such that only miracles will be able to restore them to a condition to enjoy the restored environment. He who opened the eyes of the blind and healed the lame, as part of the evidence of His Messianic ministry, will on that future day restore on a global scale: "Then the eyes of the blind shall be opened, and the ears of the deaf shall be unstopped. Then the lame shall leap like a deer, and the tongue of the dumb sing" (vv:5-6). This is prophecy, not allegory. At His First Coming He healed many, but not all. The lame-from-birth man at the Temple gate, for instance, was left for Peter and John to heal.

Claiming premature and partial fulfilment of such prophecies does our Lord a disservice. The closing verses of this chapter have been set to music: "And the ransomed of the LORD shall return, and come to Zion with singing, with everlasting joy on their heads. They shall obtain joy and gladness, and sorrow and sighing shall flee away" (verse 10). I have heard them sung as if this was currently being fulfilled. Visitors may be carried away by the emotion, but, in the cold light of day, they are likely to feel disillusioned. When it is really fulfilled, there will be no room for disillusionment.

19 July

"The wolf also shall dwell with the lamb, the leopard shall lie down with the young goat, the calf and the young lion and the fatling together; and a little child shall lead them..... They shall not hurt nor destroy in all My holy mountain, for the earth shall be full of the knowledge of the LORD as the waters cover the sea."
(Isa 11:6,9)

This is a wonderful Millennial chapter, meant to be taken at face value. The final sentence has been appended to each verse of a well-known hymn, one which visualises the progress of a triumphant Church, rather than something which can only follow Armageddon and Christ's Return. It asks, "Where is the time, the time that shall surely be?" Given the correct timing, everything in these prophecies is guaranteed, but the Rapture and Tribulation Period **must** come first! The Church has many tasks, but none includes lifting the curse imposed on the earth at the Fall in Eden. Only our Creator has the power to make such stupendous changes - in His time.

The chapter has more to say about Israel's future regathering (verses 11- 12), confirming that they are to come from so much further afield than at any time in history. We also read of the end of the three thousand year old rivalry between Judah and Ephraim, the Northern and Southern kingdoms (v 13). The chapter closes with one of several descriptions in the Prophets of huge geological changes, uplifts and depressions, which have to take place around the time of Christ's Return. In verse 15 we read of the elimination of "tongue of the Sea of Egypt", what we now know as the Gulf of Aqaba, a horn of the Red Sea. God, probably during the Flood, made provision for facilitating these end-time changes. Sixty years ago I was stationed in the Kenyan section of this great broken Rift Valley chain. Being aware of some of these prophecies, whilst also studying advanced geography, I used to be thrilled to look at the valley sides and into the nearby Longonot volcano and to think that God had His eye upon all these things, and on me, His humble servant. In our camp we had leopards almost on our doorstep; I would not have risked any goat! But it should always be a thrill to know that a final restoration of this sad old planet lies ahead.

20 July

"No more shall an infant from there live but a few days, nor an old man who has not fulfilled his days; for the child shall die one hundred years old, but the sinner being one hundred years old shall be accursed..... They shall not build and another inhabit; they shall not plant and another eat; for as the days of a tree, so shall be the days of My people, and My elect shall long enjoy the work of their hands." (Isa 65:20, 22)

We recall that no unsaved mortal will be welcomed into the Millennial Kingdom. Evidently all or many of them will do what Adam, Methuselah and other ancients failed to do – live for a thousand years. But of course children will be born to them; "For they shall be the descendants of the blessed of the LORD, and their offspring with them" (verse 23). None will be exempt from repenting and exercising saving faith; the efficacy of Christ's vicarious death at Calvary lasts throughout the Millennium, and beyond.

We have already seen that Satan will be bound out of reach in the Abyss or bottomless pit throughout. But God once accused him: "You have said **in your heart**...." (Isa 14:13). So, throughout the Millennium, while open rebellion will never be tolerated, people will be able to entertain sin **within their heart**. Some will perish prematurely. We will look at the outcome tomorrow. There is a suggestion in today's text that childhood will last much longer than in the present "three score and ten years" average lifespan. Back before the Flood the childbearing age may have started later, and was apparently greatly extended. We will have to wait for answers, but, having been raptured earlier, we will observe all from our immortal perspective.

We must never forget that, while we are living in a generation which may yet see the Rapture, the Tribulation Period and the Millennium, the first readers of Isaiah's prophecies were those whose nation was shortly to go into captivity and experience the usual fate of captives. Although it would give them no personal comfort, God wanted them to know that, regarding their descendants, He promised: "They shall build houses and inhabit them; they shall plant vineyards and eat their fruit. They shall not build and another inhabit; they shall not plant and another eat" (vv 21-22).

21 July

"And he cast him into the bottomless pit, and shut him up, and set a seal on him, so that he should deceive the nations no more till the thousand years were finished. But after these things he must be released for a little while..... Now when the thousand years have expired, Satan will be released from his prison. and will go out to deceive the nations which are in the four corners of the earth.... They went up on the breadth of the earth and surrounded the camp of the saints and the beloved city. And fire came down from God out of heaven and devoured them." (Rev 20:3,7-9)

This passage may at first sight seem surprising, but yesterday we partly answered the enigma of Satan, having been locked safely away to allow earth's final golden age, later reappearing and tempting those who will, unlike previous ages, have experienced no external tempter. What is about to happen here is to follow the Millennium. Satan would have neither the authority nor the ability to end the Millennium. His brief release is clearly authorised by God for a specific purpose.

Satan will probably have the support of a multitude of demonic fellow prisoners for this futile Post-Millennial re-run of Armageddon; Isaiah 24:21-22 suggests this. It is not to be confused with the Ezekiel 38-39 Gog and Magog invasion. For a thousand years Israel will have been the head and not the tail, and will have been seen to be God's representatives, a favoured, and at last obedient, nation. This will be the final flowering of Anti-Semitism. We have seen that many of those born during the Millennium will have willingly acknowledged and worshipped Christ, but that many others will covertly resent and resist the need to be saved. Clearly the objective of this army, summoned from all over the world, will be the earthly city of Jerusalem.

God's response is going to be immediate. Walter Scott observes: "The nations converge on Jerusalem. Christ does not intervene.... All is silent in the camp and city. The apostate nations march into the jaws of death. Their judgment is sudden, swift, overwhelming. God deals with the hosts of evil." The Devil is immediately consigned to Hell. This must happen in order to fulfil the prophecy, "He (Christ) must reign till He has put all enemies under His feet" (I Cor 15:25).

Major prophecies from a Minor Prophet

22 July

"Thus says the LORD of hosts: 'Return to Me,' says the LORD of hosts, 'and I will return to you,' says the LORD of hosts." (Zech 1:3)

Despite His using this title of supreme authority, the Lord demonstrates that He is promising to return to Israel only subject to their returning to Him. The Bible itself never calls some prophets "minor" and others "major". Zechariah understood the emotion of longing to return, and could empathise with the Lord's appeal in this verse. He was born in exile and lived in Babylonia as a child. The 137th Psalm, which opens with: "By the waters of Babylon, there we sat down and wept", is ascribed to the then young Zechariah. He would have witnessed the fall of Babylon, and in due course returned to his ancestral home of Jerusalem. He is thus a most apt prophet for his mission. We have already looked at his famous prophecy of the Lord's First Coming, "Behold, your King cometh.... just and lowly, riding upon an ass" (9:9). He started writing the earlier part of the book in 520 BC; chapters 9 to 14 may have been written much later; but he was the sole author.

There are three prominent men in the book, Zechariah the Prophet, Joshua the High Priest and Zerubbabel, the governor and uncrowned royal heir of the Messianic line. But as we read on, like Nebuchadnezzar peering into the fiery furnace, we see a fourth; and "His form is like the Son of God" (Dan 3:25). Christ is seen as the Prophet, Priest and King, the Rider on the red horse of Zechariah 1:8, as the Angel of the Lord, as the Foundation Stone, as the Capstone, as the Just and Lowly King, as the Pierced One, as the Conqueror of the nations, as the Saviour of Israel and much more. We cannot take time to look at them all.

The earlier part of the book contains eight visions, each authoritatively interpreted by an angel. The Expanded Open Bible says, "Christ is portrayed in His two advents as both Servant and King, Man and God"; He is portrayed both factually and symbolically in the earlier visions, and in simple terms in the latter chapters. It is doubtful whether any other book in the Old Testament confirms so clearly that the Son, as well as the Father, shares the triune name of Jehovah."

23 July

"'Jerusalem shall be inhabited as towns without walls, because of the multitude of men and livestock in it. 'For I', says the LORD, 'will be a wall of fire all around her, and I will be the glory in her midst.'"
(Zech 2:4-5)

How can anyone read Zechariah and fail to believe God's long term purposes for Jerusalem and Israel? Believing this is not an end in itself. In these days, when this ancient people, who have been through so many centuries of prophesied exile and hardship, are once again at the centre of the world's most persistent trouble spot, we have overwhelming evidence of the reliability of the Bible. The legacy of the Augustinian proposal that all Scripture should be taken literally, except prophecy, which should be taken allegorically, is a fiendishly cunning way of blinding eyes to the signs of the times.

In this section I am including short extracts from my *"The Minor Prophets and the End Times"*. The vision from which today's text is taken is of angels enquiring about a measuring line which will have been used to measure what is evidently the future Jerusalem. The previous vision stopped short of the Millennium, but in this vision we come to it, when the scattering will finally have been reversed. God was guaranteeing a Millennial Jerusalem, too extensive and populous to enclose. "'I' says Jehovah, 'will be a wall of fire all around her, and I will be the glory in her midst'". What a stupendous promise! The One who made it is our God and Saviour, who is just the same to all those who shelter beneath His shadow.

Other prophets tell of a fertile age for plants; here we are told of livestock within the city. The Millennium will evidently be an agrarian age, with labour pleasurable and satisfying, in a planet free from the curse and sickness. God never intended man to be idle. No environmentalist will need to agitate about carbon footprints when earth's balance is restored! It goes on to speak of Israel's enemies: "For thus says the LORD of hosts: 'He sent Me after glory, to the nations which plunder you; for **he who touches you touches the apple of His eye.'"** (2:8). That is as true today as it was two and a half thousand years ago, as many nations have found to their cost.

24 July

"'Hear, O Joshua, the high priest, You and your companions who sit before you, for they are a wondrous sign; for behold, I am bringing forth My Servant the BRANCH. For behold, the stone that I have laid before Joshua: upon the stone are seven eyes. Behold, I will engrave its inscription,' says the LORD of hosts, 'and I will remove the iniquity of that land in one day.'" (Zech 3:8-9)

One has to know a little of what was happening in the newly returned captives, and in Jerusalem under restoration, to see the significance of these prophecies. The opening verses of chapter 3 largely concern Joshua, the then High Priest, seen clad with the sins of his people and under attack from the accusing Satan, but then cleansed, restored and mitred. He is as a "brand plucked from the burning" of the furnace of Babylon. Satan still hates Israel intensely. Joshua is addressed in precedence before Zerubbabel, the governor, because, with the discontinuing of the kings of David's line until the Messiah (Jeremiah 22:30 & Ezekiel 21:26-27), the high priests were to be the recognised national leaders until Christ's crucifixion.

This Joshua was to have a responsible and honoured role in the Temple courts both thereafter and hereafter! According to Haggai (2:23), Zerubbabel is to be active in his resurrection body in the Millennial Jerusalem.

In today's verses and those following, Joshua finds that the Messiah will be the Servant of Jehovah, as in Isaiah, and the BRANCH as in Isaiah 4:2 and Jeremiah 23:3-6, and the Chief Corner Stone to be laid (Isaiah 28:16). He will be both the suffering Messiah Ben Joseph as well as the kingly Messiah Ben David. In that single day of national recognition and repentance described in chapter 12, God will be able to remove their iniquity. Those verses from Jeremiah 23 about the BRANCH should be read with this vision. Unger's Bible Dictionary states: "A branch is the symbol of kings descended from royal ancestors, and in conformity with this way of speaking, Christ, in respect of His human nature, is called 'a root out of the stem of Jesse, and a branch..... out of his roots' (Isaiah 11:1; Jeremiah 23:3; Zechariah 3:8; 6:12), just as Christians are called branches of Christ, the Vine, with reference to their union with Him (John 15:5-6)."

25 July

"This is the word of the LORD to Zerubbabel: 'Not by might nor by power, but by My Spirit,' says the LORD of hosts. 'Who are you, O great mountain? Before Zerubbabel you shall become a plain! And he shall bring forth the capstone with shouts of "Grace, grace to it!"'" (Zech 4:6-7)

This is the fifth of Zechariah's night visions, and the last which we can take time to consider. The angel had shown him a golden menorah or lampstand, like that in the Temple, which was a copy of the heavenly one. The foundation stone of the Second Temple, which later Jesus often visited, had recently been laid by Zerubbabel. He saw in vision the bowl of oil above the pipework leading to seven cups, illustrating the never-failing supply of God's Spirit for His work, even before the unique Church Age personal gift, indwelling and sealing of that Spirit. "'Not by might, nor by power, but by My Spirit,' says the Lord of Hosts" is often quoted out of context, although usually appropriately. Here is a reminder that God's light is spread not by the sword or political might but by His Spirit. Any religion propagated by the sword is no true faith.

Zerubbabel was being assured that, having laid the foundation stone, he should later put in place the capstone as well, a signal honour for this Spirit-filled man of God who had been born a refugee. The mountain which was to be turned into a plain appears to be metaphoric, rather than a reference to the end-time geological changes, which have certainly to take place. Apparently insuperable problems were going to be moved. These inauspicious beginnings, of an edifice much less magnificent than Solomon's Temple, were not to be despised ("the day of small things").

Prophetically the Capstone, which will be the crowning glory, is the coming Messiah, who, as we know from many Scriptures, including the previous vision, is also the Chief Corner Stone. The end-time significance is confirmed by the fact that God's Holy Spirit was never poured out on Israel in this manner in historical times. Previously Israel had failed miserably as a light to the Gentiles (Ezekiel 5:5). But in the Millennium, God has assured her: "The Gentiles shall come to your light, and kings to the brightness of your rising" (Isa 60:3).

26 July

"Thus says the LORD: 'I will return to Zion, and dwell in the midst of Jerusalem. Jerusalem shall be called the City of Truth, the mountain of the LORD of hosts, the Holy Mountain.' Thus says the LORD of hosts: 'Old men and old women shall again sit in the streets of Jerusalem, each one with his staff in his hand because of great age. The streets of the city shall be full of boys and girls playing in its streets.'" (Zech 8:3-5)

In chapter 8 we have one of the most comprehensive descriptions of the Millennial earth of any of the prophets. The blessings promised in Deuteronomy 28:1-14 had almost always been available, but had never been fully enjoyed. But now God confirms and enlarges upon the predictions of the earlier night visions, reasserting His great zeal for Zion. We are told of future peace and prosperity, of the summoning of the remaining exiles of Israel, of a restored ecology, of Israel's curse becoming a blessing, of a restored spiritual state, of fasting turned to feasting and of the conversion of the world, with the nations looking to the Jew for leadership. Who dares to claim that God does not have future plans for Israel? At long last God's will **will** be done on earth as it is in Heaven.

Today's text tells of old men and old women sitting and of boys and girls playing in the streets of Jerusalem. As G Campbell Morgan says in a remark reflecting the transformed nature of God's Millennial Age, "the streets will be fit for boys and girls to play in; and boys and girls will be fit to play in the streets". These "blessed of My Father" will have their strength renewed and diseases, deformities and disabilities righted at the outset (Isaiah 35:3-6).

In Genesis 1:27 we read: "So God created man in His own image; in the image of God He created him; male and female He created them." In the Millennium God's will is going to be recognised without question. When God, through His prophet, says men and women and boys and girls, He means just that. Parliaments and judiciaries in formerly Christian nations who defy their Creator over gender issues can only bring judgment upon themselves and those whom they represent. Christianity is thus being reviled by pagan nations, and we are surely suffering the consequences.

27 July

*"Yes, many peoples and strong nations shall come to seek the
LORD of hosts in Jerusalem, and to pray before the LORD.
Thus says the LORD of hosts: 'In those days ten men from every
language of the nations shall grasp the sleeve of a Jewish man,
saying, "Let us go with you, for we have heard that God is with
you.""'"* (Zech 8:22-23)

There is so much in the Old Testament to support this statement. We
have already encountered a few, and will see more of significance
in chapter 14. But it is doubtful whether any others are so simple or
succinct. During the Church Age it has been Christians who have had
this responsibility as ambassadors for Christ. During the Tribulation
period it will be the 144,000 sealed Jews; but in the Millennium the
whole nation will have this wonderful priestly responsibility. For all
those centuries they have been "an astonishment, a proverb and
a byword among all nations where Jehovah will drive you" (Deut
28:37), in fulfilment of the conditional curse which they had invoked.
Jew and Gentile alike are individually accountable to their Creator.
For both there is only one means of salvation; "We shall be saved
in the same manner as they" (Acts 15:11). It is easy to forget that,
while God's covenants with Israel guarantee ultimate restoration in
their own Land and other unique benefits, included in these plans
has always been the blessing of Gentiles through Israel. This was
no afterthought, as foolish people have occasionally suggested. It
was prophesied five and a half centuries before Christ's presentation
and rejection of Himself as Messiah. Again we are reminded of
God's four-thousand-year-old promise to Abraham of blessing to
the nations of the earth. But what a long time of being side-lined
they have brought upon themselves! However, as Malcolm Davis
comments: "What a complete reversal of fortunes the LORD can
accomplish when conditions in His people are right!"

We perceive from this text that there will still be a responsibility for
everyone in the Millennium to seek to know the Lord; faith leading
to salvation will still be required. But at least there is going to be
no doubt as to whom the Lord will have commissioned to be His
representatives, when His presence, following His visible Coming in
Power, will be seen in His Shekinah Glory.

28 July

"His dominion shall be 'from sea to sea, and from the River to the ends of the earth." (Zech 9:10)

We have already visited the famous previous verse which foretells Christ coming as King with salvation, lowly and riding upon an ass. However this chapter opens with a remarkably detailed account of events in and around Israel during the Inter-Testament years. The Apocrypha was written during that period; it is informative historically, but not inspired. Zechariah 9:1-8 is inspired; God was not about to leave His people without authoritative predictions for intervening centuries. The faithful of this period must have marvelled at, for instance, the way, strategically illogical, but exactly as prophesied, that Alexander the Great's armies bypassed Jerusalem, whilst sacking other cities. Daniel from 10:12 to 11:35 tells of the same period, but more from an angelic perspective, explaining how spiritual battles impacted on events on earth, especially after Alexander's empire has been divided into four. Ezekiel also tells of dramatic events at this time, such as the fate of Tyre. These are fascinating prophecies, both for the historian and the Bible student wishing to specialise. We must pass on, but not until we have once again mentioned that the atheist researcher would love to discredit the Bible by proving that these passages were written after the event. But he cannot, because they were not!

Today's text follows immediately the prophecy of Christ's coming on a donkey. Too late they will have to recognise as King of the whole world, as well as King of Israel, the One whom the Jerusalem leaders rejected. "The River" (Euphrates) in Scripture marks the border of the Promised Land. Verses 13 to 15 have both Inter-Testament and Tribulation applications; Judah and Ephraim have to be used by God as bows in His hands to defeat Greece's prototype Antichrist and the end-time Beast. It describes the Maccabaean resistance – a heroic patriotic Jewish campaign, the theme of one of Handel's oratorios.
It would be easy to forget individuals whilst concentrating on kings and empires. But God does not undervalue them: "The LORD their God will save them in that day, as the flock of His people. For they shall be like the jewels of a crown, lifted like a banner over His land" (9:16). Can we claim to be thus honoured?

29 July

"Behold, I will make Jerusalem a cup of drunkenness to all the surrounding peoples, when they lay siege against Judah and Jerusalem. And it shall happen in that day that I will make Jerusalem a very heavy stone for all peoples; all who would heave it away will surely be cut in pieces, though all nations of the earth are gathered against it." (Zech 12:2-3)

Zechariah introduces the final three chapters as a "burden of the word of the Lord against Israel" (12:1). These include the world-wide military assault of Jerusalem and its environs, which we look at briefly today, the national repentance and conversion of Israel, and Jerusalem's role as the global centre of worship.

Jerusalem is to be both an "intoxicating cup", maddening her foes and God's; it is also to be a "burdensome stone", something infuriatingly impossible to off-load. We have already seen how every nation will want to take Jerusalem as a prize, not a ruin; nuclear warfare would thus be excluded. When we look later at the build-up to Armageddon, we will see that this campaign, near the end of the Great Tribulation, is part of the crazy, demon-inspired attempted personal assault on Christ, something described in Psalm 2: "He who sits in the heavens shall laugh; the Lord shall hold them in derision. Then He shall speak to them in His wrath, and distress them in His deep displeasure" (verses 4-5).

In contrast with the earlier Northern invasion of Ezekiel 38-39, God wants His faithful remnant to share in the victory: "In that day the LORD will defend the inhabitants of Jerusalem; the one who is feeble among them in that day shall be like David, and the house of David shall be like God, like the Angel of the LORD before them" (12:8).

Details of the campaign are not given. It seems that the unfaithful of Jerusalem, who have sold themselves to Satan's Beast, will suffer in the final hand-to-hand urban warfare for the city: "For I will gather all the nations to battle against Jerusalem; the city shall be taken, the houses rifled, and the women ravished. Half of the city shall go into captivity, but the remnant of the people shall not be cut off from the city. Then the LORD will go forth and fight against those nations" (Zech 14:2-3).The faithful remnant are saved. No earthly commander could exercise such control in battle.

30 July

"And I will pour on the house of David and on the inhabitants of Jerusalem the Spirit of grace and supplication; then they will look on Me whom they pierced. Yes, they will mourn for Him as one mourns for his only son, and grieve for Him as one grieves for a firstborn." (Zech 12:10)

The precise timing relative to chapter 14 is difficult to determine. Some see chapters 12 and 14 as parallel, but disclosing different aspects of the same event. They believe that it will be only at Christ's Coming in Power that they will see Him whom they pierced. But perhaps the work of the Holy Spirit, the Spirit of grace and supplication, will prompt recognition *before* the Messiah is actually seen. Whenever it occurs, the grief is going to be thorough and genuine, deeply felt at national, tribal, family and individual level (12:12-14). As FB Meyer says, it will be "sorrow unto life" rather than "sorrow unto death".

The phrases "Look on Me whom they pierced" and "Mourn for Him" in verse 12:10 may seem an odd mix of personal pronouns, but they are based on the earliest manuscripts. Unbelieving Orthodox Jews have the greatest difficulty with this verse.

During the Great Tribulation a final sifting of Israel will have taken place, leaving only repentant believers at the moment of Christ's Return. "And it shall come to pass in all the land, says the Lord, that two thirds in it shall be cut off and die, but one third shall be left in it: I will bring the one third through the fire, will refine them as silver is refined, and test them as gold is tested" (Zech 13:8-9). Amos 9:9-10 describes the process as grain being sieved, with no genuine grain falling to the ground and being lost. God says to them: "I will make you pass under the rod, and I will bring you into the bond of the covenant; I will purge the rebels from among you" (Ezekiel 20:37).

They will be included in 'My Redeemed', the ransomed of the Lord upon whose heads will be everlasting joy (Isa 35:10). Those who will have earlier exercised faith by heeding Jesus' injunction to flee when the Abomination of Desolation is set up will, we assume, have been saved already and will be waiting His recall from their place of refuge.

31 July

"And Jehovah will go forth and fight with those nations, as when he fought in the day of battle. And his feet shall stand in that day upon the mount of Olives, which is before Jerusalem toward the east, and the mount of Olives shall cleave in the midst thereof toward the east and toward the west." (Zech 14:3-4 DBY)

Chapter 14 contains perhaps the simplest and most straightforward prophecy regarding the opening and continuing conditions of the Millennium. It shouts the truth and is, therefore, never read in many churches. Darby and the ASV are correct in their use of "Jehovah" as an alternative for "LORD"; it is a reminder of Christ's Deity and of the triune name of God. In verse 9 we are reminded that: "The LORD shall be King over all the earth", for until then Christ is not crowned on earth. The future split in the mount from which He ascended proves that this cannot conceivably be taken allegorically. Verses 12 to 15 add to what Revelation tells us of Armageddon.

For a thousand years the redeemed "Blessed of My Father" will come willingly yearly to Jerusalem to keep the Feast of Tabernacles, and their offspring will be required to come too, whether willingly or unwillingly: "And it shall come to pass that everyone who is left of   all the nations which came against Jerusalem shall go up from year to year to worship the King, the LORD of hosts, and to keep the Feast of Tabernacles" (14:16). Punishments for those who do not attend are given in verses 18-19, reminding us that, following the Millennium, there is to be a very brief rebellion (Revelation 20:7-10). In the past and during the Great Tribulation Jerusalem temples have been or will be desecrated. This will not be true of the future Temple described in the closing chapters of Ezekiel. "In that day 'HOLINESS TO THE LORD' shall be engraved on the bells of the horses. The pots in the LORD'S house shall be like the bowls before the altar" (Zech 14:20).

Some have queried the closing statement: "In that day there shall no longer be a Canaanite in the house of the LORD of hosts" (v 21). Canaanites during the Captivity "defiled the priesthood and the covenant" (Neh 13:29-30). Pollution will not be tolerated; worship will not be allowed to be contaminated.

Some General Prophecies from the Gospels

1 August

"Do not think that I came to destroy the Law or the Prophets. I did not come to destroy but to fulfil. For assuredly, I say to you, till heaven and earth pass away, one jot or one tittle will by no means pass from the law till all is fulfilled. Whoever therefore breaks one of the least of these commandments, and teaches men so, shall be called least in the kingdom of heaven; but whoever does and teaches them, he shall be called great in the kingdom of heaven."
(Matt 5:17-19)

We now devote thirteen days to prophecies with no specific end-time content. The very last commandment in the Old Testament is "Remember the Law of Moses, My servant, which I commanded him in Horeb for all Israel, with the statutes and judgments" (Mal 4:4). Horeb is Sinai, where the Ten Commandments were given; the Church has never been exempted.

The timing was significant. Jesus knew that He was about to challenge and be challenged by religious leaders who were devoted to the letter of the law, but ignored the spirit of the law. To them the law meant understanding the fine details of ceremonies and practices and left little room for mercy and true justice. Effectively, for them the law had become a burden which they could lay on the shoulders of others, whilst congratulating themselves on their own expertise. Jesus wanted His disciples and potential disciples to appreciate that, while He was contending with these leaders, He was in no way whatsoever making even the smallest detail of the law itself obsolete. God gave us the law for our own good, and it will outlast the world.

Breaking God's laws is called sin, which can be remedied only by Christ's sacrifice; however our spiritual position in God's Kingdom is dictated by our humble obedience to these laws. In our modern world those of our religious leaders who tamper with and dare to change God's laws, and encourage others to break them, can only attract God's judgment. It may draw the admiration of a sinful world; but what a price to pay! John Heading comments: "The 'great in the kingdom of heaven' is the Lord's assessment of those who 'do and teach'"; he goes on to quote James 1:22: "Be doers of the word, and not hearers only, deceiving yourselves."

2 August

"For after all these things the Gentiles seek. For your heavenly Father knows that you need all these things. But seek first the kingdom of God and His righteousness, and all these things shall be added to you." (Matt 6:32-33)

Jesus had been talking about priorities. It is possible for a believer to do the "right things", but to fail to do the important things. And what is important to one may be more or less important to another, because we have a variety of gifts, and the Lord has not put all of us in the same circumstances. Jesus had also been talking about things that worry us, some of them perfectly legitimate things: "Therefore do not worry, saying, 'What shall we eat?' or 'What shall we drink?' or 'What shall we wear?'" (verse 31). He was addressing Jews, so He made the comparison with the Gentiles. Applying it to ourselves, as Gentile believers, the comparison should be with unbelievers. We should not worry, or be anxious. How many believers are really obedient here - obedient all the time?

Again I quote John Heading's commentary on Matthew: "Rather 'the kingdom of God' should be our first priority. Discipleship implies forsaking all that one has (Luke 14:33), not necessarily abandoning personal possessions, but regarding them as God's property and using them for Him and not for self."

Do we ever consider that worrying can be sin? Worrying can lead to depression, and depression can lead to ineffectiveness in our discipleship. Our Enemy is not slow to take advantage of such situations; and we have to overcome by the blood of the Lamb. Some congregations have more than their fair share of depression; it is hard to admit to weakness and easy to blame others. Sometimes there are external factors, but so often it is a matter of forgetting that "your heavenly Father knows that you need all these things." And He is the One who has all the resources of Heaven and earth at hand. He knows that we need to be stretched and have our faith tested if we are to be of service. He sympathises and empathises when we are genuinely going through deep waters, and is there with us. The old hymn-writer was right in saying that there is no other way to be happy in Jesus but to trust and obey.

3 August

"When He had called the people to Himself, with His disciples also, He said to them, 'Whoever desires to come after Me, let him deny himself, and take up his cross, and follow Me. For whoever desires to save his life will lose it, but whoever loses his life for My sake and the gospel's will save it. For what will it profit a man if he gains the whole world, and loses his own soul? Or what will a man give in exchange for his soul?'" (Mk 8:34-37).

Each of these statements of Jesus contains at least one prophecy – there are two here, one with a negative and one with a positive outcome. There are also two questions, designed to make people think. These are eternal matters. Norman Crawford points out that the word "will" in the AV/KJV, rendered "desire" in the NKJV, is very strong, and could be translated "is determined". There is nothing casual in following Jesus. Nowadays the term "making a commitment" is sometimes used as an alternative to "being saved". It is a very poor alternative; we can withdraw a commitment at any time, but cannot be "unsaved". Commitment may simply be about Jesus' ethical teaching, or His compassion, or healing. Being saved implies confessing our sins in repentance, admitting that none other can save, and then trusting completely His vicarious death on our behalf.

Now currently, in what were considered Christian nations, believers are unlikely to suffer death for their faith; however there may be lesser social or judicial consequences. Each one of us should be prepared for this. In Muslim countries and sometimes elsewhere the consequences of naming Christ as our Saviour can indeed be life-threatening. But it was also true of those to whom Jesus first spoke of these matters. Probably all the Apostles died for their faith; we cannot be absolutely sure.

This is Jesus' first recorded mention of the Cross. The implications were not lost to this Galilean audience, as the Romans had not long before crucified hundreds of Galilean insurrectionists. We live in a culture where it is smart to love ourselves. Advertisements coax us to buy trivia because "you deserve it". An old chorus says, "My sins deserve eternal death, but Jesus died for me." At the very heart of Christianity is self-denial, with a divine guarantee that, in the long term, we will never be losers.

4 August

"And He said to them, 'Assuredly, I say to you that there are some standing here who will not taste death till they see the kingdom of God present with power.'" (Mk 9:1).

Today's text is not itself about the Transfiguration, but rather the fact that, within their lifetime, those addressed would see "the kingdom of God present with power", something which in our reckoning lies two thousand or more years later. The Transfiguration is recorded in Matthew, Mark and Luke, each account providing something not mentioned by the others. All three Gospels show it to have followed Peter's declaration that Jesus is the Christ, and his rebuke for remonstrating about the fact that his Lord was to be crucified. A few days later He took only three disciples, Peter, James and John, to the mountain summit; later He took the same three to Gethsemane for a vital contrasting experience. The impression made upon Peter was lasting, something to qualify him for future leadership roles. He records: "For we..... were eyewitnesses of His majesty. For He received from God the Father honour and glory when such a voice came to Him from the Excellent Glory: 'This is My beloved Son, in whom I am well pleased.' And we heard this voice which came from heaven when we were with Him on the holy mountain" (II Pet 1:16- 18).

On the mountaintop they would have been given the supreme privilege of seeing sublime realities outside the realm of time, and Peter was able to confirm later how this was a unique partial preview of the Second Coming. Later still in his Revelation, John was to witness and record much more about that Coming. But here, before His death and resurrection, the three were to hear the heavenly confirmation of the Deity of the One whose companions they were upon the dusty roads of the Holy Land, with Calvary ahead. Luke tells us what Moses and Elijah were discussing with Jesus; they "spoke of His decease which He was about to accomplish at Jerusalem" (9:30-31). When John had a preview of that same Coming, it was the One who could say: "I am He who lives, and was dead, and behold, I am alive forevermore" (Rev 1:18). As creatures of time we can see the contrast between the crucifixion, decease and the Return in Power, but may miss the eternal correlation.

5 August

"Assuredly, I say to you, wherever this gospel is preached in the whole world, what this woman has done will also be told as a memorial to her." (Mk 14:9)

Here we have a lovely example of how God deals with individuals, whether within multitudes or individually. This is about something which had happened in Bethany, just outside Jerusalem, in the home of Simon the Leper, only two days before Jesus' crucifixion. Mary, the sister of Martha and Lazarus, fellow villagers of Simon, had brought an alabaster flask of spikenard and broken it over Jesus' head. Jesus had accepted it as an act of anointing for His forthcoming burial. Mary went on to anoint His feet. One has to read Matthew's, Mark's and John's Gospels for the full account. This should not be confused with an earlier anointing of Jesus' feet in Galilee by a reputedly "sinful woman".

One feels that the Gospel writers might not have related this incident, which the disciples, prompted by Judas Iscariot, had regarded as the wasteful and probably foolish act of an emotional woman. But Jesus could see into her heart, and perceived the overwhelming love that was represented in the act of pouring out something which would have cost an average man's yearly income. Many outwardly more valuable services must have been performed by others of Jesus' followers which were never given this level of recognition. Jesus' statement is emphatic - "assuredly I say to you". It carried the full authority of the soon-to-be-resurrected Son of God, and all of us who have read the Bible have seen the evidence. Probably, as the Apostles began their ministry: "You shall be witnesses to Me in Jerusalem, and in all Judea and Samaria, and to the end of the earth" (Acts 1:8), they would recall that on this occasion in Bethany Jesus had already foretold their successes.

It is significant that this Mary was not listed among those women who took spices to the tomb on that Easter Sunday. She, having recently seen Jesus' power over death in the raising of her brother Lazarus, may have realised that there would be no need. Harold Paisley comments: "The beautiful words, 'She hath done what she could' are also preserved alone by Mark, being a true standard for all service. The Lord only expects what we have the ability to perform."

6 August

"I will arise and go to my father, and will say to him, 'Father, I have sinned against heaven and before you.'" (Lk 15:18)

Here is a personal prophecy made by one with low expectations. The speaker we have come to know as the Prodigal Son, the subject of one of three parables, all of which conclude with great joy when something lost is found. Only the Lord Jesus could speak with authority of the heavenly Father, who is represented here by a grieving but ever-watchful human father. Jesus told us so much about the prerequisites for and results of salvation.

The son, who had left home, gone to a far country and wasted his prematurely claimed share of his father's wealth on riotous living until he was penniless, is, of course, a picture of the unsaved person, particularly one from a devout home, suddenly admitting his desperate plight, and repenting. When things were as bad as they could possibly be, he admitted that **he** was the problem! It is significant that Pharisees and scribes were present (15 v 2), religious leaders whose pride forbade them to admit that they too needed to repent. Before God, their eternal position was more precarious than that of the Prodigal Son.

In his abject poverty the son realised that the least of his father's servants was far better off than he; he had to swallow any remaining pride and return to his father, not seeking reinstatement, but simply food and shelter. He wanted to make amends for his ingratitude and sins. One of the main lessons of the parable is that there is no requirement for the repentant sinner to make amends. There is no way that he can repay the price of his sin; furthermore, there is no need, because Christ has already paid it at Calvary.

We are given an insight into the heart of the loving Heavenly Father, who is ever on the lookout for lost sheep. Here the father saw him afar off and ran out to meet him. God took steps to meet us in our sin long before we appreciated our need. The father ordered that he should be re-clothed, no doubt removing his filthy garments. Our salvation takes the form of the best robe, the costliest, that bought with the precious blood of Christ. There is no second class salvation, no alternative to new life in Christ.

7 August

"The next day John saw Jesus coming toward him, and said, 'Behold! The Lamb of God who takes away the sin of the world!.... I did not know Him, but He who sent me to baptize with water said to me, 'Upon whom you see the Spirit descending, and remaining on Him, this is He who baptizes with the Holy Spirit.'" (Jn 1:29,33)

The first verse is one of the best known in Scripture. The second is probably rarely quoted. Evidently it was the Holy Spirit who had previously prophesied personally to the Forerunner, John the Baptist, so that there might be no mistake who the Lamb of God was. Having identified Him by the unmistakable sign of the descending Dove, John, who had seen this clearly, had no hesitation in proclaiming prophetically of the One who was to fulfil the role of the ultimate Lamb, the Paschal Lamb, who was to take away the sins of the world, the one of whom Heaven and earth must yet proclaim, "Worthy is the Lamb who was slain!"

Those present had depended upon the Law, which could never save. Later Paul wrote: "But now the righteousness of God apart from the law is revealed, being witnessed by the Law and the Prophets, even the righteousness of God, through faith in Jesus Christ, to all and on all who believe" (Rom 3:21-22). Believing is the condition for claiming what the Law could not do. It is significant that this episode is found in the first chapter of John, rather than nearer the crucifixion of the Lamb. Faith or lack of faith is remarked upon throughout our Lord's ministry.

Jesus could not be manifested to Israel until John the Baptist had come baptising for repentance. As FB Meyer writes: "Only when there has been repentance and confession of sins, which John's baptism signified, is a sinner prepared to receive the Saviour." Murray McCheyne put it this way: "Only a broken-hearted sinner can receive a crucified Christ." Now the Baptiser could testify: "I have seen and testified that this is the Son of God" (Jn 1:34). Beware of the cultish lie that this was the point at which Christ became the Son of God.

8 August

"No one has ascended to heaven but He who came down from heaven, that is, the Son of Man who is in heaven. And as Moses lifted up the serpent in the wilderness, even so must the Son of Man be lifted up." (Jn 3:13-14)

John 3:16 is better understood within its context, so we pause to look at two introductory verses. The first is one of the most profound in Scripture, an insight given by Christ into the Godhead. The second contains a prophecy which was shortly to be fulfilled. FB Hole writes profoundly: "A paradox greets us. He came down *from* heaven, yet He was *in* heaven. If however we remember how the Gospel started, the paradox disappears. Here is the Word who was God and became flesh. In becoming flesh He certainly came down from heaven; yet He never ceased to be God who is in heaven. But He said 'the *Son of Man* which is in heaven.'" Yes, and evidently we are intended to learn thereby that we are not at liberty to dissect in our minds His Person, as some are inclined to do. The cults are guilty of this, but sometimes so are we, in defending our faith against the cults.

It was as the Son of Man that He had to be lifted up. FB Meyer writes: "Other men and women die because they have born. Our Lord was born that He might die." Christ's was given the maximum publicity possible on that hilltop. But it was emphatically not martyrdom, where the perpetrators would have had the sole initiative. This was planned and rigorously controlled by God, Christ ever having the ability to change His mind – and leave every one of us facing Hell!

In the wilderness Moses' serpent was made in the likeness of the offending serpents which had been judgmentally plaguing the people. Christ, fulfilling His own prophecy, was lifted up because God "made Him who knew no sin to be sin for us, that we might become the righteousness of God in Him" (II Cor 5:21). He died in the likeness of sinful men. The brazen serpent had to be looked up to in faith and obedience in order to be free from the temporary plague; we must look up to Christ in saving faith to be eternally saved from the awful penalty of our sin.

9 August

"For God so loved the world that He gave His only begotten Son, that whoever believes in Him should not perish but have everlasting life. For God did not send His Son into the world to condemn the world, but that the world through Him might be saved." (Jn 3:16-17)

The best known verse in the entire Bible is both history and prophecy! The two are inextricably interconnected. The giving would have been pointless without the eternal life granted, and the granting would now be impossible without the prior giving. In verse 17 we read of Christ being "sent". Yesterday in verse 13 we find Jesus saying that He "came"; His coming was both active and passive, both obedient and voluntary.

Little words can easily be overlooked, such as the "for" which connects these statements with the eternal truths we looked at yesterday, and the "so" which tells of the overwhelming magnitude of God's love, which is demonstrated by His giving His only begotten Son. The NIV and some other translations lose something vital by using terms such as "one and only". The "begotten" distinguishes this Son from millions of adopted sons. As Archbishop Trench writes: "He is co-equal with the Father, being eternally generated; yet He was born, begotten, not created." Hebrews 1:6 reminds us that He brought His Firstborn into the world, and angels were commanded to worship Him; He had not abandoned His Deity.

This "perishing" which believers are spared is not of the body, but of the whole being in the sphere of eternity, as is the life which we are given in Christ. And this life does not have to await the resurrection; it is ours from the moment of saving faith, and indeed was known of "in eternity past", if we may put it that way. This amazing love of God, demonstrated in the giving of His only begotten Son, releases us from the condemnation of the broken law. It is by default that unbelievers are condemned, having failed to accept the very best that God has to offer: "He who believes in Him is not condemned; but he who does not believe is condemned already, because he has not believed in the name of the only begotten Son of God" (3:18). The academic Nicodemus had difficulty with these truths; yet the simplest soul can read John 3:16 and be eternally saved.

10 August

"Jesus said to her, 'Woman, believe Me, the hour is coming when you will neither on this mountain, nor in Jerusalem, worship the Father..... But the hour is coming, and now is, when the true worshippers will worship the Father in spirit and truth; for the Father is seeking such to worship Him.'" (Jn 4:21,23)

Perhaps, following his resurrection, Jacob will be amazed to learn how the Lord Jesus Christ was to use his well to encounter a sinful Samaritan and bring salvation to many in her city! Perhaps, with his soul conscious in Heaven, awaiting that resurrection, he already knows. We cannot be certain. The woman had been sensitive enough to come there at mid-day to avoid her gossiping neighbours, and had found Jesus, who was tired, sitting there. He had broken accepted protocol by asking her for a drink, before going on to deal with her spiritual situation. Horatius Bonar comments: "This is Godhead stooping down to visit and care for one solitary soul; it is the Good Shepherd casting His eye on a stray sheep by the wayside, and stooping to pick it up and carry it on His shoulders. The way in which God meets with the sinner is shown us here. God deals with him alone, and face to face. God speaks to the sinner and the sinner speaks to God."

Initially, when Jesus had pin-pointed her sin, the woman tried to change the subject by asking a technical "religious" question. The Samaritans were descendants of the foreigners whom the Assyrians had planted in the region when they deported the Northern Kingdom. They had inter-married with some of the remaining Jews, and were therefore looked down upon by both Jews and true foreigners. They were very conscious of their second-class status, which partly explains why the woman had been surprised by Jesus' request for a drink. She said: "Our fathers worshipped on this mountain, and you Jews say that in Jerusalem is the place where one ought to worship" (Jn 4:20). "This mountain" was Mount Gerizim; understandably the Jews would not allow them to worship at Jerusalem; this was their substitute where they worshipped the God of the Jews. Jesus halted her with His response, looking beyond Pentecost and beyond the later sacking of Jerusalem. Before long, neither location would be accessible. However, what matters is worshipping the Father "in spirit and truth."

11 August

"For the Father judges no one, but has committed all judgment to the Son, that all should honour the Son just as they honour the Father. He who does not honour the Son does not honour the Father who sent Him. Most assuredly, I say to you, he who hears My word and believes in Him who sent Me has everlasting life, and shall not come into judgment, but has passed from death into life."
(Jn 5:22-24)

Honouring the Son as they honour the Father must have been a difficult concept for the disciples to accept. They had seen Him only in His physical limitation and lowly conduct. Yet it is because of these and His sinless life that Jesus Christ is honoured as a Man, as well as because He is God. In His Deity it would have been unnecessary for the Father to have ordained such honour, which He had received naturally from angels before the foundation of the world.

The connection with John 3:16 is inescapable. But here Jesus tells us that it is He to whom all judgment has been committed. Paul was mocked by the many and accepted by the few, when he declared: "He has appointed a day on which He will judge the world in righteousness by the Man whom He has ordained. He has given assurance of this to all by raising Him from the dead" (Acts17:31). That judgment day draws ever nearer. But it is because of His humanity, something which was never possessed by the Father or Holy Spirit, that He is thus qualified – "that Man". "Behold the Man!" cried Pontius Pilate before His impending death. "Behold the Man who was dead and alive for ever more" is, in effect, what the Father declares in honouring His so uniquely qualified Son.

This is not the only text where we are told that, as believers, we are already in possession of everlasting life. Eternal security is a much vilified truth, but an important one. Denying it betrays a lack of faith, because it implies that we can still come into judgment for sins which were dealt with forever at Calvary. This is not about the judgment of our service, which, though important, is never a life-and-death matter. To deny eternal security is to class it as a false prophecy, a most serious accusation.

12 August

"I do not pray for these alone, but also for those who will believe in Me through their word; that they all may be one, as You, Father, are in Me, and I in You; that they also may be one in Us, that the world may believe that You sent Me." (Jn 17:20-21)

What an awesome privilege we have been given to listen in to a conversation between God the Father and God the Son on the betrayal night! What we call the Lord's Prayer should be termed the Disciples' Prayer, for *this* is the Lord's Prayer, His High Priestly prayer, interceding both for Himself and for us. The Holy Spirit later transmitted it word-for-word to the, by then elderly, Apostle so that we might know of our Saviour's passionate plea in the Garden of Gethsemane, with three of His sleepy disciples not far off. They were to be temporarily left desolate without Him; but here He is also caring for the future multitude of believers, the offspring of their witnessing. We were there in Gethsemane in the mind of our Lord!

Much folly has down through the centuries been perpetrated by those wishing to take over the Father's role, attempting to achieve some sort of organisational uniformity in what effectively has been a controlling empire-building activity. Jesus prayed, "that they also may be one **in Us**". This unity is impossible for man to replicate, when we consider the eternal unity of the Holy Trinity. Initiatives like the World Council of Churches, where the Vatican considers itself to be a separate entity, willing to spread its umbrella over the dregs of Protestantism, have been striving for the lowest common denominator of faith, rather than the highest common factor, to put it into arithmetical terms.

Of course, there have been hurtful and damaging rifts among believers for frivolous reasons, but there has also been praiseworthy and necessary separation, as in "come out of her, My people that ye be not partakers of her sins" situations. We cannot explore these here. God has already answered this prayer of Jesus: "There is neither Jew nor Greek, there is neither slave nor free, there is neither male nor female; for you are all one in Christ Jesus" (Gal 3:28). Were we only to behave thus, the world might be more impressed and less unbelieving.

13 August

"Father, I desire that they also whom You gave Me may be with Me where I am, that they may behold My glory which You have given Me; for You loved Me before the foundation of the world." (Jn 17:24)

Just stop and consider our status as revealed here: "they also whom You gave Me." Admittedly this was primarily about the Eleven who had accompanied Him for three years, but we know from our last reading that we are included. Again there are two complementary truths; we were **given** by the Father and **purchased** by the Son! It is futile trying to prioritise between eternal truths; we need only consider that at that moment, as He neared His death, this is what mattered to Him most.

What a contrast from Isaiah's vision of the pre-incarnate Christ, the King high and lifted up: "Woe is me, for I am undone! Because I am a man of unclean lips, and I dwell in the midst of a people of unclean lips; for my eyes have seen the King, the LORD of hosts" (Isa 6:5). Unlike Isaiah, there is no need for the coal from the altar; the blood from the altar of the Cross avails for us.

John Heading, referring to Jesus' words, writes: "We must note carefully the word 'before', implying the period before the creation..... Thus the Lamb was 'foreordained *before* the foundation of the world' (I Pet 1:20), and we have been chosen in Him *before* the foundation of the world" (Eph 1:6). Every statement seems more wonderful than the one before, when we consider His worthiness and our unworthiness. Moreover this beholding Christ's glory is not going to be momentary, as with Isaiah; it will be eternal. When we shortly look at the "holy city, New Jerusalem" we shall find: "They shall see His face, and His name shall be on their foreheads" (Rev 22:4).

Earlier in His prayer Jesus had asked: "And now, O Father, glorify Me together with Yourself, with the glory which I had with You before the world was" (Jn 17:5). But here there is to be *added* glory – the glory of the Victor over death. "For it was fitting for Him, for whom are all things and by whom are all things, in bringing many sons to glory, to make the captain of their salvation perfect through sufferings" (Heb 2:10).

Short and long term Prophecies of Ezekiel

14 August

"The word of the LORD came expressly to Ezekiel the priest, the son of Buzi, in the land of the Chaldeans by the River Chebar; and the hand of the LORD was upon him there.....And He said to me: 'Son of man, I am sending you to the children of Israel, to a rebellious nation that has rebelled against Me; they and their fathers have transgressed against Me to this very day.'"
(Ezek 1:3; 2:3)

God's dealings with Ezekiel were unique, and probably started when he reached the priestly age of thirty. Jeremiah at roughly the same time was preaching to the remnant majority in Jerusalem, warning them that, contrary to the predictions of false prophets, their city would be destroyed and the people exiled for seventy years. Ezekiel and Daniel had been among the early group of captives taken from Jerusalem to Babylonia. Daniel was taken to the capital, where eventually he was promoted to the most elite circles and dealt with kings; his prophecies were about nations and mainly the long-term future. Ezekiel was taken to one of the rural Jewish settlements. His ministry was to fellow Jews within Babylonia.

Both Ezekiel and Jeremiah faced much cynicism and opposition from their own religious leaders. The same thing happens when one expounds latter-day prophecy to the average twenty-first century church. We have noted elsewhere how bitterly Ezekiel complained to God that the people assumed that he was merely speaking in parables, rather than forecasting the future (20:49). People still do this. The closing nine chapters of the book contain detailed prophecies about Israel and the Millennium. Because this does not fit into the programme of the average Amillennialist, millions of Christians are being denied part of God's gracious revelation of the future. We have much to learn from this prophet of God's dealing with an unbelieving people who claimed to represent God. Ezekiel's credibility rose a little when Nebuchadnezzar sacked Jerusalem and carried captive the bulk of Jerusalem and Judah. Later, according to Jewish tradition, Ezekiel was martyred for preaching the unpalatable truth. 'Church people' today who ignore Bible prophecy forfeit something which the Holy Spirit incorporated into Scripture for their benefit.

15 August

"Like the appearance of a rainbow in a cloud on a rainy day, so was the appearance of the brightness all around it. This was the appearance of the likeness of the glory of the LORD. So when I saw it, I fell on my face, and I heard a voice of One speaking. And He said to me, 'Son of man, stand on your feet, and I will speak to you.' Then the Spirit entered me when He spoke to me, and set me on my feet; and I heard Him who spoke to me." (Ezek 1:28-2:2)

This is not unlike the experience of John in Revelation (1:17). Firstly Ezekiel sees (and hears) a vision of the glory of the Lord with a magnificence unparalleled in the Old Testament; "Then I looked, and behold, a whirlwind was coming out of the north, a great cloud with raging fire engulfing itself; and brightness was all around it and radiating out of its midst like the colour of amber, out of the midst of the fire" (1:4).

The prophet describes what he then saw in three stages. First, he sees four cherubim, mighty angelic beings, earlier seen in Eden and later in Revelation 4 as the "mysterious guardians of the ineffable throne in heaven" (Sidlow Baxter). Next, in verse 16, he records what he describes as complex multi-directional wheels with amazing speed, manoeuvrability and unity of purpose, incorporating many eyes. Sixty years ago, whilst stationed in Sharjah I was sent a Christian magazine article which seriously suggested that this was a prophecy about flying saucers, which were very much in the news at the time. Science fiction does occasionally draw on Bible data, but it also uses occult sources. God is the only "time lord!" This seems simply to illustrate that God's throne chariot, if we may describe this part of the vision thus, features both His omnipresence and omniscience, as in judgment He surveys His wayward people and foretells imminent punishment and ultimate, though still very distant, restoration.

Finally, Ezekiel sees a theophany, a representation of God Himself: "And above the firmament over their heads was the likeness of a throne, in appearance like a sapphire stone; on the likeness of the throne was a likeness with the appearance of a man high above it" (1:26). How can any fail to take seriously the prophecies of Ezekiel, when given this Divine accreditation?

16 August

"You also, son of man, take a clay tablet and lay it before you, and portray on it a city, Jerusalem. Lay siege against it, build a siege wall against it, and heap up a mound against it; set camps against it also, and place battering rams against it all around. Moreover take for yourself an iron plate, and set it as an iron wall between you and the city. Set your face against it, and it shall be besieged, and you shall lay siege against it. This will be a sign to the house of Israel." (Ezek 4:1-3)

This is one of a number of prophetic symbols which God required Ezekiel to give to people who stubbornly refuse to believe Jerusalem's impending judgment. Back in Jerusalem, at roughly the same time, Jeremiah was predicting the same thing (chapters 25 and 29). Complacently, they were convinced that God would never allow His own temple to be destroyed; blindly they refused to admit their own sinfulness. Preaching had made no impression. God was allowing His servant to be considered eccentric, but at least they would take notice of him. Ezekiel has powerful messages for the generation in which we live. Like the Jews of those days, God will not hear our prayers about other matters until we have confessed our sins.

Then God instructed Ezekiel to do something even more remarkable – and uncomfortable! For 390 days he was to lie on his left side and to "bear the iniquity of the house of Israel" (verse 5), and then on his right side for a further 40 days. Each day was to represent a past year (verse 6). The longer of the two periods applied to the Northern Kingdom, sacked by Assyria, and dispersed, never to return until a yet future day. The shorter period applied to Judah before the later Babylonian captivity. "Jehovah's Witnesses" make the most ridiculous calculations based on this "day for a year" never repeated formula, which was about history, not prophecy, relating it to a totally irrelevant event in Daniel 4, and predicting that Christ would return invisibly in 1914! Should you encounter them, you will find that they are incredibly vulnerable in this matter.

The third symbolically presented prophecy in Ezekiel 4, involved the prophet eating ceremonially unclean bread cooked on dung fires, indicating that Jerusalem, in its siege famine, would eat polluted food (vv 16-17).

17 August

"Yet I will leave a remnant, so that you may have some who escape the sword among the nations, when you are scattered through the countries. Then those of you who escape will remember Me among the nations where they are carried captive, because I was crushed by their adulterous heart which has departed from Me, and by their eyes which play the harlot after their idols; they will loathe themselves for the evils which they committed in all their abominations." (Ezek 6:8-9)

The impending punishment and exile of Jerusalem and Judea occupies several chapters. But with judgment there is mercy. Despite the intentions of Israel's enemies, which, sadly, have often included Christians, God has always taken steps to preserve a Jewish remnant. This applies both to the seventy year Babylonian captivity and the much longer *Diaspora*.

We read tomorrow of the fate of those not exiled. There was to be recognition and repentance in Babylon, not unlike the future Tribulation Period repentance, of which we read in Zechariah. "And they shall know that I am the LORD; I have not said in vain that I would bring this calamity upon them." (Ezek 6:10). The adultery is of course the illicit relationship with the idols of neighbouring nations, which "crushed" or deeply hurt God. A few of the more righteous kings of Judah had tried to stamp it out, but it was in the hearts of the majority and soon reappeared. Following the return from Exile Judah never resumed the former idolatry. Ezra, Nehemiah, Zerubbabel and other leaders were exceptionally strict, and there was a limited spiritual revival, though eventually this became the sterile Judaism of the Scribes and Pharisees, who in the parable of the Prodigal Son (Luke 15:11-32) were represented by the privileged elder son, over whom there was no rejoicing in Heaven, and who considered themselves in no need of any repentance. There are other applications of this parable. The good news in the midst of looming disaster was the God-guaranteed faithful remnant. This must have been of great consolation to Ezekiel, whose prophecies were to end with the promise that God **would be there** – in the Millennium (48:35). God never leaves Himself without witnesses. During the Church Age the Church has, of course, taken over Israel's role.

18 August

"'Go through the midst of the city, through the midst of Jerusalem, and put a mark on the foreheads of the men who sigh and cry over all the abominations that are done within it.' To the others He said in my hearing, 'Go after him through the city and kill; do not let your eye spare, nor have any pity. Utterly slay old and young men, maidens and little children and women; but do not come near anyone on whom is the mark; and begin at My sanctuary.' So they began with the elders who were before the temple." (Ezek 9:4-6)

Here, in vision, a man with an inkhorn was being addressed; God was sealing all those who were not guilty of idolatry and who hated what they saw happening. Many God-fearing people had been in the earlier smaller deportation to Babylon. There was to be a huge slaughter at the coming siege and sack of the city. God was overruling and ensuring that the most idolatrous would be slain, starting with the elders before the temple, those held most responsible.

We cannot take time to look at the vision of Jerusalem, which Ezekiel was given as he was plucked up by the Spirit by a lock of his hair so that he could view from God's perspective the abominations that were being practised in the Temple area. Chapter 8 tells of three separate abominable practices witnessed by Ezekiel, each with its own group of devotees.

Firstly (verse 3), there was "the image of jealousy", apparently an image of Asherah, described by Fred Tatford as, "The queen of heaven and goddess of love and sex. Virtually sexual desire had been introduced into Jehovah's temple and its patron deity guarded the entrance." Secondly (verse 7), Ezekiel was shown a hole dug into the Temple wall where secretly seventy elders were offering sacred incense to all manner of creatures, portrayed around the walls of this chamber, as in Egyptian religion, claiming that the Lord did not see them. Finally (verse 13), he was shown an even greater abomination, a crowd of women "weeping for Tammuz", a fertility deity dating back to Nimrod's time, and portraying an annual resurrection, crediting to him, rather than to God, the change of seasons and arrival of the rains. II Kings and II Chronicles record much, but God chose Ezekiel to relate these depths of degradation.

19 August

"Say now to the rebellious house: 'Do you not know what these things mean?' Tell them, 'Indeed the king of Babylon went to Jerusalem and took its king and princes, and led them with him to Babylon. And he took the king's offspring, made a covenant with him, and put him under oath. He also took away the mighty of the land, that the kingdom might be brought low and not lift itself up, but that by keeping his covenant it might stand." (Ezek 17:12-14)

This introduces one of a number of parables which are difficult to understand now without some knowledge of history, but must have been vivid and invaluable to the godly living in the midst of what was being portrayed. Chapter 17 describes a great cedar tree representing the royal house of David. Two eagles are portrayed, the first representing Emperor Nebuchadnezzar of Babylon and the second Pharaoh Hophra of Egypt. Nebuchadnezzar, as the first eagle, had already taken the king of Judah to Babylon along with useful people such as craftsmen, and had appointed Zedekiah as caretaker prince of Judea, having made him swear by God his allegiance. As long as Zedekiah remained true to this covenant, all was peaceful. In the parable Zedekiah is described as a vine leaning toward the second eagle. He was in fact reneging on his oath given in the Lord's name, seeking the help of Egypt to free him from his covenant.

The result was that Nebuchadnezzar laid siege to Jerusalem, as we have seen earlier. The idolatry which we have seen perpetrated in Jerusalem under this godless puppet king was, of course, also contributory to the double judgment. Zedekiah was taken, his sons slaughtered before his eyes, which were put out before he was taken in ignominy to Babylon. In verse 19 God speaks of the oath which Zedekiah despised. We have here among many other things an insight into God's righteousness in honest dealing with others, when we are meant to be His representatives.

This sad chapter closes with the lovely Millennial promise (verses 22-24) of a future tender twig, representing Christ, which will sprout from the crown of the cedar tree. There would be no further kings of Israel until: "On the mountain height of Israel I will plant it; and it will bring forth boughs, and bear fruit, and be a majestic cedar."

20 August

"Son of man, say to the prince of Tyre, 'Thus says the Lord GOD: "Because your heart is lifted up, and you say, 'I am a god, I sit in the seat of gods, in the midst of the seas,' Yet you are a man, and not a god, though you set your heart as the heart of a god…. They shall throw you down into the Pit, and you shall die the death of the slain in the midst of the seas.'" (Ezek 28:2,8)

From chapter 26, Ezekiel prophesies judgments against neighbouring nations like Philistia. Chapters 26 to 28 are devoted to the downfall of Tyre, a city which had been assigned to the tribe of Asher in Joshua's time, but never possessed by Israel. What troubles we store up for ourselves by failing to occupy what God has promised!

Tyre was a small, but immensely wealthy, kingdom on the Lebanese coast with a little heavily fortified offshore island with two excellent harbours, which traded with much of the known world. God addressed its ruler, the Prince of Tyre, who personified his nation, and had mocked God and gloated over the fall of Jerusalem. Through Ezekiel God prophesied Tyre's fate, which was to come in two stages, immediately through Nebuchadnezzar, who sacked the city, and later through Alexander, whom Tyre defied and taunted. Alexander, using the debris of the on-shore city, built a wide causeway to the point where he could use siege weapons. The Prince boasted godhood and wisdom greater than Daniel, who then served Nebuchadnezzar, and was known to be endued with wisdom. Every detail of Ezekiel's prophecy, to the very laying bare of the rock so that fishing nets could be dried there, was fulfilled. In accordance with 27:36, Tyre has never been rebuilt.

God evidently saw Tyre as a particular client state of Satan, the long since fallen 'Covering Cherub'. From 28:14 Satan is addressed as the King of Tyre. Together with Isaiah 14:12-17 we are given an amazing insight into Satan's glorious, but ultimate pride-filled, status as Lucifer before his fall, preceding this creation. No created being since has enjoyed such privilege or been promised such an awful fate. "Know your enemy" has always been a sound military policy, and clearly God wants us to be aware of, but never preoccupied with, our Enemy. Throughout the New Testament we are regularly supplied with warnings.

21 August

"Again He said to me, 'Prophesy to these bones, and say to them, "O dry bones, hear the word of the LORD!" Thus says the Lord GOD to these bones: "Surely I will cause breath to enter into you, and you shall live. I will put sinews on you and bring flesh upon you, cover you with skin and put breath in you; and you shall live. Then you shall know that I am the LORD."'" (Ezek 37:4-6)

Christendom should be much wiser and more aware of where we are in God's programme, and thus more effective in witnessing to a frightened world. Would that more Christians, "Hear the word of the Lord", as commanded! God ensures that the attention of a fragile latter day world is rarely diverted from the Middle East. Ask many 'Reformed' Christians, and they will tell you that the bones of the nation Israel are dry, very dry and in fact dead, ready to be replaced, but never to come together with the breath of Almighty God. The old song, "Dem bones, dem bones, dem dry bones", popular in its day and rather amusing, failed to persuade many to discover what the Lord actually said and why in this unconditional prophecy.

It is clearly stated in the first verse that it was the Spirit of the Lord (can there be any greater authority?) who showed Ezekiel this vision of his nation's coming deathly state and future resuscitation. This is about the nation as a whole, rather than individuals. Bones are heard by the prophet to rattle as they come together (verse 7), with God putting sinews and flesh upon them (verse 8), and breath or spirit entering them (verse 9) so that they stood up, "an exceedingly great army" (verse 10).

At verse 11 the scene changes and deals with the individuals, with the bones in graves, rather than scattered: "'Behold, O My people, I will open your graves and cause you to come up from your graves, and bring you into the land of Israel..... I will put My Spirit in you, and you shall live, and I will place you in your own land. Then you shall know that I, the LORD, have spoken it and performed it,' says the LORD" (verses 12,14). Who dares doubt? This is to follow the Lord's Return in Power.

22 August

"Take a stick for yourself and write on it: 'For Judah and for the children of Israel, his companions.' Then take another stick and write on it, 'For Joseph, the stick of Ephraim, and for all the house of Israel, his companions.' Then join them one to another for yourself into one stick, and they will become one in your hand."
(Ezek 37:16-17).

Ezekiel was told to do this in the presence of elders, who needed this powerful visual aid illustrating God's guarantee of their nation's far distant reunification. Our God is the God of the remarkable. His dealings with Israel since Jacob's day have never ceased to be a remarkable testimony to His faithfulness, and refusal to be thwarted by puny mankind. But equally remarkable is the stubbornness and ability of people in possession of Bibles to reject the evidence.

Consider the facts, which are utterly without parallel in human history. In 931 BC Israel was divided into two separate kingdoms, the one under David's descendants, the other under a succession of imposters. The Northern Kingdom in 722/1 BC was exiled from the Land, never to return, until partially in the 20th Century. In the 7th Century BC the Southern Kingdom was exiled to Babylon for seventy years, and again in 70 AD, with no return except the tiniest trickle of individuals until modern Zionism. This partial return, still in spiritual blindness, but with great mental and physical energy, complies perfectly with the need for many Jews to be in the Land to undergo the Tribulation Period.

Only God know the tribal descent of each Jew, or from which of the two kingdoms they come. A few do seem to know, and others have family traditions with limited degrees of accuracy. But Ezekiel's is a very specific unconditional prophecy which must await the Lord's Return. Thereafter we have God's assurance: "I will make them one nation in the land, on the mountains of Israel; and one king shall be king over them all; they shall no longer be two nations, nor shall they ever be divided into two kingdoms again" (37:22). This lovely prophecy ends with the promise: "My tabernacle also shall be with them; indeed I will be their God, and they shall be My people. The nations also will know that I, the LORD, sanctify Israel, when My sanctuary is in their midst forevermore" (37:27-28).

23 August

"Son of man, set your face against Gog, of the land of Magog, the prince of Rosh, Meshech, and Tubal, and prophesy against him..... After many days you will be visited. In the latter years you will come into the land of those brought back from the sword and gathered from many people on the mountains of Israel, which had long been desolate; they were brought out of the nations, and now all of them dwell safely." (Ezek 38:2,8)

With Ezekiel 38 and 39 we are suddenly plunged into the 21st Century or later. If we believe God's prophetic word, we should not need confirmation from current affairs. But when we do see developing before us the scenario painted by a prophecy, it demands our immediate attention, and we are greatly encouraged. These chapters should be read in full; there is not space to quote everything relevant in two days' readings. A massive but abortive invasion of Israel, unparalleled by anything in history is described here. From 38:5 & 6 we note that Persia (Iran), Libya and the area south of Egypt (Put) are immediately identifiable. It is almost certain that Turkey and Caucasian nations are to be included and there seems little doubt that Russia is described. Gog appears to be Russia, the only nation with the ability to coordinate such an invasion by such diverse nations. More than twenty years of my Army service were involved with the Soviet Union, in linguistics, intelligence, military press analysis and sometimes face-to-face, including a Soviet embassy visit. I met senior generals, attaches and the like. At the same time I was deeply aware of these Ezekiel prophecies, but saw nothing contradictory and much confirmatory in my experiences. Then, quite suddenly, *perestroika* and *glasnost'* arrived in the late 'eighties, and seemed to turn the old Soviet Union into a friendly neighbour without colonial superpower ambitions. But it was difficult to allay one's suspicions over the Russian identification of the nation which Ezekiel said was to come from the uttermost North.

But, conforming to prophecy, once again Russia is deeply involved actively supporting some of Israel's most bitter enemies. The balance of military power is shifting in her favour; her imperialism is ever more aggressive, like the description of Gog.

24 August

"I will turn you around and lead you on, bringing you up from the far north, and bring you against the mountains of Israel. Then I will knock the bow out of your left hand, and cause the arrows to fall out of your right hand. You shall fall upon the mountains of Israel, you and all your troops and the peoples who are with you."
(Ezek 39:2-4)

Here God addresses Gog, the leader of this vast end-time invasion. The AV/KJV statement of a sixth being spared is a mistranslation; none of the invaders are to escape, and their homelands are to suffer. It is silly to quibble about the description of ancient weapons; the prophecy had to make sense down through the ages.

The invasion is to take place between the Rapture and Coming in Power, but the precise timing is not specified. The first half of the Tribulation Period seems the more likely. Any international opposition is to be merely verbal (38:13). It could well be that Satan, as backer of both the Beast's empires and Gog's allies, will cynically encourage the defeat of the latter to allow the Beast to expand his influence from the third of the world, which he is to dominate. However it is God Himself who is to be seen to have defeated the invading forces, without Israel lifting a finger. Chapter 38:18-22 describes the means which God will use, including an earthquake, giant hailstones and the invaders slaying each other, as with the Midianites in Gideon's day (Judges 7:22). They will fall upon the mountains of Israel without coming near Jerusalem. Both the world at large, and Israel in particular, are to take note: "Thus I will magnify Myself and sanctify Myself, and I will be known in the eyes of many nations. Then they shall know that I am the LORD" (38:23); "So I will make My holy name known in the midst of My people Israel, and I will not let them profane My holy name anymore" (39:7).

God's dealing with the nations, whether in mercy or judgment, always has an impact. Satan's policy is to divert attention from God, poking fun at those who recognise the hand of God, and focusing upon secondary causes. Let us observe keenly and intelligently the signs of the times, particularly in the Middle East, and realise that our redemption is drawing nigh.

25 August

"In the visions of God He took me into the land of Israel and set me on a very high mountain; on it toward the south was something like the structure of a city..... And the man said to me, 'Son of man, look with your eyes and hear with your ears, and fix your mind on everything I show you; for you were brought here so that I might show them to you. Declare to the house of Israel everything you see.'" (Ezek 40:2,4)

The final nine chapters of Ezekiel give the most detailed description in the Bible of Israel in the Millennium. Three sections cover the Millennial Temple, the worship and the revised geography with land allocation. It was God who gave Ezekiel this vision, in which he saw 'a Man', evidently not mortal, with a measuring line and rod, who was to be Ezekiel's guide throughout the vision. He ordered Ezekiel to show all that he saw to the house of Israel.

All he was shown was entirely different from what had existed previously. "In the vestibule of the gateway were two tables on this side and two tables on that side, on which to slay the burnt offering, the sin offering, and the trespass offering" (40:39). The reinstitution of animal sacrifices is one reason why some reject the literal Millennial Temple. They point out quite correctly that the deeply symbolic Old Testament sacrifices could not save, but forget that they were nevertheless ordained by God. They had simply pointed forward to Calvary. Why should it be considered strange that future symbolic sacrifices, also clearly ordained by God, should not point back to Calvary, as a potent reminder of what God has done in Christ Jesus?

After the Judgment of the Nations (Matthew 25:31-46), Christ will be represented in the earthly Jerusalem by the Shekinah Glory: Ezekiel relates: "And the glory of the LORD came into the temple by way of the gate which faces toward the east. The Spirit lifted me up and brought me into the inner court; and behold, the glory of the LORD filled the temple" (43:4-5). God's prophet had been alive when reluctantly the glory had departed: "And the glory of the LORD went up from the midst of the city and stood on the mountain, which is on the east side of the city" (11:23). In his newly resurrected body Ezekiel will see its return!

26 August

"'This is the land which you shall divide by lot as an inheritance among the tribes of Israel, and these are their portions,' says the Lord GOD. 'These are the exits of the city. On the north side, measuring four thousand five hundred cubits'..... 'All the way around shall be eighteen thousand cubits; and the name of the city from that day shall be: THE LORD IS THERE.'" (Ezek 48:29-30,35)

Joshua (1:3-4) was told: "Every place that the sole of your foot will tread upon I have given you, as I said to Moses." This is the everlasting title to the Land, as far as the Euphrates, which to date Israel has hardly ever fully controlled and never occupied without being challenged. In the Millennium it will be theirs entirely. Some, but not all, of the boundaries can be precisely identified; but certainly much of Syria and Jordan and the whole of Lebanon will be included. Tribal allocations are given in chapter 48.

The fact that Millennial Jerusalem is described as being "beautiful in elevation, the joy of the whole earth, is Mount Zion on the sides of the north, the city of the great King" (Ps 48:2), suggests that the Millennial city and its environs, will be centred on the northern side of the Zechariah 14:4 divide. Geographical features unlike anything known hitherto in the Promised Land are described, including an ever-deepening river which is to flow from the threshold of the Temple both East and West, "healing" the Dead Sea and allowing for a multitude of fish.

The city itself is to occupy a most prominent position, which will inspire pilgrims from afar off: "They will see the land that is very far off" (Isa 33:17). "Now it shall come to pass in the latter days that the mountain of the LORD'S house shall be established on the top of the mountains, and shall be exalted above the hills; and all nations shall flow to it" (Isa 2:2, also Mic 4:1). It is to be very much smaller than the eternal New Jerusalem described in Revelation 21. The New Jerusalem and earthly Jerusalem will, however, share various other features. There is no reason to take this other than literally in view of all the other global changes. Sadly, we must now leave Ezekiel with its many detailed yet compact prophecies ancient and modern.

Seven Trumpet blasts of Revelation

27 August

"When He opened the seventh seal, there was silence in heaven for about half an hour. And I saw the seven angels who stand before God, and to them were given seven trumpets. Then another angel, having a golden censer, came and stood at the altar. He was given much incense, that he should offer it with the prayers of all the saints upon the golden altar which was before the throne."
(Rev 8:1-3)

The very silence is significant, full of both expectancy and foreboding, and conforms to the half hour of silent worship during the burning of incense in the earthly Temple. Since the time when a trumpet blast was heard from Mount Sinai, when Moses ascended to receive the Ten Commandments, trumpets have been ordained by God for important happenings. The portents described in Exodus 19:16 and Revelation 8:6 are remarkably similar. At Sinai the people trembled; in the Tribulation period those on earth will not hear the trumpets, though one suspects that we in Heaven will do, but there will still be trembling on earth as the judgments begin to take effect. Whether the prayers mentioned are those of God's people of all ages crying for justice, or only Tribulation saints, we are not told. But what happens is God's response. As Charles Ryrie puts it, "As prayer ascends, judgment descends." As with the seven Seals, there is a contrast between the first four and remaining three.

Fitting every event of Revelation 4 to 19 into something like a railway timetable is pointless. Graham Scroggie talks of the seventh seal opening out into the seven trumpets, rather than the trumpets following the seals. Certainly the Seals, Trumpets and later Bowls of Wrath start sequentially, and each seems to progress faster and with greater intensity than the former. I am one of those who suspect (but dare not be adamant) that they are coterminous, each taking us to the end of the Great Tribulation. Jim Allen writes: "When the last trumpet is blown the tribulation is over, the millennium is introduced." It is debatable whether the Trumpet judgments start in the latter part of the Beginning of Sorrows (before the mid-point) or early in the Great Tribulation. It has been suggested that the three series are repetitions of the same events, concentrating on different aspects, but the contrasts are far too great for this.

28 August

"So the seven angels who had the seven trumpets prepared themselves to sound. The first angel sounded: And hail and fire followed, mingled with blood, and they were thrown to the earth. And a third of the trees were burned up, and all green grass was burned up." (Rev 8:6-7)

Jim Allen describes the first trumpet results as "a terrible atmospheric storm on earth that leaves an area completely devastated as a mark of its passing." Seventy years ago I read a devotional Revelation commentary written by my great-aunt, Ethel A Girdlestone, a godly lady who led my parents to saving faith; it is brief but contains some gems. Her comments on chapter 8 include: "The sounding of the first trumpets produce great plagues upon the earth, sea, rivers, vegetation and the heavenly bodies." Back then I believed in faith this literal interpretation; I still do, but can now see how these consequences would follow naturally. Some respected earlier commentators see the trumpet judgments and later bowl judgments as being symbolic. Whether we can explain them scientifically is no reason to doubt God's predictions. Probably long ago few realised that the time would come, as it now has done, when everything depicted would make scientific sense, both in actions and consequences.

Tim La Haye suggests that we compare them with plagues pronounced by Moses in Egypt, likening the symbolic sounding of the trumpet and the symbolic raising of Moses' rod. He asks: "Why should the result on earth be less physical than the event in Moses' day?" Jim Allen takes the same view, and quotes Exodus 9:23-24: "And Moses stretched out his rod toward heaven; and the LORD sent thunder and hail, and fire darted to the ground. And the LORD rained hail on the land of Egypt. So there was hail, and fire mingled with the hail, so very heavy that there was none like it in all the land of Egypt since it became a nation." What God did then He can do again, only this time on a grander, global scale.

From the Seals, which we considered back in June, we learned that during the Tribulation Period there will be a steady decrease in the world's population due to various prophesied factors, including starvation. "Green grass" includes young cereal crops, while a third of the trees destroyed will greatly affect fruit production.

29 August

"Then the second angel sounded: And something like a great mountain burning with fire was thrown into the sea, and a third of the sea became blood. And a third of the living creatures in the sea died, and a third of the ships were destroyed." (Rev 8:8-9)

Again we follow the old principle that if the plain truth makes sense, we should seek no other sense. John describes as well as he can what he was actually shown. Was this a gigantic object from outer space, such as we shall see at the third trumpet blast, or could it be a monstrous subterranean volcano breaking through the ocean surface? Either seems possible. The volcanic island of Hawaii has the biggest mountain in the world, when measured from ocean floor to summit; its origins probably date to the Flood. The 1883 Krakatoa is the best known comparable eruption in recent history, when there were 36,000 immediate deaths, untold damage caused by huge tsunamis and world-wide climatic repercussions; most of the mountain disappeared into the semi-submarine caldera. One feels that such a future volcano would be within reach of the Tribulation epicentre of Israel, and probably within the Mediterranean Sea, which already has many volcanic hot spots.

We can leave the discussion of the outer space objects, which this second trumpet manifestation may yet prove to be, until tomorrow's study. Either would have similar effects on marine life and shipping. Marine life has become more fragile in recent decades owing to mankind's unscrupulous disregard for the welfare of this part of God's creation. This is what conservationists, well-intentioned, but most of whom leave God out of their reckoning, constantly warn us about. As we consider the devastation, we are reminded of the future need for our Creator to reshape the surface and atmosphere of the planet before its repopulation during the Millennium. He who pronounced His creation "very good" in Adam's day (Gen 1:31), will doubtlessly be able to do the same in the Millennium!

There is some doubt as to whether the "one third" stated with the first four trumpet judgments indicates one third of the world-wide intensity or severity of the trumpets, compared to the later bowls of wrath, or whether only a third of the globe, probably the Beast's Revived Roman Empire, will be affected. We can discuss this later.

30 August

"Then the third angel sounded: And a great star fell from heaven, burning like a torch, and it fell on a third of the rivers and on the springs of water. The name of the star is Wormwood. A third of the waters became wormwood, and many men died from the water, because it was made bitter." (Rev 8:10-11)

Ominous readings like these are not only informative, but remind us that the Almighty God of judgment is on our side. Now while the destructive object under the second trumpet blast could be interpreted as coming either from outer space or from within the earth (a minority view), this one definitely falls from the sky. There are three obvious possibilities: (a) a huge meteorite or bit of space debris, white hot as it enters our atmosphere, (b) an asteroid or rocky mini-planet from between Mars and Jupiter, which had left its orbit, possibly through collision with another asteroid, or (c) a comet, a rare visitor to our part of the Solar System, having its own unique elliptical orbit. A comet probably best answers the description of the third trumpet. Gigantic meteorite strikes occasionally occur, such as the 1908 Tunguska aerial explosion, with its enormous crater and vast area of devastation in Siberia. Astronomers are aware of such possibilities, even without scriptural support. Scientific measures to divert possible asteroid strikes are being researched.

God says that both events will happen, and John indicates that both will inflict enormous damage and instil colossal fear. The death of sea creatures at the second trumpet and the lethal embittering of drinking water of the third are consistent with what experts would expect were one to land in the sea and the other somewhere on a land surface. In 1986 a nuclear power station reactor at Chernobyl in the Ukraine exploded, causing enormous devastation and resulting in a huge exclusion zone. There was much excitement when it was pointed out that "chernobyl" is a variety of wormwood, which is mentioned in this prophecy in Revelation. Christian friends, knowing that I was a Russian interpreter, telephoned me for my reactions! I could confirm the translation, but had no authority whatsoever to draw any further correlation, beyond acknowledging that God in mercy permits reminders to draw attention to His infinitely more reliable prophecies and warnings for those who have yet turn to Him, seeking redemption.

31 August

"Then the fourth angel sounded: And a third of the sun was struck, a third of the moon, and a third of the stars, so that a third of them were darkened. A third of the day did not shine, and likewise the night." (Rev 8:12)

There may be overlapping between trumpets, the effects of some may be more lasting than others. We are back with the problem of how to understand the "one third" formula with the first four trumpets, and most commentators are wise enough not to be adamant. This is the petrifying intervention by the Creator in His own creation - the stars and planets, things which the vast part of the world's population assume to be inviolable. Jesus Christ Himself warned: "And there will be signs in the sun, in the moon, and in the stars; and on the earth distress of nations, with perplexity, the sea and the waves roaring" (Lk 21:25). The sea roaring is likely to be associated with the second trumpet and the resultant tsunamis. These are easily understood specific prophecies of things that are to follow the Rapture with increasing intensity. Lesser occurrences may take place as pre-Rapture signs of the times.

We have not as yet experienced noticeably these shortened daylight hours or reduction of solar and other astronomical illuminations. As a country dweller, and one who lived through the wartime black-out, I have to remind myself that hundreds of millions of people suffer so much light pollution, that the stars and moon are almost forgotten as light sources. Such may be the disruption to power supplies as the Tribulation progresses, that the moon and stars may again appear prominent. God may actually alter the amount of light He allows to penetrate the stratosphere, or may somehow modify the daily cycle. Jim Allen lists several of the ways in which this could be achieved. It does not seem feasible that this will apply only to the Beast's empire, but again we cannot be certain.

Many of these judgments will be recognised as 'Acts of God'. There are to be only two reactions, repentance leading to salvation and embitterment leading to further rejection. Nobody will be able to sit on the fence. Putting off being saved until after the Rapture would indeed be folly in view of what is to happen on earth.

1 September

"And I looked, and I heard an eagle flying through the midst of heaven, saying with a loud voice, 'Woe, woe, woe to the inhabitants of the earth, because of the remaining blasts of the trumpet of the three angels who are about to sound!' Then the fifth angel sounded: And I saw a star fallen from heaven to the earth. To him was given the key to the bottomless pit." (Rev 8:13-9:1)

"Eagle" is a well-supported correction to the "angel" of some versions. This will evidently be no more audible to those on earth than will be the trumpets, but listeners in Heaven will be aware; three phenomena of unprecedented severity are about to afflict the earth. The principle of the plain sense making sense has held good for those trumpet judgments which have affected the visible environment. However when we come to the unleashing of invisible spiritual forces, we must accept that John could only describe in words which conjure up some of the dreadfulness of the coming scenario.

The last three trumpets, as we come to them, are described as "woes". Post-Tribulationists do not like to be reminded that, according to their perceived programme, the Church is to be raptured at the third woe!

This "star" is an angel, described as being capable of receiving a key. The bottomless pit", also known as Tartarus, has been the prison of the worst fallen angels since the Flood; they are described by Jude (v 6) as "angels who did not keep their proper domain, but left their own abode..... reserved in everlasting chains under darkness for the judgment of the great day". They have to be released for five months, presumably literal earthly months (9:5). A mighty horde of these accursed beings, long past hope of repentance, luridly described as locusts with a sting in the tail, is to be released, but permitted by God to plague, but not to kill, only those who do not have "the seal of God in their foreheads" (9:4). They are not permitted to harm such vegetation which may have regrown. During the Great Tribulation, which will evidently have started by this point, God's control, probably augmented by holy angels, is to be very rigorous indeed. "In those days men will seek death and will not find it" (9:6). Evidently they will be afraid of the consequences of suicide.

2 September

"Then the sixth angel sounded: And I heard a voice from the four horns of the golden altar which is before God, saying to the sixth angel who had the trumpet, 'Release the four angels who are bound at the great river Euphrates.'" (Rev 9:13-14)

What is revealed at the sixth trumpet or second woe will make complete sense to believers undergoing the experience, but is somewhat enigmatic to us now. Many fallen angels or demons are confined to specific areas on earth. Here are four powerful fallen angels "bound" in the area of the Euphrates, associated since the time of Nimrod with rebellion and falsehood. We see more of the Euphrates when we come to the 6th Bowl. After thousands of years, at a specified time (hour, day, month and year – verse 15) they are to be released, and will be responsible for the death of a third of the world's population which have survived the earlier Seals. Satan simply cannot overrule God's timetable. He is to be given certain short-lived liberties to do his worst during the Tribulation Period, but will never be able to exceed them. "When the enemy comes in like a flood, the Spirit of the LORD will lift up a standard against him" (Isa 59:19).

Available to them is an army of two hundred million "horsemen" (v 16). Whether these are demons or demonically inspired humans is impossible to confirm. China has boasted that she could muster an army of such size. The description of these creatures, as John is shown them (vv 17-19), is lurid indeed and conforms to nothing known to warfare ancient or modern. However it is a heavenly perspective, and there is no doubt that the effects felt on earth will be horrific.

Verses 20-21 tell us that the rest of mankind will not repent and turn to God, but will sin more and more, stubbornly clinging to the idolatrous bestial worship of which we will see more when we come to chapter 13. The effects of the 6th Trumpet will last some time; only at 11:14 are we told: "The second woe is past. Behold, the third woe is coming quickly". That is of course the seventh Trumpet, which contains the remaining judgments including the Bowls of Wrath. What happens in the meantime we will consider in October in the section entitled "Personalities and Parentheses in Revelation".

Prophetic gleanings from Jeremiah

3 September

"Then the LORD put forth His hand and touched my mouth, and the LORD said to me: 'Behold, I have put My words in your mouth. See, I have this day set you over the nations and over the kingdoms, to root out and to pull down, to destroy and to throw down, to build and to plant.'" (Jer 1:9-10)

I have to confess that, whenever I have read through the Bible, I have looked forward to Isaiah more than to the following Jeremiah, partly because, of the two, Isaiah has more about Christ's First Coming, and is generally more positive. But we dare not call any message of God negative, even although its impact on sin and sinners is negative. We would be grossly misrepresenting God. And it is God who put these words in Jeremiah's reluctant mouth. As J Sidlow Baxter remarks, "The man and his message and his times are inseparably bound together and must be interpreted together." Seventy years has passed since my old pastor wrote that, and at least fifty had passed between Isaiah and Jeremiah. In both cases there has been a plummeting of national moral standards. Jeremiah has much to say relevant to the state of Christendom today.

The sequence of pulling down and building up cannot be reversed, and those who attempt to do that today have no chance of success. Good King Josiah had led national repentance, but much was superficial and short lived. Then came the final succession of four wicked kings, the last of David's line until the Millennium. William Kelly's comments are: "All these disgraceful representatives of the royal family were men of great importance, and the state, too, had a measure of independence entirely beyond what was known beyond the return from captivity." Much of what we have seen in Jeremiah is at the Jerusalem end of what we saw in Ezekiel.

But God did not send an Elijah to them; instead He sent his "Weeping Prophet", perhaps the most sensitive of all God's inspired authors. We do well to take note. The world is too good at portraying us as unloving and relishing our task of proclaiming God's judgment on sin. It has been said: "The LORD's servants are immortal until their work is done." If we are within His will, we need never fear what man may do to us.

4 September

"'Return, O backsliding children,' says the LORD; 'for I am married to you. I will take you, one from a city and two from a family, and I will bring you to Zion. And I will give you shepherds according to My heart, who will feed you with knowledge and understanding… At that time Jerusalem shall be called the Throne of the LORD, and all the nations shall be gathered to it, to the name of the LORD, to Jerusalem. No more shall they follow the dictates of their evil hearts'" (Jer 3:14-15,17).

Jeremiah does not date his messages; however this is evidently within the reign of Josiah and before the worst extremes of idolatry described in Ezekiel. Often, as here, Jeremiah jumps directly from his own time to the Millennium, though usually with provisos such as repentance and renewal. In fact, one can argue that there was here an offer of immediate reconciliation; the prophecy of the seventy year Babylonian captivity was still several chapters ahead. Was there ever a more loving call for restitution? Under Mosaic Law the Lord was entitled to put Judah away from Him for ever, in view of their spiritual adultery with idols and those forces which were behind them. But He still asserts that, both spiritually and nationally, He is their Husband. Sadly many "backsliding children" would never heed the gracious invitation to return. Here again is the doctrine of the faithful remnant surviving to the end of the Great Tribulation; the Lord will not cast off forever. "Though He causes grief, yet He will show compassion" (Lam 3:31-32).

When Jeremiah was preaching, the Ark of the Covenant, with its Mercy Seat, representing God's meeting place through the shed blood and presence among them, was still in the Jerusalem Temple. But, within the lifetimes of many of his hearers, the Ark was to be taken to Babylon, never to return. However this was to be no obstacle to God's future earthly throne returning one day to Jerusalem. We have confirmation in the closing chapters of Ezekiel, where, despite details of the Millennial Temple being given, no Ark is included. Jerusalem is to be the throne of God for all the nations during the Millennium, with no opposition from local alternatives.

At a personal level, we are reminded that it is we, not God, who place obstacles to Christ's reigning in hearts.

5 September

"They have lied about the LORD, and said, 'It is not He. Neither will evil come upon us, nor shall we see sword or famine. And the prophets become wind, for the word is not in them. Thus shall it be done to them.'..... An astonishing and horrible thing has been committed in the land: the prophets prophesy falsely, and the priests rule by their own power; and My people love to have it so. But what will you do in the end?" (Jer 5:12-13, 30-31)

What Jeremiah wrote about Judah more than two and a half thousand years ago could be applied to 21st Century Christendom. He was addressing people, who though unfaithful, at least believed in God. They were "religious". What they chose not to believe were His righteous demands and warnings of impending judgment. They were scathing about the words of Jeremiah and other prophets of God. On the other hand false prophets had arisen – "a horrible thing". What was worse, they were doing it in God's Name. The 26th chapter, too long to summarise here, relates one of the worst examples and the fate of the perpetrator. At the same time the priests were devising and preaching popular, non-challenging theology on their own authority. God's comment is: "and My people love to have it so." Does that not sound familiar? I have personally encountered recently church-goers who complain about too much preaching about repentance. Yes, there are faithful preachers out there who deliver what God has laid on their heart. But they tend to be classed as "Jeremiahs". Poor old Jeremiah, that his name should have become a byword for negativity!

But then God asks a most pertinent question: "But what will you do in the end?" What were they to do at the final, dreadful, bloodthirsty sack of Jerusalem? What will today's scoffers do when the Rapture occurs, and, having failed to meet Christ for deliverance, will face the wrath of the Antichrist?

In his Lamentations, Jeremiah wrote at a time when a minority had been taken captive to Babylon, and the false prophets, still denying their national sin, as many do today, prophesied a speedy repatriation: "Your prophets have seen for you false and deceptive visions; they have not uncovered your iniquity, to bring back your captives, but have envisioned for you false prophecies and delusions" (Lam 2:14).

6 September

"I have made the earth, the man and the beast that are on the ground, by My great power and by My outstretched arm, and have given it to whom it seemed proper to Me. And now I have given all these lands into the hand of Nebuchadnezzar the king of Babylon, My servant; and the beasts of the field I have also given him to serve him. So all nations shall serve him and his son and his son's son, until the time of his land comes; and then many nations and great kings shall make him serve them." (Jer 27:5-7)

We are reminded of God's sovereignty in dealing with kings, empires and nations. It was of Nebuchadnezzar that God, through Daniel, announced: "You, O king, are a king of kings. For the God of heaven has given you a kingdom, power, strength, and glory" (Dan 2:37). It was Nebuchadnezzar who, having learned some very hard lessons, declared to his subjects: "Now I, Nebuchadnezzar, praise and extol and honour the King of heaven" (Dan 4:37). It was his grandson, Belshazzar, who was informed, a matter of hours before it happened: "Your kingdom has been divided, and given to the Medes and Persians" (Dan 5:28). Would that the nations of the world learn today that the same Almighty God is no less in control now than He was then.

At the time that Jeremiah was prophesying, Nebuchadnezzar and his Babylonian army had taken over world leadership from Assyria, who had in turn replaced Egypt. All were hereditary oppressors of Israel, and Nebuchadnezzar had already captured Jerusalem, set up a puppet king, Zedekiah, and was soon to return and sack the city. Jeremiah was commissioned to tell the people that God actually required them to surrender to this emperor

Later we find the city leaders asking the king to have Jeremiah slain for demoralising the people by foretelling the imminent sacking of the city by the Babylonian army (38:3-4); "This man does not seek the welfare of this people, but their harm." They did not in fact kill him, but threw him into a miry dungeon. It was an Ethiopian who petitioned the king to allow him to rescue him. Motivation may be excellent human resources management (God created men and women, not human resources!), but when it flies in the face of God's laws, it must be abandoned.

7 September

"The LORD has appeared of old to me, saying: 'Yes, I have loved you with an everlasting love; therefore with lovingkindness I have drawn you..... They shall come with weeping, and with supplications I will lead them. I will cause them to walk by the rivers of waters, in a straight way in which they shall not stumble; for I am a Father to Israel, and Ephraim is My firstborn.' Hear the word of the LORD, O nations, and declare it in the isles afar off, and say, 'He who scattered Israel will gather him, and keep him as a shepherd does his flock.'" (Jer 31:3,9-10)

This passage has shorter term relevance for those soon to be deported for seventy years to Babylon; but it also has a long term relevance for all Israel, plus some for the Church today. God's promises to Israel are both conditional and unconditional. It is quite extraordinary how the Jews of Jeremiah's day believed the unconditional and scorned the conditional, and how many Christians today do exactly the opposite regarding Israel. Chapters 31 to 33 lie at the very heart of Jeremiah's prophecies and contain God's most faithful promises, including the one where it is God, who, having scattered Israel, will not only regather Israel in a second Exodus, but will keep and shepherd them.

Even the Judeans of Jeremiah's day must have been surprised by the mention of Ephraim, whose firstborn right over Manasseh goes back to Genesis 48:19. Ephraim was a leader in the Northern Kingdom's apostasy and was now exiled by Assyria and disowned by God. But even Ephraim, who is not to be included among the Tribulation Period witnesses (Revelation 7:5-8), has to be restored and honoured in the Millennium. A few verses later we read of Rachel, mother of Joseph and grandmother of Manasseh and Ephraim, weeping bitterly for her children and being comforted by the Lord (v 16); the "slaughter of the innocents" by Herod is only one of two prophetic applications.

One lesson for Church Age believers is that the backslider who has strayed, perhaps since teenage years, may still be restored, when coming with "weeping and supplication", having been "drawn by lovingkindness". Sadly fellow believers may continue to condemn what the Lord has long since forgiven, and can prove an obstacle to reconciliation. There are lessons for us all in Jeremiah.

8 September

"They shall ask the way to Zion, with their faces toward it, saying, 'Come and let us join ourselves to the LORD in a perpetual covenant that will not be forgotten.' My people have been lost sheep. Their shepherds have led them astray; they have turned them away on the mountains. They have gone from mountain to hill; they have forgotten their resting place….. Thus says the LORD of hosts: 'The children of Israel were oppressed, along with the children of Judah; all who took them captive have held them fast; they have refused to let them go. Their Redeemer is strong; the LORD of hosts is His name. He will thoroughly plead their case, that He may give rest to the land, and disquiet the inhabitants of Babylon.'" (Jer 50:5-6,33-34)

Jeremiah had been prophesying the doom of Moab, Ammon, Edom and Syria, countries which had for many centuries been regularly at war with Israel. Now, in chapters 50 and 51, we come to two of the recurrent themes of Jeremiah, Israel's ultimate restoration and judgment upon her oppressors. Here Jeremiah was forecasting Babylon's short- and long-term doom; the latter we will encounter in Revelation 17 and 18. The charge against Babylon has been repeated down through the centuries, even among 'Christian' nations: "All who found them have devoured them; and their adversaries said, 'We have not offended, because they have sinned against the LORD'" (50:7). God cannot be impressed by those who would rewrite the history of the Holocaust. He has ever been intensely aware, and the perpetrators have invariably suffered. Observe how He viewed them: "Because you were glad, because you rejoiced, **you destroyers of My heritage**" (50:11).

Even today in some churches which class themselves as evangelical, because of *their* Amillennial tradition, one may encounter quite stiff resistance to prophecies regarding Israel's future restoration, which can only be Millennial. "'In those days and in that time,' says the LORD, 'The iniquity of Israel shall be sought, but there shall be none; and the sins of Judah, but they shall not be found; For I will pardon those whom I preserve'" (Jer 50:20). Israel's strong Redeemer is also our Redeemer; is He any less trustworthy regarding Israel than He is the Gentile Church, or vice versa? God forbid!

The Holy City
The New Jerusalem

9 September

"As it is written: 'Eye has not seen, nor ear heard, nor have entered into the heart of man the things which God has prepared for those who love Him.' But God has revealed them to us through His Spirit. For the Spirit searches all things, yes, the deep things of God."
(I Cor 2:9-10)

We referred to these two verses back in April regarding the Rapture and what lies beyond. We return to the theme of what lies beyond, especially for resurrected, by then immortal, believers. We will also consider further how these are to relate to mortals on earth during the Millennium. As we have seen in our studies hitherto, Scripture tells, much about a gloriously restored planet under Christ's direct rule – wonderful, but more or less comprehensible. However, the fact that, if we are believers now, we will be in incorruptible bodies then, is thrilling indeed; but much of what we shall experience then is beyond mortal comprehension. Paul in today's text refers back to Isaiah 64:4, and adds a "But.....". In the New Testament, particularly in the final two chapters of Revelation, New Testament saints are told more. What we are told can be perceived spiritually, rather than intellectually.

The Holy City, the New Jerusalem, is formally introduced in Revelation 21; we shall be reminded tomorrow that there are in fact a few earlier references to it. What we have to keep in mind, and this can be difficult, is that this is not part of our creation, which is passing – temporary. Here are grounds for rejoicing and confidence.

Some think of God's dwelling place as being part of a 'parallel' universe, but this would put it on the same plane as our own, that which appears to extend thousands of light years to the farthest galaxies, incorporating black holes and various other astronomical wonders. But it seems that, in reality, God, should He wish, could, in a moment, stretch out His hand and draw home everything in this creation. CS Lewis, in his final Narnia book, "The Last Battle" got somewhere near it, though sadly he also incorporated elements of Greek mythology. We are about to look now at a most privileged revelation - the Holy City, the New Jerusalem.

10 September

"Now I saw a new heaven and a new earth, for the first heaven and the first earth had passed away. Also there was no more sea. Then I, John, saw the holy city, New Jerusalem, coming down out of heaven from God, prepared as a bride adorned for her husband."
(Rev 21:1-2)

The timing of the first statement of today's text is indisputable. John is being taken in vision beyond the end of this earth and perhaps, though we cannot be sure, beyond the end of this visible universe. "Heaven" can mean (a) the atmosphere, (b) the cosmos or visible universe or (c) God's dwelling place. It is inconceivable that it is God's dwelling place which will have passed away.

We must now face an important question; is this Holy City and its accompanying new earth something which will not exist until following the end of this old world? Evidently the new *world* must await the passing of the old one. However we will already have occupied the City, the bridal home. Moreover we know where it is at present; it is within the Father's House, as yet unoccupied, awaiting not the end of the world, but the First Resurrection. Two statements stand out as to our accompanying Him and simply cannot be denied: "That where I am, there you may be also" (Jn 14:3) and "And thus we shall always be with the Lord" (I Thess 4:17). The first was when He promised the Eleven that He was going to prepare a place for them. The Thessalonians text confirms the timing of our occupation.

How do we fit this in with the Day of Pentecost statement about the ascended Christ? We have already seen confirmation from Acts 3:20-21: "Whom heaven must receive until the times of restoration of all things," in other words the Millennium. Does this mean that, for a thousand years, mortals and immortals would have to live together on earth, perhaps in the way that Jesus lived, often invisible, with His disciples for those forty days after His resurrection? Does it mean that, for the duration of the Millennium, we would have to abandon the place the Lord has gone to prepare for us? The answer to both questions is that it will not be like that. Our **home** will be the Holy City, the New Jerusalem. But how can this be if we are to relate to earth and its mortal inhabitants?

11 September

"Then one of the seven angels who had the seven bowls filled with the seven last plagues came to me and talked with me, saying, 'Come, I will show you the bride, the Lamb's wife.' And he carried me away in the Spirit to a great and high mountain, and showed me the great city, the holy Jerusalem, descending out of heaven from God" (Rev 21:9-10).

We must ask whether this descent of the New Jerusalem is the same event as that described in yesterday's text (Rev 21:2). Evidently it is not; it is a prior one, describing what is to happen at the beginning of the Millennium. We have in Isaiah 65 a splendid precedent for this reversal of sequences: "For behold, I create new heavens and a new earth; and the former shall not be remembered or come to mind" (verse 17); this sounds remarkably like Revelation 21:1 which we quoted yesterday. However it is immediately followed by a "But", and we find ourselves on this earth in the Millennium, reading texts which we saw back in July's readings.

Revelation chapters 21 and 22 are generally agreed to fall into three main parts:-
• 21:1 to 21:8 Starting with "a new heaven and a new earth" and referring exclusively to what follows the end of the world.
• 21:9 to 22:5 Starting with "the bride, the Lamb's wife", revealed as "the holy city, New Jerusalem", covering both the period of the Millennium and beyond.
• 22:6 to 22:20 An epilogue, addressed to all irrespective of timing.

So critical are answers to a consistent understanding of the Millennium, that, when I was researching for my book, *"The Millennium – Restoration After Retribution"*, I consulted twenty-six Pre-Millennial commentaries. I believe that the above is the majority view; the fact that John is shown this by one of the pre-Armageddon "Bowl" angels (Revelation 16:1) surely confirms that events in this old earth below are covered: "And the nations of those who are saved shall walk in its light, and the kings of the earth bring their glory and honour to it (21:24), and the leaves of its trees are for the healing of the nations" (22:2).

12 September

"And he who talked with me had a gold reed to measure the city, its gates, and its wall. The city is laid out as a square; its length is as great as its breadth. And he measured the city with the reed: twelve thousand furlongs. Its length, breadth, and height are equal." (Rev 21:15-16)

The Holy City is not a state, as some assume; it is a place, even although its dimensions may exceed anything with which our earthbound imaginations can cope. The Greek *'topon'* always means a place, a locality, room or similar. Our Lord has gone to prepare a *place* for us; whatever else He is preparing, a place is what He promised in that upper room that night so long ago, not merely a state or a condition. As John de Silva in one of the most comprehensive and helpful books on the subject, *"Outlines in Bible Prophecy"*, writes: "Abraham did not look for a mystical dwelling place, but one that was as literal as the tents of his day. The structural features of the New Jerusalem indicate it is literal. The occupants are *distinct* from it (Hebrews 12:22-23). The very dimensions also prove that it is a literal place." Yes, while it is rather more than a place, that does not mean that it is not a place! The fact that it is as high as it is long and broad could mean that it is either a cube or a pyramid. There is limited value in speculating; it will make perfect sense to us one day.

More important is how it will relate to earth and how the inhabitants of the two will communicate with one another. As they are two separate creations, one cannot measure the gap in distance. Even in the present age Paul remarked: "So that they should seek the Lord, in the hope that they might grope for Him and find Him, though He is not far from each one of us; for in Him we live and move and have our being" (Acts 17:27-28). In the Bible we have ample proof of the proximity of God in many respects, and of, from the human perspective, an insuperable gap in others. We will see tomorrow some indications of the "commuting" of immortal believers between their celestial home and the Millennial world.

13 September

"Then, the same day at evening, being the first day of the week, when the doors were shut where the disciples were assembled, for fear of the Jews, Jesus came and stood in the midst, and said to them, 'Peace be with you.'" (Jn 20:19)

This may seem an odd verse for our current theme; its relevance should quickly become obvious. The Bible gives only one precedent for those resurrected never to die again appearing on earth; this may give us some guidelines as to how immortal saints, visiting earth during Millennium, will be able to behave and to be perceived by mortals. That precedent is the Lord Jesus Christ Himself, during the forty days between His Resurrection and Ascension. Before His death, He had periodically broken natural laws, as when He walked on the water. But that was miraculous, or supernatural – the exercise of Divine power over the nature which He had created. But later, in His resurrection body, He was simply behaving naturally when, for instance, He passed effortlessly through walls. Trench points out that the Greek of Jesus' greeting in John 20:21 is the equivalent of the Hebrew *'shalom lakem'*, which is always an assurance of safety, that all is well, and that the disciples had no need to be alarmed by this sudden manifestation. So surely it is likely to be in the Millennial earth with immortal visitors.

We have noted that at least some of these immortal saints will have divinely delegated tasks or offices upon earth, so they will evidently be coming and going to and from earth below. What Jacob saw momentarily of angels ascending and descending was the norm! However those on earth in their **mortal** bodies will not enter the New Jerusalem, although they will enter the Millennial earthly Jerusalem. It goes without saying that, within the New Jerusalem, immortals will be visible to one another, as will our Lord Himself be.

The physical empathy of the almighty risen Lord with the disciples is reflected in His question, "Children, have ye any meat?" His resurrection body was still in sympathy with their body. We cannot explain it; we can only accept it. Fellowship between mortal and immortal is assured, as no doubt such delegated ruling authority and administrative discipline, as is required, will seem natural (see Revelation 3:21).

14 September

"And there shall be no more curse, but the throne of God and of the Lamb shall be in it, and His servants shall serve Him. They shall see His face, and His name shall be on their foreheads."
(Rev 22:3-4)

Anything that may be perceived as an attempt to analyse the Godhead requires such care. Whilst we are still in these frail bodies, shades of opinion among those who accept the great central truths may be expected, especially regarding the future. Yet it is important not to leave unanswered questions as to how the Lord Jesus Christ will be perceived or seen (a) by immortal saints in the Holy City, (b) by mortal earthly inhabitants. There are very clear differences. Within the Holy City it is stated that we shall see His face; indeed we will have seen His face since our resurrection or Rapture. But we have noted elsewhere that, except perhaps very briefly at the Judgment of the Nations (Matthew 25:31-46), He will be seen only in the form of His Shekinah Glory in the Jerusalem Temple (Ezekiel 43:1-5). When despairing unbelievers eventually see the Lamb of God, whom they rejected, it will precede their consignment to eternal punishment.

Seven times between Revelation 21:9 and 22:5 we read of the Lamb: "The bride, the Lamb's wife." (21:9); "On them (the foundations) were the names of the twelve apostles of the Lamb" (21:14); "The Lord God Almighty and the Lamb are its temple" (21:22); "The Lamb is its light" (21:23); "Those who are written in the Lamb's Book of Life" (21:27); "The throne of God and of the Lamb" (22:1); also in 22:3. The Lamb was first identified as a Man in Isaiah 53:7 and as the Man Christ Jesus in the Baptist's cry, "The Lamb of God who takes away the sin of the world" (Jn 1:29). However, as Jim Allen, in his most comprehensive recent commentary, points out, referring to I Peter 1:18-20, His appointment as the Lamb was ordained before this world began. "You were not redeemed with corruptible things.... but with the precious blood of Christ, as of a lamb without blemish and without spot. He indeed was foreordained before the foundation of the world". That which preceded time, as we know it, will surely also outlast time altogether. Indeed, "The Lamb is all the glory in Immanuel's Land!"

15 September

"Also she had a great and high wall with twelve gates, and twelve angels at the gates, and names written on them, which are the names of the twelve tribes of the children of Israel..... Now the wall of the city had twelve foundations, and on them were the names of the twelve apostles of the Lamb." (Rev 21:12,14)

This follows the description of the Millennial descent of the Holy City. When we recall that the first inhabitants of the City will have been the newly Raptured or resurrected Church, we may be tempted to wonder how Israel with its twelve tribes is to fit in along with the Church, which has been the Lamb's wife, since before Christ's Coming in Power.

Dr Sale Harrison writes: "The twelve foundations have inscribed in them the names of the twelve apostles of the Lamb (v. 14). This is well explained in Ephesians 2:19-20. '(Ye) are built upon the foundation of the apostles and prophets, Jesus Christ Himself being the chief corner stone.'" The prophets are part of our foundation, as well as the Apostles. Jim Allen is very much aware of the perceived problem, but answers it well. "With the fact in mind that those of the 'Wife of Jehovah' will have been raised to immortal life at the outset of the Millennium, we should ask ourselves where else would these redeemed be other than within the eternal city; it would seem unnatural that they should be confined to earth with mortals."

Dr Walvoord reaches similar conclusions. "Because of the symbolism of a bride in the New Testament, in contrast to Israel as the wife of Jehovah, some have attempted to limit the New Jerusalem as having reference only to the church..... The use of the marriage figure, however, in both the Old and New Testaments is sufficiently frequent so that we cannot arbitrarily insist that figures are always used in precisely the same connotation." These are sensitive matters, and I have quoted from authorities who write carefully and yet succinctly.

The Bride of the Lamb will have been complete in membership since the Rapture, whereas the resurrection of the Old Testament saints takes place at or just before the start of the Millennium, but still in time to claim their place in the eternal Holy City, along with, although this is not confirmed, the Tribulation martyrs.

16 September

"For 'He has put all things under His feet.' But when He says 'all things are put under Him,' it is evident that He who put all things under Him is excepted. Now when all things are made subject to Him, then the Son Himself will also be subject to Him who put all things under Him, that God may be all in all." (I Cor 15:27-28)

It is easy to perceive different roles within the Godhead. There is never any conflict, though Jesus, purchasing our redemption, took on various contrasting roles. Immediately before today's text we read: "Then comes the end, when He delivers the kingdom to God the Father, when He puts an end to all rule and all authority and power. For He must reign till He has put all enemies under His feet." Thus it is said: "And God will wipe away every tear from their eyes; there shall be no more death, nor sorrow, nor crying. There shall be no more pain, for the former things have passed away" (Rev 21:4).

John Heading quotes from these verses of Paul, in commenting on the opening verses of Revelation 21: "Notice the difference in style, when these verses are contrasted with the rest of Revelation. There is now no separate mention of the three Persons of the Godhead – only 'God' is mentioned..... the Godhead shall be all in all, reigning eternally and unitedly. The distinctions necessary for His work on the first earth appear to be veiled in this passage speaking of the eternal state. 'I and My Father are one' (Jn 10:30)." Dr Sidlow Baxter comments, not in contrast, but in addition to the above thought: "As Hebrew 13:8 says, our Lord, by His incarnation is now 'Jesus Christ', the same yesterday, today and *unto the ages'*..... That is why in the Apocalypse, the throne is said to be that of 'God and the Lamb unto the ages of the ages'. Eternity will not nullify that office of the Lamb which bought us everlasting life at such great cost, even when 'God is all in all'".

The unrepentant, unsaved "shall have their part in the lake which burns with fire and brimstone, which is the second death" (v 8). We considered the Great White Throne back on 29th January; now even that is past, though its consequences live on, utterly separate from the Holy City.

A selection from the Minor Prophets

17 September

"For the children of Israel shall abide many days without king or prince, without sacrifice or sacred pillar, without ephod or teraphim. Afterward the children of Israel shall return and seek the LORD their God and David their king. They shall fear the LORD and His goodness in the latter days." (Hos 3:4-5)

We looked briefly at Hosea on 28th May. We know only this prophet's father's name and his wife's and children's names and that he was a contemporary of Isaiah. God told Hosea to enter into a marriage with a potentially unfaithful woman, Gomer, whose conduct would reflect Israel's conduct towards her Husband, Jehovah. Hosea's name is a variation of Joshua and Jesus, in other words it means 'saviour'. He was to be saviour and redeemer as well as husband to Gomer. The pain and shame which Hosea experienced was very real. God wanted this faithful servant of His to endure what, for centuries, He had endured with a faithless nation, and to record his experiences for future generations to read. How very much we learn about God's love and purpose, short and long term, here.

Only Hosea's eldest, Jezreel, was positively identified as his child, Lo-Ruhamah, a daughter was second, whilst the youngest of three, a son, was Lo-Ammi. God carefully named these children, giving two negative prefixes, 'Lo-'. Gomer had sold herself to a number of lovers. The references to pagan practices in 2:11-13 suggest that she had served as a shrine prostitute, a common and sometimes lucrative practice at that time, but one which would have added to the shame involved in redeeming her. The parallel with God and Israel is constantly referred to in Hosea. Five times within fourteen chapters we have the cycle of Israel's sin, punishment and ultimate restoration, each with a different emphasis; today's text concludes the first of these.

We and many generations before us are the beneficiaries of this man's trauma. We have to be cautious about generalisations about backsliders, because the question always arises as to whether they have been saved in the first place. But many have, and are reminded of the welcome that awaits our penitential return, even though our 'exile' has been long, painful and costly. What a waste if, having trusted in Christ in our youth, we "fear the LORD and His goodness (only) in our latter days"!

18 September

*"I **will** return again to My place till they acknowledge their offence. Then they **will** seek My face; In their affliction they **will** earnestly seek Me."* (Hos 5:15)

Today's text is one of the most sombre in the Bible. Hosea was preaching and writing before the 722/1 BC exile of the Northern Kingdom. God, who was, as with the Laodicean Church, standing outside at the threshold, was not to "return to His place" for twenty-seven plus centuries. Only Judah and adherents were to be privileged to experience His Son's coming forth "from His place" after seven centuries, again, as far as the bulk of Judah was concerned, to return rejected to His own place until His glorious Coming Forth on that future day.

Do we ever forget that the Bible is the infallible Word of God, and that, whenever He gives no conditions, He will not be thwarted, and that much in the Bible is simply not open to negotiation? Any challenge or disbelief is sin. Hosea's book is rich in divine assurances, and we may be reassured that our salvation is equally safe in His hands. Throughout the book, sometimes in the midst of gloom and doom where they are least expected, we encounter the wonderful promises of restoration already referred to, confidently bridging the intervening centuries. Note the triple affirmative in today's text. Let us look at some of them briefly, some have already been quoted, but bear repetition:-

"In the place where it was said to them, 'You are not My people,' there it **shall** be said to them, 'You are sons of the living God'" (1:10). "'In that day' says the Lord, 'you **will** call Me "my Husband", and no longer call Me "my Master"'" (2:16). "'I **will** betroth you to Me forever; yes, I **will** betroth you to Me in righteousness and justice'" (2:19). "I **will** say to those who were not My people, 'You are My people'" (2:28). "'They **shall** come trembling like a bird from Egypt, like a dove from the land of Assyria; and I **will** let them dwell in their houses, says the Lord'" (11:11). "O Israel, you are destroyed, but your help is from Me. I **will** be your King" (13:9). "I **will** heal their backsliding; I will love them freely.... I **will** be like the dew to Israel" (14:4-5).

19 September

"My God will cast them away, because they did not obey Him; and they shall be wanderers among the nations." (Hos 9:17)

We have seen much evidence in other Old Testament books of God's purposes for Israel declaring His faithfulness in the blessings and curses which he gave through Moses in Deuteronomy 28 and 29. But actually Hosea's book alone provides sufficient evidence. My own fairly wide experience of Protestantism in several countries indicates that whenever one encounters a church which claims to be evangelical, but denies God's future purposes for Israel, there is inevitably a hardness of heart and that strange imbalance which drives people towards either the Calvinist or the Arminian extremes, as if God were incapable of being able to honour both "Whosoever will may come" and "You have not chosen Me but I have chosen you." The two are equally true, but how they are equally true is comprehended spiritually rather than intellectually.

Let us ask four key questions, seeking answers in Hosea's book:- (a) To whom does the promised restoration apply? The answer is simple. The ones who are promised restoration are those "who shall be wanderers among the nations" (9:17). Having sown the wind, they were to reap the whirlwind (8:7). Nowhere in the book is there the faintest hint that those who are to be disciplined and those who are to be restored are not one and the same. Already, said Hosea, they were "among the Gentiles like a vessel in which is no pleasure" (8:8). (b) Has the promised restoration occurred already? Certainly no restoration as described here has ever taken place to date. "I have spoken by the prophets, and have multiplied visions; I have given symbols through the witness of the prophets" (12:10). (c) If it has not occurred yet, when will restoration take place? Chapter 3:5 simply says that it will be in the latter days. "Afterward the children of Israel shall return and seek the Lord their God and David their king," and several times uses the expression "In that day". In Chapter 13:10-11 **Jehovah** (13:4) declares unambiguously: "O Israel.....I will be your King." (d) Will it be a physical as well as spiritual restoration? If the wandering among the nation has been geographical, how can any assume that the restoration can be less so – geographical as well as spiritual?

20 September

"How can I give you up, Ephraim? How can I hand you over, Israel? How can I make you like Admah? How can I set you like Zeboiim? My heart churns within Me; My sympathy is stirred. I will not execute the fierceness of My anger; I will not again destroy Ephraim. For I am God, and not man, the Holy One in your midst; and I will not come with terror......They shall come trembling like a bird from Egypt, like a dove from the land of Assyria. And I will let them dwell in their houses', says the LORD." (Hos 11:8-9,11)

Here God is addressing the guiltiest of the soon-to-be-exiled Northern tribes, but, being God and not man, He cannot give up His covenant people. The cities of the plain referred to were neighbours of Sodom and Gomorrah and shared their destruction. But God gives us an awesome insight into His own heart of love. Does His heart ever churn for us? Is His sympathy stirred? Do we underestimate His holiness, which compels mercy as well as penalty?

As I write, there are fifteen inches of snow in our back garden. I had already chosen my text for the day when I opened the back door to find two hungry pheasants and sundry smaller birds waiting. While the frequent visiting pheasant was fairly confident; her friend was clearly petrified, edging back and forward, terrified lest I, looming over her, should molest her, but equally petrified that if she did not get her share of peanuts she would starve. In the end hunger won! My mind went to this latter day prophecy of Hosea. Ephraim and her neighbouring tribes will be conscious of three thousand years of rebellion, but, as the Great Tribulation nears its end, they will be afraid not to be afraid. We have seen something of the details in Zechariah 12. Surely God's Holy Spirit will bring to mind these wonderful words of promised restoration. When a name is attached and God's reassurance is thus personalised, fear is more easily overcome. When Hezekiah confessed "I mourned like a dove" (Isa 38:14), God sent the prophet personally to him.

"Fear not, for I have redeemed you; I have called you by your name; you are Mine" (Isa 43:1). We are not the first addressee, but we are also a covenant people and each believer can claim this.

21 September

"So I will restore to you the years that the swarming locust has eaten, the crawling locust, the consuming locust, and the chewing locust, My great army which I sent among you." (Joel 2:25)

This prophet's name means "Jehovah is God". Joel has been called the prophet of God's sovereignty, and has much to say about the Day of the Lord, which means any time of dramatic divine intervention in the affairs of men, but also specifically refers to the Tribulation and beyond. The emphasis in Joel is upon the judgmental: "For the day of the LORD is great and very terrible; who can endure it?" (2:11). Actual locust swarms with their devastation are prophesied in the opening verses. Human "locusts" are suggested in 1:6-7. "For a nation has come up against My land..... He has laid waste My vine and ruined My fig tree; he has stripped it bare and thrown it away; Its branches are made white." God can judge or bless any nation, and we may well consider whether the United Kingdom, once a world leader in evangelism and missionary endeavour, is not beginning to suffer under the hand of God for publicly defying His ancient laws and welcoming paganism. Only confession and repentance can restore us.

There are two dangers in Joel for those who take prophecy seriously, namely that too much will be assumed to refer primarily to the latter days on the one hand, or that too little will be on the other! God had messages of warning, comfort and reassurance for His people, who still had centuries to survive before their Messiah first came. He did not neglect them. There is little doubt that, because of their sinfulness, God was about to send genuine locusts; the various stages of their development is described in chapter 1; but they also foreshadow invading armies. Had the first been heeded, there would have been no need for the second. Both the ancient and future Assyrian invasions are included, but the language suggests the massive end-time invasions which we have considered elsewhere. But what is most important is what is indicated in today's verse; everything, whether it be several centuries BC or yet in the future is in view. God is going to restore what all locusts, be they insect, human or demonic, have consumed or destroyed.

22 September

"And it shall come to pass afterward that I will pour out My Spirit on all flesh; your sons and your daughters shall prophesy, your old men shall dream dreams, your young men shall see visions, and also on My menservants and on My maidservants I will pour out My Spirit in those days." (Joel 2:28-29)

Peter on the day of Pentecost added "says God" after the first few words, because in verses 17 to 21 of Acts chapter 2 he is quoting the Septuagint version of Joel, where, as in the Hebrew version, these constitute a separate chapter. The Acts citation is much better known than the Joel original. Peter had been pointing out that those who were praising God in a multitude of foreign languages were not drunk, it being early in the day, but rather "This is what was spoken by the prophet Joel." People demanded explanations. The answer was that it was the same Holy Spirit at work. Old Testament people did not think of the Holy Spirit as a Person, so this to many of them was revolutionary.

The whole quote includes Joel's prediction of spectacular wonders in the heavens and earth involving the sun and moon (2:30-31); Peter concludes with Joel's, "And it shall come to pass that whoever calls on the name of the LORD shall be saved" (v 32). Nowhere does Peter suggest that the whole of Joel's prophecy is being fulfilled then and there. He is merely explaining that the manifestation which the crowds are witnessing is an outpouring of God's Holy Spirit, something promised for the latter days in several other Old Testament passages, but occurring most dramatically at the outset of the Church Age.

Even this wonderful Pentecostal outpouring was less universal than will be the latter day one, as the Tribulation Period is about to pass into the Millennium, because, as, Joel continues: "In Mount Zion and in Jerusalem there shall be deliverance, as the Lord has said, among the remnant whom the Lord calls." At Pentecost there were no "wonders in heaven, no blood, or fire or vapour of smoke"; so the apostle could not possibly mean that the prophecy was then really fulfilled. On the other hand there was another wonder; Jewish pilgrims from much of the known world had been filled with the Holy Spirit and were about to return with the Gospel to distant homes.

23 September

*"'Let the nations be wakened, and come up to the Valley of
Jehoshaphat; for there I will sit to judge all the surrounding nations.
Put in the sickle, for the harvest is ripe. Come, go down; for the
winepress is full, the vats overflow - for their wickedness is great.'
Multitudes, multitudes in the valley of decision! For the day of the
LORD is near in the valley of decision......The LORD also will roar
from Zion, and utter His voice from Jerusalem; the heavens and
earth will shake; but the LORD will be a shelter for His people, and
the strength of the children of Israel."* (Joel 3:12-14,16)

The final chapter of Joel is entirely latter day and addresses both
Gentiles and Judah. It is important to have the sequence of events
from Revelation 19:11 to 20:15 in our mind. Joel deals only with the
Jerusalem sector; we can leave Armageddon itself to other prophets!
Judgment of the Nations will come in two phases, firstly military,
secondly civilian, so to speak. Firstly, the colossal armies will be
destroyed by the sword of the Lord's mouth (Zechariah 14:12,
Revelation 19:21) as He returns in glory. Secondly, all survivors of
the Gentiles will be gathered into the Valley of Jehoshaphat (Joel 3:2)
for the Judgment of the Nations. Some might dispute whether both
are included in this prophecy, but it seems profitable at least to look
at them. The spectacular valley which lies between Jerusalem and
the Mount of Olives will be occupied on both occasions, though in
very different ways. The invading nations will aim to capture the city
virtually intact. God commands agricultural implements to be modified
into weapons (verse 10) as He challenges them to open confrontation.

Once the armies have been annihilated, there is to be a further quite
different judgment or assizes in the Valley of Jehoshaphat; Gentiles
survivors are to be judged and momentous segregating decisions
are to be made. Civilian numbers will have been reduced to a
fraction by wars, plagues, famines, earthquakes, martyrdom and
other disasters, from the opening of the first four Seals of Revelation
6 to the global earthquake of the seventh Bowl in Revelation 16. We
looked at the criteria for this Judgment of the Nations back on 13th
January; do please refer. Any 'Replacement Theologian' ambivalent
about Anti-Semitism should read the six closing verses of Joel.
Palestinian partitionists should read 3:2.

24 September

"Surely the Lord GOD does nothing, unless He reveals His secret to His servants the prophets. A lion has roared! Who will not fear? The Lord GOD has spoken! Who can but prophesy?" (Amos 3:7-8)

The first statement gives great assurance to those who trust in the Lord, but should strike terror to those who do not. A well-known verse in Psalm 119 reads: "Your word is a lamp to my feet and a light to my path." (verse 105). Long ago, when I ran leadership courses, I quoted this to illustrate the difference between an aim and an objective. The traveller at night needed to see the light on the watchtower of the town to which he was journeying, but he also needed a lamp to ensure that he could deal with dangers along the way. God has in His word of prophecy given us that final light, but we have to trust Him daily for the steps of the way which we may encounter only at the last minute, often changing our short term plans. Amos was one of those to whom God had revealed secrets and had given sufficient authority, credibility and, indeed, compulsion for people to pay attention. Here the context is one of reprimand for failing to heed God's prophet. Even the warning roaring of the lion was being ignored. Ivan Steeds remarks: "If God has not spoken, then one man's guess is as good as another; but He has spoken, as He has in His word; that at once settles everything for the one who fears Him."

Earlier (v 3) Amos asks: "Can two walk together, unless they are agreed?" Seeing two out walking together indicates a degree of friendship or trust. Amos had spoken because he had been walking with God, listening to Him, and passing on what had been vouchsafed to him. He is thus seen as being trustworthy, not for his own sake, but for God's. Each one of us shares the same responsibility, but can be trusted only if we are walking with God, when those who know us best will be duly alerted, and even the casual observer may take note.

Amos had been announcing that God's judgment had come. Is it not our responsibility to point out cause and effect upon society when our nation turns its backs on its Creator?

25 September

"Woe to you who desire the day of the LORD! For what good is the day of the LORD to you? It will be darkness, and not light."
(Amos 5:18)

The foolish people whom Amos had been addressing had been calling out for the Day of the Lord. We have seen that this term more often applies to judgment. Whatever else it means, it will always be appropriate to actual circumstances, rather than to wishful thinking. Amos has already, in his first two chapters, condemned neighbouring nations; his own nation was delighted and actually looked forward to the Day of the Lord with respect to these, but ignored what God was saying about them. It was inconceivable to them that they of all people were ripe for judgment. This was one of three intensifying condemnatory warning addresses in Amos to Israel regarding her abuse of privileges and special status. "You only have I known of all the families of the earth; therefore I shall punish you for all your iniquities" (3:2).

"Woe to you who desire the day of the LORD!" (5:18); such a desire is folly. Repentance was what was needed. In Great Britain our last national day of prayer was during the Second World War; those who have occasionally advocated one since have been treated with contempt. Intercessory prayer for the nation is still as appropriate as when Nehemiah and Daniel uttered their classic passionate intercessions (Nehemiah 1:4-11 & Daniel 9:1-19).

Our country too has the Word of God, but will not learn. A compassion for minorities is one thing; discarding a Christian heritage to appease something alien is entirely different. Dire consequences are elaborated in Scripture. The euphoric singing of 'Land of Hope and Glory' in the Albert Hall surely no longer conforms to God's assessment of our spiritual status – if it ever did. The 'Bible loving Scotland' of former years has become 'Bible scorning Scotland' at parliamentary, judicial and ecclesiastical levels, with only a minority of dissenters. Paganism in many forms has become established, assertive and even fashionable. "Prepare to meet your God, O Israel!", cries the prophet (4:12). Prepare to meet your God, O Britain, O America, O Australia, O Canada, O modern Israel!

26 September

"'Behold, the days are coming,' says the LORD, 'When the ploughman shall overtake the reaper, and the treader of grapes him who sows seed; The mountains shall drip with sweet wine, and all the hills shall flow with it. I will bring back the captives of My people Israel; they shall build the waste cities and inhabit them; They shall plant vineyards and drink wine from them; they shall also make gardens and eat fruit from them.'" (Amos 9:13-14)

We move from doom and gloom to the delightful. Israel's final chapter is to be a blessed one. We touched on this very briefly in July. After the Lord returns and the Judgment of the Nations has taken place, there is to be a reversal, not only of the catastrophes of the Tribulation, but of the Fall itself; it will be Eden restored. Sowing and reaping seasons of the different crops will overlap; it will almost be instant harvest. Productive vineyards will again be terraced on the hillsides, and these will drip with sweet wine. The remaining captives of Israel will be brought home, and the desolate cities will be rebuilt and inhabited. We think of the amazing revised Millennial geography of Ezekiel 47 and, for instance, of fishermen casting nets at En Gedi (47:10).The barren En Gedi I once visited is currently no angler's paradise!

"'I will plant them in their land, and no longer shall they be pulled up from the land I have given them' says the Lord your God" (9:15). And that land includes the West Bank, all Jerusalem and much more, including at least a significant part of what is today Jordan! The Land is God's to allocate; He has already made and declared His long-term dispositions. It has not happened yet; and it certainly does not make sense to apply it to the Church. How could the statement that they shall no longer be pulled up from the Land God has given them apply to the Church? It makes complete sense on the other hand for Israel. Has the statement ever been as descriptive of any other nation? God's promises may tarry, but they never fail. However, militant Replacement Theology is on the march and is becoming increasingly defensive and bitter towards those who believe in God's promises of restoration for Israel. On whose side are we marching?

27 September

"Then saviours shall come to Mount Zion to judge the mountains of Esau, and the kingdom shall be the LORD'S". (Obad 1:21)

We are so used to using the noun 'saviour' of the Lord Jesus Christ, that we are reluctant to use it of anyone else; however it is the most accurate term, although latter day "deliverers" empowered by God gives the same sense; we meet them again in Zechariah 12. Obadiah deals with the sins of Esau. The Edomites were descendants of Esau and very much aware of the fact that Israel or Jacob was Esau's brother, the closest kin of all nations to Israel. God stressed this kinship and its consequent responsibilities (verse 10). This rivalry went back to the twins struggling within Rebekah's womb. One brother was accepted by God and the other rejected. The birthright transferred to Jacob was a permanent bone of contention (Genesis 25:27-34). The one brother, though far from faultless, trusted God, whilst the other remained aloof and independent. Herod was an Edomite. Edomites massacred Jews who had settled in their land (II Chronicles 21:8-11). They were among the chief encouragers of every invader of Israel.

One feature of Bible prophecy which liberal theologians cannot stand is the accuracy, which confirms the inspiration, of Bible prophecy. In due course the proud Edomites suffered a series of humiliating defeats over several centuries, corresponding closely to Obadiah's prophecy. He prophesied around 850 BC, but sceptics suggest nearer 300 BC, to escape the implications of inspiration! Christian nations should display a brotherly role towards Israel, born not of genealogy, but of adoption, and should take a courageous stand against Anti-Semitism. God will honour such a stand. God holds Christian nations more accountable, rather than less. Jeremiah 49:7-22 and Amos 9:12 make it clear that God still recognises Edomite descendants or at least inheritors by race or geography. Some are to survive into the Great Tribulation. Around 3,750 years ago Jacob cried to God: "Deliver me, I pray, from the hand of my brother, from the hand of Esau; for I fear him" (Gen 32:11). God appeared to him that very night and blessed him, giving him his new name of Israel. The Kingdom is God's; He never breaks His covenants, though His time-scales are not ours. Obadiah's prophecies still await future vindication in God's dealing with Transjordan Arab neighbours.

28 September

"I will surely assemble all of you, O Jacob, I will surely gather the remnant of Israel; I will put them together like sheep of the fold, like a flock in the midst of their pasture; they shall make a loud noise because of so many people. The one who breaks open will come up before them; they will break out, pass through the gate, and go out by it; their king will pass before them, with the LORD at their head." (Mic 2:12-13)

What exquisite language! What a glorious picture is painted in a few words. I have had to discipline myself over the lovely book of Micah. I wanted to include at least five readings but had to leave room for others! I commend its seven short chapters for a single reading. Note the contrast of the above quote with Micah's opening declaration. "For behold, the LORD is coming out of His place; He will come down and tread on the high places of the earth. The mountains will melt under Him, and the valleys will split like wax before the fire" (1:3-4). Such contrasts are usually explained by either a different group of people being discussed or by some spiritual revival or downfall occurring. Today's text is about His coming for His own of Israel.

This is the first of Micah's Millennial promises, and was given in time to be communicated to the ten Northern tribes before their exile of twenty-seven centuries or so. A lovely reassurance was slipped in in a timely manner. We do not know exactly how long there was between this first discourse of Micah and the siege and fall of Samaria, but it was only a few years. The Shepherd-heart of God is in evidence, and the response is to be like the loud bleating of sheep being led - not herded as in most Western farms. Their king will pass before them, with the Lord at their head. This is a particularly gracious promise to the nation which has suffered from so many centuries of false shepherds. From such passages as Ezekiel 45 & 46 we know that in the Millennium, when Jesus will rule over the whole world from Jerusalem, Israel will have a prince with a mortal body, a latter day David, but Jehovah will be at their head.

29 September

"Now it shall come to pass in the latter days that the mountain of the LORD'S house shall be established on the top of the mountains, and shall be exalted above the hills; and peoples shall flow to it. Many nations shall come and say, 'Come, and let us go up to the mountain of the LORD, to the house of the God of Jacob; He will teach us His ways, and we shall walk in His paths.' For out of Zion the law shall go forth, and the word of the LORD from Jerusalem." (Mic 4:1-2)

There is no need to take this elevated location figuratively. What is more natural than that in the great earthquakes prophesied in Revelation, when mountains and much else will be moved, the Millennial capital should be thus gloriously elevated as an impressive focal point for the crowds of eager Gentile pilgrims of whom Zechariah also writes?

Micah was a contemporary of Isaiah, though starting his ministry a little later. He lived near the Philistine border; which was often as dangerous then as living is today near the Gaza Strip. As a prophet, he pleaded with his people, but dealt severely with the ever-optimistic false prophets. Do we plead or simply preach? He had already pictured the Lord's coming dramatically in judgment: "Behold, the LORD is coming out of His place; He will come down and tread on the high places of the earth" (1:3); that passage and what follows is descriptive of Christ's Coming in Power.

If we go back a single verse from today's text, we read: "Therefore because of you Zion shall be ploughed like a field, Jerusalem shall become heaps of ruins, and the mountain of the temple like the bare hills of the forest." Here is another of these dramatic contrasts we mentioned yesterday. However the interval between the fulfilment of these verses is one of at least twenty-seven centuries! Today's declaration of the establishment of the Millennial Kingdom capital is assured by God, but has yet to materialise. We read of the ultimate reunification of all the tribes of Jacob in such passages as Ezekiel 37:22. When one buys electrical products one is liable to be offered an extended guarantee for a price which favours the insurers and is rarely if ever worthwhile. How many Christians regard God's guarantees to Israel equally sceptically?

30 September

"He shall judge between many peoples, and rebuke strong nations afar off; they shall beat their swords into ploughshares, and their spears into pruning hooks; nation shall not lift up sword against nation, neither shall they learn war anymore." (Mic 4:3)

The opening verses of Isaiah 2 and those of Micah 4, including the above, are almost identical. Because of the general context, it seems more likely that Isaiah was quoting Micah, rather than vice versa. God has allowed both to be preserved. While only the "blessed of the Lord" shall enter the Millennial kingdom, there may be a settling-in time for the new regime by people whose only experience may have been the Antichrist's reign. And, of course, there will be a need to reclaim and inhabit territory which emerges from the aftermath of the Great Tribulation, with valleys exalted and hills made low. Just decisions will be made by the One who knows all the facts.

War and violence will be ended. There is an old saying that we cannot have peace without the Prince of Peace, and, of course, it is true. Any other peace is temporary and fragile because those who seek it tend to have private agendas, and sin is never absent. The Post-Millennial dream of Utopia without a prior Great Tribulation has no basis in prophecy. Sadly, the beating of swords into ploughshares or their modern equivalents is not realistic as yet. Tragically even peaceful nations have always had to have the means of defence against predators. The conditions described in the first two verses will never be *achieved*; rather they will be *imposed* by God Himself. At last total disarmament will be ordered with confidence. Following the horrors of the Great Tribulation and destruction of the armies, it will surely be welcomed by the survivors. The First World War was not the hoped for "war to end all wars"; but Armageddon will be, because Jesus Christ will be the Victor.

Everyone sitting beneath his own vine and fig tree (4:4) was the common expression for peace and prosperity. It will be a natural outcome of the lifting of the Edenic curse (Genesis 3:17-18). Labour will be sweet and rewarding. Obviously we cannot be sure, but there are indications that all or most people will be involved in traditional occupations and will personally reap their own rewards.

1 October

"But you, Bethlehem Ephrathah, though you are little among the thousands of Judah, yet out of you shall come forth to Me the One to be Ruler in Israel, Whose goings forth are from of old, from everlasting." (Mic 5:2)

This verse is better known in its quote by the chief priests and scribes in Matthew 2:6. Their interest, like too many modern counterparts, was purely academic; in their view prophecy was all very well, provided it did not impinge upon them personally.

At the time of writing, Israel's ruler or overlord was Nebuchadnezzar. The future promised Ruler of Israel was to come from no magnificent royal city; but rather an insignificant village in Judah. David's family had had little social status within the tribe. In II Samuel 23:1, in his closing address, David recognised how God had exalted him from a very lowly estate. Nevertheless he was from Judah and was chosen by God to perpetuate Jacob's deathbed promises that, "The sceptre shall not pass from Judah, nor a lawgiver from between his feet, until Shiloh comes; and to Him shall the obedience of the people be" (Gen 49:10). The significance would not have been lost upon Micah's generation. The coming One is Shiloh, the Lion of the Tribe of Judah, the Root of David (Revelation 5:5). His Deity is declared by Micah, He is the One "whose goings forth are from of old, from everlasting". This, like Isaiah 9:6-7, which we return to in December, is a key verse for dealing with cults who deny Jesus' Deity. Bethlehem here is recognised as the actual small village to the south of Jerusalem; it comes complete with its ancient Post Code or Zip Code; it is Bethlehem Ephrathah, not the northern Bethlehem or any other supposed 'house of bread', although that is what the name actually means.

Even today many fail to recognise that this verse 2 is more about His Second Coming than His First, because Jesus at His First Coming never assumed the role of Ruler. When He ascended to Heaven it was to sit down with His Father on His throne (Revelation 3:21), not to occupy David's throne; that was promised but has yet to be fulfilled. At His First Coming, His prophesied birthplace was easily established, but His Nazareth domicile gave the right amount of excuse for those who wished to avoid the truth.

2 October

"Who is a God like You, pardoning iniquity and passing over the transgression of the remnant of His heritage? He does not retain His anger forever, because He delights in mercy. He will again have compassion on us, and will subdue our iniquities. You will cast all our sins into the depths of the sea. You will give truth to Jacob and mercy to Abraham, which You have sworn to our fathers from days of old." (Mic 7:18-20)

The prophet, in wonder, addresses his God with a question. And of course the answer, imparted to a nation which had been seeking false gods, is "Nobody!" A well-known hymn, one with a splendid tune, is "Great God of wonders". The refrain is, "Who is a pardoning God like Thee? Or who has grace so rich and free?" It is applied to the Church of today, and is perfectly acceptable, because ours is the very same God whom Micah was addressing. However, it is sad that so many refuse to recognise that this question ends a book which is about the sinfulness of ancient Israel and her ultimate restoration. None can read the whole book of Micah without appreciating this. But sadly nowadays few bother to read the Bible through from Genesis to Revelation, an invigorating and beneficial annual discipline. Israel had transgressed, Israel had gone astray and Israel has to be pardoned. It will be pardoned. The extent of God's pardon for past, present and future repentant sinners is limitless, being underpinned by a Divine compassion which does not ignore sin, but, in the mercy in which He delights, deals with it in His Son, and, having dealt with it, casts it where it cannot be resurrected.

God's pardon follows God's complaint; it does not precede it. By the time Micah wrote today's text, he was an old man. He had been recording his personal prayer to the Shepherd of Israel on behalf of the flock of His heritage. When the pitiful minority of Judah who chose to return from Babylon started to rebuild Jerusalem, they were intensely aware that they were a reproach and were being laughed at and despised (Nehemiah 2:17-19). Nehemiah prayed fervently, declaring the situation, confessing the people's sin and asking that their reproach might be turned on the heads of their enemies (4:4). God heard and answered. He is a pardoning God!

3 October

"Behold, on the mountains the feet of him who brings good tidings,
Who proclaims peace! O Judah, keep your appointed feasts,
perform your vows. For the wicked one shall no more pass through
you; he is utterly cut off." (Nah 1:15)

We encounter the same lovely sentiments in the better-known Isaiah 52:7. There it applies to future restoration; here it applies to Judah, who is massively reassured by God through Nahum that the marauding Assyrians, that most bloodthirsty and atrocity-committing nation, which had just defeated Egypt and was attempting to conquer the whole world, would not conquer Judah. Assyria was shortly to sack Samaria (722 BC) and would exile the Northern Kingdom. But we know from Isaiah 37:36 and II Kings 19:35 that Sennacherib's Assyrian armies would attempt to destroy Jerusalem, openly defying Jehovah, who would have 185,000 slain by an angel in a single night. Nahum's name means "Comfort" – God used him to comfort Judah, but in no way to comfort Assyria, whose doom he foretold. Long ago I heard that verse 2:4, "The chariots rage in the streets..... they run like lightning", was prophetic of modern traffic. This I would query. As far as Nahum's original readers were concerned, this was descriptive of the sudden swift destruction of the existing nation.

In May we looked at Jonah's reluctant mission to Nineveh, the hated Assyrian capital. To Jonah's chagrin, the city repented, and the judgment predicted by that prophet, with the credibility of having been swallowed by a fish and survived, was averted. But that was now long in the past; as Al Maxey puts it, "they repented of their repentance". When God warns and there is no possibility left of further repentance, His patience may end. The dual message of Nahum is that judgment cannot be averted indefinitely, and that God is always aware of the victims of evil, especially when these are His own people. Some have been critical of the rejoicing over Assyria's coming downfall. As Christians we are not tasked to judge on our own initiative, but Christian nations have been used by God to defeat tyrants. It is His right to choose the means, be they willing or unwilling.

4 October

*"Though the fig tree may not blossom, nor fruit be on the vines; though the labour of the olive may fail, and the fields yield no food; though the flock may be cut off from the fold, and there be no herd in the stalls - **yet** I will rejoice in the LORD, I will joy in the God of my salvation."* (Hab 3:17-18)

Habakkuk's book opens with the cry: "O Lord, how long shall I cry and You will not hear". Throughout the rest of the book there are reminders of the fact that God always hears, even if He does not always choose to answer immediately. It closes with today's text. That "yet" reflects a man of faith in God, whate'er betide.

This book was written by one who cared passionately, and was deeply perplexed about the state of his nation and of the world. Yet he had a deep-seated faith in the holiness of God, to whom he took his troubles. His name is thought to mean 'embrace', and one feels that he wanted to take his wayward people in his arms, and plead to God for them and for the destruction of their enemies. He was deeply aware of his nation's sinfulness. Many pray for our own nation's well-being, without acknowledging the righteousness of God's dealings with her. Habakkuk was more perceptive.

Unlike most other books, the dialogue is between the prophet and his Creator; God clearly respects His prophet, instructing him to record it on clay tablets (2:2). This is a man of faith who was determined to believe in the face of adversity, and who in the end had his expectations of God vindicated and his confidence re-enforced. In this respect it is a blueprint for believers with similar concerns in today's world.

There are three major themes. Firstly, Habakkuk's concern about the forthcoming Babylonian invasion; secondly, his wrath against their aggressor; thirdly, the promise of Babylon's fate only a few generations later, and the assurance of the ultimate fate of all Gentile empires. The book ends with one of the Bible's finest declarations of personal faith.

5 October

"The LORD has taken away your judgments, He has cast out your enemy. The King of Israel, the LORD, is in your midst; you shall see disaster no more. In that day it shall be said to Jerusalem: 'Do not fear; Zion, let not your hands be weak.'" (Zeph 3:15-16)

I recently came across a commentary which said of Zephaniah: "No hotter book lies in the Old Testament..... It is everywhere fire, smoke and darkness." Certainly from the opening verse until 3:9 that description may not be inappropriate. But then it suddenly it becomes sweetness and light. The Amillennialist, with his foreshortened, bankrupt prophetic programme simply cannot comprehend these wonderful truths. Immediately before the dramatic change of tone from cursing to blessing is the intervening Great Tribulation in a nutshell: "'Therefore wait for Me,' says the LORD, 'Until the day I rise up for plunder; My determination is to gather the nations to My assembly of kingdoms, to pour on them My indignation, all My fierce anger; all the earth shall be devoured with the fire of My jealousy.'" (3:8). What so many refuse ('refuse' rather than 'cannot') to recognise is that it is the same God who declares both and means both. True restoration on earth is to follow the Great Tribulation. Twice Jesus Himself alluded to Zephaniah in connection with His Second Coming.

The book opens with a declaration of coming judgment against the whole world, but three verses later this is narrowed down to Judah. They would suffer along with these captors, plus bearing all the other consequences of the sin which had led them into captivity.

Zephaniah preached during the reign of good King Josiah. Zephaniah was a kinsman of the king through Hezekiah; indeed, God may have used Zephaniah to influence Josiah for good. Commentators talk of Josiah's 'revival', but Gaebelein's 'reformation' is probably more appropriate, as the godly king imposed spiritual reforms and iconoclasm upon a somewhat reluctant nation, who apparently still craved for the idols and shrines which they were ordered to destroy. Any revival was limited to a tiny portion of a single tribe. There was little work of God's Spirit within the hearts of the people. Is Western Christianity not at a similar stage? Our task is to hold fast, preaching the Gospel of Grace until our Lord calls us home.

6 October

"For thus says the LORD of hosts: 'Once more..... I will shake heaven and earth, the sea and dry land; and I will shake all nations, and they shall come to the Desire of All Nations, and I will fill this temple with glory,' says the LORD of hosts." (Hag 2:6-7)

No prophet more frequently quoted God as his authority, and no prophet was more successful in accomplishing his mission. He wrote in 620 BC, having arrived as a youngster from the Babylonian captivity. Very soon after the return from Babylon under Zerubbabel, the altar had been erected in the Temple court, so that burnt offerings could be sacrificed (Ezra 3:2). However, at the time of writing, building work had been discontinued for sixteen years as the result of discouragement and opposition; they had turned their attention to rebuilding their own homes. Haggai's awakening call was heeded. There was encouragement and reassurance both for the immediate future and longer term "For I am with you,' says the Lord of hosts (2:4); 'My Spirit remains among you, do not fear!'" (2:5).

God promised that "the glory of this latter temple shall be greater than the former" (2:9). Hundreds of years after this the proud and ambitious Edomite, Herod the Great, sought to be seen as the one who was identified in this prophecy. He lavished a fortune on the total refurbishment and costly adornment of this Temple. He blasphemously wanted to be seen as "The Desire of all Nations" (2:7).

In 2:6 God says that He "will shake heaven and earth, the sea and the dry land." We think of similar prophecies elsewhere and realise that this is the closing stage of the Great Tribulation. This does not mean that the shaking is *limited* to geographical and cosmological features. From Hebrew 12:26-27, where Haggai is quoted, we learn that everything which is shakeable will be shaken. Spiritual powers and temporal rulers and their kingdoms are included. One reason why there is such resistance to the literal shaking is the fact that the Desire of Nations is said here to be coming *following* this shaking, as per Pre-Millennialism. But of course the Prince of Peace, when He first came to that temple, was rejected, so that He could suffer and become our peace (Ephesians 2:14-15). Consequently the latter Temple which will completely fulfil the prophecy has yet to be built.

7 October

"'Behold, I send My messenger, and he will prepare the way before Me. And the Lord, whom you seek, will suddenly come to His temple, even the Messenger of the covenant, in whom you delight. Behold, He is coming,' says the LORD of hosts. But who can endure the day of His coming? And who can stand when He appears? For He is like a refiner's fire and like launderers' soap."
(Mal 3:1-2)

This is one of God's attention-demanding 'Beholds' in Malachi. Malachi, which means "My messenger", may have been his title or his name. He wrote around a century after Haggai and Zechariah; there were to be no further authoritative books until the New Testament. The Apocrypha is never quoted in the New Testament and is not part of Holy Scripture. Malachi was clearly the spiritual leader of his day and dealt with the kind of spiritual problems which Nehemiah encountered – a nation which had at least abandoned its pre-exilic idolatry, but assumed that its formal religious observations were all that was required. Malachi found that people were offended because God was displeased by the moral and spiritual laxity of the priests, by the failure to give tithes to the Lord's work, apathetic worship and intermarriage with Gentile outsiders. It sounds all too familiar to us.

Malachi was not the only messenger, neither was the later John the Baptist. Here Christ is called the Angel or Messenger of the Covenant, a title recalling the various theophanies or visible appearances of the pre-incarnate Son of God, such as in Joshua 5:13-15, or in Judges 13:9- 21, when He declared His name to be Wonderful. The covenant of which He was then Messenger was the still existing old covenant. Those addressed are said to delight in Him, but are warned in the next verse of the less delightful refining and purifying role at His appearance, when many will be unable to stand.

Here we are taken forward to His Second Coming. Malachi then catalogues the categories who will be purged, ultimately for not fearing Jehovah of Hosts. This is about Israel's judgment, rather than the separate Judgment of the Nations. But all should take note, especially those who, not having accepted Jesus as Saviour, have no hope of the prior Rapture. It is not too late to turn to Him and be saved, and to delight in Him.

8 October

"Behold, I will send you Elijah the prophet before the coming of the great and dreadful day of the LORD. And he will turn the hearts of the fathers to the children, and the hearts of the children to their fathers, lest I come and strike the earth with a curse." (Mal 4:5-6)

Before considering this final Old Testament 'Behold', let us turn briefly to a previous lovely statement, displaying the tenderness with which God treats His own – not necessarily for tremendous exploits, but simply for repenting, obeying, meditating upon and honouring Him. "Those who feared the LORD spoke to one another, and the LORD listened and heard them, and a book of remembrance was written before Him.... 'They shall be Mine,' says the LORD of Hosts, 'on the day that I make up My jewels'" (3:17). The Bema or Judgment Seat of Christ which follows the Rapture is for the Church. But the Lord has other saints too, and their worthy deeds done for Him are not to be forgotten. Chapter 4 begins with, "For behold, the day is coming, burning like an oven". What a contrast within two consecutive verses between the fates of the wicked and of the redeemed! God now directs His attention to *those who fear His name*. The Old Testament closes with the assurance of the brilliant dawning of the Millennial day, with speedy healing of the wounds and terrors of the past night. The New Testament closes with the promise for the Church of the gracious and lovely token of our meeting in the clouds, before that sunrise.

The final "Behold" tells of Elijah, whom God is to send "before the great and dreadful day of the Lord". John, when asked, denied that he personally was Elijah (Jn 1:21). The only New Testament cross reference which seems to match is in Revelation 11:3-12, where two witnesses appear miraculously and perform miracles similar to Elijah's. Evidently they will be instrumental in keeping a sizeable minority from giving their allegiance to the Beast, from venerating the Abomination of Desolation and from accepting his fatal Mark. We return to this in our next section. The last word of the Old Testament is 'curse'; Jesus' public ministry begins with the word "Blessed" (Matt 5:3)!

Personalities and Parentheses in Revelation

9 October

*"**There should be delay no longer**, but in the days of the sounding of the seventh angel, when he is about to sound, the mystery of God would be finished, as He declared to His servants the prophets."* (Rev 10:6-7)

We have already observed that what lies in the future in Revelation commences with chapter 4. We have seen that, between the Rapture of the Church and Christ's Coming in Power, there are to be three series of seven judgments, namely opened Seals, Trumpet blasts and emptied Bowls or Vials of Wrath. But space devoted to these series is rather less than that devoted to various other personalities and happenings. We have touched on some of the earlier ones already, and must now deal briefly with some of the remainder, starting at chapter 10.

Today's text is part of a declaration by a mighty angel. The AV/ KJV "Time shall be no more" in 10:6 is seriously misleading, and is one of the few verses which those who try to turn Christ's Second Coming into a single event can cling onto. Through His prophets God has declared that His patience with fallen mankind will end at His appointed time; His intervention in judgment is about to reach its climax. Other texts which we shall encounter confirm that this is the start of the three-and-a-half-year Great Tribulation. Some of the parentheses introduced between the three series start earlier or finish later. Coordinating them with the Seals, Trumpets and Bowls can prove problematical, and differences of opinion are legitimate.

Earlier in the chapter we read of seven thunders, whose voices John hears, but is told to "seal them up". Any, like the "JW" cult's Judge Rutherford, who, of their own initiative, claim to be able to interpret these thunders, fall under the dreadful condemnation of Revelation 22:18. What we are to learn is that significant things are to happen at that time, which are not revealed to us, even though they may remain   the happy hunting ground of the cults. The chapter closes with John being told to eat a little bittersweet book before being told: "You must prophesy again about many peoples, nations, tongues, and kings" (10:11). Dare we fail to heed this Book of Revelation to which our risen Lord attached His blessing? Dare we distort, deny or encourage others to ignore it? Sadly, some leaders do dare.

10 October

"And the angel stood, saying, 'Rise and measure the temple of God, the altar, and those who worship there. But leave out the court which is outside the temple, and do not measure it, for it has been given to the Gentiles. And they will tread the holy city underfoot for forty-two months.'" (Rev 11:1-2)

We have already seen much scriptural evidence for a rebuilt Tribulation Period Jerusalem Temple. John was writing at least twenty years after the destruction of the Second Temple. There has been no temple in Jerusalem since, so this must be the future one, where the Abomination of Desolation, prophesied by Daniel and confirmed by Jesus Himself, is to be set up. After the Rapture, the Beast or Antichrist has to establish his power base and find a means of authorising the rebuilding of the Temple, so that he, in terms of II Thessalonians 2:4, can fulfil his ambitions: "Who opposes and exalts himself above all that is called God or that is worshipped, so that he sits as God in the temple of God, showing himself that he is God." He is to convince the many, but not the godly minority. All the materials and fitments for this temple are ready in Jerusalem for speedy erection. In fact, as soon as the altar has been set up, a matter of days, it will be considered to be functional, and cynically the Beast will allow sacrificial and other rituals to recommence until, after three and a half years, he breaks his covenant and presents himself as the Messiah.

How the Beast will negotiate or impose the erection of this temple we do not yet know. An understandable element in current Islamic militancy over the Temple Mount is the fact that it is known that Orthodox Jews believe from various authentic prophecies that the Temple will be rebuilt, either on a completely cleared Temple Mount or in the space between the existing Al Aqsar Mosque and the Dome on the Rock. Muslims have an interest in their preservation.

Today's text confirms that God will recognise this future temple as His by right, and orders it to be fully assessed. However He will allow the outer court to be trodden by the Gentiles during those first three and a half years, as per Luke 21:24. Thereafter the entire Temple will be defiled. Jewish Tribulation converts are being given advance notice that God will be in full control.

11 October

"And I will give power to my two witnesses, and they will prophesy one thousand two hundred and sixty days, clothed in sackcloth..... These have power to shut heaven, so that no rain falls in the days of their prophecy; and they have power over waters to turn them to blood, and to strike the earth with all plagues, as often as they desire." (Rev 11:3,6)

Many amazing things are due to happen during the Tribulation Period. God is going to take unprecedented steps to warn people as well as to punish, and there is no need to interpret these witnesses other than literally, even if there are doubts as to their personal identity. They appear upon the Jerusalem scene suddenly and apparently miraculously. Their powers identify them as servants of God, and remind us of Elijah, who never died, and Moses, whom God buried secretly. Both had appeared on the Mount of Transfiguration; but, as neither is named here, we cannot be adamant, and Enoch, who never experienced death, is another possible candidate.

There is considerable debate as to whether their mission is to be the first or second three and a half years. In the second half all the judgments - Bowls and perhaps Trumpets - are so clearly identified as direct acts of God, that their personal curses would seem superfluous. Their activities would, however, seem to fit the earlier Seals.

They will be Divinely-protected from the Beast, who, only at the end of their mission, will murder them. So devastating will their God-given mission have been that people are to exchange celebratory gifts, something which would never happen at the end of the Great Tribulation. Their bodies are to lie unburied in Jerusalem: "Now after the three-and-a-half days the breath of life from God entered them, and they stood on their feet, and great fear fell on those who saw them. And they heard a loud voice from heaven saying to them, 'Come up here.' And they ascended to heaven in a cloud, and their enemies saw them" (11:11-12). A few have tried use this to prove a Mid-Tribulation Rapture. But if we consider the mission of these two witnesses – and there are only two – and compare the Church's mission with theirs, there is no "Mid-Trib" case to prove.

12 October

"Now a great sign appeared in heaven: a woman clothed with the sun, with the moon under her feet, and on her head a garland of twelve stars. Then being with child, she cried out in labour and in pain to give birth..... She bore a male Child who was to rule all nations with a rod of iron. And her Child was caught up to God and His throne." (Rev 12:1-2, 5)

So very much is revealed in chapter 12, which spans two thousand years and more, that we must take time and read it in full. It is about warfare past and present in Heaven and upon earth, and explains many ancient mysteries. It is about Christ and Satan, angels and demons and Israel both faithful and unfaithful. The great signs are more than allegories; they are vivid representations.

The woman is neither Mary nor the Church, as various parties have asserted. Mary's future in no way conforms with what happens in this chapter and the Church did not give birth to the Messiah! The woman is Israel, the symbolism going back to Genesis 37, with Jacob, Rachel and the twelve tribal patriarchs. The Church Age, which follows His Ascension "catching up", is passed over. Israel is shown in many passages to have given birth to the Messiah, after lengthy, largely self-inflicted trauma. The Manchild is carefully identified with prophecies concerning His coming Messianic reign.

The next sign is the "great, fiery red dragon having seven heads and ten horns, and seven diadems on his heads." (v 3); we will see the significance of the description later. Satan, described thirteen times as the Dragon, was waiting for Christ to become incarnate in the hope that he could destroy Him at His birth and again at His death; he was of course outwitted. His fury has been diverted to Israel who gave Him birth. Before the Dragon's defeat we are given here details found nowhere else in Scripture of the proportion of the army of fallen angels. It seems that when Satan originally fell, he brought with him a third of the heavenly host. "His tail drew a third of the stars of heaven and threw them to the earth. And the dragon stood before the woman who was ready to give birth, to devour her Child as soon as it was born." (v 4).

13 October

"And war broke out in heaven: Michael and his angels fought with the dragon; and the dragon and his angels fought..... So the great dragon was cast out, that serpent of old, called the Devil and Satan, who deceives the whole world; he was cast to the earth, and his angels were cast out with him." (Rev 12:7,9)

Throughout history Satan and his fallen angels have had access to Heaven; this is first recorded in Job chapter 1 and I Kings 22. This is about to end at the mid-point of the Tribulation period, with his precipitate casting out and humiliation, allowing both God's righteous wrath and the Dragon's diabolical wrath to be felt on earth during the Great Tribulation. Obviously we have no way of visualising what form this warfare will take, but it will be at least as meaningful as the deadliest warfare of mankind.

The cry in Heaven is: "Now salvation, and strength, and the kingdom of our God, and the power of His Christ have come, for the accuser of our brethren, who accused them before our God day and night, has been cast down." (v 10). Do we appreciate that, whilst on earth, we, the "brethren", give Satan 'ammunition' to accuse us, and that were Jesus Christ not our Great High Priest interceding for us, we would be defenceless? Even on earth, Tribulation believers will be able to overcome by the effective spiritual shield and spiritual weapon: "And they overcame him by the blood of the Lamb (shield) and by the word of their testimony (weapon), and they did not love their lives to the death" (vv 10-11). While the heavens rejoice, woe is declared to the spiritually defenceless upon earth because of the Devil's wrath, intensified because he knows that his remaining liberty is very short indeed (v 12).

And even then Satan will not be able to touch the faithful of Israel who have heeded Jesus' Olivet Discourse warning (Matthew 24:16) to flee to the mountains when the Abomination is set up (confirming the timing): "But the woman was given two wings of a great eagle, that she might fly into the wilderness to her place, where she is nourished for a time and times and half a time, from the presence of the serpent" (Rev 12:14). We can speculate endlessly about the miraculous details, but rejoice in the basic facts.

14 October

"Then I stood on the sand of the sea. And I saw a beast rising up out of the sea, having seven heads and ten horns, and on his horns ten crowns, and on his heads a blasphemous name."
(Rev 13:1)

The final verse of chapter 12 fits better into chapter 13. Some manuscripts say, "he" (the dragon) "stood on the sand of the sea"; it seems to be more logical. We have seen the so-called "trinity of evil" in several other passages, but Revelation chapters 12 and 13 give the fullest account. John F Walvoord writes: "The beast out of the pit is Satan (11:7). The beast out of the sea is the world dictator (13:1). The beast out of the land is the religious leader of that day (13:11)." The Greek describes these as ravenous or wild beasts.

The Beast mentioned from verses 1 to 10 is the one whose diabolical character is to be revealed only at the mid-point of the Tribulation Period, when he usurps the Temple, claiming to be Christ and sharing his blasphemous "glory" with the Dragon, as a parody of the Father and Son. His description matches that of the Dragon in 12:3 with seven heads and ten horns. John declares: "I saw one of his heads as if it had been mortally wounded, and his deadly wound was healed. And all the world marvelled and followed the beast" (Rev 13:3). It is generally thought that this means that the parody extends to mimicking Christ's death and resurrection

"So they worshipped the dragon who gave authority to the beast; and they worshipped the beast, saying, 'Who is like the beast? Who is able to make war with him?'" (v 4). Up to that point, as the revived Roman Prince (Daniel 9:26), he may have controlled only a third of the world. Now he claims world-wide worship. "So they worshipped the dragon who gave authority to the beast; and they worshipped the beast, saying, 'Who is like the beast? Who is able to make war with him?'" (v 4) "All who dwell on the earth will worship him, whose names have not been written in the Book of Life of the Lamb slain from the foundation of the world" (v 8). Verse 5 reminds us that, mercifully, this lasts only forty-two months.

15 October

"Then I saw another beast coming up out of the earth, and he had two horns like a lamb and spoke like a dragon. And he exercises all the authority of the first beast in his presence, and causes the earth and those who dwell in it to worship the first beast, whose deadly wound was healed." (Rev 13:11-12).

In this second Beast we have a parody of the Holy Spirit. Thereafter he is usually referred to as the False Prophet. Overtly he appears to be less aggressive than the first Beast, but internally he is dragonish and, as a satanic miracle worker, gains increasing credibility, not only by taking credit for the first Beast's "resurrection", but by performing acts to impress the watching world at a time of crisis, when the godly repentance-demanding alternative is unpalatable to the majority.

He exploits the age-old longing for idolatry and sets up an image of the first Beast - what Jesus (Matt 24:15) referred to as the Abomination of Desolation of Daniel 9:27. The image itself is to be given some form of demonic life – idolaters love this sort of thing: "He was granted power to give breath to the image of the beast, that the image of the beast should both speak and cause as many as would not worship the image of the beast to be killed" (Revelation 13:15). It is to be a murderous image as well as a magic one. We are not told much elsewhere of Satan's ability to work miracles, but in bringing this world to a climax, God is evidently going to allow him temporarily such dramatic powers.

The False Prophet has become known for his 666 Mark. We have mentioned this twice already. The number signifies the triple falling short of God's standards; it is the mark of a man; the Man of Sin (v 18). Everybody on earth will be required by the False Prophet to have implanted or otherwise imposed a mark, without which it will be illegal to buy or sell. God will require outright refusal to bear this mark of allegiance to Satan. Chapter 14:11 reads: "And the smoke of their torment ascends forever and ever; and they have no rest day or night, who worship the beast and his image, and whoever receives the mark of his name." Being a believer during the Great Tribulation will, for many, mean martyrdom.

16 October

"Then I looked, and behold, a Lamb standing on Mount Zion, and with Him one hundred and forty-four thousand, having His Father's name written on their foreheads..... These are the ones who follow the Lamb wherever He goes. These were redeemed from among men, being firstfruits to God and to the Lamb." (Rev 14:1,4)

Malcolm Davis talks of Revelation 14 containing seven cameos of salvation and judgment. Charles Ryrie observes that most of the chapter is like a table of contents for the remainder of the book.

Most commentators see those in today's text as being the same as the 144,000 in Revelation 7; I agree. The fact that they are seen upon Mount Zion links them with the Jewish identity emphasised in chapter 7. Neither a heavenly nor an earthly location is confirmed in the text; however, as Jim Allen points out, many Old Testament prophecies show that it is from the literal Mount Zion that Christ will reign during the Millennium. He adds: "These Scriptures are now fulfilled and the Lamb is publicly associated with His servants; their suffering in the dark days of tribulation over, they are associated with Him as He sets up His kingdom." Each of these faithful preachers of the Gospel, ("these My brethren" of Matthew 25:40) has been preserved alive to enter the Millennium with honour, as the firstfruits of the Great Tribulation.

Then John sees "another angel flying in the midst of heaven, having the everlasting gospel to preach to those who dwell on the earth - to every nation, tribe, tongue, and people - saying with a loud voice, 'Fear God and give glory to Him, for the hour of His judgment has come; and worship Him who made heaven and earth, the sea and springs of water.'" (14:6-7). Satan at this juncture is busy persuading mankind to join belatedly his ancient rebellion (Isa 14:12-15) against his Creator, setting himself up as an alternative, less demanding, deity. Salvation begins by rejecting the Satanic claims and giving our Creator God the glory due. In verse 13 reassurance is given to those still to be martyred: "'Blessed are the dead who die in the Lord from now on.' 'Yes,' says the Spirit, 'that they may rest from their labours, and their works follow them.'" How fundamental is that last statement. Our works never precede us to gain us entry!

17 October

"Then one of the seven angels who had the seven bowls came and talked with me, saying to me, 'Come, I will show you the judgment of the great harlot who sits on many waters, with whom the kings of the earth committed fornication, and the inhabitants of the earth were made drunk with the wine of her fornication.'" (Rev 17:1-2)

Chapters 15 and 16 describe the Bowls of Wraths, to which we return soon. We now come to the two 'difficult' chapters describing Mystery Babylon and Babylon the Great, the world's great apostate religious harlot and the world's godless political-commercial system. We deal with the religious mystery "harlot" first.

After the Flood God told Noah's offspring: "Be fruitful and multiply, and fill the earth." (Gen 9:1). They defied that command and built a city, Babel, with a ziggurat or zodiacal observatory to worship the host of heaven, an Antediluvian hangover passed on by Ham, Nimrod's grandfather (Genesis 11:4). Babel thus embodied the first false religion. God destroyed it and scattered its citizens. As the embryo nations were dispersed, a variety of apparently divergent religions blossomed to suit each emerging culture. In Babel the worship of the mother and child Queen of Heaven cult developed. By the time of Balaam Babylon honoured 1,300 deities. Following the defeats by Medo-Persia and Greece, its importance declined and its proud Pontifex Maximus title passed via Pergamum to the Vatican, which still claims it! Mystery Babylon is still being cynically manipulated by Satan, evidently becoming multi-faith following the religious crisis left by the Rapture, when a united religious front against Christ will be required. In 17:3 we find she is being carried or supported by the First Beast of Revelation 13:1-2, but not for much longer, as we shall see tomorrow.

One much debated problem is whether Mystery Babylon is to be an actual rebuilt city near the old site; Saddam Hussein tried and failed. Revelation 17:9 reads: "Here is the mind which has wisdom: The seven heads are seven mountains on which the woman sits." The Roman church has for centuries been embarrassed by the likeness to her famous city on seven hills. Babylon had no hills. Moreover we are reminded of the revived end-time Roman Empire of the prince of Daniel 9:26. When the time comes, believers possessing Bibles will be left in no doubt.

18 October

"There are also seven kings. Five have fallen, one is, and the other has not yet come. And when he comes, he must continue a short time......The ten horns which you saw are ten kings who have received no kingdom as yet, but they receive authority for one hour as kings with the beast." (Rev 17:10,12)

Obviously this chapter needs to be read in full; there is much scope for debate, especially regarding the identity of the earlier kings, who are usually thought to represent the seven successive ancient empires from Egypt, through Assyria, Babylon, Medo-Persia, Greece, ancient Rome (that which "now is" as John writes) and latter day Rome, etc; but certain things are already clear. We learn more about the antecedents of the First Beast, but find that he now has ten subordinate kings, albeit very briefly (v 12), making him a latter day Revived Roman Emperor. Since 1948 I have read various suggestions, some cautious, some ingenious, some rash, about the identity of the ten 'horn' latter day kings, based upon the international situation as it was at various different junctures. The birth of the Common Market and Treaty of Rome caused quite a stir; even Scottish Nationalism and Hadrian's Wall, and more latterly 'Brexit', featured in debate. Others pointed out that the old Roman Empire extended right round the Mediterranean Sea, which the European Community has never done. By all means let us watch the signs of the times, but let us not become too preoccupied by those features which do not point directly to our Lord's return **for** us.

We noted yesterday from verse 3 that the Harlot rides the Beast, so we might have expected the ten kings also to support her, because they oppose Christ, the Lamb (v 14). But, no! Mystery Babylon will have served its purpose. At the mid-point of the Tribulation Period all worship is to be directed to the Beast. That which has served since the Tower of Babel can at last be discarded: "And the ten horns which you saw on the beast, these will hate the harlot, make her desolate and naked, eat her flesh and burn her with fire. For God has put it into their hearts to fulfil His purpose, to be of one mind, and to give their kingdom to the beast, until the words of God are fulfilled" (17:16-17).

19 October

"Babylon the great is fallen, is fallen, and has become a dwelling place of demons, a prison for every foul spirit, and a cage for every unclean and hated bird! For all the nations have drunk of the wine of the wrath of her fornication, the kings of the earth have committed fornication with her, and the merchants of the earth have become rich through the abundance of her luxury." (Rev 18:2-3)

The religious harlot will have been dispensed with as the Great Tribulation commences. But Babylon the Great will not be discarded by Satan and his emissaries, but rather destroyed suddenly by God's decree, causing praise and joy from all God's people: "Rejoice over her, O heaven, and you holy apostles and prophets, for God has avenged you on her!" (v 20).

Already corruption, fraud, greed, selfishness and utter carelessness as to the consequences of one's behaviour and risk taking are increasingly common, as well as the fragility of stock markets. It may well be that the Rapture and sudden disappearance of thousands of key people will provoke a financial crisis so unprecedented that the Beast, as he rises quickly to power, will take control in the form of Babylon the Great, perhaps as a brand new world commercial centre, conceivably on the ancient Babylonian site. This is, of course, only a suggestion; but whatever actually happens, it will bear the hallmark of the Devil and his deputies. What is made very clear is that this post-Rapture entity is something in which no believer must be involved: "Come out of her, my people, lest you share in her sins, and lest you receive of her plagues" (v 4). It is probable that for every one who profits, a dozen will suffer loss in this time when love will have grown cold. For the underprivileged masses it will be a case of survival at any cost, with believers at the very bottom of the prosperity ladder.

Those who are listed as profiteers are shown in old-fashioned terms, of course, and the luxuries in which they trade and profit are likewise listed in terms of two thousand years ago. It does not take much imagination to up-date them. What is noticeable is that "bodies and souls of men" are listed as trading commodities! (verse 13). Are vulnerable people to be seized for their body parts for the wealthy?

Prophecies in the Pauline Epistles

20 October

"Or do you despise the riches of His goodness, forbearance, and longsuffering, not knowing that the goodness of God leads you to repentance? But in accordance with your hardness and your impenitent heart you are treasuring up for yourself wrath in the day of wrath and revelation of the righteous judgment of God."
(Rom 2:4-5)

The potential for choosing readings in Paul's epistles is enormous; but there are only so many days in the year! We cannot use a thematic approach here, as the Apostle quickly moves from theme to theme. We have frequently quoted from these and later epistles within other readings. In these epistles we find the most basic truths of the Gospel of grace as well as some of the most profound, and very much more.

In chapter 2 Paul deals with Jewish attitudes towards Gentiles, but there is much of general application too. Salvation is resisted and ultimately lost through hard and impenitent hearts. A friend of mine regularly preaches his heart out to what one might call a mixed congregation of evangelicals and others; he has told me that the chief complaint is his regular preaching of repentance! Repentance, that change of heart which sorrows for sin, is something which is allowed and encouraged by the goodness of God. This is what is being resisted. God in His divine generosity forbears. We should value His longsuffering. Instead, and Paul deliberately uses the verb 'to treasure' for that which should be feared; he is pointing out that what is being amassed is to be met with wrath in that day which so many simply refuse to admit is yet to come. God's righteous judgment is spurned in our courts and now in all too many churches; but the day of wrath is to be revealed.

As believers, and particularly as preachers, it is our duty to call sin 'sin'. The requirement should be obvious, because as Paul goes on to say of God: "who will render to each one according to his deeds: eternal life to those who by patient continuance in doing good seek for glory, honour, and immortality; but to those who are self-seeking and do not obey the truth, but obey unrighteousness - indignation and wrath, tribulation and anguish, on every soul of man who does evil" (Romans 2:6-8). It is our privilege and responsibility to publicise these alternatives.

21 October

"Therefore, having been justified by faith, we have peace with God through our Lord Jesus Christ, through whom also we have access by faith into this grace in which we stand, and rejoice in hope of the glory of God." (Rom 5:1-2)

These two verses finish with the future, but a future based upon the past and present. The Greek verb tense for the passive "having been justified" implies that point of time at which, as individuals, we were saved. Until that moment there had been no peace; thereafter that peace has been there to be enjoyed. The NKJV and some other margins give an alternative ancient manuscript rendering: "Let us have peace." The suggestion is not that the peace is elusive, but that we may not be enjoying its full benefits. As believers we may be fearful of the security of our salvation; that is anything but a peaceful situation. It leads to faltering in our Christian lives, rather than standing; it robs us of our rejoicing. It stems from a wavering faith, as if we still had some responsibility for completing what Christ achieved for us. In fact, whether we waver our not, having been bought with the greatest price the universe can demand, that of the precious blood of Christ, we do stand or have a standing in God's eyes, though not our own. There are only two positions which a person may occupy relative to God – enmity or peace, in that sequence, for, when we move from one to the other, we pass through no intermediate state.

WE Vine points out that the keynote of this chapter is "through Christ". All that we have for time and eternity is through Christ. All that we are spared through time and eternity is through Christ. Here is the access to saving faith – faith pinned on Christ's finished work. Our hope in the glory of God, which would be unbearable for us without that finished work, is a sure, underpinning hope rather than baseless optimism, which is all too common on the fringe of Christianity. The glory of God in which we hope is not some kind of Mormon blasphemous ultimate deification of the believer; the glory of God is the outward manifestation of His divine attributes, with a splendour utterly and inconceivably unimaginable to our minds this side of the resurrection or Rapture.

22 October

"For if we have been united together in the likeness of His death, certainly we also shall be in the likeness of His resurrection, knowing this, that our old man was crucified with Him, that the body of sin might be done away with, that we should no longer be slaves of sin." (Rom 6:5-6)

Paul has been writing about our being baptised figuratively into Christ's death, not in order to be saved, but having been saved. We must first have life in Christ in order symbolically and in obedience to identify with Him. As FB Hole remarks, "Baptism in itself achieves nothing vital, and alas, millions of baptised persons will find themselves in a lost eternity. Believer's baptism is the natural sequence; it confirms death to our former spiritual state without Christ and our new life in Him, demonstrating our passing through death, burial and resurrection. The resurrection is of course anticipated, but we should immediately begin to walk in newness of life".

The expression "united together" is very strong, and occurs nowhere else in the Bible. That which was demonstrated symbolically becomes reality when we are resurrected to be with Him who is our Forerunner. Some will not taste death, but even they will appear in the likeness of His resurrection.

Here we see the bearing of Christ's death and resurrection upon our sinful nature. In talking of our "old man", Paul is personifying what we are naturally as members of Adam's race. Though descendants of Adam, we have been crucified with Christ. It is something received by us only by faith. The body of sin has not merely to be cancelled, but destroyed. The power of sin over us whilst we are yet in these bodies is what Paul implies has to be dealt with now. All too often we behave as if this were not true, and our witness and the joy of our salvation suffer. But even Paul admitted failure here. "For I delight in the law of God according to the inward man. But I see another law in my members, warring against the law of my mind, and bringing me into captivity to the law of sin which is in my members". (Rom 7:22-23). He goes on to explain the reason with which we can identify; we too are in a battle in which by God's grace we must be overcomers.

23 October

"The creation itself also will be delivered from the bondage of corruption into the glorious liberty of the children of God. For we know that the whole creation groans and labours with birth pangs together until now. Not only that, but we also who have the firstfruits of the Spirit, even we ourselves groan within ourselves, eagerly waiting for the adoption, the redemption of our body." (Rom 8:21-23)

This is part of a complex argument covered in verses 18 to 30, but it is much too important to ignore; we must all take it aboard. It contrasts the present suffering with the future glory, but makes it clear that the first is not to be compared with the greatness of the second. Our eternal heavenly state must not be seen as simply a consolation prize for what has gone before. In II Corinthians 4:17 Paul gives that true perspective, far too rarely evident in modern believers: "For our light affliction, which is but for a moment, is working for us a far more exceeding and eternal weight of glory."

Creation has been groaning since Adam, under whose authority it had been put, fell, taking creation with him. And we in our mortal lives are still subject to certain of its conditions, and therefore groan. Vine comments: "Redemption here is the future actual liberation of the body from its present condition of sinfulness, weakness, decay and death". Our groaning is only until the full benefits of the adoption, which we already possess with regard to God, are realised. But, since the day of our individual salvation, we have the "firstfruits of the Spirit" indwelling us as our absolute guarantee on which our hope is based; in the meantime we eagerly wait. There would be no eagerness but for the surety of that redemption. Fallen creation's hope, the removal of the Edenic curse in the Millennium follows, rather than precedes, our redemption. Our hope realised, the reversal through Christ of Adam's fall, is to end earth's groaning. In the Old Testament Prophets and under the Trumpet and Bowl judgments of Revelation, we see that creation's groaning has still to reach its climax. How many well-meaning conservationists stop to consider that it is mankind's sinfulness and rebellion against the Creator, rather than against the creature, which has resulted in the increasingly worse state of our global environment?

24 October

*"But what does it say? 'The word is near you, in your mouth and in your heart' (that is, the word of faith which we preach): that if you confess with your mouth the Lord Jesus and believe in your heart that God has raised Him from the dead, **you will be saved**. For with the heart one believes unto righteousness, and with the mouth confession is made unto salvation.'"* (Rom 10:8-10)

From the complexity of yesterday's study, we turn to one of the most basic prophecies (and yes, it is a prophecy) in the Bible. Sixty-five years ago I was one of the young people who gathered, complete with soap box, at the Mound in Edinburgh, that city's equivalent of Hyde Park Corner, on a Sunday afternoon and shouted out a number of Gospel verses – in the Authorised Version of course! "Romans ten and nine" was as much a favourite as "John three sixteen"; it was shorter and therefore more memorable. The AV/KJV has the advantage of the specifically singular "thou", rather than "you". "If thou shalt confess with **thy** mouth....., and believe in **thy** heart....., **thou** shalt be saved." It was for the individual when Paul wrote; it is still for the individual today.

In verse 8 Paul had been talking about that which had been brought nigh in the Old Testament by the Law, what people ought to do, but had now been brought nearer by what Christ had actually done once for all, to be received in faith.

There can be no salvation without Christ. There can be no salvation without God having raised Him from the dead. There can be no salvation without belief in our heart, rather than simply our head, confirmed by our preparedness to confess this faith and the name of the One in whom it is placed. If the faith is merely head knowledge there may be reluctance to confess openly; it will be questionable. If it is truly in the heart, confession of faith will be natural. Righteousness, being made right with God, is instantaneous when we believe. Salvation involves more than just freedom from the penalty of sin, essential though that be. Some of the benefits still lie ahead, but it is received under the same conditions with its two emphases of faith and confession. If we trust in this divine promise, we should trust in them all.

25 October

"I say then, has God cast away His people? Certainly not! For I also am an Israelite, of the seed of Abraham, of the tribe of Benjamin. God has not cast away His people whom He foreknew. Or do you not know what the Scripture says of Elijah, how he pleads with God against Israel, saying." (Rom 11:1-2)

Back in June we devoted a section to Israel in Bible prophecy; let us now devote a further day to remind ourselves how central Israel has been to God's plan of mercy both for the Jews and Gentiles. Paul was careful to specify "Israelite", rather than "Jew ", confirming that God had all the tribes in mind. Moreover he stressed that they were foreknown by God. We are taken back to the call of Abram, through whom all the tribes of the earth would be blessed, through whose promised Descendant salvation would be wrought. Paul was refuting the foolish and stubborn teaching, still with us, that God cast away His original people once Christ had been raised and the Church had been born. It was a most timely statement, for in a very few years the armies of Rome would be besieging and destroying the Israelite capital city, and commencing the second, longer stage of the *Diaspora*. Paul was writing to believers in Rome; those who were Jewish would soon be banished and the remaining Gentiles would be persecuted.

Confessing God's future purposes for Israel is not popular with our Enemy – we noted recently that when Satan is cast out and denied further admission to Heaven (Revelation 12:13), he will pursue all Jews who have not been given sanctuary by God. Replacement Theology is a favourite tool of all who deny the Rapture of the Church before the Tribulation period, because Israel and Jerusalem feature so prominently in the vacuum which must be left by the called-home Church.

Paul goes on to ask: "For if their being cast away is the reconciling of the world, what will their acceptance be but life from the dead?" (11:15). This question makes no sense to Replacement Theologians, and yet they, *assuming* they are saved, are the beneficiaries of Israel's temporary being laid aside. As we look at Israel's isolated place on the world stage, let us never forget Paul's inspired question and answer: "Has God cast away His people? Certainly not!"

26 October

"Even as the testimony of Christ was confirmed in you, so that you come short in no gift, eagerly waiting for the revelation of our Lord Jesus Christ, who will also confirm you to the end, that you may be blameless in the day of our Lord Jesus Christ. God is faithful, by whom you were called into the fellowship of His Son, Jesus Christ our Lord." (I Cor 1:7-9)

Paul was addressing a church which had had a promising start, and had initially been enriched. Sadly Paul was to hear of internal divisions, as different parties aligned themselves with Paul, Apollos and Peter, and only a few directly with Christ (1:12). It was sheer folly, because none of the three named faction leaders (what we might call 'celebrities' nowadays) was in competition with the others. How easy it is for us to take our eyes off the Lord and invent human heroes. But Paul recognised that there was still much to commend in Corinth and his desire was that these young believers should be blameless in the day of the Lord Jesus Christ – not to be confused with the day of the Lord from which the Church is to be spared. Rather Paul is anticipating the *Bema*, of which we will have more to say tomorrow.

The "testimony of Christ" refers back to the genuineness of their salvation; they had shown evidence of conversion. Paul wanted them to be lacking in no gift; however the gifts were to be secondary in importance to the coming revelation of Christ. Here was a congregation or assembly which, as we find in later chapters, was to become preoccupied with gifts, and in particular with the least important gifts, forgetting that these were to be temporary means of bearing fruit, which will be assessed and rewarded at the revelation of our Lord Jesus Christ. The word for gift here is *charisma* or gift of grace, and should be primarily seen as the whole panoply of gifts, rather than individual ones, which are distributed as the Holy Spirit sees fit. The earnest, enthusiastic expectation of the Lord's Return is virtually guaranteed to promote spiritual enrichment if it is centred on Him, and not upon anticipated personal benefits.

And just look at the variety of titles accorded to our Lord within those three short verses! Look, and ponder again who He is.

27 October

"Therefore judge nothing before the time, until the Lord comes, who will both bring to light the hidden things of darkness and reveal the counsels of the hearts. Then each one's praise will come from God." (I Cor 4:5)

In the previous chapter Paul had being writing about the *Bema* or Judgment Seat of Christ, an important and under-considered subject, found most often in the two Corinthian epistles, which concerns the Church following the Rapture. He had been writing about the testing of our witness and those deeds performed following our conversion, in order to judge whether they are to be deserving of reward or commendation. Now Paul turns to Christ's future evaluation of our motives, especially within the body of the Church – our relationships with our fellow-believers.

In the earlier chapters of this epistle we find Paul dealing with the schisms that had occurred within the Corinthian congregation. A variety of rival factions had quickly emerged. While this should not happen within the Church of God, it frequently has done throughout Church history, in contrast with the sometimes legitimate requirement for internal discipline. Paul here cautions the Corinthians against premature conclusions. The time is coming when those wronged or slighted will be vindicated and those guilty will be exposed. This must be taken seriously; Christ's evaluation will be unerring, and wrong motives will be exposed, leading no doubt to many surprises. In dealing with the Bema, we must remember that this is not about the punishment of sins committed after our having been saved. Our sins were dealt with once for all at Calvary. But we must not therefore conclude that those who have often sinned following conversion are to be judged no more strictly than those whose lives have been Christ-like. If we are living in a right relationship with our Lord, we will, naturally, as a matter of course, regularly confess our sins in order to maintain fellowship with Him: "If we confess our sins, He   is faithful and just to forgive us our sins and to cleanse us from all unrighteousness" (I Jn 1:9). This is not a case of being saved time and again or 'maintaining' our salvation. But it is the kind of exemplary Christianity which on that day will require nothing hidden to be exposed, and will multiply our joy when we see Him face-to- face.

28 October

"In the same manner He also took the cup after supper, saying, 'This cup is the new covenant in My blood. This do, as often as you drink it, in remembrance of Me.' For as often as you eat this bread and drink this cup, you proclaim the Lord's death till He comes."
(I Cor 11:25-26)

Matthew (26:29), Mark (14:25) and Luke (22:18) all give accounts of the Last Supper, and, with minor variations, relate how Jesus said that He would not partake of the fruit of the vine until He drank it anew with them in His Father's Kingdom. He told them that they were to do this in remembrance of Him – in remembrance of His death. Incredibly important though His subsequent resurrection was, the death from which He arose was equally important and central to our own salvation.

Paul's account covers most of the same important points, but it was not based upon what the others had told him, but rather upon what he personally received from the Lord after the Church Age had begun, when this memorial supper was already being practised, as we know from Acts. Paul added nothing to elaborate this simplest of memorial feasts. Ceremonies and rituals which have been developed down through the centuries have no justification in any of the four Bible accounts, neither is there any suggestion of re-enactment or miraculous properties. Emphasised by Paul, however, is the fact that this simple celebration is a proclamation or preaching of Christ's death. Also stated only in Paul's account is the fact that it is only "Till He comes".

We learn from the Gospels that, in the Millennial Kingdom, and therefore as far as Jesus and His disciples are concerned, in their immortal bodies, they will taste the fruit of the vine again. It does not say that they will repeat the Lord's supper, because the One who died and rose again will be in their midst. Whereas Paul, with the Lord's authority, tells us that we are to partake of this memorial feast only **until He comes**, and evidently not thereafter in Heaven. It is simple earthly bread and simple earthly wine. But its eating and drinking is a command, as is the reverence and self-examination which is required. Some Protestant denominations are guilty of infrequency, and are thus sparing in their proclamation of our Saviour's death. Excuses are pitiful.

29 October

"If in this life only we have hope in Christ, we are of all men the most pitiable. But now Christ is risen from the dead, and has become the firstfruits of those who have fallen asleep."
(I Cor 15:19-20)

Paul is talking of people who exist, people on the verge of Christianity, who by definition have never been saved. Their situation is described as being pathetic, pitiable. They have taken on the responsibilities of Christianity and would probably consider themselves to be Christians, but they have none of the immense benefits and blessings of Biblical Christianity. The Christ whose name they claim to honour has not, in their minds, risen from the dead. He was, according to them a good man, even the best of men, a wonderful example, one who took pity upon others, one who died a martyr's death; but that is all. His resurrection, they believe, is fanciful, imaginary, wishful thinking or merely "the life that never, never dies", as one popular modified pagan song puts it. It may bring a little temporary comfort at funerals, but not much, because there is no substance to this kind of "faith", no basis for confidence, except possibly the forlorn hope that God will approve. At least overtly non-Christians are marginally less pitiable, in that they do not have this false hope.

Then Paul bursts forth with the greatest possible contrast and with divinely imparted confidence: "But now Christ **is** risen from the dead!" Yes, He was dead. Hallelujah! In dying He accomplished one of His essential aims in having become man. His was a vicarious death, a victorious death, and effective death, a ransoming death. But it was not the end, because death could not keep its prey. God raised Him·from the dead in fulfilment of eternal plans. He raised Him not to be alone, but to be the Firstfruits of them that slept. The Greek word translated "Firstfruits" is singular, as He is the sole life-giver of the many who are to share in His resurrection. It is that impending resurrection which allows the term "fallen asleep" to be appropriate and not merely a palliative: "For it was fitting for Him, for whom are all things and by whom are all things, in bringing many sons to glory, to make the captain of their salvation perfect through sufferings" (Heb 2:10).

30 October

"There are also celestial bodies and terrestrial bodies; but the glory of the celestial is one, and the glory of the terrestrial is another. There is one glory of the sun, another glory of the moon, and another glory of the stars; for one star differs from another star in glory. It is sown in dishonour, it is raised in glory..... It is sown in weakness, it is raised in power." (I Cor 15:40-43)

Paul had been answering two anticipated questions which some Corinthians would ask: "How are the dead raised up? And with what body do they come?" (verse 35). Then he tells them how foolish they were; they should have had at least some comprehension. Jesus had to tell the two on their way to Emmaus how foolish they were; Paul had to do so here. We should not expect to be spoon-fed with basic doctrines, but should be capable of comparing Scripture with Scripture.

Paul points out that material, physical bodies vary from one to another in glory or appearance, as do the celestial bodies of sun, moon and stars. They should have appreciated that it is God who gives the appropriate body as He chooses, and believers should never have to ask **how** God does anything; that is left to agnostics. As for the kind of body, it should have been obvious that when a seed is planted and dies, the new body which emerges will be the identifiable replacement, but it will have different resurrection properties. However all will not possess the same degree of glory. But when Church believers die or are raptured, they will receive their immortal bodies from God: "who will transform our lowly body that it may be conformed to His glorious body, according to the working by which He is able even to subdue all things to Himself" (Phil 3:21). In contrast with our present state, these will be bodies of incorruptibility, glory and power.

At the Christian graveside we are no doubt very much aware of the lowliness of the body which we are committing to the ground. Do we realise that when we next see our loved one, they and we will be in bodies conformed to His likeness? Failure to do so suggests that we are not confident that He is "able even to subdue all things to Himself"; our expectations can be too low.

31 October

"Knowing that a man is not justified by the works of the law but by faith in Jesus Christ, even we have believed in Christ Jesus, that we might be justified by faith in Christ and not by the works of the law; for by the works of the law no flesh shall be justified." (Gal 2:16)

Now why, one might ask, is this text included in a series of prophetic passages? Every promise of God, every guarantee, every assurance is a prophecy, just as every unconditional prophecy is a promise, guarantee or assurance.

This is of course fundamental Christian doctrine. If we personally do not need to be reminded of it, somebody in our family or among our friends will do. I recall, as a newly saved teenager, trying to preach the Gospel and reason with my grandmother. Looking back, I doubt if I did it well, because I was applying Biblically-based logic rather than giving a simple testimony, emphasising Christ's part rather than my own. She was a regular church attender, was a natural organiser who had devoted considerable time and energy to the "Band of Hope" – work among alcoholics, and might have been regarded as a pillar of the community. Indeed, she was probably 'better' than I was in most respects. I was very fond of her, hence my desire to witness to her. Probably other readers have had similar experiences; they are worth sharing.

Basically she believed in justification by the works of the law – "do enough good and hopefully you will qualify for Heaven." The Gospel of grace confirms that nobody is "qualified" for Heaven because we are sinners, and whether we are sinners great or small, that sin excludes us unless it is totally wiped out. That is what justification means, being made right, just or perfect in God's sight. There can be no comparatives or degrees of justification. Of course some believers are more worthy than others, but their works never form the foundation of their salvation. Christ and His finished work (one cannot over-emphasise that 'finished') comprise the foundation which cannot be added to, but can be built upon. Asserting that good works can justify effectively implies that Calvary was unnecessary and that there was no need for Christ to die. The implications are terrifying – but wrong. This is why a simple understanding of such verses as the above is so vital.

1 November

"For he who sows to his flesh will of the flesh reap corruption, but he who sows to the Spirit will of the Spirit reap everlasting life. And let us not grow weary while doing good, for in due season we shall reap if we do not lose heart. Therefore, as we have opportunity, let us do good to all, especially to those who are of the household of faith." (Gal 6:8-10)

The context of today's verse is bearing one another's burdens (v 2) and the fellowship or "household of faith" (v 10). Christ is the great Burden Bearer, and we are privileged to follow in His footsteps here. It is a principle referred to throughout both Old and New Testaments, that, as long as we are alive and conscious, we are sowing. Both as believers and non-believers we sow seed and reap the results. It is obvious that what we sow will be mirrored in what we reap at harvest time, though in mercy God sometimes intervenes and we do not reap all or indeed any of what we have sown to the flesh, as opposed to the spirit, especially if we have examined ourselves and confessed to wrong or inadequate sowing. I am inclined to agree with Hogg and Vine that it is not the Holy Spirit who is implied here, despite the capital 'S' in some versions, but means our own spirit as opposed to our body, which leads to corruption. There may be earthly harvests from the liberal sowing of quality seed, but the final reaping is that which we shall receive at the *Bema* or Judgment Seat of Christ, and that is eternal. If we grow "weary in well doing", we will reap less. We are responsible for encouraging not only others, but ourselves! It should be a mutual activity within the fellowship.

We must never assume that eternal life is the fruit of our sowing. As Gaebelein puts it, "The life is looked at here, of course, in its practical character, in its fruits and activities. The life itself, the life which produces this, is no matter of reaping at all, it is what we must have to be Christians. Nevertheless, we can reap it as a practical thing, and the witness of it is that, even though reaped here upon earth, it is something which has eternity in it."

2 November

"The eyes of your understanding being enlightened; that you may know what is the hope of His calling, what are the riches of the glory of His inheritance in the saints, and what is the exceeding greatness of His power toward us who believe, according to the working of His mighty power which He worked in Christ when He raised Him from the dead and seated Him at His right hand in the heavenly places, far above all principality and power and might and dominion, and every name that is named, not only in this age but also in that which is to come." (Eph 1:18-21)

Some passages are so overwhelming in their glory that we are unable to comment even remotely adequately. Paul, the last, and in his own mind, the least of all the Apostles, has been given the incredible gift of description concerning that which is divine and holy, primarily regarding the Triune God, but also regarding our status in Him. Joseph Parker writes: "How deeply anxious the Apostle Paul is that we should all be better men. He does not seek our admiration; he does not come to decorate the house, but in the grace of God to recreate the householder. The cogency of his reason adds to the passion of his appeal. With less logic Paul would have less love. This is no paradox, but a simple commonplace; it is really because he reasons conclusively that Paul loves so ardently."

None of us aspires to compete with Paul in his spirituality and eloquence. But do we pray for greater comprehension of God's love for us? The eyes of Paul's understanding were enlightened. Are ours? Do we know what is the hope of His calling? Do we comprehend the riches of the glory of His inheritance in the saints, among whom we are numbered? Have we even attempted to evaluate the exceeding greatness of His power toward us who believe? Do we truly appreciate the working of His mighty power which He worked in Christ when, with all the powers of Hell desperately ranged against Him, God the Father raised His Son from the dead? Do we picture Him having been seated at His right hand in the heavenly places until He makes His enemies His footstool? Do we appreciate that the highest place that Heaven affords is eternally His by sovereign right?

3 November

"Even when we were dead in trespasses, made us alive together with Christ (by grace you have been saved), and raised us up together, and made us sit together in the heavenly places in Christ Jesus, that in the ages to come He might show the exceeding riches of His grace in His kindness toward us in Christ Jesus."
(Eph 2:5-7)

Here is a passage which may have puzzled us, because of the verb tenses. There is no perceived problem in our having been dead in trespasses; if we have been saved by grace, that indeed was our former status. We can understand our having been made alive together with Christ, despite the fact that He was made alive first and we have followed to newness of spiritual life. But how, we may ask, can we, still in our mortal bodies, be already raised up together and made to sit in heavenly places? William Kelly raises a related question which is easier to answer, but which helps to put the whole into perspective: "Is it not a fuller statement of the blessing that belongs to us as Christians now, which could not be predicated of any till the resurrection and ascension were facts?" This we can accept more easily.

FB Hole points out that Paul uses two prepositions, 'with' and 'in', and adds: "We have already been actually quickened in the sense of John 5. 25, though we wait for the quickening of our mortal bodies. As quickened we live in association *with* Christ, because of living of His life. We have not yet been actually raised up and seated in the heavens, **but Christ has, and He is our exalted Head**. We are in Him, and consequently raised up and seated *in* Him."

We may be tempted to say that this is all very well, but that it is not the reality which we experience. But it is the reality as God sees it, and that is infinitely more important. Kelly puts it this way: "The difference is in the mind of God and how it bears upon His glory." One glorious day we will experience our position in Christ in all its fullness. Within any fellowship there are likely to be some who live in the light of these profound but wonderful truths, and others who are still undergoing what they call nowadays a learning curve.

4 November

"I thank my God upon every remembrance of you, always in every prayer of mine making request for you all with joy, for your fellowship in the gospel from the first day until now, being confident of this very thing, that He who has begun a good work in you will complete it until the day of Jesus Christ." (Phil 1:3-6)

Paul had a high opinion of the church at Philippi, that Roman colony where he and Silas had been beaten and imprisoned.. They were ever in his prayers. Would he have said the same about our fellowship? *Ever* remembrance? The New Testament sets us standards to meet.

When he talks about the good work done in them, he is evidently referring to their conversion, their being saved. These would have included the jailer and his family. We are reminded that our conversion is the start of a journey which should have no halts, rest periods or backslidings, but only progress to that point where our next step is our resurrection or Rapture - the Day of Jesus Christ. Paul had such works in mind when he wrote to Titus (2:14): "who gave Himself for us, that He might redeem us from every lawless deed and purify for Himself His own special people, zealous for good works." When we find 'He' referring to God but without a particular Member of the Holy Trinity specified, we may usually take it to refer to the Father, though He will accomplish this through the Holy Spirit for the glory of Jesus Christ on His day.

That day is, of course, in contrast with the Day of the Lord, which is for those left behind, or saved later and having therefore to undergo the Tribulation Period. Wherever one of the names of Jesus is included in the definition, the *Parousia* is meant. There is no exact equivalent word in the English language; 'presence' is the nearest we can get, but it is a formal word meaning more than that, such as 'coming to be present.' We looked at the definition of *Parousia* on 29th April and 2nd June, but, because it is so important, we remind ourselves that, in its New Testament use, it implies the Rapture and what happens in Christ's presence immediately thereafter, including the Marriage of the Lamb. It does not refer to the many things which will be happening on earth below.

5 November

"Therefore God also has highly exalted Him and given Him the name which is above every name, that at the name of Jesus every knee should bow, of those in heaven, and of those on earth, and of those under the earth, and that every tongue should confess that Jesus Christ is Lord, to the glory of God the Father." (Phil 2:9-11)

This is the second half of one of the most famous passages in Scripture, where three verses are devoted to our Saviour's humiliation and three to His exaltation, all being within the context of "Let this mind be in you which was also in Christ Jesus!" (v 5). It is our mind, not our body, which is challenged. One of the most blasphemous fallacies originating in recent centuries is the '*kenosis* theory', which teaches that Christ emptied Himself of His Deity when He became Man, effectively making Him fallible and unreliable. He was by nature very God; what He did at His incarnation was not to detract from His Godhood, but to add to it. He took on a second nature, a human nature, in which He humbled Himself and became obedient to the accursed death of the cross.

His exaltation at the hands of His Father is of His human nature; He had not died as God, but He had died as Man and had, as such, to be vindicated. The Holy Spirit has chosen to devote several passages to this theme, and we should not dare to do otherwise It is not actually stated that the name above every other name is Jesus, but most would assume this to be the case. Certainly the passage concludes "Jesus Christ is Lord"; and the word Lord here, as usual in the New Testament, is *Kurios*, which, since the time of the Septuagint Greek New Testament, is used to translate Jehovah. This is further confirmation that Jesus shared the exclusively Divine title of Jehovah.

All creation has eventually to acknowledge that Jesus Christ is Lord or Jehovah, and that His exalted status is His by right. In Revelation chapter 5 (vv 8-14) we find all classes, angelic and human, acknowledging this: "Worthy is the Lamb who was slain!" Whether in the future this is to happen in unison at a single moment, or as great ocean breakers following one after another upon a reef, we cannot say.

6 November

"For our citizenship is in heaven, from which we also eagerly wait for the Saviour, the Lord Jesus Christ, who will transform our lowly body that it may be conformed to His glorious body, according to the working by which He is able even to subdue all things to Himself." (Phil 3:20-21)

We live in a sad age where people come to our country from other religious backgrounds, clamour for citizenship and thereafter resist the Christian culture and traditions which underpin most of what is still worthy in our land. And among many in authority there is a craven fear of defending such standards which we have in the past enjoyed. Perhaps we would find that the excuse given among new arrivals is that their imported culture should take priority and that they should be free to reap the benefits of the sowing of others.

In contrast, here is a simple statement: "Our citizenship is in Heaven", the place whence our Lord will soon come to take us **home**. We are not citizens of this world, but have been left here as representatives. There is a lovely old hymn based upon II Corinthians 5:19- 21, too long to quote in full: "I am a stranger here, within a foreign land..... ambassadors to be of realms beyond the sea, I'm here on business for my King." Our business in an alien world is a positive one, not the hostile one of some current embassies; we invite men and women to become reconciled to God.

We looked at verse 21 on 1st June, but add a few comments. The bodies in which we appear as ambassadors are no different from those among whom we minister, just as our Saviour whilst on earth had a lowly body. But this is all going to change one day. His body is already glorious. In our world many are engaged in sport, potentially an innocent and healthy interest, though with unpleasant reminders of mortality. But we have the confidence, shared by all true believers, that one day we are to have immortal bodies conformed to His glorious body; and our confidence is based entirely upon Him "according to the working by which He is able even to subdue all things to Himself." Elsewhere Paul reminds us to keep in spiritual training, which has no age limitations; but our confidence is in Christ.

7 November

"And He is the head of the body, the church, who is the beginning, the firstborn from the dead, that in all things He may have the pre- eminence. For it pleased the Father that in Him all the fulness should dwell. and by Him to reconcile all things to Himself, by Him, whether things on earth or things in heaven, having made peace through the blood of His cross." (Col 1:18-20)

Bill Freel compares this passage with I Corinthians 12:14-16, where, in Paul's analogy, the Church is Christ's body in a **metaphorical** sense, whereas the body is regarded as a **mystical** reality, adding: "As our Lord appeared in a body of flesh, so now He dwells in the Church, which is regarded as His larger incarnation." And of that Church He remains the Firstborn from the dead, those currently asleep in Him awaiting to join Him in resurrection fullness. It is the Father's will and pleasure, and surely ours also, that He should have the pre-eminence and Headship.

It is easy to make perfectly acceptable generalisations about the difference between believers and unbelievers. But we should remember that, as long as we are in these "bodies of death", we are capable of behaving in a carnal manner. This will be noticed by others, and will thus undermine our witness and give us an uneasy relationship with our Saviour without destroying it: "For to be carnally minded is death, but to be spiritually minded is life and peace. Because the carnal mind is enmity against God; for it is not subject to the law of God, nor indeed can be" (Rom 8:6-7).

It is our business to preach reconciliation, but only Christ can actually reconcile fallen mankind with a sinless God. Reconciliation is possible only through the costly work of the cross. He is our peace. But there must be a willingness to be reconciled to God; none is forced reluctantly into Heaven. Nobody is saved as a second best option or with regrets for what is being given up. Reconciliation is the end of enmity, but many prefer to remain alienated towards God, whose love they resent. When the awfulness of this rejection eventually dawns on them, it will be too late. Reconciliation and peace through the blood of His cross is complete for those in Heaven or Heaven-bound, but still optional for those as yet undecided on earth.

8 November

*"I now rejoice in my sufferings for you…..for the sake of His body, which is the church….. to fulfil the word of God, the mystery which has been hidden from ages and from generations, but now has been revealed to His saints. To them God willed to make known what are the riches of the glory of this mystery among the Gentiles: which is **Christ in you, the hope of glory**."* (Col 1:24-27)

Yesterday we looked briefly at the subject of the Church as Christ's body, and of course we could say much of the sufferings which Paul endured for the sake of the young churches which he founded or visited, or ministered to in his writings. That ministry is still available for us today, as is that of other less profuse New Testament writers. Through the ages many faithful leaders have suffered for their charges, and the Lord has not forgotten: "Shepherd the flock of God which is among you, serving as overseers…. and when the Chief Shepherd appears, you will receive the crown of glory that does not fade away" (I Pet 5:2,4).

The word 'mystery' does not mean the type of cabalistic secrets held by initiates into the dark arts, often paying a dreadful price. Here it simply means that God had chosen us for His own good reasons, which we have occasionally touched upon. As FB Hole says: "It concerns Christ and the church, and more particularly the bringing in of the Gentiles in one body." Much of Paul's suffering was of course at the hands of the jealous representatives of his own nation, who could not contemplate such generosity from 'their' God. The knowledge which was formerly a mystery has been made available to all believers. The language used here reflects the wonder and glory which God wished should be attached to this revealed mystery. "Christ in you, the hope of glory" is actually addressed to Gentile readers. Of course it does not exclude Jewish believers, but to Paul's first readers, most of whom had never met Paul, it must have been a most astonishing and thrilling declaration.

Bill Freel writes: "The hope of glory is not just a blessing of a future world, for it already exists. It is the hope of glory of the eternal kingdom. Because the Lord lives within us, the hope of glory is assured."

9 November

"When the Lord Jesus is revealed from heaven with His mighty angels, in flaming fire taking vengeance on those who do not know God, and on those who do not obey the gospel of our Lord Jesus Christ. These shall be punished with everlasting destruction from the presence of the Lord and from the glory of His power, when He comes, in that Day, to be glorified in His saints and to be admired among all those who believe, because our testimony among you was believed." (II Thess 1:7-10)

We appear to have skipped over First Thessalonians; but, back in April, we explored that little epistle for teaching on the Rapture. The context of today's text is persecution which the Thessalonians had been suffering since they had first believed. Acts 17:1-10 relates the first preaching of the Gospel at Thessalonica, and the fierce opposition of militant Jews who set the city in an uproar and dragged the new leaders before the local authorities. These Jews were well-versed in the Scriptures and should have been awaiting the Messiah. The greater our knowledge, the greater is our guilt and consequent punishment. Paul here goes on to foretell in the most dynamic way the coming fate of those who oppose the Gospel. Few other epistles have anything to compare with the vigour of this act of lawful vengeance, God's prerogative, not ours. It is a reflection of how He is constantly aware of and cares for His suffering saints. The Thessalonians were at one of the most ferocious points on the battle front.

The reference is of course to Christ's Coming in Power. We are never told that the dead in Christ will rise at the same juncture as Christ is destroying His enemies; the Rapture will have occurred earlier. The word rendered 'revealed' means uncovered. The Heavens will not have been opened to view to rebellious defiant bearers of the Mark of the Beast, those willingly ignorant of God. Suddenly, as they have allowed themselves to be gathered for Armageddon, the skies burst asunder to reveal the One who has been there all the time, now with His escort of mighty angels and the saints who are His Bride. How the "fire" will appear we cannot yet say, but it was sometimes associated with the Old Testament theophanies or pre-incarnate appearance of Christ and with His Shekinah Glory.

10 November

"Now, brethren, concerning the coming of our Lord Jesus Christ and our gathering together to Him, we ask you, not to be soon shaken in mind or troubled, either by spirit or by word or by letter, as if from us, as though the day of Christ had come." (II Thess 2:1-2)

Paul, during his brief stay at Thessalonica and in his first epistle, had taught the new believers the basics of eschatology; would that more leaders did the same today. However they were still confused and had to be corrected by Paul; we are the beneficiaries of the error of our forebears. It is generally accepted that manuscripts which say "Day of Christ" are wrong; several versions give "Day of the Lord" in margins. The context confirms this. Had the Day of Christ arrived they would have already been raptured! As it was, they were worried about the persecution and other trials which they were suffering, and wondered whether the Great Tribulation had arrived. Paul in the following verses went on to explain that this could not have happened: "Let no one deceive you by any means; for that Day will not come unless the falling away comes first, and the man of sin is revealed, the son of perdition, who opposes and exalts himself above all that is called God or that is worshipped" (vv 3-4).

Note how Paul starts his explanation with a warning; people (presumably Jews in this instance) were prepared to deceive or to distort end-time teaching. One of the most effective ways of doing this is to say absolutely nothing. The coming Antichrist is rarely if ever preached to most congregations, yet the Bible has so much to say about him. Those 'Preterists' who say that the vast majority of predictive prophecy was fulfilled in the early Church period are guilty of the most serious and irresponsible diversion, effectively undermining the faith of those who should remember our Lord's injunction, that when we see these things **begin** to come to pass, we should be looking **up**, anticipating the Rapture. Currently Russian imperialism is once more figuring ominously in the news, and even Christians look surprised if they are directed to Ezekiel 38 & 39 at what appears to be being foreshadowed. Instead of being "troubled either by spirit or by word or by letter", let us be thrilled by the signs, and search the Scriptures.

11 November

"For bodily exercise profits a little, but godliness is profitable for all things, having promise of the life that now is and of that which is to come." (I Tim 4:8)

Over the past three weeks, as we have delved into Paul's writings; we have touched on some profound truths. Here we return to simpler, but nevertheless important, matters. Believers who participate in sport may find this challenging, particularly should they have read only the AV/KJV Bible's misleading: "For bodily exercise profiteth little". Paul was not saying that; he was not dismissing physical exercise, which has its place. Indeed, there are many instances where our work for our Lord and our responsibility for family and friends suffer if we fail to keep physically fit. It is a matter of priorities. Physical fitness is for this life only; godliness reaps eternal rewards. It was the same Paul who wrote regarding his thorn in the flesh, which was probably a physical infirmity: "My grace is sufficient for you, for My strength is made perfect in weakness. Therefore most gladly I will rather boast in my infirmities, that the power of Christ may rest upon me" (II Cor 12:9).

However Paul occasionally gives illustrations from the well-known Greek sports world, without denigrating such activity. Many Christians are keen or talented sportsmen or women; some have even witnessed through this medium. But sometimes we are confronted with problems. Forty years ago the film "Chariots of Fire" was a splendid testimony to Eric Liddell's refusal, because it was to be held on a Sunday, to run the Olympic 100 metre final, which he was expected to win. He even defied his King (George V), who was furious and almost commanded him to run. But God vindicated Eric, and, instead he won the gold medal at a different distance for which he was less qualified. It so happened that my father had been in the same Edinburgh club, and ran in relay races with Eric. His name was frequently cast up to me as a boy as the embodiment of almost every human virtue, and, child-like I was not amused; but I could not but admire his later missionary exploits! I too, merely a regimental sprint record breaker, later declined Sunday athletics.

The "life that now" is will soon draw to a close; the "life to come" is eternal. Let us discipline ourselves and keep in training chiefly for that.

12 November

"For the grace of God that brings salvation has appeared to all men, teaching us that, denying ungodliness and worldly lusts, we should live soberly, righteously, and godly in the present age, looking for the blessed hope and glorious appearing of our great God and Saviour Jesus Christ." (Titus 2:11-13)

The Revised Version correctly renders the first statement: "The grace of God hath appeared, bringing salvation to all men." The ASV is similar. The NKJV has not changed the AV's sense. As Vine comments, "God's grace has not appeared to all men, but is laden with salvation for all." He goes on to remind us that God's grace has been manifested not only in Christ's Incarnation but is effective in His death and resurrection, giving limitless provision of salvation. The NKJV correctly changes "present world" to "present age". In this present age, not only does the Gospel bring us salvation, but teaches us to live godly lives, which do not further our salvation, but do further our fellowship with God and bring eternal benefits.

The closer our walk with God, the more constant our blessed hope will be, the more we will long to see our Lord face-to-face. I think it is Hal Lindsey who refers to the popular jibe of some Christians being so heavenly minded that they are of no earthly use, whereas a far greater modern problem is that of Christians being so earthly minded that they are of no heavenly use! John writes: "Beloved, now we are children of God; and it has not yet been revealed what we shall be, but we know that when He is revealed, we shall be like Him, for we shall see Him as He is" (I Jn 3:2). Are we so preoccupied with this age and this world that we have ceased looking? Has that coming appearance lost its glory in our minds? Our "looking for" is a command, a duty, not a supplementary trivial pursuit for the few.

The way that that "appearance" is described indicates that Paul was applying both the "great God" and "Saviour" to the one Person of the Trinity, rather than distinguishing between the Father and the Son. It is the Father's will that this should be Christ's Day. This is yet further confirmation of the Deity of the Lord Jesus Christ, which believers should stress when defending their faith.

More Prophecies from Isaiah

13 November

"When the Lord has washed away the filth of the daughters of   Zion,
and purged the blood of Jerusalem from her midst, by the spirit of
judgment and by the spirit of burning, then the LORD will create above
every dwelling place of Mount Zion, and above her assemblies, a
cloud and smoke by day and the shining of a flaming
fire by night. For over all the glory there will be a covering." (Isa 4:4-5)

At various time throughout the year we have quoted Isaiah, and will be returning to him for our closing week. This prophetic chapter 4 of Isaiah is sandwiched between two severe chapters dealing with the situation in the prophet's time. This is about the coming Millennium, but it is just as true from God's perspective as were the short-term prophecies which applied to Isaiah's day. Israel will have gone through the Great Tribulation, she will have been sifted and refined, and will have emerged purged and sanctified. Judgment and burning will be behind her.

We recognise the Shekinah Glory, the pillar of cloud by day and flame by night, which led the Children of Israel through the wilderness and separated the camp of Israel from that of the Egyptians (Ex 14:20). It was the visible sign of the Lord's presence. Ezekiel had witnessed something of the reluctance of the necessary removal of the symbol of Divine presence as it departed from the desecrated Temple and hovered over the Mount of Olives (Ezekiel 11:23). We also saw how, on that future day, when the Millennial Temple is established, this Glory will return from the very direction in which it departed so long ago (Ezekiel 43:2-4).

But here we learn something else. The cloud by day and flaming fire by night will apparently no longer appear as a pillar or leading beacon, for there will be no further moving, no exiles, no scattering of Israel. Rather we are to visualise a canopy, a screen, a covering or shield above the city. Indeed, every household is to be covered, as will every assembly or gathering to worship (and these will be daily and also seasonal). We know that the Lord Jesus Christ, inhabiting the Holy City, New Jerusalem, will not normally be visible to mortals on earth, but the evidence of His overshadowing presence will be visible by all who approach Jerusalem.

14 November

> *"'And now, please let Me tell you what I will do to My vineyard: I will take away its hedge, and it shall be burned; and break down its wall, and it shall be trampled down. I will lay it waste; it shall not be pruned or dug, but there shall come up briers and thorns. I will also command the clouds that they rain no rain on it.' For the vineyard of the LORD of hosts is the house of Israel, and the men of Judah are His pleasant plant. He looked for justice, but behold, oppression; for righteousness, but behold, a cry for help."* (Isa 5:5-7).

The tenderness of the appeal of this song to the Beloved nation is touching beyond human words. And yet there is a warning, which applies to Church Age believers as much to Israel of old, against presuming against the God of love and mercy. Israel is God's vineyard; He had done everything possible to encourage its growth, prosperity and security, but all in vain. They had been fully equipped for their task of blessing and glorifying God's Name, and had cleared out the pagan "stones". The false sense of security, the assumption that that God would not deal severely with their neglect, was foolish. What we have here is the state of the nation at the time when God asked for a volunteer spokesman, and Isaiah responded with, "Here am I, send me." (Isaiah 6:8-9).

When Jesus was confronted in the Temple by the chief priests and elders regarding His authority (Matt 21:23), having answered them, He went on to tell the parable (vv 33-41), of the vinedressers and the son. The extent to which their obtuse minds were blinded reflects Isaiah's commission, because when He asked what the owner of the vineyard would do to the murderers of the son, they replied: "He will destroy those wicked men miserably, and lease his vineyard to other vinedressers who will render to him the fruits in their seasons." (v 41). They could not come to terms with the fact **they** were the "wicked men"; and when in due course the vineyard was indeed leased for the following age to others, namely the Church, they would persecute them also. We might ask whether the modern leaders of those to whom it was leased are any better? What has happened to justice and righteousness in established Christian countries?

15 November

*"The burden against Damascus. 'Behold, Damascus will cease
from being a city, and it will be a ruinous heap.'"* (Isa 17:1)

Isaiah, like some of the other prophets, was required to declare or unload burdens against a number of named nations. The contents of these burdens are mainly historical, but some have latter day elements in terms of Tribulation judgment or Millennial blessing. I have avoided dealing with most of these, but am aware that currently people are asking about Syria and its capital. This verse has been quoted to predict Damascus' near future destruction. However the prophecy has already been fulfilled once at the hand of Assyria. Israel's Northern Kingdom had relied upon a godless alliance with Syria, and paid the price with her own destruction. Amos has a similar prophecy regarding Damascus, but the personally named kings proved it to have been long ago fulfilled: "'But I will send a fire into the house of Hazael, which shall devour the palaces of Ben-Hadad. I will also break the gate bar of Damascus..... The people of Syria shall go captive to Kir,' says the LORD" (Amos 1:4-5).

Damascus was an established city in Abraham's day. It lay within the territory of the Promised Land; David put a garrison in the city (II Samuel 8:6), which became part of Solomon's kingdom, and during the Millennium Israel's borders will pass close to it (Ezekiel 47:18, 48:1). My older commentaries, while not ruling out a latter day relevance, see verse Isaiah 17:1 as being mainly or exclusively of historical significance.

Please appreciate that I am not dismissing out-of-hand any latter day relevance; I am simply being more cautious than some recent sensational writers. We must be deeply aware of the current build-up of Middle East forces bitterly opposed to Israel. Syria was one of the neighbouring nations humiliated by Israel in 1948, and is currently allied with and heavily supported by Iran and Russia, nations which feature in the great latter day Ezekiel 38/39 invasion of Israel (see August 25 and 26); but we believe that to lie beyond the Rapture. Syria has featured prominently since 2010 in what international commentators (but not serious Bible students!) at the time thought was a breakthrough in Arab liberalism, but turned out to be one of the bloodiest episodes in modern civil war. These things should keep us looking up!

16 November

"Then it shall be in that day, that I will call My servant Eliakim the son of Hilkiah;..... The key of the house of David I will lay on his shoulder; so he shall open, and no one shall shut; and he shall shut, and no one shall open. I will fasten him as a peg in a secure place, and he will become a glorious throne to his father's house."
(Isa 22:20,22-23)

Here is what we call a 'type' of Christ, somebody who foreshadows the Lord Jesus Christ in certain respects; Joseph, the rejected brother who became saviour to his family, is one of the best known examples. Eliakim, having replaced the evil Shebna, a 'type' of the latter day Antichrist, became chamberlain or steward to King Hezekiah, a godly monarch over an only superficially reformed Judah which, two generations later, would be taken into captivity by Babylon.

Eliakim's description constitutes an honourable CV, one which the risen Lord Jesus later applied to Himself: "And to the angel of the church in Philadelphia write, 'These things says He who is holy, He who is true, He who has the key of David, He who opens and no one shuts, and shuts and no one opens'" (Rev 3:7). Needless to say, the lesser (Eliakim) is the type of the greater (Christ). Eliakim was the trusted servant who was to have access to the royal treasury and all the king's resources. Henry Ironside, commenting on the Revelation verse and its relevance to Isaiah 22, writes: "To those who look up to Him as their divinely-given Guide and Protector, He opens up the treasure house of divine truth, revealing to them the precious things which God has stored away in His word." Are we individually utilising these amazing facilities? Ironside continues: "Eliakim was to be as a nail, fastened in a sure place. The reference is to the wooden peg, driven into the supporting post of a tent. Upon this peg were hung vessels used in camp-life and the garments of those dwelling in the tent." Within our fellowship, do we share such characteristics of reliability and usefulness? As long as the divine nail or peg remains in place we are secure. Ironside aptly concludes: "While the old creation fell in Adam, the new creation stands in Christ, upon whom all the glory of the house of God is suspended."

17 November

"Your dead shall live; together with my dead body they shall arise. Awake and sing, you who dwell in dust; for your dew is like the dew of herbs, and the earth shall cast out the dead. Come, my people, enter your chambers, and shut your doors behind you; hide yourself, as it were, for a little moment, until the indignation is past. For behold, the LORD comes out of His place to punish the inhabitants of the earth for their iniquity; the earth will also disclose her blood, and will no more cover her slain." (Isa 26:19-21)

Now this lovely and most descriptive of prophecies is sometimes taken to refer to the resurrection of individual Old Testament saints. Indeed I have said so myself and am happy to see that Malcolm Davis agrees: "This will occur at the end of the Tribulation when the Old Testament saints and the Tribulation martyrs will be raised from the dead to enter the Millennial Kingdom." However William Kelly, Henry Ironside and WE Vine all believe that the **prime** significance is the collective national resurrection of Israel, comparable to the dry bones of Ezekiel 37 coming together, gaining flesh and the breath of life. The one does not rule out the other, and both fit in to some extent with the invitation to seek refuge.

The idea that the entering into their chambers till the indignation is past proves that the Old Testament saints are to take part in the Rapture simply does not fit. If we turn to Revelation 12:14, where Israel is pictured as the woman who gave birth to the Messiah, we do see a further potential fulfilment: "But the woman was given two wings of a great eagle, that she might fly into the wilderness to her place, where she is nourished for a time and times and half a time, from the presence of the serpent." The timing fits perfectly with this Isaiah 26 passage, the "indignation" when the Lord visits the earth in judgment being the three and a half years of the Great Tribulation, when Satan, the Dragon, would destroy God's faithful remnant of Israel if he could. Whether this refuge proves to be a specific location such as Petra, guarded by angels, or simply the wilderness of the nations, we cannot be sure. But if God guarantees it, it will be effective.

18 November

"There will be on every high mountain and on every high hill rivers and streams of waters, in the day of the great slaughter, when the towers fall. Moreover the light of the moon will be as the light of the sun, and the light of the sun will be sevenfold, as the light of seven days, and the day that the LORD binds up the bruise of His people and heals the stroke of their wound." (Isa 30:25-26)

This is one of the many passages in Isaiah where the prophet jumps suddenly from the grim present or near future to gracious Millennial glory. The "bruising" and "wounding" of Israel was to continue with greater or lesser intensity for centuries, and is, indeed, still happening. This is God's perspective. From verse 18 He looks beyond the exile, the Dispersion, Inquisition, Pogroms, and Great Tribulation or Time of Jacob's Trouble to the glorious Millennial kingdom, when the blessings offered three and a half thousand years ago will at last materialise. It is a national perspective rather than an individual one. Individuals will live and die, having been saved or not saved. Just as the Church is sometimes considered collectively in the New Testament, so is Israel in the Old.

This is about the time following the collapse of the old system at Armageddon, when the curse imposed at the Fall will at last be lifted. Most of the benefits will be shared with the Gentiles, for the Fall predates Israel by millennia. Male and female will benefit equally. "To the woman He said: 'I will greatly multiply your sorrow and your conception; in pain you shall bring forth children; your desire shall be for your husband, and he shall rule over you.'" (Gen 3:16). Evidently childbirth will no long be painful. It was to Adam that God said: "Cursed is the ground for your sake.... In the sweat of your face you shall eat bread" (3:17-19).

Atmospheric conditions may revert to those of creation: "Thus God made the firmament, and divided the waters which were under the firmament from the waters which were above the firmament" (Gen 1:7). The brightness of the heavenly bodies, which would be intolerable under present global conditions, will be a blessing. Consider the tenderness of the healing and binding; He is our God as well as Israel's, and cares for us equally.

19 November

"Behold, a king will reign in righteousness, and princes will rule with justice. A man will be as a hiding place from the wind, and a cover from the tempest, as rivers of water in a dry place, as the shadow of a great rock in a weary land." (Isa 32:1-2)

Here is a lovely description of the Lord Jesus Christ as both King and Saviour. Our minds go back to that early morning scene when, after an illegal overnight hearing, the chief Priests brought Jesus in front of Pilate: "he said to the Jews, 'Behold your King!' But they cried out, 'Away with Him, away with Him! Crucify Him!' Pilate said to them, 'Shall I crucify your King?' The chief priests answered, 'We have no king but Caesar!'" (Jn 19:14-15). Our natural inclination would have been instant vindication and release of the Prisoner, rather than the two thousand or so years' interval which Almighty God chose to allow before that solemn opening line from Isaiah 32 could be declared. Pontius Pilate, representing the Roman Emperor, reigned in weakness and unrighteousness. Such deputies as he had were no better, whereas in the Millennium the Apostles and those appointed Old Testament heroes, only a few of whom have already been identified, will, in their immortal bodies, share the administration of justice when He returns to reign. Ironside describes them as "those who were faithful to Him in the time of His rejection."

At present every believer is living in the dispensation of Christ's rejection. The old hymn aptly puts it: "Our Lord is now rejected and by the world disowned; By the many still neglected, and by the few enthroned." Today's text reminds us that, "The Crowning day is coming by and by!" It is **His** crowning day that is in mind here, rather than the Judgment Seat of Christ.

Although it is not plainly stated, the "Man" who is thereafter described is surely the Son of Man Himself, the title He often used personally of Himself regarding His return. It was He who bore the storm which should have been ours as guilty sinners; it is He to whom we turn when requiring a hiding place from God's wrath, when the spiritual elements would overwhelm us. It is He who refreshes us when this barren world would otherwise be a howling wilderness. He is our sheltering Rock.

20 November

"Behold, the Lord GOD shall come with a strong hand, and His arm shall rule for Him; behold, His reward is with Him, and His work before Him. He will feed His flock like a shepherd; He will gather the lambs with His arm, and carry them in His bosom, and gently lead those who are with young." (Isa 40:10-11)

Many years had passed and much had happened since Isaiah's earlier writings; but it is the same Isaiah. Our Lord Himself and Luke and Paul, who quoted both parts of the book, never referred to a second or 'Deutero-Isaiah', the invention of unbelievers who cannot accept the miraculous elements of Isaiah's later prophecies. The chapter begins with the repeated word "Comfort!" and later gives some of the numerous divine credentials for His ability to comfort and care: "'To whom then will you liken Me, or to whom shall I be equal?' says the Holy One. 'Lift up your eyes on high, and see who has created these things'" (verses 25-26).

This is about when the Lord returns in power after the Great Tribulation. 'Tending' is more accurate than 'feeding'. "'Thus they shall know that I, the LORD their God, am with them, and they, the house of Israel, are My people,' says the Lord GOD. 'You are My flock, the flock of My pasture; you are men, and I am your God,' says the Lord GOD." (Ezek 34:30-31). It seems clear that, not only adults, including pregnant women, but also children will survive the privations and persecutions of the Great Tribulation, and need tending.

While the scenario is primarily about Israel, one feels that the Gentile Tribulation saint survivors, elsewhere likened to sheep, the "Blessed of My Father", in the Judgment of the Nations (Matt 25:34), will also be catered for with extreme love and tenderness. Neither need we exclude the Church in the present age from such care. When we sing, "The Lord's my Shepherd, I'll not want," we do not pause to say that such truths are not for us. In Church epistles we read: "As it is written: 'For Your sake we are killed all day long; we are accounted as sheep for the slaughter'" (Rom 8:36); "For you were like sheep going astray, but have now returned to the Shepherd and Overseer of your souls" (I Pet 2:25).

21 November

"Sing, O heavens! Be joyful, O earth! And break out in singing, O
mountains! For the LORD has comforted His people, and will have
mercy on His afflicted. But Zion said, 'The LORD has forsaken me,
and my Lord has forgotten me.' 'Can a woman forget her nursing
child, and not have compassion on the son of her womb? Surely
they may forget, yet I will not forget you. See, I have inscribed you
on the palms of My hands; your walls are continually before Me.'"
(Isa 49:13-16)

What misery God's people may bring upon themselves by their
preoccupation with their own achievements – or lack of them – when
God is actually commanding the Heavens to rejoice and break out
in singing, because of the deliverance which He has accomplished.
The Lord may have comforted His people, but many may not have
been listening. This compassionate 49th chapter follows three more
severe chapters. Here we find the Lord Jesus taking upon Himself
personally, as the faithful Servant of Jehovah, the failed role of
the nation of Israel. And there is a lovely reference to His future
incarnation: "And now the LORD says, Who formed Me from the
womb to be His Servant, to bring Jacob back to Him, so that Israel
is gathered to Him" (49:5). There are at least two ways of looking at
Zion's opening statement. In one it is God who is getting the blame,
and in the other they are blaming themselves, but underestimating
the extent of God's love and forgiveness. Even born-again Christians
can be just as guilty of underestimating God's faithfulness when
allowing guilt to persevere, especially if we are tempted to believe
that we have put ourselves beyond repentance. Here God compares
His love with that of a mother, indeed, greater than that of a mother,
because even a mother's love may fail; He assures us that His love
never fails.

It is the work of Christ as the Servant which is to accomplish the
ultimate return to the Promised Land. Malcolm Davis writes: "He
will lead a new Exodus and mediate a new covenant for Israel,
protecting them from all harm on the way back to the Land. This will
bring universal joy and singing on account of the Lord's compassion
on His people."

22 November

"Arise, shine; For your light has come! And the glory of the LORD is risen upon you. For behold, the darkness shall cover the earth, and deep darkness the people; but the LORD will arise over you, and His glory will be seen upon you. The Gentiles shall come to your light, and kings to the brightness of your rising." (Isa 60:1-3)

Much nonsense has been claimed by what has called itself the 'one true church', despite it never having had any authority over some Eastern areas of 'Christendom'. It was not in the epistle to the Romans that Paul said: "Therefore take heed to yourselves and to all the flock, among which the Holy Spirit has made you overseers, to shepherd the church of God which He purchased with His own blood" (Acts 20:28). The true Church is that which is made up of blood-bought individuals, free of any organisational label.

But, in contrast, throughout the Millennium there is to be one true redeemed Israel; there is to be no false Israel, no substitute Israel, only the original Israel restored. It is to her, at the very outset, when darkness has finished reigning in the Tribulation world, that God commands: "Arise, shine; For your light has come! And the glory of the LORD is risen upon you." He adds that this glory is to be seen. He has appointed her unique Millennial role. Ironside comments: "This is to be taken literally. God will deal thus with His people Israel and bring the nations that once antagonized and persecuted them into this blessed harmony in the last days."

It is so easy to detach the first two verses from the rest of the chapter and to try to draw spiritual lessons. But the Gentiles are as significant as Israel. Following the brief reference to Israel's regathering, we read: "The wealth of the Gentiles shall come to you. The multitude of camels shall cover your land, the dromedaries of Midian and Ephah; all those from Sheba shall come; They shall bring gold and incense, and they shall proclaim the praises of the LORD" (vv 5-6). The blessing is to be mutual. One suspects, but cannot be absolutely sure, that most of the technical inventions of recent centuries will become obsolete, and that far greater happiness will be achieved with traditional artefacts and commodities in that coming peaceful and righteous reign.

23 November

"Who is this who comes from Edom, with dyed garments from Bozrah, this One who is glorious in His apparel, travelling in the greatness of His strength? –'I who speak in righteousness, mighty to save.' Why is Your apparel red, and Your garments like one who treads in the winepress? 'I have trodden the winepress alone, and from the peoples no one was with Me. For I have trodden them in My anger, and trampled them in My fury; their blood is sprinkled upon My garments, and I have stained all My robes. For the day of vengeance is in My heart, and the year of My redeemed has come.'" (Isa 63:1-4)

There is much to cover, so I will overlook the interesting question of why Edom is singled out from other guilty parties, and concentrate on the comparatively short Day of Vengeance of our God being followed by the much longer Year of the Lord's Redeemed. This is immediately post-Armageddon. The One who is questioned and who answers is the Lord Jesus Christ, the Mighty to Save. The Day of Vengeance is part of what is sometime termed 'Christ's Mission Statement', that which He quoted from Isaiah 61:1-2 in the Nazareth synagogue after His wilderness temptation, stopping in mid-sentence after "The Acceptable Year of the Lord", and announcing, "Today this Scripture is fulfilled in your hearing" (see Lk 4:16-21). This Acceptable Year which Jesus had just inaugurated will not end until the Rapture; the Day of Vengeance, which immediately follows in that Isaiah text, ends with Armageddon events; the Year of My Redeemed follows Armageddon. It is the best possible news and the worst possible news, depending how one relates to Christ.

The redness of His garment and the treading of the winepress of God's wrath have sometimes been wrongly assumed to refer to Jesus' loneliness in Gethsemane and what followed. But there He was the One who bore the wrath of our God as He carried our sins in His body on the tree. Here the wrath is His, as we will be reminded as we shortly look at the Revelation Bowls of Wrath. In this act of judgment, what is called His "strange work" (Isaiah 28:21), in which He takes no delight, none on earth will be able to help. His delight commences thereafter as He welcomes His mortal redeemed into His earthly kingdom.

24 November

"'For as the new heavens and the new earth which I will make shall remain before Me,' says the LORD, 'So shall your descendants and your name remain. And it shall come to pass that from one New Moon to another, and from one Sabbath to another, all flesh shall come to worship before Me,' says the LORD. 'And they shall go forth and look upon the corpses of the men who have transgressed against Me. For their worm does not die, and their fire is not quenched. They shall be an abhorrence to all flesh.'"
(Isa 66:22-24)

As so often in Isaiah, the contrasts are immense. Again in this final chapter we have God's eternal guarantee for Israel and the assurance that all will come to Jerusalem to see the glory of the One who had been the "despised and rejected of men": "It shall be that I will gather all nations and tongues; and they shall come and see My glory" (v18). The old feast days, new moons and Sabbaths will be restored, to commemorate rather than to anticipate Christ's work of redemption. The new Temple will indeed be a house of prayer for all nations.

Commenting on this passage, William Kelly writes: "As His honour is thus maintained, so is His fear." We do not enjoy talking about death and eternal punishment. But note that the Speaker is God Himself. In March 2018 part of the elaborate five hundred year old ceiling in St Peter's Basilica collapsed only hours after a Vatican spokesman publicly declared that there is no Hell and that those who do not repent will simply disappear. There is some debate as to whether the source was the Pope himself. Now it is not for me to declare cause and effect, but one does wonder. Countless millions would be delighted could it be authoritatively said that there is no Hell. But God says that there is, and it is He who is created it, initially for the Devil and his angels. However the bodies talked of here will not yet have taken part in the second resurrection. Apparently they will be displayed somewhere in the environs of Jerusalem as a reminder, a merciful reminder against rebellion for those born during the Millennium. I cannot help but think of the mummified corpse of Lenin in Red Square – and no, I did not queue up to see it!

Seven Bowls of Wrath of Revelation

25 November

"Then one of the four living creatures gave to the seven angels seven golden bowls full of the wrath of God who lives forever and ever. The temple was filled with smoke from the glory of God and from His power, and no one was able to enter the temple till the seven plagues of the seven angels were completed." (Rev 15:7-8)

We come now to the final and most severe of the three series of judgments upon the earth. These must happen in quick succession towards the end of the Great Tribulation. Unlike the plagues upon Egypt, there is no reason to believe that the effects of one poured out bowl will terminate before the next one starts. Periodically we find both human and angelic voices proclaiming God's righteousness and justice in judgment, as with the angel declaring: "You are righteous, O Lord, The One who is and who was and who is to be, because You have judged these things" (16:5); it is utterly appropriate and necessary that we should publicly accord our Saviour such accolades, for He alone is worthy.

What we might call the 'build-up' to the Bowls of Wrath ('vials' in the AV/NKJ) starts with the angelic invitation: "Thrust in Your sickle and reap, for the time has come for You to reap, for the harvest of the earth is ripe" (Rev 14:15). Two days ago, reviewing Isaiah 63:1-4, we saw Christ having completed this treading of the grapes of wrath. I used the word 'invitation', because this holy angel has no actual authority to command the Son of God. These mighty beings have a perspective based on very much wider vision and experience than we have; but we too have the duty to acknowledge our Lord's right, recognising that only the sinless Son of Man is qualified to judge.

What is described here may be said to be symbolic. But it is symbolic of an intensely real future happening, which in Heaven we shall one day witness. The curtains of the heavenly Tabernacle of Testimony are drawn apart and seven angels emerge carrying the golden bowls which are **full** of the wrath of God. In mercy and incredible patience He has long held back, but this is His righteous wrath in full measure. As with the Tabernacle of old, the smoke screens God's glory from witnesses, lest they should perish.

26 November

"Then I heard a loud voice from the temple saying to the seven angels, 'Go and pour out the bowls of the wrath of God on the earth.' So the first went and poured out his bowl upon the earth, and a foul and loathsome sore came upon the men who had the mark of the beast and those who worshiped his image."
(Rev 16:1-2).

Periodically we are reminded of the plagues upon Egypt. The area of Goshen, where the Children of Israel lived, was exempt when the plagues arrived. God does not always spare us from the misfortunes that afflict our society, but He has the right and sometimes exercises it. During the Great Tribulation the world will become polarised as never before into those who worship God and those who worship Satan; currently hundreds of thousands sit on the fence until their deathbed. So here the plague is limited to all who had accepted the lethal Mark of the Beast, thus effectively worshipping Satan through his deputy. Then there can be no reprieve, no repentance or ability to repent. Let us recall that refusal to accept the Mark of the Beast will make buying and selling impossible, causing incredible hardship. But their suffering will be temporary, and known to God, whereas that of the bearers of the Mark will be eternal.

This plague is not unlike the seventh of those imposed by God through Moses: "And the magicians could not stand before Moses because of the boils, for the boils were on the magicians and on all the Egyptians. But the LORD hardened the heart of Pharaoh; and he did not heed them, just as the LORD had spoken to Moses." (Ex 9:11-12). What priests and deputies the Beast and False Prophet will have we are not told, but if the prophets of Baal tell us anything, it is that there could be a multitude to enforce the worship of the Beast and his image – a sort of Tribulation secret police force. But none will be exempt. Lest we are tempted to say 'only boils' in comparison with the following more dramatic Bowl plagues, we should take note that the first Bowl is upon man rather than his environment. Boils so often result in septicaemia and can be deadly as well as loathsome; one can only guess at the potential death toll.

27 November

"Then the second angel poured out his bowl on the sea, and it became blood as of a dead man; and every living creature in the sea died. Then the third angel poured out his bowl on the rivers and springs of water, and they became blood. And I heard the angel of the waters saying: 'You are righteous, O Lord, The One who is and who was and who is to be, because You have judged these things. For they have shed the blood of saints and prophets, and You have given them blood to drink. For it is their just due.'"
(Rev 16:3-6)

While there is scope for devoting a day each to the second and third Bowls, it seems profitable to deal with them together, as both concern water – that of the sea and rivers. The first Egyptian plague had a similar effect, but was confined to the Nile, as God was dealing with one defiant nation rather than with a rebellious world. These Bowls resemble the second and third Trumpets of Revelation 8, but with triple intensity or geographical coverage. With the trumpets we are told how God is to achieve the result, with what appear to be comets, meteorites or asteroids cast into the sea; here we are simply told of the results. It is worth bearing in mind that man has been polluting the sea with ever more devastating results, despite the warnings of environmental experts. Such social conscience as the world still has will evaporate during the Tribulation Period, when it will be each for himself, ignoring the long-term consequences. God will give the world what it deserves.

The results of both bowls will be devastating. When the second angel pours out his bowl into (not on) the sea and it becomes as blood, the oceans will be deprived of all life, whether microscopic, whale-like or intermediate. A major source of food will vanish and the stench and pollution will be unimaginable. Rivers and springs will suffer a similar fate. Only static sources, which are extremely limited, may be spared sufficiently to allow people to survive at all. Competition for these will be furious.

It is here that the declaration of God's righteousness, which we quoted two days ago, is announced. The punishment will fit the crime. God always takes seriously the persecution of his saints, whether by forces human or demonic.

28 November

"And I heard another from the altar saying, 'Even so, Lord God Almighty, true and righteous are Your judgments.' Then the fourth angel poured out his bowl on the sun, and power was given to him to scorch men with fire. And men were scorched with great heat, and they blasphemed the name of God who has power over these plagues; and they did not repent and give Him glory." (Rev 16:7-9)

Here from the altar itself is another declaration of the righteousness of God in these judgments. We are becoming so accustomed to the "nanny state" mentality of our modern judicial and penal systems that we need to be reminded of God's standards, which we know in our heart of hearts to be reasonable and just.

As with the foregoing Seals and Trumpets, this series of seven also breaks down into contrasting groups of four and three. The Book of Revelation anticipates the folly of allegorical interpretation. I have often pointed out to members of the JW sect that "every **eye** will **see** Him" (1 v 7) has a double emphasis of visibility, shattering one of their main teachings. So here it is not a debatable case of *either* scorching *or* fire, but both. Here is a contrast with the fourth Trumpet, where a third of the sun's light will have been cut off. Power "will be given" to the sun to behave in this way. It will be much more than a heat wave. This is going to be intolerable heat with, no doubt, accompanying sunstroke, sunburn and loss of physical energy; think of the recent Californian wildfires as a tiny foretaste. While there is no actual mention of melting polar ice-caps, these can be anticipated.

The lie of evolution as an alternative to believing in a Creator God will at last be universally exposed. No longer will men regard what is happening as natural phenomena. Just as the Egyptian magicians eventually admitted, "this is the finger of God", without repenting, so men and women will at last recognise that this is Divine intervention, but will refuse to acknowledge God's righteousness. As Jim Allen in his Revelation commentary writes: "'They repented not' is the scriptural record as they refuse to admit their sin as the first step to taking sides with God. To do this would be 'to give Him glory'..... but now, like Pharaoh of old (Exodus 8:32), hearts are hardened and men plunge to destruction."

29 November

"Then the fifth angel poured out his bowl on the throne of the beast, and his kingdom became full of darkness; and they gnawed their tongues because of the pain. They blasphemed the God of heaven because of their pains and their sores, and did not repent of their deeds." (Rev 16:10-11)

Some of the Bowl judgments are clearer than others; sometimes, as here, we have to take time, and, having taken time, admit that this side of the Rapture we cannot be sure. After all, it is Bible believers living through the experiences described who will need to know, and who **will** know. The question arises as to what is meant by the throne of the Beast (whose identity we do not dispute) and his kingdom. Equally competent students of end-time prophecy are divided on certain minor issues. This must never be allowed to undermine our confidence in God's gracious revelation.

We have already learned much from Daniel. We learned that the fourth (Roman) empire revealed to Nebuchadnezzar is to have a latter day extension or revival following an interval of indeterminate length between the legs and the feet of Nebuchadnezzar's prophetic image dream. We know from the same dream that the latter day Roman Empire, whose prince will be the Beast, will have an empire made up of two incompatibles, iron and ceramic clay, possibly indicating apostate Christianity and Islam. We know that Rome was the capital of its empire, but we see indications of Babylon being brought in. We know that it is the Jerusalem Temple which the Beast will usurp, and where he will make his blasphemous claims. So, while the Beast is to have world-wide influence, his actual territory or 'throne' may equate to that of ancient Rome. We cannot be sure. So it may well be that it is only this part of the world which is to be plunged, into this tangible, impenetrable, pain-inflicting darkness under the fifth Bowl. Exodus 10:22-23 gives us an interesting precedent. "So Moses stretched out his hand toward heaven, and there was thick darkness in all the land of Egypt three days. They did not see one another; nor did anyone rise from his place for three days." As before, there will remain satanically inspired bitter resistance against and hatred of God.

30 November

"Then the sixth angel poured out his bowl on the great river Euphrates, and its water was dried up, so that the way of the kings from the east might be prepared….. For they are spirits of demons, performing signs, which go out to the kings of the earth and of the whole world, to gather them to the battle of that great day of God Almighty." (Rev 16:12,14)

Again we do not have all the answers, but are meant to study what we do have. We may be so conscious of the united front of the entire world against Christ, that we may assume that the nations will be allied in other respects during the tribulation. That could not be further from the truth. Let us remember Jesus' prophecy, as expanded later in Seals, Trumpets and Bowls: "For nation will rise against nation, and kingdom against kingdom. And there will be famines, pestilences, and earthquakes in various places" (Matt 24:7). Even the Beast, should   he want to, will not be able to stop unprecedented international, inter- racial, inter-cultural and inter-personal conflict.

Having long accepted the majority understanding that the drying up of the Euphrates was only to facilitate the way to Armageddon, I am now inclined to agree that, as Jim Allen points out, this may be to allow the kings of the East (or 'from the sunrise') to cross the natural border and attack the Beast and his empire. We noted at the sixth Trumpet that God had long imprisoned four fallen angels at that significant river, and they are to be released at that Trumpet. The physical drying up of that ancient river will have a huge psychological impact, as if an invitation were to be given to attack the Beast's realm, with its spiritual capital at Jerusalem and its political one either at Rome or perhaps in a rebuilt Babylon on the banks of the Euphrates, the destination of wickedness in Zechariah's enigmatic vision (5:5 -11).

But would the Beast countenance seemingly personal attacks? It is difficult not to accord even most evil tyrants some principles, but that is foolish when we are dealing with the utterly-unprincipled Satan and his two deputies. Cynically he may rule his empire, cynically he may sacrifice it as, in a passage which we considered back on 25 January, he assembles his forces to confront Christ at Armageddon.

1 December

"Then the seventh angel poured out his bowl into the air, and a loud voice came out of the temple of heaven, from the throne, saying, 'It is done!' And there were noises and thunderings and lightnings; and there was a great earthquake, such a mighty and great earthquake as had not occurred since men were on the earth. Now the great city was divided into three parts, and the cities of the nations fell. And great Babylon was remembered before God, to give her the cup of the wine of the fierceness of His wrath."
(Rev 16:17-19)

We are on the very brink of Armageddon and Christ's Return in Power. What is about to happen is to be proclaimed by the voice of God, from the very throne of Heaven, rather from a mighty angel. There is little doubt that hitherto the mightiest earthquake or series of earthquakes ever were during the Flood, when the world that emerged had a completely new pattern of continents, with mountain chains buried in the depths of the ocean and ocean floors uplifted in great sierras. The immediate Post-Diluvian settling accomplished more in a few years than modern man assumed to have taken many millions of years. And yet a few areas appear to have been relatively unaffected. So, preparatory to the succeeding Millennium, God will arrange an even greater earthquake, though leaving the area of the Holy Land geologically modified, but still recognisable. One contrast with the Genesis Flood is that then earth's inhabitants were not in a position to witness the hand of God; this time many millions are evidently going to be spared long enough to meet Christ either at Armageddon or at His following Judgment of the Nations.

The text goes on to describe the accompanying hailstones, each about the weight a man could carry, each eliciting further blasphemy from men and women. Particularly if we are antiquarians, we may be horrified by the idea that every city, and no doubt every ancient monument and every 'antique' is to be destroyed. And yet it happened before at the Flood, and we cheerfully accept that. All is going to be necessary in order to allow a completely new start in the Millennium. The "blessed of My Father" who enter the Millennium will have no such lingering regrets as we might express. Let us simply trust that God knows best.

Prophecies in Hebrews to Jude

2 December

*"But to the Son He says: 'Your throne, O God, is forever and ever'..... And: 'You, LORD, in the beginning laid the foundation of the earth, and the heavens are the work of Your hands; they will perish, **but You remain**; and they will all grow old like a garment; like a cloak You will fold them up, and they will be changed. But You are the same, and Your years will not fail.'"* (Heb 1:8,11-12)

The first chapter of Hebrews is a classical passage for trouncing cults and apostasy. It is unparalleled in demonstrating the Deity of the Lord Jesus Christ, who is presented there equally as God and Man. Most of the above citations squeezed into the above three verses are from the Psalms, but include one from II Samuel 7:14. What these brief citations of the Old Testament do is to add the Holy Spirit's authority that it is indeed Christ, the Messiah, who is the subject of these earlier pronouncements; and moreover, when we read them together Christ is demonstrated to be Jehovah. The author of Hebrews, who may or may not be Paul (we cannot be sure), was addressing believing Jews, most, if not all, were saved after Christ's death and resurrection, who required clarification or confirmation of New Testament truths, especially regarding the Person of Christ. To us, as genuine latter day Gentile saints, these are fundamental truths. But we are the beneficiaries of their need to be convinced, and our appreciation of who our Saviour is appropriately enhanced. At the time of writing and first reading of this epistle, these must have been real eye-openers, if we may use that expression.

We are taken back to Christ as the Creator, and forward to the Millennium and beyond. Christ is addressed as Creator, Sustainer and Finisher. When Jesus became Man, His adversary, the Devil, was to do all within his power to ensure that He, the Man who is God, should not 'remain' even as long as the works of His hands! As it is, it is He the Creator-Christ who will one day fold this creation up, and put away for ever that evil adversary as well.

When we are reminded that He 'remains', we should consider where He is now, risen, ascended and seated at His Father's side, whence He shall come to take us, that we too may behold His glory.

3 December

"Inasmuch then as the children have partaken of flesh and blood, He Himself likewise shared in the same, that through death He might destroy him who had the power of death, that is, the devil, and release those who through fear of death were all their lifetime subject to bondage." (Heb 2:14-15)

It is so easy to pass over superficially the most profound truths, absorbing their general purport, but missing much of its deepest significance. A Pridham captures succinctly what these verses are actually telling us; they are the measure of the amazing love of God in Christ reconciling the world to Himself, as well as the basis of our confidence in that present world where the Devil seems to some to be holding ever increasing sway. He writes: "That the Lord Jesus might enjoy the children as the gift of God, He must first take away the yoke of the oppressor. But because the right of Satan to destroy was founded upon the victory of sin, which made man the lawful prey of death, He who loved the children, though as yet they knew Him not, took also flesh; that in their stead He might undergo that death which should forever spoil the devil of his claim."

I turn again to FB Hole: "Only death could meet the tragic situation in which we were found..... Death is actually passed as the Divine sentence upon all men because of sin, and Satan, who at the outset manoeuvred men into disobedience, now wields the power of death..... nothing but DEATH could annul *death*. And it must be the death of a MAN to annul death for *men*. All this was fulfilled. The Captain of our Salvation, by taking part in flesh and blood, became a true Man, and for us He died."

As the faith of some is shaken by what we see around us, so those who take the Bible's end-time prophecy seriously are thrilled, and their confidence is boosted by the almost incredible recent proliferation of the signs of the times. Not far over the prophetic horizon delineated by the coming Rapture we hear echoed the command: "Therefore rejoice, O heavens, and you who dwell in them! Woe to the inhabitants of the earth and the sea! For the devil has come down to you, having great wrath, **because he knows that he has a short time**" (Rev 12:12).

4 December

"(The LORD has sworn and will not relent, 'You are a priest forever according to the order of Melchizedek'), by so much more Jesus has become a surety of a better covenant. Also there were many priests, because they were prevented by death from continuing. But He, because He continues forever, has an unchangeable priesthood." (Heb 7:21-24)

The Lord Jesus was constituted a Priest for ever by a Divine oath, something which was not accorded to Aaron, where priest followed priest. The unique Melchizedek was mortal, but his ancestry is not disclosed, that he might serve as a contrasting example or prototype of Christ's everlasting Priesthood and better covenant.

One of the most fundamental errors of the emerging early church, as apostasy took hold, was the appointment of human priests, effectively attempting to usurp Christ's everlasting and unchangeable priesthood. The implications are heretical, attempting to impose oneself as a mediator or go-between between God and man. It becomes worse when Mary is added to the cycle. It allows laziness to creep into our relationship with God, where people think that they can delegate to the priest, the 'professional', given the responsibility for interceding with the Almighty. Some impose vain repetitions and 'penances', and dare to tell people that their sins are forgiven. Jesus said "Do not call anyone on earth your father; for One is your Father, He who is in heaven."(Matt 23:9); "For there is one God and one Mediator between God and men, the Man Christ Jesus" (I Tim 2:5); "The Son of Man has power on earth to forgive sins" (Lk 5:24). We take no pleasure in exposing false teaching within what calls itself Christianity, but we have a responsibility for plucking others as 'brands from the burning', whenever the most basic truths of the Gospel are ignored, distorted or by-passed.

Overseers and other leaders are legitimate appointments within any congregation or assembly; they must not be dismissed as irrelevant. Their responsibility is God-appointed and therefore necessary. But theirs is anything but an unchangeable responsibility. Leaders come and go; thus the contrast at every level with our one and only unchangeable Great High Priest is immeasurable.

5 December

"And as it is appointed for men to die once, but after this the judgment, so Christ was offered once to bear the sins of many. To those who eagerly wait for Him He will appear a second time, apart from sin, for salvation." (Heb 9:27-28)

It is strange how some verses or parts of verses tend to become detached from their settings; the first sentence of today's reading is typical. Separated, the integral parts lose something, especially any sense of contrast. In Christ sin, for the believer, is put away with; it was dealt with at Calvary; it is removed as far as the East is from the West. Yes there is, of course, the Judgment Seat of Christ to be faced by the believer, but not this judgment, which is for the natural man - the one whose sins might have been forgiven, but were not. For them there can be no eager expectation. Our appointment with death was kept by our Saviour when He appeared the first time. He will not reappear with a portfolio of our sins – even our cancelled sins. That is why we can wait eagerly with confidence, rather than apprehensively.

The Judgment Seat of Christ or the *Bema* is rarely mentioned, compared with the judgment which the unredeemed must face; so let us neither forget it, nor be so preoccupied with it that we lose the eagerness of our expectation. "Most assuredly, I say to you, he who hears My word and believes in Him who sent Me has everlasting life, and shall not come into judgment, but has passed from death into life" (Jn 5:24). Are we living in the light of this truth? Failing to live there amounts to doubting Him as well as doubting ourselves.

Let us remember further that what was once a mystery is no longer a mystery: "Behold, I tell you a mystery: We shall not all sleep, but we shall all be changed" (I Cor 15:51). When He appears for us a second time, it will be nothing to do with sin; that is what He dealt with once for all at His first appearing. Do we doubt that? Rather we have saving faith. He is to appear in order to give us complete deliverance from those lingering results of sin which still afflict us whilst here in our mortal bodies. His later coming **to** the world will be in stark contrast.

6 December

"These all died in faith, not having received the promises, but having seen them afar off were assured of them, embraced them and confessed that they were strangers and pilgrims on the earth. For those who say such things declare plainly that they seek a homeland. And truly if they had called to mind that country from which they had come out, they would have had opportunity to return." (Heb 11:13-15)

This follows several commendations of the life of Abraham and one of Sarah. Abraham's faith regarding his call to leave his homeland had a double significance. He was to leave Ur of the Chaldees, sojourn at Haran till his father died and then go down to the Promised Land, where promises were made by God, but no permanent right of occupation was given. Being forbidden to put down roots, he lived tents to his dying day. It is in Hebrews that it is confirmed that this man of faith had a permanent heavenly destination of which God had made him aware, as well as an elusive temporary earthly one. There could in theory have been a return to Ur, but, having placed his faith in God, there could be no going back to his original spiritual state.

Abraham and the others listed in this Hebrews 11 'roll call of faith' are our examples to be emulated. We have been called out of this world; it is not our home, and if we feel too comfortable here our spiritual life is stagnating. We have work to do, because our bodily existence here is legitimate, though only God has full control of its duration. Like Abraham, we have faith not only to invest in God, but to display to the world. Abraham's ultimate test of matured faith was displayed in his unquestioning obedience by offering up Isaac. 2,500 years later, in his Koran, Muhammad substituted his claimed ancestor, Ishmael, to give him spurious credibility! Nobody knows better than God how to vindicate such faith as Abraham's. We have to question faith which does not contain an element of patience. We are required to have patience here without losing that sense of not belonging, which is called separation. These Old Testament heroes saw the promises from afar; we are privileged to witness God-given signs which assure us that the fulfilment of the promises cannot be far off. We must "count Him faithful that promised."

7 December

"Therefore Jesus also, that He might sanctify the people with His own blood, suffered outside the gate. Therefore let us go forth to Him, outside the camp, bearing His reproach. For here we have no continuing city, but we seek the one to come." (Heb 13:12-14)

The study of Bible prophecy is of limited value if it has no influence over our present life on earth. It should be energising and purifying. Here is another instance of our eternal glorious future dictating how we are to live in the meantime, and drawing on the example of our Saviour. Twenty-three times between Exodus 29 and Deuteronomy 33 the expression "outside the camp" is used for a number of sacred purposes. Calvary or Golgotha was outside the 'camp' or city of Jerusalem. The site within the city where the majority of tourists visit simply does not conform to the three requirements, namely (a) to be outside what was the city, (b) to the North and (c) resembling a skull. The other site near the Garden Tomb complies with all three – even today the resemblance to a skull is startling.

The original readers of the Hebrews epistle were being warned that continuing to practise Levitical rituals was effectively putting Christ 'outside' while remaining within what was now obsolete. The 'camp' is for those who rely upon that human priesthood, which denies His everlasting Priesthood, and dares to re-enact Calvary. The veil was rent from top to bottom. Any altar rail or altar screen with the priest on one side and the congregation on the other insults our Lord.

We continue with yesterday's theme of our having no permanent home on earth, no continuing city. Here, however, the emphasis is upon identifying with our Lord's exclusion. The longer we have to await the Rapture, the more likely it is that we shall have to bear His reproach if we actively witness to our faith. Christian students are now understandably reluctant to enter professions for which they are ideally suited, simply because they are likely to be required to accept or even promote transgender and other principles. No wonder there are shortages in certain professions, if there is a requirement to defy publicly the clearest of God's commands! Millions of others know within themselves that the Bible is true, and that its laws are there for the benefit of mankind; but they may not feel the same moral obligation to their Creator.

8 December

"Therefore be patient, brethren, until the coming of the Lord. See how the farmer waits for the precious fruit of the earth, waiting patiently for it until it receives the early and latter rain. You also be patient. Establish your hearts, for the coming of the Lord is at hand." (Jas 5:7-8)

Our blessed hope is the Rapture, when the Lord will come to take us home. At times we are inclined to ask, "How much longer, Lord?" But when we pause to reflect, we have to ask ourselves, what would have happened to us personally had the Lord returned for His Church ten, twenty or fifty years ago? We may even find ourselves asking the Lord not to return until a certain person dear to us is saved. I have to confess to thinking how much better it would be for some loved one to be saved after the Rapture, and undergo the dreadful Tribulation Period than not to be saved at all. All these thoughts are natural, and no doubt the Lord understands. However our requirement is simply to be patient.

James' readers, most of whom would be closer to the land than the average modern reader, would be well aware of the anxiously awaited early and latter (autumn and spring) rains. Occasionally the rains might fail, with disastrous consequences, but the coming of the Lord at the time which He knows to be best is guaranteed. And let us recall that we are the main harvest. Let us also remember that we are workers in the whitening fields, making the best use of our time to win others to increase that harvest. The good farmer waits patiently; but he does not sit back and wait!

Everything around us in the world seems to be collapsing or in danger of collapsing in an increasingly fragile and volatile environment. That is hardly surprising when we consider how man has challenged as never before foundational moral principles. Increased learning has led, not to increased conformity with our Creator's standards, but to the turning of backs on them and venturing into the lethal unknown, where the dangers far outweigh the benefits for all but a greedy elite, who, as they will soon discover, are doubly answerable to God. But believers are commanded to establish their hearts, not their minds, in view of that longed for Harvest Home which is at hand.

9 December

"Blessed be the God and Father of our Lord Jesus Christ, who according to His abundant mercy has begotten us again to a living hope through the resurrection of Jesus Christ from the dead, to an inheritance incorruptible and undefiled and that does not fade away, reserved in heaven for you, who are kept by the power of God through faith for salvation ready to be revealed in the last time." (I Pet 1:3-5)

Peter introduces his next thought with a peon of praise, something which we should do as we contemplate God's blessing for us for the past, present and future. Nowadays, when the influence of Islam is spreading and few dare to confront it, we must pause to compare "Allah who has no son" with "the God and Father of our Lord Jesus Christ". None but our God has boundless mercy, none other provides a lively hope, none other raised for us a Forerunner or "Firstfruits" from the dead. **Therefore** none other can legally or logically, rather than arbitrarily, guarantee such an inheritance.

What a description is provided of that inheritance. The Islamic inheritance is carnal, with a quite extraordinary balance in favour of males. I read the Koran whilst preparing my book, *"Israel, the Church and Islam"*, and am saddened by the lack of awareness of the width of the gulf between Christianity and Islam, which is commonly portrayed as "just an alternative". Unlike our present condition, however blessed that may or may not be, it will neither fade nor pass away. It is securely located in God's Third Heaven. I include a quote from Boyd Nicholson: "What encouragement this would be to those sojourners whose meagre resources would count for little in the provincial banks of imperial Rome. Their wealth was a spiritual inheritance kept on deposit in the reserves of heavenly places and secured by the power of God."

Our faith plays a part, but it is the power of God in which that faith is invested which guarantees our inheritance. The faith mentioned here is in what is future as well as in what is past. It is the completion of that which cannot be reversed, which was wrought when we first placed our saving faith in the Lord Jesus Christ. As yet we can only faintly visualise the fulness of the glory of that salvation, which has "yet to be revealed in the last time."

10 December

"In this you greatly rejoice, though now for a little while, if need be, you have been grieved by various trials, that the genuineness of your faith, being much more precious than gold that perishes, though it is tested by fire, may be found to praise, honour, and glory at the revelation of Jesus Christ, whom having not seen you love. Though now you do not see Him, yet believing, you rejoice with joy inexpressible and full of glory." (I Pet 1:6-8)

We continue from the point where we left off yesterday, with a passage which concerns us in so many ways, short-term and longer-term, including warning, challenge, self-discipline, comfort and reassurance, plus a reminder of the amazing fact that our activity on earth, as witnessed by others, can bring glory to our Saviour in Heaven. What we greatly rejoice in is the expectation of that as yet unseen inheritance guaranteed for us by the power of God.

But now Peter introduces that "now for a little while", which we share with his readers. Here is an assurance that the sometimes grievous testing of the genuineness of our faith is sanctioned by God. Their testing may have been more severe at a time when they were liable, especially in Rome, to be persecuted for both their Jewishness and for their Christianity. This is not the refining of the Judgment Seat of Christ, of which we have read elsewhere, but that refining through faithfully enduring persecution which will result in praise, honour and glory at His Coming, without any further need to be tested.

Peter, who had been an eye-witness of Christ's majesty on the Mount of Transfiguration (II Peter 1:16-17), was addressing those scattered Jews who had never seen Him in the flesh; he could say of them what he could never now say of himself, "whom having not seen you love". Note that second "now" in this passage. The "unspeakable" of the AV has changed its meaning over the years; however Peter is talking of that inexpressible joy as being present whilst actually undergoing such persecutions – the kind of joy which Paul and Silas experienced in the Philippian prison, something about which Christians enjoying unchallenging lives know little. That "if need be" is at our Lord's discretion in love, for our profit and the enhancement of our faith, and always within His ability to see us through.

11 December

"Yet if anyone suffers as a Christian, let him not be ashamed, but let him glorify God in this matter. For the time has come for judgment to begin at the house of God; and if it begins with us first, what will be the end of those who do not obey the gospel of God?"
(I Pet 4:16-17)

This is the only use of the title "Christian" in the Epistles, but the Holy Spirit has sanctioned it, and it is a privilege thus to be associated in name with our Saviour. Peter has been writing about suffering, but also about reproach and blame. Suffering for evil-doing is forbidden to the believer, for it reflects on our Saviour's Name. It is all very well for Christians to claim to be suffering manfully or in silence, but this is no great virtue if this has nothing to do with our Christians lives, and especially if it has been our own fault in the first place! Unbelievers may be equally courageous. Suffering in any way for our Christian witness is entirely different. We are, of course, never told to take pride in this kind of "suffering for righteousness' sake"; it is for Christ to praise us, not ourselves. If the world praises us for something done in the Lord's name, it is up to us to ensure that it is He who receives the glory.

Twice already we have considered the widespread distortion of the prophetic programme through Fourth Century and later statements in Creeds such as "From thence He shall come to judge the quick and the dead," which give the utterly unscriptural impression that rewards and eternal punishment will be dispensed at the same tribunal, and fail to distinguish between believer and unbeliever.

FB Hole refers to Ezekiel chapters 8 and 9, when God instructed that judgment should start at His Sanctuary. The principle still holds true. It is a solemn thought, because any wrong-doing within the fellowship is under God's scrutiny, and it is His right to deal with it openly and fairly. We should all take note. When there was external persecution, there was little room for the half-hearted and uncommitted. If the Lord tarries, we may have to face active persecution, unprecedented since the Reformation, for taking even a passive stand against ever- increasing convenience abortion and that which the Bible teaches us are perversions.

12 December

"And so we have the prophetic word confirmed, which you do well to heed as a light that shines in a dark place, until the day dawns and the morning star rises in your hearts; knowing this first, that no prophecy of Scripture is of any private interpretation, for prophecy never came by the will of man, but holy men of God spoke as they were moved by the Holy Spirit." (II Pet 1:19-21)

Peter's readers needed to be convinced of what they should have automatically regarded as certainties. The need for convincing is widespread today. The prophetic word is regarded as something supplementary for a few specialists, rather than something given to us all by the Holy Spirit. We are the losers and our position in the world where we are ambassadors suffers. Far too often the Old Testament, including its unfulfilled unconditional prophecies, is regarded as obsolete. But Bible prophecy sheds reliable light in a filthy (rather than dark) place. Even within the fringes of evangelical Christianity there are still those who have not learned the lesson of the last few decades, that there is to be no gradual spiritual evolution from a fallen world to a more blessed or Utopian state. The lie is promoted by false prophecies and imaginative song writers. There is a stubborn resistance to deeper study of a precious resource which is available for us until the rising of the Morning Star, the Rapture of the Church, which is to precede, by a short period of lingering darkness, the Millennial dawn, when the Sun of Righteousness, of which Malachi writes, "shall arise with healing in His wings", (4:2). The light shed should not only illumine our minds as to the facts of our Lord's Return for us, but should encourage and motivate us to make the best use of our remaining time.

The fact that no prophecy is private, or of its own, interpretation, indicates that it cannot be viewed independently of other prophecies; Darby renders it thus: "the scope of no prophecy of scripture is had from its own particular interpretation". There is an overall consistency in God's plan of the ages. When in doubt, we must compare prophecy against prophecy. Some prophecies may have a special emphasis, but when one seems in our minds to contradict the others, it is we, not the prophecy, which are faulty.

13 December

"Be mindful of the words which were spoken before by the holy prophets, and of the commandment of us, the apostles of the Lord and Saviour, knowing this first: that scoffers will come in the last days, walking according to their own lusts, and saying, 'Where is the promise of His coming? For since the fathers fell asleep, all things continue as they were from the beginning of creation.'" (II Pet 3:2-4)

Peter was now approaching the martyrdom of which Jesus had forewarned him, and was aware of the dangers which were to follow, especially of the scoffing at the prophecies of the Lord's Return. It is a feature which has increased rather than decreased down through the centuries, and over the past two hundred years it has been reinforced by the pseudo-scientific idea of continuity about which Peter hints. This was greatly enhanced by Darwin's theory of evolution, though it goes back rather further. The idea is that, in contradistinction to the actions of the Creator, everything in the universe has developed at the pace which we observe today. "All things continue as they were from the beginning of creation" suggests that Peter is talking exclusively about deceived believers. But in his day everybody, of whatever religion, believed in some kind of creation. Nowadays one might talk of everything continuing at the same pace since the "Big Bang" or whatever theory happens to be in vogue. However, as John Walvoord remarks, "Peter accused the scoffers of having a short memory and forgetting purposely..... Though they passed by the question of the origin of all things, by saying God created it, they fail to realise that this God has supernatural powers over natural laws and can change any or all of them as He wills."

George Waugh points out how Peter warns how arrogant and blasphemous the errorists had already become, and foretells an increase in their numbers towards the close of the age. They walk according to their lusts in a permissive society. Total rejection of the truth of Christ's Return is simply the first step towards disbelieving any coming judgment for sins and any need for repentance. Waugh writes: "These are mockers, mockingly taunting the real and genuine teacher and deliberately deceiving the unwary saint." It is our responsibility to protect our ever more vulnerable young people from such predators.

14 December

"But, beloved, do not forget this one thing, that with the Lord one day is as a thousand years, and a thousand years as one day. The Lord is not slack concerning His promise, as some count slackness, but is longsuffering toward us, not willing that any should perish but that all should come to repentance." (II Pet 3:8-9)

This verse has been used to deny the literal Millennium, despite its being stated six times in Revelation 20 as being a thousand years. It is a ridiculous argument which could be used equally foolishly against any other specified periods of time in Scripture, but tends not to be, because it is the Millennium which is chiefly under attack. Not only is a thousand years as a day to God, but the reverse is equally true.

What Peter is asserting is God's timelessness, something which may be difficult to grasp intellectually but easy to accept spiritually. Peter had been dealing with the disappointment among some believers that Christ's Return had not already occurred. They were impatient, as if God, "who desires all men to be saved and to come to the knowledge of the truth" (I Tim 2:4), were being forgetful and failing to keep His promise! The two thousand years since the promise was made should be no grounds for doubting. Here is another reason for God having given us the signs of the times to keep us alert without faltering. What size of Church would there have been had Christ returned within three or four decades of the promise being made? God requires us to accept His, rather than our own, perspective on time. Praise the Lord for God's perspective! Ours is the resultant blessing. Were a thousand believers to recommend a time for Christ's Return, we would have a thousand different answers!

God, in longsuffering mercy, gives mankind extended opportunity, just as before the Flood he waited more than a hundred years before imposing judgment. It is sad that some should be so preoccupied with their assumption that God is failing in His promise, that they virtually dismiss that promise altogether, unaware of God's unwillingness that any should perish. Millions are perishing because they reject God's way of salvation. It is within His permissive will, but not within His personal will. Is the distinction so difficult to grasp?

15 December

"Therefore let that abide in you which you heard from the beginning. If what you heard from the beginning abides in you, you also will abide in the Son and in the Father. And this is the promise that He has promised us - eternal life." (I Jn 2:24-25)

There a contrast between the way in which those two Apostles, Peter and John, express key truths. The Holy Spirit chose very different personalities to deliver equally inspired words of Scripture. What does John mean by "that which we heard from the beginning"? John started this chapter by addressing us as babes or little children, rather than as sons. We are indeed sons if we are redeemed, but angels are also described as sons of God (Job 1:6), and all men are described as His offspring (Acts 17:29). John wants no misunderstanding; children are exclusively redeemed, born of God's Spirit. As children we are being taken back to the beginning of our new life in Christ, to the day we heard and believed. Often in our daily lives we need to be taken back to that point where our abiding in the Son and the Father began. As FB Hole writes: "The Son comes first, since we can only continue in the Father as we continue in Him. To 'continue' is to abide in the conscious knowledge and enjoyment of the Son and the Father, possible for us as we are born of God and have received the Anointing..... Now we may possess that life and be in it; and this is for all of us, for these were written to the babes in the family of God."

I recall many years ago being shocked to hear what I thought of as a mature Christian woman relating a spiritual crisis which she had just experienced, saying: "I said to myself, 'Stay saved, Mary, Stay saved!'" (naturally I have changed the name) She genuinely believed that she could be saved, become unsaved and then be saved afresh. Now there is no denying the fact that we may indeed have periods of backsliding in our Christian lives, and suffer loss of both usefulness and reward. But the above is an impossible situation for the true child of God.

Arthur Gooding points out: "The promise is sure; it is guaranteed by the identity of the Promiser and by the repetition of 'promise..... promised'".

16 December

"Beloved, now we are children of God; and it has not yet been revealed what we shall be, but we know that when He is revealed, we shall be like Him, for we shall see Him as He is. And everyone who has this hope in Him purifies himself, just as He is pure."
(I Jn 3:2-3)

The world *should* already see something of Christ in us, as indeed we should in each other. But our future state is to be grander still. Currently we are nothing very special to look at, let alone to admire. Before His resurrection and ascension, the Lord Jesus was for us despised and rejected of men. As believers, we may similarly be despised and rejected of men. If we are, let us take comfort in knowing that He is aware, understands and approves. In order to see Him as He really is, we ourselves must in that day be truly like Him; the fact that at present we tend to consider ourselves unworthy is only natural. One day we are to bear His image in order that we may gaze upon His beauty and holiness; "They shall see His face, and His name shall be on their foreheads" (Rev 22:4).

AMS Gooding writes: "He will appear to the saints at the Rapture, to the world at His appearing. At the former we shall be changed to be like Him; at the latter we shall be seen by the world to be like Him. The day will be coming where it will be evident that we are the children of God." However this does not mean that we should not even now display at least some evidence of this wonderful status. Some unbelievers really do take notice of witnessing believers, and may thus be influenced to seek our Saviour for themselves. Purifying ourselves to be like our peerless Saviour is indeed impressive evidence. As believers we all have the hope. But do we also have the purity?

Gooding reminds us that in these verses we are celebrating the accomplishment of God's eternal purposes for man. He quotes: "let us make man in our image, after our likeness", adding "Genesis 3 tells us how man, not content with the true likeness to God which was his by creation, grasped at the deceptive likeness held out as the serpent's bait." The result was ungodliness leading to death.

17 December

"Now to Him who is able to keep you from stumbling, and to present you faultless before the presence of His glory with exceeding joy, to God our Saviour, Who alone is wise, be glory and majesty, dominion and power, both now and forever. Amen." (Jude 1:24-25)

This wonderful doxology concludes a book which deals with apostasy, and is therefore potentially depressing. The Holy Spirit furnished Jude with information not found elsewhere in Scripture, such as Enoch's prophecy (verse 14). We must never accept apostasy as inevitable; it is our duty to challenge it should it dare to manifest itself within our midst. Apostasy was rife in Jude's day, how much more it is today: "I found it necessary to write to you exhorting you to contend earnestly for the faith which was once for all delivered to the saints" (1:3). Jude's description of the apostate is one of the most solemn denunciations in Scripture: "They are clouds without water, carried about by the winds; late autumn trees without fruit, twice dead, pulled up by the roots; raging waves of the sea, foaming up their own shame; wandering stars for whom is reserved the blackness of darkness forever" (1:12-13).

But suddenly we are reminded that **He is able** to keep us from falling. Who is able? God is able! Before we come to that glorious final Book of Revelation the believer is assured that the keeping power of God is able to keep us from doctrinal error and anything approaching apostasy. Should we fall, and many over the centuries have fallen, and Church history bears eloquent testimony to the variety and depth of false teachings, we have nobody but ourselves to blame. Darby renders the word translated as 'faultless' as 'blameless', a thrillingly comforting thought in view of the evil which currently abounds.

But, as John Walvoord comments, "A Christian is assured that the day will come when he will be presented to God as a trophy of His grace and that he will be without fault and with great joy." Albert McShane points out that the angels who sinned were once in this sphere of glory before being cast out, but that we are the preserved ones who will be permanently set in it and never be deposed. The attributes of "God our Saviour" which close this doxology guarantee this for all eternity.

Christ's seven rewards for Overcomers

18 December

"To the angel of the church of Ephesus write, 'These things says He who holds the seven stars in His right hand, who walks in the midst of the seven golden lampstands..... He who has an ear, let him hear what the Spirit says to the churches. To him who overcomes I will give to eat from the tree of life, which is in the midst of the Paradise of God.'" (Rev 2:1-2,7)

We return to the seven epistles to the churches in the province of Asia. In April we considered their merits and faults; now we consider the promises for their overcomers. The risen Lord introduces Himself differently as appropriate to each church's characteristics, using His description as recorded in Revelation 1. The rewards offered seem also to differ, until we notice the repeated injunction: "He who has an ear let him hear what the Spirit says to the churches." Every description of the Lord applies to every church and every reward is available to all, but He has chosen specific ones as being particularly appropriate to each church.

The lampstands are the churches. Ephesus needed to be reminded that this is not a distant Christ, but one who takes an intense interest in them, walking among them.

But who are the overcomers? John writes: "Whatever is born of God overcomes the world. And this is the victory that has overcome the world - our faith. **Who is he who overcomes the world, but he who believes that Jesus is the Son of God?** (I Jn 5:4-5). In fact the overcomers are simply the believers within the churches. Probably almost all within the Ephesus church were believers, but, as the years passed, the Gospel was watered down and standards dropped; there would progressively be proportionately fewer and fewer, with revivals periodically helping to restore the believing numbers. When we come to the end of Revelation, we find only two classes of people – believers or unbelievers, saved or unsaved. There is no intermediate group of 'non-overcoming saved'. All the redeemed in Heaven will inherit some blessings.

Tim Lahaye writes: "The Tree of Life, of which those who overcome are given the opportunity to eat, is unquestionably the tree from which Adam and Eve were forbidden to eat after their sin. A symbol of eternal life, it is to have a prominent place in the paradise of God."

19 December

"And to the angel of the church in Smyrna write, 'These things says the First and the Last, who was dead, and came to life..... He who overcomes shall not be hurt by the second death.'" (Rev 2:8,11)

The little church at Smyrna, one of only two which the risen Lord did not publicly criticise or admonish, and which was about to suffer severe persecution, is given the shortest description of Christ and the briefest promise. But what a description and what a promise!

In chapter 1 we read of One declaring: "'I am the Alpha and the Omega, the Beginning and the End,' says the Lord, 'who is and who was and who is to come, the Almighty.'" (v 8), John turned to see the Speaker and saw in the midst of the lampstands "One like the Son of Man" (v 13) who is the Almighty! These matters are devastating to the cults, but immensely reassuring to persecuted churches. Theirs is a risen Lord who was once dead and was raised to life and is able to keep His promises.

We have already looked at the subject of the second death: "But the rest of the dead did not live again until the thousand years were finished. This is the first resurrection. Blessed and holy is he who has part in the first resurrection. Over such the second death has no power" (Rev 20:5-6). By looking at this positive mirror image of the apparently negative promise to Smyrna and the post-Apostolic age which it typifies, we see a guarantee of participation in the first resurrection, meaning, for the Church, the Rapture, as well as further blessings attached. The One who is making the promise stated that He holds in His hand "the keys of Hades and death" (1:18), and has control of access and exclusion. Hades and death are not the same; one is temporary and the other eternal. We may be puzzled by the choice of promises, but I think we may safely conclude that the believers in Smyrna who first read this little epistle would have been thrilled rather than puzzled that the risen Lord had chosen this particular promise. The persecutors had been encouraged by the local Jewish community. As we know from the Gospels, unsaved religious people with their spiritual pride can be experts at taunting and belittling the faith of others. But Christ knew and understood.

20 December

"And to the angel of the church in Pergamos write, 'These things says He who has the sharp two-edged sword:…. To him who overcomes I will give some of the hidden manna to eat. And I will give him a white stone, and on the stone a new name written which no one knows except him who receives it.'" (Rev 2:12,17)

When we see how Christ introduces Himself to the Pergamos (or more correctly Pergamum) assembly, our thoughts turn to Hebrews 4:12: "The word of God is living and powerful, and sharper than any two-edged sword….. and is a discerner of the thoughts and intents of the heart". We immediately see the relevance of this symbol of justice and absolute truth in a city with specific Satanic associations and emperor worship, and a congregation which was falling into apostasy and false doctrine, typifying the period in Church history when, among other falsehoods, the Augustinian lie was perpetrated that everything in Scripture should be taken literally except prophecy. Once that lie was accepted, others followed in quick succession.

Manna had been God-given food for a needy people in desert conditions. This hidden manna suggests alternative heavenly nourishment in a society of supposedly advanced culture, but spiritually wilderness conditions. Now the purpose of the white stone is not specified, but many assume it to refer to the common contemporary practice of the judge giving a white stone when an accused was found innocent and a black one when he was found guilty. The purpose of the name written on the stone reminds us of the retained identity of the redeemed individual for eternity. In Eastern religion and New Ageism the ultimate aim is "self actualisation" or "absorption in into the infinite". Any reader who has trained as a teacher or has studied psychology elsewhere will remember this being the pinnacle of achievement in New Age Abraham Maslow's pyramidal "Hierarchy of Needs", effectively the inversion of Christ's superior Beatitudes. Within the Church, the Bride of Christ, we remain individuals with, apparently, a personal name shared by Christ and ourselves. Alford suggested, and I agree, that the "the stone's value rests in the new name of the recipient which is his title to eternal glory." In this age of latter day apostasy, it is thrilling to know that our Lord does not ration His rewards to overcomers!

21 December

> *"And to the angel of the church in Thyatira write, 'These things says the Son of God, who has eyes like a flame of fire, and His feet like fine brass..... And he who overcomes, and keeps My works until the end, to him I will give power over the nations. He shall rule them with a rod of iron; They shall be dashed to pieces like the potter's vessels - as I also have received from My Father; and I will give him the morning star.'"* (Rev 2:18,26-28)

We have already seen Christ identified as the Son of Man (1:13), but here we see Him as the Son of God. Both contrasting equally valid titles must always be borne in mind; they are never chosen casually. Walvoord writes: "His title here is in keeping with the character of the judgment pronounced upon this church. The diversion from the true worship of Jesus Christ the Son of God was so serious that it called for a reiteration of His Deity." There is anger here as well as purifying judgment. Do we as individuals or congregations not need to be reminded of who our Lord is? The evidence suggests that many nominal Christians had crept into the midst. We live in an age where the bigger the congregation, the more who come into that category.

As with Pergamum, Christ's displeasure with the congregation in no way limits the honour He accords to the true believer and overcomer. The reference is to the Millennium, as we have seen elsewhere. We must be careful to distinguish between what we are to share with Christ at that time and what He is to do Himself. We are to be privileged, as immortal members of the Church in the New Jerusalem, to join Him in His power over the nations, but we are not to be granted the right, nor would we then want that right, to apply a rod of iron or to break any like a potter's vessel. That is His right alone, and it is accorded to Him as the Son of Man by His Father.

Jim Allen writes: "The morning star is the harbinger of the dawn as its shining precedes the sunrise. Tried believers are encouraged by Christ to look ahead to the establishment of the kingdom and the sharing with Him of rule."

22 December

"And to the angel of the church in Sardis write, 'These things says He who has the seven Spirits of God and the seven stars..... He who overcomes shall be clothed in white garments, and I will not blot out his name from the Book of Life; but I will confess his name before My Father and before His angels.'" (Rev 3:1,5)

Next to Laodicea, the Lord's message to Sardis is the most severe. As ever it is the angel or (perhaps better) human messenger who is directly addressed. Leaders are accountable for the spiritual life of the church. We read in Revelation 1:4 of "seven Spirits who are before His throne" and in 5:6 of "the seven Spirits of God" in a scene where the Occupant of the Throne is central. It is commonly agreed that the seven-fold character of the Holy Spirit, as described in Isaiah 11:2, is intended. This is a very searching depiction of Christ who walks amidst the churches: "The seven stars are the angels of the seven churches, and the seven lampstands which you saw are the seven churches" (1:20). A complacent church, where only a few are worthy, not having defiled their garments, needs this vision of Christ. The Sardis church seems to typify the self-satisfied Post-Reformation church, where doctrine, which is not criticised in this little epistle, had been corrected, but where spiritual life was stagnant.

Here only a minority seem to be regarded as overcomers or true believers. They are told that they are to be clothed in white – both the imputed righteousness of Christ's salvation and their sanctified, separated state in a carnal church. Jim Allen, referring to Zechariah 3:1-7, where garments had been defiled in Babylon but were now purified, sees here the Millennial priestly function, pointing out that the verb tense indicates that investiture still lies ahead.

Blotting out of names from the book of life is seen by some to indicate that one can be saved and thereafter lost, in contradistinction to many assertions that this is not the case. The explanation, seems to be that God, who is not willing that any should perish, caused all human names to be recorded in the Book of Life, to be erased only after salvation is rejected. The Sardis overcomers were thus being reminded that this would not be their fate.

23 December

"And to the angel of the church in Philadelphia write, 'These things says He who is holy, He who is true, He who has the key of David, He who opens and no one shuts, and shuts and no one opens..... He who overcomes, I will make him a pillar in the temple of My God, and he shall go out no more. And I will write on him the name of My God and the name of the city of My God, the New Jerusalem, which comes down out of heaven from My God. And I will write on him My new name.'" (Rev 3:7,12)

Philadelphia is the second of the seven little churches which our Lord chose not to criticise publicly. We note how the Lord introduces Himself to the Philadelphian believers. He is described as "holy and true". Holiness is something which we have come to understand, but the word translated "true" here is interesting. I turn again to Jim Allen who quotes WE Vine and points out that the Greek word which John uses twenty-two times in his writings speaks of absolute reality, as in "true bread" (John 6:32), which does not imply that all other bread was actually false, but rather that this was the very essence of truth and reality, compared with which anything else was inferior. Back on 16th November, in another context, we looked at the implications of the key of David. Here we see it as being appropriate to a church which seizes its opportunities to evangelise and go into the world preaching the Gospel. When we do this faithfully, the Lord keeps doors open. Currently so many doors are being closed in our presence.

Philadelphia had suffered devastating earthquakes, sometimes with only broken pillars left standing and the survivors fleeing. The idea of being symbolically a pillar of God's temple would have had a special appeal, as would bearing the name of the New Jerusalem described as in Revelation 21:2 & 10, with all the freedom of citizens who may have the task of ministering in the Millennial earth below. The original members of the Philadelphian church had refused to deny the name of Christ; in that day they are to be honoured by having inscribed upon them Christ's new name, which remains as yet undisclosed: "He had a name written that no one knew except Himself" (19:12).

24 December

"And to the angel of the church of the Laodiceans write, 'These things says the Amen, the Faithful and True Witness, the Beginning of the creation of God..... To him who overcomes I will grant to sit with Me on My throne, as I also overcame and sat down with My Father on His throne.'" (Rev 3:14,21)

The Lord introduces Himself in three ways to this self-satisfied lukewarm church which typifies latter day Christianity. Paul writes: "For all the promises of God in him are yea, and in him Amen" (II Cor 1:20 KJV); a church compromising with so many truths must be reminded that Christ is the absolute, the final authority. A church whose witness to the world has been diluted and distorted must realise that He is the Faithful and True Witness. Some, particularly among the cults, have argued from the word "Beginning" that Christ was a created being – "JW's", for instance, claim He was the first creation through whom Jehovah created all other beings. But "All things were made through Him, and without Him nothing was made that was made" (Jn 1:3), and He most certainly did not create Himself! "He is before all things, and in Him all things consist" (Col 1:17); "through whom also He made the worlds" (Heb 1:2) – all the worlds.

One might have assumed that overcomers in this church might be offered a lesser reward; but, far from it, its prospects equal or surpass some of the others. We must realise that two thrones are referred to by Christ here, His Father's throne and His own. When in Revelation 4 and 5, John, having been caught up to Heaven in the Spirit, sees the Father's throne, and in due course Christ, whom he sees as the overcoming or prevailing Lamb, coming from the midst of that throne: "as I also overcame and sat down with My Father on His throne". William Newell writes: "Christ's throne is the throne of His father David at Jerusalem" (he gives numerous Old Testament references plus Lk 1:32 and Acts 15: 14-18) adding: "But our Lord's royal inheritance by the Davidic covenant extends to His heavenly bride, the Church, as Eve shared the dominion that God gave the first Adam." "When the Son of Man comes in His glory, and all the holy angels with Him, then He will sit on the throne of His glory" (Matt 25:31).

The Zeal of the Lord of Hosts will perform this

25 December

*"For unto us **a Child** is born, unto us a Son is given; and the government will be upon His shoulder. And His name will be called Wonderful, Counsellor, Mighty God, Everlasting Father, Prince of Peace."* (Isa 9:6)

I am very much aware of the fact that Christ was born in mid-autumn rather than on what we call Christmas Day, which is an adaptation of the pagan winter solstice or Yuletide festival. However I am equally aware that millions who never, except at Christmas or funerals, enter a Christian place of worship hear sung some of the most sublime truths, such as "Veiled in flesh the Godhead see, Hail the incarnate Deity", "He came down to earth from Heaven, who is God and Lord of all," and similar lines. Besides, I wish to end the year with one of the most Christocentric Messianic prophecies in Holy Scripture. So I am proceeding without further explanation.

The context of this verse is a sinful Israel, due in both the near and distant future to require a Divine Deliverer from Northern invaders. However as that Deliverer is Christ, who saves all willing mankind of all nations and ages, I wish to concentrate over the next few days on the wonderful features of His Person listed here, as a fitting end to our studies.

Commenting on the opening statements, Ironside says: "In these two expressions we see the humanity and Deity of our Saviour. The child born refers to His humanity….. He was a true Man, spirit, soul and body, as born of Mary." First He was to be born a Child. Only God could have condescended to do this. Not only was it an outstanding demonstration of His infinite love, it was a necessity so that He could become our Kinsman Redeemer – one of us. It would not have sufficed for Him to appear on the scene as God having taken on an adult human likeness. This He had already done several times before Isaiah's time in what we refer to as theophanies; but His later incarnation was entirely different, being born to live, die and be raised again to life, that He might deliver us from the pain and penalty of death. As WE Vine, referring to Isaiah 7:14, remarks, "verse 6 is an expansion of Immanuel. He is partaker with 'the children' of flesh and blood" (Heb 2:14).

26 December

*"Unto us **a Son** is given; and the government will be upon His shoulder....."* (Isa 9:6)

Several of the thoughts here are taken or adapted from a little goldmine of a book sent to me recently by Ritchies, the publishers, "*The Glories of Our Lord*" by HC Hewlett. He writes, for instance: "Noting that 'son' speaks of dignity, we think of our Lord's Sonship as stated in John 1:18: 'No man hath seen God at any time; the only begotten Son, which is in the bosom of the Father, he hath declared him' (KJV). It is a unique Sonship. 'Only begotten' does not refer necessarily to birth, but to that which is unique in character and nature as with Isaac, who was thus distinguished from Ishmael. The equality with God is implied in this Sonship, where Son is an expression of dignity rather than subjection and still less of inferiority." This Sonship indicates intimacy; the Son dwells in the bosom of the Father, a strange expression to us, but common enough in Bible times in family and other close attachments.

This Sonship indicates the eternity of the relationship. It is not the result of the incarnation, as comes over so clearly in our Lord's High Priestly prayer in John 17. Earlier that evening He said: "I came forth from the Father and have come into the world. Again, I leave the world and go to the Father" (Jn 16:28). This Sonship gives us a unique and unprecedented revelation of God. His own characteristics displayed during His life and ministry on earth tell us so much of the Father who sent Him, for instance: "I have come in My Father's name". (Jn 5:43). "This is the will of the Father who sent Me, that of all He has given Me I should lose nothing" (Jn 6:39); "My Father, who has given them to Me, is greater than all; and no one is able to snatch them out of My Father's hand." (Jn 10:29). And let us never forget that the Son was **given**. Our redemption cost the Father more than we can ever know.

Regarding the prophecy, "The government shall be upon His shoulder", we have looked several times at prophecies which foretell His Millennial reign. Here that is tied in with the Child born, the Son given and all those Divine attributes.

27 December

*"And His name will be called **Wonderful, Counsellor**..... "* (Isa 9:6)

This is in the future case because it had still to be applied collectively to Christ as the One to be born and given. While we do not dispute that He is a wonderful Counsellor, we have here two separate Hebrew nouns. He is independently both Wonderful and Counsellor. When the Pre-incarnate Christ appeared to Samson's parents as the Angel of the Lord, they dared to enquire what His name was. He replied: "Why do you ask My name, **seeing it is wonderful**?" (Judg 13:18). They had wanted to make an offering and were told: "if thou wilt offer a burnt-offering, thou shalt offer it up to Jehovah" (Judg 13:16 DBY). When they made their offering, "He did a **wondrous** thing while Manoah and his wife looked on - it happened as the flame went up toward heaven from the altar - the Angel of the LORD ascended in the flame of the altar! When Manoah and his wife saw this, they fell on their faces to the ground" (Judg 13:19-20). This was God! He was equally wonderful in who He was and what He did. No angel would have dared to accept an offering; this was the clearest evidence that Christ is Jehovah and to be worshipped.

Only the Father understands the mystery of godliness: "God was manifested in the flesh, justified in the Spirit, seen by angels, preached among the Gentiles, believed on in the world, received up in glory" (I Tim 3:16).

As Ironside says, "He is called Counsellor because He comes to us as the Revealer of the Father's will. That is what is implied in His divine title, 'the Word'" The Psalmist prophesies: "The kings of the earth set themselves, and the rulers take counsel together, against the LORD and against His Anointed" (Ps 2:2), Well, we know what their 'counsel' recommends and even enforces nowadays, and it is in defiance of God's holy laws; their futile blasphemous counsels brings no happiness, no prosperity, no peace, and will ultimately bring damnation. Lawrence Richards writes: "The Old Testament views God's counsel as His fixed purpose. It was important that Israel when facing national crises received guidance from God." Isaiah had been talking of such crises and promises in the coming Messiah, a Counsellor sufficient for their needs, and for ours today."

28 December

*"And His name will be called….. **Mighty God**….."* (Isa 9:6)

This cannot be watered down just because it is applied to God the Son, rather than God the Father; He who temporarily laid aside His glory for a season was no less mighty. At His arrest He said: "Or do you think that I cannot now pray to My Father, and He will provide Me with more than twelve legions of angels?" (Matt 26:53). He had the authority, but was happy to let His Father wield it for Him when it was appropriate. Thus we have confirmed that He is Emmanuel – God with us. We see Him in His utmost humility as He is made sin for us on the Cross. We see Him at His sublime height when He is exalted above the highest Heavens to His Father's throne. In both cases only His Deity, His Godhood is sufficient for both positions, and for all that He set out to accomplish. It is in our eternal interests that He became God manifest in the flesh. It is in our eternal interests that He holds all things in His almighty power.

Throughout the New Testament we find confirmation of Christ's Emmanuel description. The first to publicly acknowledge the immense truth that had previously evaded Him was the doubting disciple: "Thomas answered and said to Him, 'My Lord and my God!'" (Jn 20:28); Paul wrote with that confirmatory "Amen": "Of whom are the fathers and from whom, according to the flesh, Christ came, who is over all, the eternally blessed God. Amen" (Rom 9:5). He is contrasted with, rather than likened to, the holy angels:

"But to the Son He says: 'Your throne, O God, is forever and ever" (Heb 1:8). We find Him as the Revealer of the Godhead: "And we know that the Son of God has come and has given us an understanding, that we may know Him who is true; and we are in Him who is true, in His Son Jesus Christ. This is the true God and eternal life" (I Jn 5:20).

We close with Ironside: "He was also the eternal Son of the Father who had come from the glory that He had with the Father from all past eternity, given in grace for our redemption, who linked His Deity with our humanity, apart from sin, and thus was God and Man in one blessed, adorable Person."

29 December

*"And His name will be called..... **Everlasting Father**....."* (Isa 9:6)

I am not the only person to admit to having been surprised to see this description of Christ, the Son, along with the other titles which seem so much more comprehensible. Some commentators pass this over quickly; we cannot. Actually a better rendering would be "Father of Eternity", as in the Septuagint, "Father of the Ages", or even, as in the Vulgate, "Father of the coming age". Ironside and Ellicott point out, and surely we would not disagree, that the Son is not to be confounded with the Father, though He and the Father are one (Jn 10:30). Because He is the One in whom all ages meet, He is rightly designated Father of Eternity: "whom He appointed heir of all things, through whom also He did make the ages" (Heb 1:2 YLT); He actually created time! Commenting on the rendering "Father of Eternity", WE Vine writes: "There is a twofold revelation in this: (1) He inhabits and possesses eternity (Isaiah 57:15); (2) He is loving, tender, compassionate, an all wise Instructor, Trainer and Provider." Hewlett writes: "The word 'father' is used in the Old Testament for the author of anything, for the nourisher and preserver, and also of one who excels in any particular quality."

The point is that this title of Father of Eternity, especially in this context, is not about His relationship as God the Son with God the Father, something with all believers, who are naturally Trinitarian, understand or at least accept. We find it in John 3:16, we find it in so many places, especially in the New Testament. It is not that the title 'Everlasting Father' as applied here to Christ is more profound, nor is it obscure. It is simply one of those things which is rarely discussed. As puny mortals we are in danger of trying to analyse the eternal God. As Hoste and Rodgers write: "We cannot by searching find out God, except in as far as He is pleased to reveal Himself. God has never condescended to prove His existence, not yet explain His mode of Being; but He reveals Himself in His Works and Word; and even then we need God the Spirit to teach us. The great truth of the Old Testament is the Unity of the Godhead."

30 December

*"And His name will be called….. **Prince of Peace**."* (Isa 9:6)

No eyebrows are raised as we come to this lovely title. We remember that the context of this verse is a succession of past wars, where only the One who bears these titles would prove to be the Deliverer. First in view with Isaiah had been the bloodthirsty Assyrians, who were very soon to sack Samaria and take the Northern Kingdom of Israel captive, thus inaugurating the first and greater stage of the Dispersion, which is to end completely only following Armageddon, when latter day Assyrians also seem to participate.

At His birth, the angels proclaimed: "Glory to God in the highest, and on earth peace, goodwill toward men!" (Lk 2:14). The Prince of Peace had arrived. His own rejected Him and peace was postponed for around two thousand years. The 1914 to 1918 war proved not to be the "war to end wars". The many in those days who were familiar with Bible prophecy were considered wet blankets, but were of course proved to be right. The same thing happened again a few decades ago. The war to end wars still lies ahead and culminates with Armageddon, when the Warrior King, having crushed all opposition, will be acknowledged as Prince of Peace and reign in absolute peace for a thousand years, before that very brief but necessary final rebellion which we considered on 21 July. "My people will dwell in a peaceful habitation, in secure dwellings, and in quiet resting places" (Isa 32:18); this will be true of the whole world as well as Israel, who was being addressed.

But we hardly need to remind readers that He is the Prince of Peace in another at least equally important respect. "Peace" (Shalom") was the risen Lord's first greeting to His assembled apostles. He had just accomplished the greatest peace mission in all eternity. Fifty-eight times in the Epistles we find the word "peace", sometimes characterising the nature of the new Church Age, but sometimes referring to the peace between God and fallen mankind accomplished on the Cross: "Having been justified by faith, we have peace with God through our Lord Jesus Christ" (Rom 5:1); "For He Himself is our peace, who has made both one, and has broken down the middle wall of separation" (Eph 2:14); "Having made peace through the blood of His cross" (Col 1:20).

31 December

*"Of the increase of His government and peace **there will be no end**, upon the throne of David and over His kingdom, to order it and establish it with judgment and justice from that time forward, even forever. The zeal of the LORD of hosts will perform this."*
(Isa 9:7)

Malcolm Davis observes: "The Lord would accomplish this victory through the virgin's Son, Immanuel, the Child born, who was really God manifest in the flesh..... He would rule the world in perfect righteousness and peace forever as David's greater Son."

Zacharias, having heard of the soon-to-be-born Christ, praised God and declared: "Blessed is the Lord God of Israel, for He has visited and redeemed His people, and has raised up a horn of salvation for us in the house of His servant David, as He spoke by the mouth of His holy prophets" (Lk 1:68-70). "I have made a covenant with My chosen, I have sworn to My servant David: 'Your seed I will establish forever, and build up your throne to all generations.'" (Ps 89:3-4).The birth of the Son was about to take place, but the earthly enthronement is to await His Return in Power. We have yet to see established the promised Kingdom which is guaranteed to outlast the Millennium and beyond the end of the world, with the tribal names inscribed on the gates of the Holy City, New Jerusalem (Revelation 21:12).

This year we have seen so much that God has accomplished throughout history and will yet accomplish. We could repeatedly declare, "The Zeal of the Lord of Hosts performed this." We have seen prophecies regarding the Rapture of the Church, the Judgment Seat of Christ, the Marriage of the Lamb, Seals, Trumpet judgments, Bowl judgments, Christ's descent and the defeat of Satan and his two deputies. We have read of the later Judgment of the Nations, the Millennial Kingdom, the end of the world, the Great White Throne and the Holy City, the New Jerusalem. Lest any should dare to doubt God's promises and His ability and determination to fulfil them, we join the prophet in declaring: **"The zeal of the LORD of hosts will perform this!**"

"He who testifies to these things says, 'Surely I am coming quickly.' Amen. **Even so, come, Lord Jesus!**" (Rev 22:20).

Index of Readings

Isa 65:20,22	July 20
Isa 66:22-24	November 24
Jer 1:7	May 27
Jer 1:9-10	September 3
Jer 3:14-15,17	September 4
Jer 5:12-13,30-31	September 5
Jer 27: 5-7	September 6
Jer 31:3,9-10	September 7
Jer 50:5-6,33-34	September 8
Ezek 1:3, 2:3	Aug 14
Ezek 1:28-2:2	Aug 15
Ezek 4:1-3	Aug 16
Ezek 6:8-9	Aug 17
Ezek 9:4-6	Aug 18
Ezek 17:12-14	Aug 19
Ezek 21:26-27	February 23
Ezek 28:2,8	Aug 20
Ezek 37:4-6	Aug 21
Ezek 37:16-17	Aug 22
Ezek 38:2,8	Aug 23
Ezek 39:2-4	Aug 24
Ezek 40:2,4	Aug 25
Ezek 48:29-30,35	Aug 26
Ezek 48:35	June 18
Dan 2:28, 37	May 14
Dan 2:44	May 15
Dan 5:26-30	May 8
Dan 7:7-8	May 16
Dan 7:13-14	May 17
Dan 9:24	May 19
Dan 9:27	May 20
Dan 11:36	May 21
Dan 12:1	May 22
Dan 12:4,9	February 24
Dan 12:7	May 23
Dan 12:9-10	May 24
Hos 3:4-5	Sep 17
Hos 5:15	Sep 18
Hos 9:17	Sep 19

Matt 5:17-19	August 1
Matt 6:9-11	March 2
Matt 6:19-21	June 7
Matt 6:32-33	August 2
Matt 8:16-17	February 7
Matt 12:17-21	February 8
Matt 13:14-15	February 9
Matt 13:3, 23	March 3
Matt 13:30	March 4
Matt 13:31-32	March 5
Matt 13:33	March 6
Matt 13:35	February 10
Matt 13:44	March 7
Matt 13:45-46	March 8
Matt 13:47-50	March 9
Matt 16:1	March 11
Matt 16:2-3	March 12
Matt 16:3	March 13
Matt 16:4	March 14
Matt 16:18	April 7
Matt 16:21	January 10
Matt 16:21	April 6
Matt 21:2-3	May 9
Matt 21:4-5	February 11
Matt 23:37-39	February 25
Matt 24:3	March 15
Matt 24:4-5	March 17
Matt 24:6	March 18
Matt 24:7	March 19
Matt 24:8	March 20
Matt 24:21-22	January 10
Matt 24:21-22	January 12
Matt 25:31-32	January 13
Matt 25:32-33	July 14
Matt 25:34-36	July 15
Matt 25:40-41	July 16
Matt 26:28-29	February 26
Matt 26:63-64	January 16
Matt 27:35-36	February 14

Acts 15:14-16	January 18
Acts 20:22-23	April 10
Acts 20:29	April 13
Acts 23:11	April 11
Acts 28:27-28	April 16
Rom 2:4-5	October 20
Rom 5:1-2	October 21
Rom 6:5-6	October 22
Romans 8:21-23	October 23
Rom 9:3-4	June 17
Rom 10:8-10	October 24
Rom 11:1-2	October 25
Rom 11:8,25	February 29
Rom 11:26-27	June 20
Rom 14:10-12	June 5
I Cor 1:6-8	October 26
I Cor 2:9-10	September 9
I Cor 3:12-13	June 6
I Cor 4:5	October 27
I Cor 15:27-28	September 16
I Cor 11:25-26	October 28
I Cor 15:19-20	October 29
I Cor 15:40-42	October 30
II Cor 5:10	January 20
Gal 2:16	October 31
Gal 6:8-10	November 1
Eph 1:18-21	November 2
Eph 2:5-7	November 3
Phil 1:3-6	November 4
Phil 1:6	June 2
Phil 2:9-11	November 5
Phil 3:20-21	November 6
Phil 3:21	June 1
Col 1:18-20	November 7
Col 1:24-27	November 8
I Thess 1:9-10	April 17
I Thess 4:13	April 18
I Thess 4:14	April 19
I Thess 4:15	April 20

Rev 3:14,21	December 24
Rev 3:17, 19-20	April 30
Rev 4:1	June 3
Rev 4:3-4	June 4
Rev 5:5-6	January 23
Rev 5:14	June 8
Rev 6:1-2	June 23
Rev 6:3-4	June 24
Rev 6:5-6	June 25
Rev 6:7-8	June 26
Rev 6:9-11	June 27
Rev 6:12-14	June 28
Rev 6:15-17	June 29
Rev 7:3-4	June 30
Rev 7:9-10	July 1
Rev 7:13-14	January 24
Rev 8:1-3	August 27
Rev 8:6-7	August 28
Rev 8:8-9	August 29
Rev 8:10-11	August 30
Rev 8:12	August 31
Rev 8:13-9:1	September 1
Rev 9:13-14	September 2
Rev 10:6-7	October 9
Rev 11:1-2	October 10
Rev 11:3,6	October 11
Rev 12: 1-2,5	October 12
Rev 12:7,9	October 13
Rev 12:17-13:1	October 14
Rev 13:11-12	October 15
Rev 14:1,4	October 16
Rev 15:7-8	November 25
Rev 16:1-2	November 26
Rev 16:3-6	November 27
Rev 16:7-9	November 28
Rev 16:10-11	November 29
Rev 16:12,14	November 30
Rev 16:14,16	January 25
Rev 16:17-19	December 1